Peter Reinhart's **Whole Grain Breads**

Peter Reinhart's
WHOLE GRAIN BREADS

NEW TECHNIQUES, EXTRAORDINARY FLAVOR

photography by **Ron Manville**

TEN SPEED PRESS
Berkeley | Toronto

This book is dedicated to my wife, Susan, who understood how hard this book would be to write, who got me through it, gave me time, space, and patience, and kept me sane. And to our oldest cat, Lily, who considered herself executive editor of all late night typing sessions, keeping me company and occasionally deleting passages with her head as it rested on the keyboard.

Ten Speed Press
P.O. Box 7123
Berkeley, California 94707
www.tenspeed.com

Distributed in Australia by Simon and Schuster Australia, in Canada by Ten Speed Press Canada, in New Zealand by Southern Publishers Group, in South Africa by Real Books, and in the United Kingdom and Europe by Publishers Group UK.

Cover and text design by Nancy Austin

The wheat diagram on page 28 is used with permission from the Wheat Foods Council.

Library of Congress Cataloging-in-Publication Data
Reinhart, Peter.
  Peter Reinhart's whole grain breads : new techniques, extraordinary flavor / Peter Reinhart ; photography by Ron Manville.
     p. cm.
     Includes index.
  ISBN-10: 1-58008-759-0 (hardcover)
  ISBN-13: 978-1-58008-759-9 (hardcover)
  1. Bread. 2. Cookery (Cereals) I. Title.
  TX769.R41875 2007
  641.8'15—dc22   2007106660

Printed in China
First printing, 2007
1 2 3 4 5 6 7 8 9 10 — 11 10 09 08 07

CONTENTS

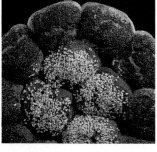

THE BREADS

ENRICHED BREADS

HEARTH BREADS

SPECIALTY BREADS

INTERNATIONAL BREADS

BAGELS AND FLATBREADS

CRACKERS

ACKNOWLEDGMENTS

First of all, there are nearly 350 recipe testers that must be thanked again and again. The passion, perseverance, and dedication of these home bakers is the secret ingredient of this book. I will list them all at the end of this section, but want to acknowledge you all, as a group, right up-front.

In addition, there are many people and companies who lent their expertise and ingredients to my research. Thank you to Susan Miller, Jeffrey Hamelman, and the King Arthur Flour Company, as well as Paula LaBine and Tim Huff of General Mills. Both companies contributed many pounds of white wheat flour for testing as well as technical consulting from Jeffrey and Tim. Bill Weekly, who was the technical baker at SAF Yeast for nearly two decades and who has been one of my main go-to consultants for years, was, yet again, there for me when I needed him. A number of cereal chemists from the American Institute of Baking were also very helpful, explaining to me the challenges of whole grain baking in layman's language. Thank you to the Wheat Council for providing the wheat kernel graphic. Jeff and Janet Ganoung, of Great Harvest Breads of Charlotte, who not only wrote an excellent essay on the nutritional benefits of whole grains but also supplied me with freshly milled wheat and whole wheat kernels. Monica Spiller, Jennifer Lapidus, Debra Wink, and Emily Buehler also contributed extensive bread science essays, background stories, and research but we just ran out of pages to include them here (see the resources on page 304 for how to access their excellent and important essays).

The Bread Bakers Guild of America is the single greatest source of collective artisan and craft baking knowledge in America and without its generous members, like Dave Miller, Michel Suas, Craig Ponsford, Didier Rosada, Abe Faber, Ciril Hitz, Richard Miscovitch, Mitch Stamm, Gina Piccolina, and many others, I would know far less than I do and would never have been able to connect the dots of my bread journey.

Johnson and Wales University in Charlotte, North Carolina, under the leadership of President Arthur Gallagher and Culinary Deans Karl Guggenmos, Peter Lehmuller, and Wanda Copper, has been exceedingly generous and accommodating, allowing me both time and space to complete this book and to test the formulas. My campus bread baking colleagues, Chefs Harry Peemoeller, Jeff Alexander, and Sadruddin Abdullah provided ongoing support and ideation. A special thanks to Chef Joseph Benedetto, who spent many hours working up the nutritional analysis on his trusty ESHA program. And to Laura Benoit for her sharp proofread.

Thanks also to Steve Bardwell and Gail Lunsford of Wake Robin Farm Breads in Marshall, North Carolina, for organizing the annual Asheville Bread Festival, a source of inspiration and key breakthroughs in the writing of this book.

Thanks to Jan Byers and folks at the Westeye Group in Charlotte for letting us use their Wolf/Sub Zero kitchen showroom for many of our photo sessions.

A very special thank you to photographer Ron Manville for his tremendous dedication, investment, and commitment to this project, and for his willingness to go beyond the call of duty to intuit and create the kind of photos for this book that I've been dreaming about for years.

Thank you to my classmates and the faculty at Queen University's creative writing MFA program for workshopping the opening chapter of this book and helping me become a better writer.

Thanks also to my agent, Angela Miller, my legal advisor, Ted Grabowski, and to my chiropractor, Dr. Ralph Burris, who kept me functional when my back wanted to quit (and almost did).

Finally, enormous thanks to the wonderfully patient and collaborative creative team at Ten Speed Press who offered the full resources of their publishing house to evoke the full potential of this book: Owner Phil Wood; Publisher Lorena Jones; Editorial Director Aaron Wehner; my tireless editor, Meghan Keeffe; Art Director Nancy Austin; and Publicist Lisa Regul. Thank you also to Jasmine Star, Mike Ashby, and Ken DellaPenta for excellent copyediting, proofreading, and indexing, respectively.

Again, thank you to the following recipe testers around the world, many of whom who helped identify problems with early prototypes and bring about the breakthroughs that are presented in this book. I hope to meet each of you and thank you personally: Peter Achleitner, Kirsi Allison-Ampe, Alice Ammons, D.J. Anderson, Burleigh Angle, Annie Angle, Raj B. Apte, Pedro Arellano, Michael Arnoldi, Deb Arsenault, Christine Ashburn, James Bairey, Stefan Baumann, Deborah Bede, Gilles Belin, Ina Bellmann, Barbara Bendix, Carla Benedict, Jim Bennett, Irene Bensinger, Barb Blackmore, Mary Blender, Gea Blok, Carla Bone, Jane Borden, Malcolm Boshier, Craig Broderson, Carlton Brooks, Bonni Brown, Diane Brown, Doris Bruntel, Ruth Brutz, Ian Buchanon, Steve Buckner, Sylvia Burgos, Dawn Burstyn, Lucy Burton, Amanda Butterfield, Michele Caplan, Bryan Carmenati, Mary Cassidy, Karen Chen, Dana Chiu, Ken Chomic, David Chow, Donna Clancy, Julie Clawson, Jim Clayton, Allen Cohn, Carol Beth Coleman, Sylvia Conard, Kevin Contzen, Margaret Cope, Ann Cornelius, Diane Cotton, Keith Craig, Lori Crews, Bill and Leisel Cruise, Ray D'Esposito, Christine Dalrymple, Lisa Danchak-Martin, Carolyn Dandalides, Jon Davis, Matt Deatherage, Cindy DeCesare, Andre de Graaf, G. Owen Delaney, Robert C. Dempsey, Arthur Denys, Kathy Destadio, Nancy DeVries, Darci DeWulf, John DeYoung, Aranka Dol, Pat Doucette, John Dougherty, Lisa Downing, Pauline Dysko, Barbara Edwards, Karina Egloff, Tony Ernst, Adila Esbhani, Arlene Etzold, Jeff McBride, Jill Farrimond, Pat Fields, Natalie Fine, Laura Fischer, Carol Fisher, Steven Flanagan, Floyd Foess, Dennis Foley, Jason Fout, Cindy Frederick, Paul Friedman, Eric Fung, Kathleen Gahan, Mario Garcia-Rios, Claire Garner, Wil Gatliff, Brian J. Geiger, Lee Geyer, Marti Giacopelli, Angelina Glas-Kanis, Dave Glaze, Lonni Goldman, Rosalynn Gorski, Halina Gostkowski, Darryl Gould, Diana Gray, Kathy Green, Melissa Greene, Barbara Grimes, Jeff Grimm, Cynthia Grob, Phil Gross, Jon Grube, Jammie Gundersen, Dan Haggarty, Rich Halbert, Mike Haney, Cindy Hannah, Matt Hansen, John Hart, Tammy Hart, Becky Hart, John Hartley, Karen Hawkins, Gordon Hayes, Kevin Hayes, Maxwell Heathcott, Suzette Heiman, Barb Hein, Dulcey Heller, Dougal Hendry, Sue Hermosillo, Sara Herpolsheimer, Trent Hill, Brenda Hock, Petra Holzapfel, Nilgun Hoodbhoy, Robert Huffman, Bob Hunter, Aaron Hyman, Connie Hyman, Jennifer Iverson, Erik Jacobs, Carol Jamison, Huiling Johnson, Joanne Johnson, Norma Johnson, Paul Johnston, Steven Benford, Michael Jubinsky, Rhonda Kaya, Kate Kelly, Cynthia Kepler, Gretchen Kern, Jen Kettering, John Kino, Soep Kipje, Dan Klinger, Tim Knight, Daina Kojelis, Katie Kondo, Bob Koontz, Alex Kowalczul, Sandy Krause, Steve Krause, Merry Gay Lape, Carol Lauffer, Kathi Lazzarini, Dorothea C. Lerman, Benjamin Licciardi, Karen Lichti, Barb Lindsay, Wan Yan Ling, Jay Lofstead, Rachael Lohr, Sandi Long, Carla Low, Floyd Mann, Tom Marino, Joy Martin, Lisa Martin, Amber Matthews, Sheila Mayer, Jeff McBride, Donna McFerren, Noelani McGadden, Lori McKiernan, Jackie Messina, Leslie Meyer, Marti Mikels, Jeff Miller, Lou Mitchell, Leigh Monichon, Mark Montgomery, Robin Mordfin, Roxanne Morgan, Francine Morin, Can Necaf, Erin Nesmith, Adam Newey, Eve Ng, Phann Ngauv, Karen Noll, Kim Ode, Ed Okie, Evan Oulashin, Fran Padilla, Jennifer Park, Greg Parks, Lynne Paschetag, Thomas Passin, Helene Payette, Joan Pelletier, Larry Peters, Carol Peters, Brandon Pettit, Suzanne Pickett, Stephen Pitman, Kathi Plomin, Josie Plungas, Maureen Potter, Martin Pozzo, Ruth Provance, Diane Purkiss, Linda Rawson, Gary Redmond, Nancy Reeve, Cathy Reichel, Hesz Rivera, Pat Robb, Susan Robeck, Emma Robertson, Chuck Robinove, Debbie Rogers, Elaine Rosenfield, Rebecca Ross, Frederick Ross, Teresa Rouzer, Caroline Rumsey, JoAnn Rupert, Eric Rusch, Harold Russ, Georgia Sabourin, Madelyn Salyer, LaDonna Saria, JoAnne Sawyer, Saudra Scarce, Lynda Schemansky, Pauline Schettini, Lynn Schick, Jane Schiraldi, Barbara Schmitt, Nancy Schol, Joe Schreiber, Robert Schroeder, Susan Schwarting, Daniel F. Schwarz, Joan Scruggs, Gail Sears, Jennifer Seiger, Phillip Seitz, Maria Enid Serrano, Kent Servant, Susanne Shavelson, Tom Shavlik, Laura Shaw, Steve Shelton, Beth Sheresh, Reed Sheridan, Jeanne Shi, Lauren Shive, Daniel Siegel, Philip Silverman, Renee Slazinski, Amy Smereck, Samantha Smith, Tami Smith, Jill Smith-Mott, Ben Sostrin, Susan Sperry, Alexander Spurgeon, Mary J. Stackhouse, Mike Stancliff, Pete Stawasz, Miriam Stengel, Camille Stephens, Carol Stevens, Lorraine Fina Stevenski, Pam Stowe, Richard Stringfellow, Mark Strobel, Amy Stromberg, Jessica Su, Matthew Swift, Susan Tarman, Hilary Tatem, Linda taylor, Debby Taylor, Adam Tenner, Susan Tenney, Keng Ngee Teoh, Eric Thompsson, Jessica Tomasi, Bill Trapp, Sue Trimble, Geraldine Tulane, Katy Valentine, Renee Van Hoy, Rita van Hulst, Nancy Wajda, Kyle Warendorf, Sue Waudby, Al Wegener, Stephen Weinberg, Beth Weiss, Jessica Weissman, Bill Welch, Evie Werthmann, Ulrike Westphal, Kathy Wetherell, Stanley Wheeler, Gary White, David Widaski, Russ Wiecking, Petra van der Wielen, Murray Wilcox, Chris Wilson-Grady, Debra Wink, Sharon Wong, Alan Woods, Jude Woods, David Wright, John Wright, Sharon Wright, Shawn Wright, Lucille Yackowski, Joy Zbinden, Dick and Maggie Zieg, John Zingheim, and Lindsey Zucker.

INTRODUCTION

Culinary instructors all know that once the preliminaries of safety and sanitation, ingredient knowledge, knife skills, and plate presentation are out of the way, the ultimate success of a chef is determined by his or her ability to deliver flavor. So too with breads: We may agree in theory that whole grain breads are better for us, but will we eat them?

Yes, but only if they taste very, very good.

Whole grain breads, while never in doubt as the healthier option, have faced the challenge of desirability ever since white bread became the popular national choice about one hundred years ago. That white bread would be more desirable than whole grain bread is not surprising. White flour is, after all, essentially sugar, in the guise of starch, with a little protein. We love sugar in whatever form it comes in; our taste buds never seem to get enough of it. White flour breads, especially if crafted with attention to proper fermentation methods, deliver flavor, nuance, complexity, and comforting satisfaction. We can train ourselves to appreciate the flavor of whole grain bread, but it takes no training at all to fall in love with white bread. And despite the theme of this book, I have always maintained that there are times when only white bread will do. But it is no secret that we will be much healthier if we primarily eat whole grain breads and save the white breads for special occasions.

While the artisanal food movement and a growing interest in eating healthier foods have combined to bring better breads to the marketplace, very few of those loaves consist entirely, or even predominantly, of whole grains. Plus, there are times when only a home-baked loaf will do, especially if you are a bread baking enthusiast. Fortunately, using the method described in this book, you'll soon be making whole grains breads that do, in fact, taste very, very good.

As a baking instructor, I teach my students that bread baking is all about the manipulation of time, temperature, and ingredients for the purpose of creating an extraordinary product, a transformational food called bread. In previous books I introduced a technique called delayed fermentation, which works beautifully to maximize flavor in white flour baguettes, focaccia, and pizza dough. When the recent low-carb, antibread craze was in high gear, I began wondering if the method could be applied to whole grain breads. Thankfully, we emerged from that craze with a deeper understanding of what constitutes a healthy diet, leading to a national rediscovery of the importance of whole grains. The time had come to test the theories and method of delayed fermentation in response to the demands of the new "bread is back" movement.

After a lot of tinkering and testing (with much-appreciated help from nearly 350 testers), the delayed fermentation method has been improved in order to meet the challenge that is whole grain baking. The formulas used in my previous books work exceedingly well, but we are now forging into frontier territory, applying the principles of what we in the artisan bread community have come to know as slow rise baking, only in a different way.

In addition to making whole grain breads that taste very, very good, the delayed fermentation method presented in this book actually makes bread baking easier, and it is a valuable technique for both home and professional application. It gives the baker more control over the product and also frees up time for other things. In many ways it is radical because it seems to go against traditional, time-honored methods. Anyone who knows me knows how much I value and honor tradition, but traditional bakers did not have refrigerators or the means to control fermentation the way we do now. And they had intuitive but not scientific knowledge about enzymes and microorganisms and their effects on food and flavor.

There has never been a time in history when we have had the ability to control things as we do now, to direct our gastronomic knowledge to create wines, beers, cheeses, and breads (all fermented foods, you will notice) of such extraordinary diversity and flavor. Our benchmarks are the great traditional versions, and our technical foundations are the time-honored methods. And now that we have come to understand how traditional methods work—why, for instance, long, slow fermentation creates a better-tasting product—we are not abandoning tradition, but rather applying that understanding to extend tradition into the present moment.

The goal of this book is to invite you into a new frontier of whole grain baking. I will show you how to make whole grain breads that taste better than any you have ever had and that are easy to make so you will choose to make and eat them, not just read about them and nod your head in intellectual agreement. This book is divided into four chapters, and because the background information is important, I hope you will read the first three before jumping into the recipes:

- **Chapter 1, "Following the Flavor: A Bread Baker's Journey Back to Whole Grains,"** provides background and context about how and why I created the methods described in this book. It gives the broad brushstrokes upon which subsequent chapters will build.

- **Chapter 2, "From Wheat to Eat: A Tutorial,"** provides a crash course on baking science, including a short history of wheat and milling, a discussion of microorganisms, and descriptions of various grains other than wheat.

- **Chapter 3, "The Theory and Process of Delayed Fermentation,"** is a step-by-step tutorial, with instructional photos, that explains how to use the delayed fermentation method, including how to make every pre-dough and starter, how to combine the individual pieces in the final mixing, and how to bake the dough. Chapter 3 is essential reading, as all of the formulas that follow will refer back to it. While not difficult, the delayed fermentation method does require some unique steps, and the dough is more fully hydrated than in most white flour breads. The question my recipe testers asked most often was "How do you know how the dough should feel?" Chapter 3 will help you answer that question.

- **Chapter 4, "The Breads,"** contains fifty-five formulas in small batch recipes that can be easily made in a home kitchen. (The formulas can be expanded to larger batches for production bakers.) This chapter also contains helpful discoveries and tips that came out of responses to recipe testers' most frequently asked questions; hopefully somewhere in the following, at least one will address the inevitable questions you are bound to have:

From this book, I hope you will take with you: new knowledge to build upon your old knowledge; the freedom to think outside the box and take bold intuitive leaps; and the ability to make whole grain bread so good that you and your family and friends will not only eat it, but actually prefer it. It can be done—you are about to do it.

Following the Flavor: A Bread Baker's Journey Back to Whole Grains

We shall not cease from exploration
And the end of all our exploring
Will be to arrive where we started
And know the place for the first time.

—T. S. Eliot (from "Four Quartets")

In September 2005, along with about two hundred other bread fanatics, I became a camper at the first Camp Bread in South San Francisco. A "fantasy camp for bread-heads," as I'd described it to friends before traveling west, it was held on a peaceful hill overlooking the San Francisco Bay, under the auspices of the Bread Bakers Guild of America. I arrived at Camp Bread well on my way to writing a book on making 100% whole grain breads using a unique method I call delayed fermentation and was scheduled to give a workshop on that very subject. The method, which I believed could revolutionize bread making, was designed to create whole grain breads that are as satisfying as classic artisanal white flour breads. I'd adapted the method from one I had learned from a Parisian baker named Philippe Gosselin, which I'd described in a previous book, *The Bread Baker's Apprentice*. I thought applying the method to whole grains would be a fairly simple task (though there were some minor inconsistencies in early testings) and had been looking forward to the trip as the perfect kickoff for my writing that fall.

I began my workshop with a caveat: Some of my whole grain prototypes were not rising as they should have after their cold overnight stay in the refrigerator, taking far too long to awaken and begin their final rise. It seemed that the large amount of yeast needed to raise this heavier dough was causing overfermentation, resulting in a dense, tight crumb and a slightly bitter, back-of-the-throat bite. I was still trying to figure out how to tweak the yeast measurement, so I informed the class that the formulas were, at this stage, just a work in progress.

I demonstrated the method on 100% whole grain multigrain seeded loaves as well as on my original Gosselin-based *pain à l'ancienne*, made with white flour. As always, the *pain à l'ancienne* performed predictably and beautifully, yielding delicious focaccia and mini baguettes of excellent flavor and texture. But the seeded whole grain bread was, again, heavier and more bitter than I wanted.

I explained the theory behind the method to the class: the balancing act of time, temperature, and ingredients; the tightrope walk of delaying the yeast fermentation by using cold water and refrigeration while simultaneously utilizing enzyme activity to break sugar threads free from larger starch chains in order to create better flavor. Then, unexpectedly, a powerful question emerged: "If the goal of the method is to promote some enzyme activity but not leavening, then why do we need to put yeast in the dough and refrigerate it? Why not just add the yeast to the dough the following day, remix it, and then treat it like regular bread dough?" I looked up to see Allen Cohn, professional business consultant but, more significantly, a serious home baker, whom I have come to know these past few years, first as a frequent student and then as a volunteer helper whenever I came to the San Francisco area to teach a bread class.

I had two reactions to his question. One was elation that someone was actually following the logic and understanding this method. The other was the kind of anxiety I feel when asked a question for which I do not have the answer. While quickly scanning my memory for stored information, I recalled the method as I originally learned it from Philippe Gosselin in Paris. He too added the yeast on the second day, just as Allen suggested, after an overnight cold phase, so I described this. But Allen, again one step ahead of me, asked, "But why even bother with the refrigeration? Is the cold refrigeration doing something that would not occur if you just left the dough out at room temperature? Is there a function to the refrigeration? Does it impact the enzyme development in some way?"

Baboom!

"Well, I'm not sure if it is, in fact, necessary since there is no yeast in the dough. However, in a bakery situation there is a lot of yeast just floating around that could inoculate the dough. I'm guessing—and this is just a guess because Gosselin never addressed it and I have a feeling even he wouldn't know the full answer—that he uses the cold fermentation simply to create a reliable outcome. I think he'd say something like, 'I do it this way because it works, and it works in exactly a predictable amount of time.' Would it work as well without the refrigeration?" Before Allen could beat me to it, I answered, "Probably yes, but then he [Gosselin] would have to change his timing and would have to take the dough to the shaping stage in two hours rather than in six, and this might throw his entire production schedule into disarray. The cold dough gives him more time, a more generous window in which to work."

I took a pause and quickly reviewed what I had just said, wondering if it made sense, if it answered the question, if it was even plausible. I knew it was only a partial answer when I saw Allen simultaneously nodding and shaking his head sideways in between the nods.

After class I thanked Allen for giving me one of those head-slapping moments to free me from the limitations of my own thinking. I had been so fixated on making the one-step mixing method work, adding the yeast on the first day (which is how my *pain à l'ancienne* differs from Gosselin's), that I had not considered a different approach. I hated adding yeast to cold dough and remixing on the second day because I did not want to wait another six hours, as Gosselin did, for the dough to warm up and ferment. But I had overlooked the possibility of not refrigerating the dough at all, but rather just treating it as if it were what bakers call a soaker. It gave me something new to test out when I got home, and I was pretty excited about it.

• • •

Had this been my only aha moment, Camp Bread would have already been a successful event for me. But after my presentation ended, I attended another by Monica Spiller, an old friend and a true wheat and yeast freak (meant in the most flattering sense). Her baker's mission is to find ways to deliver maximum nutritional value with high-quality wheat using only natural, wild yeast fermentation from a starter she calls barm, after the English term for naturally yeasted foam derived from beer. I adapted her original barm technique for both whole grain and white flour starters years ago, and after also working with many other methods for making starters, I still find it to be one of the most reliable.

What I learned next was that Monica had since added a new wrinkle to her technique: the use of an actively enzymatic grain mash. I had heard of techniques using boiling or hot water to scald flour or whole grains to induce gelatinization and thereby naturally sweeten the flavor, but I had always assumed the hot water would denature the enzymes and make them useless. Monica, however, asserted that when done correctly, scalding grains creates the perfect environment to promote activity by certain favorable enzymes while deactivating others that are troublesome. She then proved this by making such a grain mash, stirring boiling water into a bowl of whole wheat flour supplemented with a pinch of malted wheat flour (also known as sprouted wheat flour). She wrapped the bowl in a blanket to hold it within the desired temperature range (between 140°F and 150°F) for one to three hours. When we sampled the mash, it tasted as though Monica had added a big shot of corn syrup or honey to the grain; the alpha-amylase enzymes in the flour had triggered the release of that much natural sweetness from the starches.

The beauty of the mash, though, is not just its sweetness but its functionality. Monica had created a lump of sweet, enzymatic dough food, perfect for feeding to sourdough starters, but also useful for enhancing the conversion of starch to sugar in any dough. Monica is exploring these possibilities in her own work and hopes to publish her still-evolving methods and formulas soon. In the meantime, I vowed to try out her new mash technique once back in my own kitchen to see if it would solve my problem of inconsistently rising doughs.

The Camp Bread experience was enlightening and educational in so many ways. I think every attendee, even the teachers, learned something from someone else and vowed to add that newly attained knowledge to their repertoire. But when I got home my breads were still not working right. In fact, they seemed to be getting worse. Sometimes the dough felt wonderful during the mixing stage but then quit rising during the baking stage, leaving me with a flat, dense, gummy loaf. I was also having difficulty determining the proper flour hydration ratio when using mash, since the mash was wetter than normal bread dough. I was in deep trouble; it was as if I had too much information for my own good and yet not enough information to piece it all together. Somehow I had to find a way to make sense of it, tie it together, and convert it all into great bread—and do all of that before my manuscript deadline in three months.

Whole Grain Flashback

Just so you're sure to understand the intense pressure I was under to get this right, allow me to retrace my baker's mission—a journey I have been on for thirty-seven years.

I baked my first loaf of bread in 1970 while a student at Boston University. I was caught between two dueling food philosophies that were emerging at the time: the newly hip macrobiotic movement, anchored in cooked, barely seasoned foods, brown rice, and a compelling though mysterious yin-yang cosmology; and the just budding California-influenced health food scene with its fresh, organic fruits and vegetables, sprouts, abundant herbs and spices, and other aspects of a lifestyle that later came to be called holistic. Conflicted as I was by these contrapuntal worldviews, it was no surprise my inaugural loaf came out of the oven with its own identity crisis. It was made from freshly milled wheat that I bought at Boston's Erewhon Natural Foods Market. I mixed it with salt and water but no yeast, as specified in the macrobiotic recipe I was following, and it yielded a thick, dark, leathery crust surrounding an inedible wad of spongy, glutinous paste. It was awful.

The late 1960s and early 1970s were an important preamble to the American culinary awakening of succeeding decades, and bread, as one piece of the larger puzzle, served nutritional, political, and metaphorical purposes during those years. A few months after that disastrous first loaf, I found myself baking some of those symbolic loaves for a local theater group, the Stomach Ache Street Theater, an offshoot of Peter Schumann's more famous Bread and Puppet Theater of Glover, Vermont. At the end of each performance, my large, just-baked whole wheat loaves were passed among the audience members, who broke bread with the cast in a communion-like ritual that was, in many ways, more profound than the play itself. Although it was called the *Stomach Ache* Street Theater, thankfully that had nothing to do with my bread. My new recipe—the same one used at the original Bread and Puppet Theater—was made from wheat I ground the day of the performance in a hand-cranked mill, and it did include yeast. What a difference a little leaven can make. The audience would go wild over the bread, and in the years since, whenever I've run into people who had been to those productions, they remember the bread more than the content of the play.

After a few months with the theater troupe I moved on and, at the age of twenty-one, became part of a Boston restaurant collective called the Root One Café, where we served wholesome vegetarian food inspired by both the California-style and macrobiotic cosmologies. Our bread was made for us by two local bakeries, one macrobiotic and one not, both using natural leavening techniques with wild yeast starters. The macrobiotic baker made a very dense whole wheat bread that had to be sliced thinly or it would be too tough to chew. The other bakery, which we called the Seven Grain No-Name Bakery because it had no name, made a moist, multigrain bread loaded with brown rice and seeds, dense yet easy to chew, but too crumbly to hold together unless sliced thickly. I loved them both, but particularly the seven-grain bread, which I often had to patch together around freshly ground peanut butter or almond butter.

I worked at the Root One for three years and learned how to cook everything except meat. I volunteered often to make the pickups at the two bakeries, both hidden in the back of alternative vegetarian restaurants. I asked lots of questions of the young, long-haired bakers, but none of them really knew much about bread other than how to follow procedures handed down from the long-haired bakers they'd replaced. "If you follow these steps and make a few adjustments for the weather, it usually turns out pretty good" was the general attitude.

This was the era I now call the "whole grain wave" of the American bread revolution: small, counterculture enclaves like these, selling whole grain breads to promote any number of philosophies, including the popular "white flour is death" and "us against them" agendas. It represented just a sliver of society, but it started a snowball effect that has gradually grown in size and influence over the following decades. This was also the era in which I ate only 100% whole grain breads and because of that, coupled with the healthful foods we served at the Root One Café plus some yoga and a little racquetball, I was in the best shape of my life. My childhood allergies and asthma disappeared. I was lean and loving it.

• • •

While still in my midtwenties, I left the hippie world and, following my unfolding spiritual journey, became a member of a structured Christian service community, the Holy Order of MANS, where, surprisingly (to me, anyway), the diet included meat, white flour, and, most evil of all, white sugar. I immediately gained weight, and I discovered, despite my joyful vegetarian years, that I had never really lost my taste for bacon and burgers, nor even for white bread. My first job was to cook in the novitiate seminary in St. Petersburg, Florida, and one of the recipes was for simple sandwich bread. It was a basic recipe, with melted butter, scalded milk, active dry yeast, and all-purpose flour; I believe it came from *Betty Crocker's Cookbook*. It was the first time I ever made white bread and, to be honest, it was delicious and made me quite popular among the seminarians.

During the next few years I had many missionary jobs. I worked on a hospital maintenance crew in Hamtramck, a neighborhood of Detroit where, on my lunch breaks, I discovered wondrous Polish kielbasa and also the Vernors soda bottling facility, where I stopped every day on my way home to try out flavors not normally found on the store shelves. After that I was a house parent for juvenile delinquents (we called them "undisciplined youth") in Raleigh, North Carolina, where I learned about the power of just baked bedtime cookies to calm down hormone-challenged teenagers, and also discovered the healing potential of a good neighborhood pizzeria when I needed to get the kids out of the house to decompress from the day's various traumas. As I pursued my missionary vocation I was, without realizing it, developing a certain culinary ethic as well as an expanding repertoire of cooking tricks. My one constant through it all, though, was bread, which I made whenever I could and which still brought much popularity.

By the end of the 1970s, as I approached my thirtieth birthday I found myself again in the seminary kitchen, though this time in San Francisco, where I found out how much I enjoyed theology, service work, and both classic French bread and San Francisco sourdough bread. A fellow seminarian, Phillip Goodrich, made me a loaf of French bread using a recipe that he'd clearly mastered over the years. The sound of that bread's fresh crust crackling as you bit into it, followed by the sweet, creamy, but toothsome texture of the interior crumb, might even have converted health food pioneer Sylvester Graham to white flour bread. I quickly traded my Betty Crocker recipe for the six pages of instruction from Julia Child's book *In Julia's Kitchen*. Mastering that recipe became a type of spiritual exercise for me. Even the notion of misting the oven with water to create steam was new—a magic tool. The results were transcendent, and I began making fresh bread every day, even though it was easy to buy great San Francisco sourdough at every corner grocery.

A few years later I transferred to our order's retreat center in Forestville, California, not far from the Russian River. Among my responsibilities at the retreat center was developing food-related livelihood opportunities, since we were a self-supporting community. I taught myself how to make cheese, and then, recalling my happy afternoons at the Vernors soda vending machines, I started playing with various herbal combinations to make all sorts of natural tonic beverages. I even came up with a barbecue sauce, which we dubbed Holy Smoke; according to those whom we sold it to again and again, it was the best ever. I was not officially the cook there (my future wife, Susan, was), but I did bake bread often, just for fun. I entered my French bread in the Sonoma County Harvest Fair and won $100 for best in show two years in a row. My years of cooking and discovering flavors in Boston, Hamtramck, Chicago, North Carolina, and other regions were converging.

The final piece in this evolving culinary journey was *struan*. As a result of our community's research into early Christian history, we began celebrating the nearly extinct Christian harvest festival, called Michaelmas, by hosting a harvest fair at the retreat center. Our librarian, Sister Ann, discovered a Celtic blessing for a bread called Struan Micheil, a Scottish harvest loaf baked only on Michaelmas (September 29). According to the Blessing of the Struan, the bread was made of many ingredients, a few of which—like gray cailpeach, woad, and three carle-doddies— we'd never heard of (and to this day they remain a mystery). I volunteered to make some loaves

for the harvest fair with the idea of staying true to the spirit of the original, but with familiar ingredients. My first version, a multigrain bread with rye, whole wheat, and soy flour, oats, corn-meal, and honey, was rather heavy. People ate it and smiled warmly, but I recognized that look as not dissimilar to that on the face of those folks way back in Boston who politely ate my non-yeasted macrobiotic loaves and then headed to the restroom.

The following year I made it again, cutting out the rye, soy, and whole wheat flours and substituting some high-gluten bread flour and, in tribute to those moist seven-grain breads we served at Root One, some cooked brown rice. Not too bad. Everyone seemed to genuinely like it, and I felt I was on the right track. The next year I made it again, continuing to modify it, and came very close to what seemed like a great loaf of bread.

By then, in 1986, Susan and I were engaged, and we had decided to combine our culinary talents and open a small restaurant. The idea was to test out our recipes on the local community to see if any of them might become the basis of a cottage industry to support the retreat center. The menu was simple, featuring various forms of barbecue (all with a generous dose of Holy Smoke), chili, soups, salads with original dressings, natural soft drinks (my herbal concoctions), and, of course, house-baked bread. The Julia Child–inspired French bread had to be part of the daily menu, even though most of the locals were more accustomed to sourdough bread, but the real centerpiece would be *struan*, which no one outside our community had yet tasted.

We called our restaurant Brother Juniper's Café, after one of Saint Francis of Assisi's famous disciples known for his generosity and hospitality. Two days before we opened, I was still tweak-ing the *struan* recipe. When the final version came together, the dough was so beautiful, so silken and golden (from a nice shot of honey and coarsely ground polenta), that I knew, even before baking it, how good it would be. Susan reminded me, in my moment of glory, that I had bet-ter write it all down, which I immediately did, and Brother Juniper's Struan Bread was born. Within two years, Brother Juniper's Café had spawned a full-scale bread bakery, and our breads, expanded to include six varieties, were used in many restaurants and sold in dozens of Bay Area supermarkets.

Struan is still the top-selling bread in the Brother Juniper's product line, though the bakery has been sold twice since we owned it. I have made many variations of *struan* since that first loaf, including the 100% whole grain version featured here (page 102), but I do not believe I will ever love any type of bread as much as I loved the original. In a way, that loaf represented the incipi-ent stirrings of the third wave of the bread revolution—the neo-traditional wave. But I'm getting ahead of myself.

The Rise and Fall of Artisanal Bread

Around the same time that Brother Juniper's opened, innovative bakeries like Acme Bread, Grace Baking, Metropolis, and Semifreddi's opened in Berkeley and Oakland, challenging the long-held sourdough monopoly of the older San Francisco bakeries. Little by little, other like-minded small bakeries across the country followed. These are now usually referred to as *artisanal*, which simply means "crafted by hand." These new bakeries mainly focused on recreating the traditional crusty hearth breads of western Europe, ushering in what I now refer to as the "traditional wave" of the bread revolution. Other bakeries, like the Tassajara Bakery (founded and run by the San Francisco Zen Buddhist Center), Alvarado Street Bakery in Santa Rosa, Alfaro's in Santa Cruz, and our own Brother Juniper's, featured original, flavored breads that were made using both traditional and self-discovered methods. This was the third movement of the bread revolution, what I call the "neo-traditional wave."

The increasingly popular artisanal breads brought more attention to whole grain breads, and before we knew it, the whole grain, traditional, and neo-traditional waves rolled into each other and formed a bread movement that some people referred to as a renaissance or, as I prefer, a bread revolution. Bread had suddenly become like one of those twenty-years-in-the-making overnight success stories. Then, in the early 1990s, the Bread Bakers Guild of America (BBGA) came into existence, allowing all of the small individual bakeries around the country to become aware of each other and realize that there was something big going on. The bread revolution had hit critical mass.

In 1993 the BBGA—which was especially significant in spreading the gospel of high-quality bread—brought Professor Raymond Calvel to the United States from France. His three-day seminars served as needed leaven for the nascent movement, because up to that point, only a few U.S. bakers had been to Europe to study with bread masters. Calvel, who died in 2005 at the age of ninety, inspired a quantum leap in the skill of U.S. bakers and baking educators. He was both a baker and cereal chemist, and the near-perfect quality of his bread came about not because he stumbled into secret tricks, but because he questioned conventional wisdom and tracked his experiments in a scientific manner. Calvel introduced not only techniques for pre-fermented dough, but also a scientific understanding of why a pre-ferment improves bread and how mixing methods and temperatures affect the final product.

When Calvel came to Oakland, California, to teach a workshop at the Acme Bread Company, I attended with dozens of other bakers and felt, for the first time, empowered with the knowledge of how certain choices throughout the baking process dramatically affect the outcome. Like me, most of the participants were self-taught bakers, people who had stumbled into the bread world because they enjoyed it. We were not like classical pastry chefs who had been trained in academies or through long apprenticeships. Spending three days with Professor Calvel was a rare experience of a true master class and, as it should have, it changed us and, in due course, contributed to the elevation of bread in America.

After seven years of building our bakery into a business much larger than we'd ever imagined, Susan and I sold Brother Juniper's. Armed with what I had learned from Professor Calvel and other skilled bakers, I became a baking teacher myself and continued to follow the breadcrumb trail.

In 1995 I won a bread competition sponsored by the James Beard Foundation. I called my winning loaf a wild yeast country *boule*, meaning that it was a round sourdough bread in the style of French *levains*. I had at last succumbed to the mystique of wild yeast leavening and was fortunate enough to stumble into creating a method, because I did not know any better, that used an unusually high percentage of sourdough starter, and it made a pretty spectacular loaf. My final entries, baked in a professional oven at Amy's Bread in Manhattan but made with sourdough starter I brought with me from Santa Rosa, were probably the most beautiful loaves I had ever baked to that point.

The prize was supposed to be five days in Paris to study with the baker of my choice, but I was able to convince Nick Malgieri, the organizer of the competition, to let me change it from one baker for five days to five bakers for one day each. The trip to Paris became one of the most important events in my growth as a bread baker and is probably the main reason I am now able to write this book. Among the bakers I got to interview were Lionel Poilâne, Michel Cousin, and Philippe Gosselin, each of whom taught me baking techniques I probably never would have figured out on my own. The most influential encounter was unexpectedly with Philippe Gosselin, the least known (in America) of the bakers I met, who showed me the technique that earned him his award for best baguette in Paris: a delayed fermentation method unlike any I had ever seen.

The Gosselin method mixes flour and cold water together into a firm, unleavened dough, which is then chilled overnight. The following day, more water is mixed in, along with salt and yeast. It then sits at room temperature for about six hours to gradually awaken and ferment until it is nearly doubled in size. The dough, which is now wetter than standard baguette dough and more like sticky ciabatta dough, is then divided, gently rolled into short torpedoes, and tossed in flour. A few minutes later, the relaxed pieces are carefully pulled (not rolled, as is the normal way) into baguette lengths, scored with a blade, and immediately baked. Unlike standard baguettes, they do not get a final rise, but because the dough is so wet, they have terrific oven spring and end up with a very open-holed structure, a crisp crust, and a creamy crumb. They are wonderful and were easily the best baguettes I tasted during my short time in France.

I came home and started playing around with variations on Gosselin's techniques, and after completing another book already in the works before I left, *Crust and Crumb*, I immediately started on yet another baking book, this one based on the new methods I'd picked up in France. *The Bread Baker's Apprentice* was published in 2001, at a time when American bakers were becoming bread masters themselves and artisan baking was trickling down to the home baker. The book did very well and I suddenly found myself with a wonderful readership eager for more.

• • •

At the same time, BBGA-organized American baking teams began doing extraordinarily well at the periodic Coupe du Monde de la Boulangerie competitions (also known as "Bread Olympics") held in Paris every few years, placing in the top six in 1994 and 1996, and winning the gold in 1999 (a feat since repeated in 2005). The BBGA had, by then, taken the leading role in championing the concept of artisanship in bread, and fought hard for a seat at the table of the much larger retail baking industry. Within a few years, especially between 1993 and 1998, a new standard of quality bread and bread knowledge had been established, and anyone entering the world of artisan baking had new benchmarks to match, as well as access to a pool of accumulated knowledge that simply did not exist a decade earlier.

Artisan bread, as a market segment, grew rapidly throughout the 1990s until it was inevitably co-opted by the large supermarkets. The word *artisan* lost its full impact the day that Safeway began using the brand name Artisan to describe their store-baked loaves. Then, in another unexpected twist, enterprising, true artisan bakers like Nancy Silverton of La Brea Bakery in Los Angeles, Ecce Panis in New York City, and the Grace Baking Company in Berkeley, among others, figured out how to flash-freeze partially baked hearth breads, resulting in a greatly increased availability of high-quality "artisan" breads through existing mainstream markets.

Nevertheless, breads truly made by hand were still very much appreciated, and across the country, wood-fired brick oven bakeries and bakery cafés were thriving. The United States seemed on the verge of creating something akin to a European-style bread culture.

Then, with the unexpected suddenness of a sleeper wave, came the low-carb diet fad.

Is Bread Dead?

In the fall of 2003, the first National Bread Symposium was held at Johnson and Wales University in Providence, Rhode Island. The symposium brought together people from all aspects of the bread world, including equipment makers, ingredient suppliers, artisan and high-volume bakers, and baking educators. The focus was supposed to be on the new food pyramid and its support of grains in the diet, as well as on sharing ideas for how to continue building a bread culture in America. I gave the keynote address, and in it I focused on the power of bread to tell a story, to transmit cultural worldviews from generation to generation. There was a fair amount of press in attendance, but they were there for a different reason than the rest of us. They were hot on the trail of the Atkins and South Beach diet fads. The question they kept asking us was "Is bread dead?"

Everyone at the symposium fielded the question in his or her own way. My stock answer was, "Hey, bread has been around for six thousand years and it is not going away." I also predicted that when the pendulum swung back to a more balanced position, as it most certainly would, bread would not only be back as the staff of life, but it would reestablish itself through whole grains. My position was that the low-carb craze is actually doing us a favor. It is revealing the future; we have to seize it.

There was some discussion at the conference that, when the cycle came back around to embracing bread again, the challenge would be to create whole grain breads that delivered all the flavor satisfaction of white flour breads. No matter what food or diet fad is in vogue, flavor always wins. In answer to the question of whether people in the United States would actually eat 100% whole grain breads, we agreed that health is compelling, but flavor is much more so.

The "is bread dead?" angle never really made it to the front pages. I thought it would take two years for the low-carbohydrate cycle to run its course, but I was wrong; it took only one year. Not that bread ever went away; most artisan bakers reported that their sales never ebbed at all during the Atkins craze. It was the big bread companies that suffered. Soft sandwich breads like Wonder Bread took the major hit. Why? Because when folks passed through the first stage of their low-carbohydrate plans and then reintroduced bread into their diet, they turned either to inexpensive, soft "whole wheat bread" (or what too often passes for whole wheat bread, softened as it is with dough conditioners and a fairly high percentage of white flour), or to high-quality, whole grain artisanal breads. *Whole wheat* or *whole grain* became a magic phrase, offering a transition back into guilt-free enjoyment of bread which most people still craved.

With the market shifting toward whole grains, the artisan bread community now had before it the opportunity to show the public how good whole grain bread could be, just as it already had with traditional European white flour hearth breads.

Next Steps

Living in the heart of the food world and teaching at some of the finest culinary schools was, for one who had lived for many years in a seminary under a vow of poverty, like putting a kid in a candy store. Surrounded by great chef instructors and their foods, writing about food, which involved never-ending research (alright, tasting), well, the most delicate way of saying it is, I gained a lot of weight. I was eating good food, even healthful food, but just too much of it.

Meanwhile, as a writer I had reached the point where I felt I had nothing left to say about bread. *The Bread Baker's Apprentice* had accomplished something every writer dreams of, the opportunity to add something new to the canon. Having introduced the concept of delayed fermentation, I thought, I could rest in peace and write about something other than bread. So I wrote a book about pizza. Oh, it was fun! More "research," but, alas, more pounds to work off.

I hit the gym and was about to start on two books entirely unrelated to food when, invigorated by the challenge issued at the National Bread Symposium by the question "Is bread dead?" I made my first 100% whole wheat focaccia, using the *pain à l'ancienne* method. It was excellent. I wondered, "Why can't this technique work for other whole grain breads?" Soon after, an editor asked me, "Don't you still have something left to say about bread?" The day after that, I read an article in the newspaper with the headline "Carbs Are Back, Whole Grains Are In." I was off and running.

Having come full circle from my youthful whole grain days, and having learned about breads of all types, made in many different ways, I returned, thirty years later, to my bread baking roots. But now I was armed with a renewed sense of mission and a clear focus: I wanted to use delayed fermentation breads to evoke the full potential of the flavor trapped in whole grain.

Rising to the Challenge That Is Whole Grain Baking

Although bakers have been making leavened bread for well over six thousand years, it shouldn't be surprising that we still have new things to learn and new frontiers to explore. No two bakers will agree on the pros and cons of every technique; one baker's *poolish* is another's *biga* is another's soaker. In baking, the magical dance between time, temperature, and ingredients can take many forms in the relentless striving to create perfect loaves. (And just try getting agreement on just what constitutes a perfect loaf!)

But, as I have said, I ran into problems when I returned home from Camp Bread and tried to apply all that I had learned. The Spiller mash technique did not, at first, create breads as good as the ones I saw during Monica's demonstration. My biggest challenge was getting the breads to rise to full size. In whole grain breads, the gluten, which traps gas and stretches like a balloon as the gas accumulates, is compromised by the fiber from the bran. All of the techniques of the delayed fermentation method, as well as the Spiller mash technique, are designed to counteract this tendency, but theory does not always conform to reality. I was beginning to wonder whether it would ever be possible to develop whole grain formulas and methods that yielded predictable results.

It was time to get some help, so I contacted a number of people who I felt might offer insight. I also went back to the textbooks and read up on enzymes, how lactobacillus affects acidity, proteolysis (protein breakdown), hetero- and homofermentative organisms (lactic acid bacteria), wild yeast, commercial yeast, starch damage, and volatile flavor compounds. I experimented with various combinations of hydration and ingredient ratios, cold and ambient temperature ranges, long and short mixing times, and wild and commercial yeast combinations. For a time, my breads were shrinking in the oven instead of springing, a sure sign of too much enzyme or yeast activity, and my theories were breaking down faster than the dough. But little by little, the tweaks began to produce better and better loaves. I was beginning to feel hopeful again.

Eventually, I began sending out recipes for testing. Nearly 350 home bakers responded to my call for testers, and they began with great enthusiasm, filling out the response questionnaire with many details and suggestions. We began the testing with two methods for making a whole grain wild yeast starter, and signs of problems to come emerged immediately. Some of the testers reported that their mixture of whole wheat flour and pineapple juice was not performing as my confident instructions predicted. "It's just sitting there," one tester wrote, "showing no signs of growth, fermentation, or life." And some of the starters began sporting white spots, indicating the growth of molds and bacteria. They had to be discarded.

The testers were eager to begin baking the first mash bread recipe I had sent them, but many of them could not because their starter had gone moldy or had never come to life. I pulled out every reference book I had on wild yeast starters and tried to figure out what was going wrong. My own starters were performing as expected, so I was really stumped. Some of my best correspondents, like Debra Wink (the team leader for the "pineapple juice solution," see page 60), had a background in biochemistry and sent me articles and research papers on sourdough and wild yeast starters. The research confirmed my intuition that the best bread flavor in whole grain breads would be created by a combination of both wild yeast (*Saccharomyces exiguus* and other strains) and commercial yeast (*Saccharomyces cerevisiae*) in conjunction with a healthy colony of the right strains of bacteria. But this information was of no help to those testers who could not get their starter off the ground.

I recalled a video I had seen about commercial yeast production and how air is pumped into the tanks of the liquid nutrient base in which a small amount of *S. cerevisiae* has been seeded. As the brew bubbles away, the yeast cells bud and split, rapidly multiplying until the mixture is loaded with millions upon millions of vibrant yeast cells.

Then a few testers reported that they saw more growth in their starters after kneading or stirring them.

Click!

As soon as I instructed the testers to stir their starters a few times a day, even if they were not adding more flour, the starters began performing much more dynamically, springing to life, percolating away, and growing in size. Aeration became a critical part of the method, though Debra later told me she thought the stirring helped redistribute food to the yeast and that this, not the aeration, caused the starters to awaken. Perhaps it is due to both aeration and feeding, the synergy rather than one or the other; we're still not sure, but hey, it works.

Having a healthy starter did not guarantee successful bread, and many of the testers sent emails about the difficulty of, first, making their mash and, then, turning the mash into a workable dough. I had suggested using a slow cooker to keep the mash at the correct temperature for the desired three hours and kneading the mashed grains every ten or fifteen minutes to distribute the heat. During this phase in the testing, we were working with mashes in the same style as Monica Spiller's; that is, a thick, doughlike, kneadable mash that took some effort to mix. At 150°F, this was a hot piece of dough, and while some testers figured out methods of protecting their hands by using silicon pads or rubber gloves, others were dreading the new recipes that called for a large piece of mash, which meant burnt hands, not just fingertips, and extra work—and all for breads that were frustratingly tight and dense, even gummy. Our attempts at controlling enzyme attacks on the starch were not working as planned; we were getting lots of sweetness from the wheat, but at the cost of structure.

I visited Jennifer Lapidus at her Natural Bridge Bakery near Asheville, North Carolina, and watched her work with very wet dough to create beautiful *desem* loaves—the famous, crusty, wild yeast, 100% whole grain Flemish breads leavened by a cold fermentation process—out of her freshly ground wheat, Kamut, spelt, and rye (shown below). While waiting for the dough to rise, we discussed the many challenges of whole grain baking and decided to host a panel discussion at the upcoming Asheville Bread Festival to see what techniques other whole grain bakers were using and how they figured out their systems.

When I returned to Charlotte, I visited with Jeff and Janet Ganoung, the owners of our local Great Harvest Bread Company. In addition to baking 100% whole grain breads every day, both Jeff and Janet also have degrees in food science, so I picked their brains for solutions.

The information overload was sometimes paralyzing, but it was necessary. I could only hope that it would lead to a third and final "aha!" moment, but epiphanies are not something that can be contrived. Meanwhile, many of my recipe testers were dropping out due to frustration and the difficulty of the development process, but many others were sending suggestions and insights of their own.

Huiling Johnson, one of the testers, sent me information about the soup seed method, a Chinese cooking technique similar to the Spiller mash technique. It makes a thin mash that is much easier to mix and incorporate into dough than the thick mash we had been using. It did not require a slow cooker, kneading, or burning of hands, so I put my recently purchased Rival away to save for regular slow-cooking recipes. I think this was the beginning of the breakthrough, the turning point for which I had hoped and prayed.

It was after the Asheville Bread Festival, however, that good things really began to happen.

A Happy Confluence, at Last

On April 1, 2006, I attended the second annual Asheville Bread Festival, organized by Steve Bardwell and his wife, Gail Lunsford, of Wake Robin Farm Breads. The previous year, at the inaugural event, I had been invited to give the keynote address, which I did while standing on a table at the Greenlife Grocery, which was hosting the event. The Asheville festival was very different from the annual bread festival in Portland, Oregon, which I wrote about in *The Bread Baker's Apprentice.* The artisan bakeries of the Pacific Northwest are larger and more established than those of Asheville and are steeped in the knowledge of Calvel, Didier Rosada, and the Bread Bakers Guild of America. Portland is arguably one of the three best bread cities in the United States. Asheville, on the other hand, is a small, arts and crafts centered city of about seventy thousand people in the foothills of the Smoky Mountains of western North Carolina, about two and half hours from Charlotte. It is a vacation town and a stronghold of independent, countercultural artisans. It was also a good place for someone like me, wrestling desperately with the implications of thirty years of all three waves of the bread revolution, to breathe in the free-spirited air and look at everything with fresh eyes.

As planned, I moderated a whole grains panel (a new educational feature of the festival), which included Jennifer Lapidus, Brian Cook (the head baker of Weaver Street Bakery in Carrboro, next to Chapel Hill), and Gail Lunsford. The panel drew a standing-room-only crowd of both bakers and consumers, and we discussed issues like using vital wheat gluten to help the breads rise, partial versus 100% whole grain breads, and the use of wild versus commercial yeast. More importantly for me, one of the Weaver Street bakers, Emily Buehler, was in the audience, and Brian Cook, her boss, told me she had just written a book on bread science. As fate would have it (like I said, things were beginning to go my way), she has a PhD from the University of North Carolina in chemistry, and while baking at Weaver Street, she decided to write a book for people who do not have her scientific background (that pretty much includes all of us) on the science of how bread baking works.

The timing could not have been better. After the festival, Emily sent me her manuscript, and as I read her explanations of dough chemistry and how enzymes work, I began to see more ways that I could improve my bread formulas by adjusting the amount of yeast and fermentation times, and also through occasional strategic use of oil to strengthen aeration. Sometimes magic happens when people with a common interest and passion get together, and the Asheville

Bread Festival provided just the right amount of critical mass to start a winning streak of good tidings. I returned home with renewed hope, and was greeted by more help in the form of emails from recipe testers with new suggestions based on their test results. Huiling's Chinese soup seed method had opened up so many new options that there was no turning back, and some of the testers wrote in that they had never tasted better whole wheat bread than the mash versions, even with the difficulties.

What I was realizing, as more and more test feedback filtered in, was that we were on the verge of a totally unique, yet relatively easy method that brought together the threads of all the techniques and information I had previously gathered, not only during the research for this book, but from the past thirty years of my bread baking life. The realization that these streams were finally arriving at their confluence occurred when I received an email from one of my favorite recipe testers, Carol Peters, who had not been shy about her concerns regarding the early test recipes, calling them, at times, horrific. Because the recipe I had sent her to test turned out so badly, she made up a recipe of her own that turned out great, and she sent it to me. It used a very large percentage of wild yeast starter, much larger than what I had been calling for, more like the wild yeast country *boule* with which I had won the James Beard competition so many years ago. It performed, according to Carol, perfectly.

Another lightbulb came on and I realized that this might be the missing piece of the puzzle. If I were to combine the nonyeasted, room-temperature soaker dough (the Gosselin method, modified with the Allen Cohn challenge) with the Carol Peters formulation employing an equal amount of starter dough (either wild yeast starter or a commercially yeasted *biga*), perhaps the final dough would perform like epoxy and be stronger than the two individual pieces. (I use the epoxy analogy because I have long been fascinated by the idea that two resins with little or no cementing ability could create an ironclad glue when mixed together, in much the same way that glutenin and gliadin, two weak proteins, make the strong protein gluten when brought together.)

Sure enough, when I brought these two components together on Day 2, mixing them with additional ingredients such as salt, yeast, honey, and in some instances oil (thank you Emily Buehler), the dough had a liveliness and character not otherwise present. This was the dough I had been looking for. The long development time of each pre-dough, one at room temperature (the soaker) and the other in the refrigerator (either the wild yeast starter or the *biga*), allowed for maximum enzyme activity and flavor development without exhausting the yeast or using up all the sugar. The addition of commercial yeast during the final mix allowed for a fast, timely rise, which is fine because there is no need to delay it—the flavor development has already been accomplished by the delayed fermentation method (thank you Philippe Gosselin). There is no flavor advantage to a long, slow final rise, as most artisan breads require, because the flavor development has been accomplished during overnight, delayed processes. This sounds obvious and simplistic, but it took me more than a year to figure it out and realize that, while my original theories were mostly correct, they were missing this epoxy effect.

With this two-part technique, I could now add mash to the dough or create any number of variations, both original and traditional. We had, collectively, discovered something akin to a universal field theory, a new way of preparing dough that evokes the full potential from the grain, allowing the flavor and mouthfeel of whole grain breads to reach new heights. With all of these discoveries coming together so fast and furiously, I felt I was on a roller-coaster ride, hanging on for dear life, but the breads kept getting better and better. It was time to write the book!

Final Touches

The testers responded, some with enthusiasm and some frustrated because they were still having trouble making the recipes work. Most of the new problems were my fault: too many vague, incomplete, or confusing directions. Fortunately, the testing process was designed not only to work out the recipe ingredients but also to fine-tune the instructions: to discover the kinds of questions a new baker might have and to figure out how to describe the way a dough should feel or be handled, what to do if the dough is either too wet or too dry, how to mix and shape it, and what to do if the dough does not respond as the instructions indicate it should.

A bread recipe is, at best, a set of guidelines for getting close to a final version. But making adjustments to accommodate the performance of different types of flour or individual measuring methods requires another set of instructions explaining how to develop a feel for the dough. This is one of the hardest things to convey, especially in words. Many photographs were taken to illustrate how dough should look or feel, but there is no substitute for hands-on trial and error. I tell my students that the way to get a feel for dough is to actually touch it, work with it, and develop sense memories of how it feels when it feels right. It usually takes only a few tries before one gets this sense of feel, and when it happens it is a glorious breakthrough for a baker.

Thanks to the collaborative efforts of so many testers, colleagues, consultants, and friends old and new, good things began to happen. Piece by piece we figured it out and I became a mad little scientist, baking loaf after loaf and correlating the streams of new information until they converged into a newer theory that worked, and that created beautiful breads of uncommon flavor.

The following pages describe how to do it, what is happening, and why. You are about to digest a lot of information. I implore you to read the background and tutorial information in the next chapters, and to carefully study the master formula in chapter 3 before making the individual recipes. Though you may recognize some of the steps, this method is unlike any that you have tried before. It cannot be mastered by simply reading instructions and recipes. You will have to make adjustments for your particular flour; you will have to develop a feeling for the dough so that it, rather than the words on the page, can tell you what it needs and when to move on to the next stage. You will be required to make a commitment to the process and to the mystery itself.

We have taken apart conventional bread making and put it back together in a totally new and different way, and we are navigating both familiar and unfamiliar streams, yet we have the

same goal as ever: to make world-class bread and, let us hope, to make whole grain bread that people will actually want to eat—not just because it is good for them but because it brings them, and us, joy with each bite.

. . .

One final thought about the confluence of streams: New frontiers will always appear on the horizon as we master the currently converging ones. The learning never seems to stop, and I look forward, eagerly, to the discoveries of future bakers as they take these findings down other streams not yet imagined. That bread can be simultaneously so simple and yet so complex and fraught with the potential for maddening, powerful, stop-you-in-your-tracks questions and puzzles, sending you on endless searches for new ways to evoke its fullest potential, is reason enough why bread baking is now and will always remain such a compelling, fascinating metaphoric mystery. I said it before and will continually declare: Bread has been around for over six thousand years, and it is not going away.

From Wheat to Eat:
A Tutorial

There's an old culinary saying: Cooking is taking ingredients and doing something to them, while gourmet cooking is taking ingredients and doing something to them ... and then doing something else to them. It's true—all cooking partakes of transformational processes. Living things that have been harvested are recombined with other ingredients and manipulated with heat, spices, and mixing techniques to bring forth something that goes beyond the original ingredients. But bread baking goes even further. Bread is the ultimate transformational food. Its ingredients are not only radically changed from one thing into something completely different, but more significantly, and unlike any other food, bread actually goes through two transformations in its journey from the earth to the table. Let me explain.

To make bread we harvest the caryopsis (the seed) from living grass, taking the life of that grass. Usually but not exclusively, that grass is wheat. Then we grind the seed into flour, taking even its potential for future life. During the mixing stage, we combine this flour with salt and water and turn it into a claylike mixture. When infused with leaven, it gradually comes to life as it rises and becomes bread dough. (It may help to know that the dictionary definition of *leaven* is "to enliven, to vivify; to bring to life.") This is the first transformation.

After several succeeding stages of the bread making process—fermentation, shaping, resting, and so on—the baking stage arrives and a second transformation occurs. Living dough enters a hot oven, and as the internal temperature of the dough passes 139°F (the dough's thermal death point), all life ceases. In order to complete its mission of raising the dough and transforming it into bread, the leaven gives up its own life, too.

These two transformations help to explain our fascination and love for bread. Whether literally or symbolically, the ingredients are radically transformed and so, at times, is the baker. The road from wheat to eat takes many twists and turns, verging at times on seemingly mysterious, alchemical changes. And the ultimate loaf experienced, finally, at stage twelve (eating!) is a creature totally unlike the grass seeds ground into flour from which it originated.

THE LIFE AND TIMES OF WHEAT

There are over thirty thousand varieties of wheat, and many of them are direct descendants of einkorn. Einkorn was one of the first cultivated strains of wheat, mainly because the seeds were large enough to be worth all the trouble. Spelt was a similar early strain, and then came a more complex strain called emmer (or *farro* in Italy). These wheat strains dominated the fields throughout the ancient Middle East for about four thousand years, and eventually cultivated durum wheat emerged from the emmer family, it is believed, around 100 B.C.E.

Over the centuries, farming, milling, and baking processes evolved as the uses for wheat products increased and the skills required to meet the needs became more specific. Growers, for instance, observed that wheat could be planted during two distinct seasons: autumn and spring. Spring wheat is planted after the thaw, grows straight through summer, and is ready for harvest in late summer or early autumn. In contrast, winter wheat is planted in autumn. The seeds germinate, sprout, and grow a few inches before the frost hits, and then as the cold weather sets in, the plants go dormant. In spring, winter wheat comes back to life and is ready for harvest in late spring and early summer. Autumn planting doesn't work where winters are brutally cold, but where it does work, the wheat takes on very different characteristics than those of the same seeds planted in spring.

As it matures, all wheat passes through a green, grassy, chlorophyll stage, then a stalk and straw stage, until it finally heads, which means it begins to develop seeds in order to procreate. During their entire growth period, the plants are vulnerable to all sorts of factors, such as the amount of rainfall, which can be either too little or too much; insects like aphids, worms, weevils, mites, and various types of flies; weeds (the Biblical "tares"), which compete for nutrients and moisture; and molds and fungus spores, such as ergot and rust, that feed parasitically on the plants (of course, yeast is also a fungus, but one that proves to be useful later). Having survived this perilous journey, often due to the diligent care of the farmer, the grain is ready to be reaped, or harvested.

Harvesting choices are also critical to the final characteristics of the flour, and ripeness is tricky to gauge. If the grain is left growing too long and then gets rained on, it could germinate and sprout. This can greatly compromise quality, storage, and milling. Sprouted wheat cannot be milled into quality flour. And yet if it is harvested too early, the flavor and protein qualities will not reach their full potential.

But the seeds of wheat still have a long way to go on their journey to the table. They have to be collected, cleaned, and then stored in climate-controlled facilities in order to sweat off excess moisture and settle down from the shock of being plucked from living stalks. Humidity is the enemy of stored grain, and as anyone who has been in the North American wheat belt knows, summer and fall are humid times. The ideal moisture content of a wheat seed is 14%, but it usually comes from the field at 16% to 17%, depending on how much rain fell during the growing season (during dry years it can come in as low 7% to 8%). Normally, it needs ample time to dry out, and so it will typically sit in silos for about six weeks before moving on to a mill.

Bread bakers get a lot of the credit for making wonderful bread, and as a reader of this book your own interest is probably more focused on learning how to bake wheat into bread than how to mill it into flour. Farmers and millers, however, deserve their share of the credit.

From the early, early days, when the time-consuming task of taking a stone or mortar to grain could be an all-day project for an entire family, to modern methods of milling with steel rollers, the historical progression of techniques for milling grain into flour is similar to that of growing and cultivating wheat, marked by long periods of stasis and then advanced by a surge of ingenuity or technological vision. In the industrial age, for example, as Oliver Evans was just creating automated mills with continuous flow systems in the States, Hungarian millers developed gradual milling, a technique that involves breaking the grains into progressively smaller pieces. This allowed for better separation of the bran and germ particles, and for the first time, millers and bakers became more aware of the differences in performance of flours with various compositions. And by the end of the Civil War, French miller Edmund La Croix came to America and introduced a purifying system that he had developed and which effectively blew out the bran particles from the middlings (the intermediate, coarsely ground flour).

Millers were now expected to be more than just grinders of grain. They were expected to assess the various strains and blend them to spec for bakers. They were expected to perform tests to determine flour functionality, gluten content, ash content, and performance tolerances, and then to separate the yields into different categories. The miller and baker, as well as all the distribution channels that connect them, forge an essential partnership, a formal relationship that ultimately leads to bread and other wheat products.

For all of these partnerships and products to be successful though, we not only need wheat and other grains, but we need to undertand them.

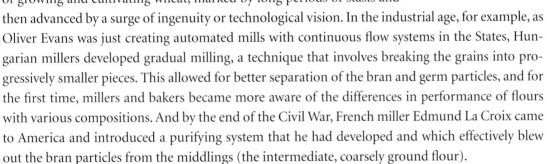

THE ANATOMY OF A WHEAT KERNEL

What we think of as grain and flour begins life growing as grass, first as a germinated seed, then as a sprout emerging above the soil, and then as green grass. New seeds emerge and mature late in the life cycle of the grass, much as they do in the grasses grown on home lawns.

When the seed is growing, it is protected by a covering, or husk, which is rubbed off before the grain is ground into flour. This is the part referred to as chaff. The dehusked seed of the grain, its fruit, is called the caryopsis. This is the part that's edible. While the term *wheat berry* is commonly used to refer to this seed, we will use *kernel* to avoid confusing it with other types of berries and fruits. Within the kernel, there are three main components: the bran, germ, and endosperm.

The *bran*, or pericarp, is composed of layers of cellulose/carbohydrate fiber, minerals, and vitamins. The innermost layer of the pericarp is called the aleurone layer, which is generating a lot of interest lately among bakers and nutritionists, as studies show it to be the most beneficial part of the bran from a health standpoint. However, like the rest of the pericarp layers, it is eliminated from white flour during the sifting process, after the kernels are milled into flour. The aleurone layer is closest to the endosperm and is often attributed to both the bran layer and the endosperm.

The *endosperm* is the largest part of the kernel, comprising approximately 75% to 80% of the total. It is designed to provide nutrition to the embryo once it sprouts. Nearly three-quarters of the endosperm is starch and the rest is protein and moisture. The amount of protein varies, depending on the hardness or softness of the wheat.

The *germ* is where the embryo dwells, surrounded by essential vitamins, minerals, and oils. This is where new life develops: future blades of grass, and then a new generation of seeds. Because it is mostly oil, the germ is the most volatile part of the kernel, the part that can spoil and become rancid.

With white flour, bran and germ are nonissues, but with whole grain flour they are a major part of the story. There are many whole grain books that deeply explore each of these components and, frankly, it can get a little overwhelming. Not all of this information is relevant to our bread baking concerns, but we do need to understand the components of wheat to some degree.

The Bran

Bran, the primary source of fiber in flour, is mostly a type of carbohydrate. It is high in phytic acid, which may help prevent colon cancer by binding with iron. Iron can cause oxidative damage in the colon by creating free radicals and this can ultimately lead to cancer. So this component of bran can actually be considered an antioxidant. Bran also contains a wide array of B vitamins, including folic acid, thiamin, biotin, and riboflavin. It also contains a number of vital minerals. Wheat bran makes up 14% to 15% of the total wheat kernel.

Wheat bran is just one of many sources of fiber, but given how much wheat we eat, it has the potential to be a major source of this important nutrient. A fiber-poor diet is a major factor in the obesity and health problems in our society. In calories alone, for instance, fiber has only half the calories of starch, even though they are both carbohydrates, a fact that could make an enormous difference in the number of calories consumed over a person's life. White flour is generally 72% to 76% extraction, that is, it contains only about three-quarters of the full wheat kernel, and it consists of pure endosperm. The bran and the germ are entirely removed. The endosperm contains most of the protein, so white flour is not all starch, but protein is usually only about 12% to 15% of the remaining flour. This means that about 75% of white flour is starch and moisture.

Even though all forms of fiber are carbohydrates, not all fiber is the same. The three primary forms are soluble fiber, insoluble fiber, and resistant starch. Soluble fiber dissolves in water and forms a gel as it passes through the body. Though much of it is indigestible, it can be fermented and partially broken down in the colon. Insoluble fiber does not dissolve in water, nor is it digested anywhere in the body. It is primarily composed of cellulose (technically, an inert carbohydrate that makes up the cell walls of plants), and it passes out of the body intact. Wheat bran is mostly insoluble cellulose, though it also contains a small amount of soluble fiber.

Resistant starch is somewhat different. These are complex carbohydrates that resist digestion and thus arrive in the colon mostly intact, where they offer some of the benefits of both soluble and insoluble fiber. One form of resistant starch is bread crust that has been hardened during cooking and does not break down until it reaches the colon, where the body's natural bacteria and enzymes can work on it. Resistant starch, along with both soluble and insoluble fiber, is labeled as dietary fiber in the nutrition panels on food packaging.

Soluble fiber has many health benefits, including the following:

- Lowering levels of total cholesterol and LDL cholesterol (bad cholesterol)
- Helping regulate blood sugar (especially beneficial for people with diabetes and prediabetic conditions)
- Helping slow down digestion for better nutrient absorption

The best sources of soluble fiber include oats and oat bran, dried beans, barley, flaxseeds, psyllium husks, most fruits and vegetables, and nuts and seeds.

The many health benefits of insoluble fiber include the following:

- Controlling the pH balance in the intestines
- Moving food through the intestines
- Promoting regular bowel movements
- Pulling toxins out of the body

The best sources of insoluble fiber include wheat bran, any whole wheat products, flaxseeds, potato skins, cauliflower, root vegetables, the skin of fruits, and green beans.

As a rule, we tend to eat three times more insoluble fiber than soluble, though most people do not get enough of either. Nutritionists recommend that we consume at least 25 grams of dietary (total) fiber per day and especially recommend getting at least half of it from grain products.

The Endosperm

Because at least three-quarters of the endosperm is starch and only a small portion is protein, let's begin our exploration of endosperm with starch.

STARCH

Although it is by far the most voluminous ingredient in flour and in bread, starch is poorly understood by many people. Here is a simple definition of starch from Emily Buehler's *Bread Science*: "A polysaccharide made of glucose rings."

Saccharide is a technical way of saying sugar, and polymer refers to a molecule consisting of repeated structural units, so a polysaccharide is essentially a chain of sugar molecules, which means it is in the carbohydrate family. Monosaccharides, or simple sugars, are single sugar chain molecules, which have a ringlike structure. They are the most basic units in the world of sugars; glucose and fructose are two common monosaccharides. As you might guess, disaccharides are molecules comprised of two simple sugar molecules joined together. Common disaccharides include maltose, made up of two glucose molecules, and sucrose, made up of glucose and fructose. These four sugars—glucose, fructose, maltose, and sucrose—are the most important in bread. Unless we add other sugar compounds to dough via ingredients like fruit juice, milk, and syrups, the internal sugar community of flour is based in these four saccharides, which are present in the starch in the endosperm.

The long chains of saccharides known as polysaccharides can be very complex and may have many branches. The types of sugars in the chain, whether the chain is branched, and the overall configuration of the molecule determine the type of starch and its various properties. This will become more important when we discuss enzymes and how they break starch chains apart.

Starch chains have two molecular personalities: amylose (straight chains) and amylopectin (branched chains). The starch in flour typically consists of about 20% to 30% amylose and 70% to 80% amylopectin. When starch gelatinizes, or gels, these sugar chains swell and absorb water. This is what we observe as thickening. (Please note, this is a very simplified explanation of what, chemically, is a very complex process involving hydrogen bonds, helix and double helix configurations, random and nonrandom branching, and all sorts of molecular drama, which, fortunately, you need not know for the purposes of this book.)

Amylose chains thicken, or gel, differently than amylopectin chains. Amylopectin tends to create a more sticky gel (it sometimes shows up as a shiny, translucent aspect of the crumb), while amylose forms tighter colloidal bonds and crystals. However, amylose does not bind water as well as amylopectin, and this is one cause of retrogradation of the starches after baking (in other words, staling). The balance of amylase and amylopectin starches that remain in the final dough greatly determines the texture and keeping properties of the loaf.

What all of this means is that starch has two functions in bread: flavor and structure. The flavor comes from the various sugar chains that break free from the polysaccharides, and the structure arises from the gelling of the starch chains as they swell from the oven heat, bursting at the seams to some extent, while maintaining and binding the water in the dough. This all happens concurrently with other oven reactions: coagulation and denaturing of the proteins, as well as the caramelizing and browning of surface sugars and proteins to create crust (including the Maillard reaction, see page 301).

Clearly, the starch profile of the flours used to make a particular bread can have a big impact on the flavor and texture of the loaf. Many factors can influence this starch profile, even milling. During milling, some of the starch molecules become damaged, ruptured actually, by the grinding tools, exposing smaller sections of the complex starch configurations to enzymes. As they are programmed to do, enzymes then latch onto and break the smaller sections free from the larger chain. Thus, bits of glucose and maltose are broken out and become available to yeast and bacteria for fermentation. These sugars also become available to our taste buds, if they are not first consumed by the microorganisms.

What all of this means is that sugar presents itself as food for yeast and bacteria, which convert it to carbon dioxide, alcohol, and acids. Sugar also presents itself for caramelization in the crust (the only place where bread gets hot enough during baking to caramelize sugar)—and as a flavoring agent for our palates. It is the freeing up of these sugars, and potential sugars still trapped in the starch, in conjunction with the protein that gives each type of bread its own unique flavor and characteristics.

PROTEIN

One thing that distinguishes wheat from the other agricultural grasses, such as rye, barley, corn, and oats, is the amount and quality of its protein, and especially its potential to generate the tenacious and elastic protein known as gluten. Before we can examine the role and significance of protein in bread making, we need to understand some basics about protein.

Proteins are an essential component of all living organisms, where they are critical both for structure and for mediating all of the processes of metabolism. Proteins are composed of more than twenty different amino acids linked together in various types of chains. The amino acid sequence of any given protein, along with any side chains, determines its shape and properties.

The amino acid chain is linked together by what is called a peptide bond. This is a complex topic, as peptide bonds involve carboxyl chains and amino chains, hydrogen bonds, covalent disulfide bonds (the strongest of the protein bonds), ionic bonds, electrostatic attractions, hydrophobic bonding, and on and on. (For those wishing to get deeper into this level of cereal chemistry, you can refer to Emily Buehler's book *Bread Science*, listed in the resources on page 304; much of what follows I learned from her.) The bottom line of all this is that proteins come in many sizes and shape. Some bend and fold upon themselves, some loop around and around, and some pleat into wavy sheets with other proteins. They can curl into a ball or form random-coil configurations. These shapes and various types of bonding are affected by heat, hydration, agitation, and exposure to salt and other ingredients.

Wheat kernels contain four major types of protein: gliadin, gluten, albumin, and globulin. Although we often think of gluten as the protein in wheat flour, it does not actually exist in wheat; it develops later, when flour is hydrated and gliadin and glutenin bond together to make the longer, stronger protein we call gluten. Albumin and globulin are water soluble, that is, they dissolve in water. But glutenin (a long-chain protein) and gliadin (a globular short-chain protein), as well as the gluten that they eventually make, are not water soluble. Rather than dissolving in water, they form a colloidal suspension, in which the protein molecules are somewhat dispersed but also somewhat organized due to the influence of many factors, including electrostatic charges. Both heat and salt can affect the colloidal structure, causing the proteins to cluster, or aggregate. Some of the bonds hold water tightly, trapping it in protein folds, while others allow for the free movement of water. All told, this interplay between protein and water is how gluten forms and develops.

The word *gluten* means "glue" in Latin, making it an apt name for this protein, as it has a sticky nature, forming and reforming bonds with other protein molecules, connecting and sticking through electrostatic or hydrogen bonds, as well as other kinds of bonds (disulfide and hydrophobic bonds), eventually creating a more complex alignment. In other words, as you work a dough and repeatedly bring its protein molecules into contact with one another, the molecules become more and more organized and tightly knit.

The long chains of glutenin provide elasticity, or springiness, to dough, while the short, globular chains of gliadin contribute to the extensibility of dough. Typically, the gluten in bread flour contains about 65% gliadin and 35% glutenin. Changes in this ratio can affect the performance of the dough, so the amount of total protein in any flour is not always the best indicator of its quality. A higher percentage of gliadin, for instance, might make the dough too slack, while too much glutenin could cause it to be too elastic and thus difficult to form into loaves. All of that said, I must offer a proviso: Although wheat does not contain gluten, per se, flours are often described in terms of their gluten content, and we've grown accustomed to hearing that various grains are high in gluten or are gluten free. Therefore, I will continue to use these conventions as I describe various grains and flours.

Millers have developed sophisticated equipment to gauge the amount and quality of gluten in doughs made from their flours, such as alveographs, extensigraphs, and farinographs. An alveograph, for example, forces air into a slice of dough, blowing it up like a balloon, in order to test its resistance and elasticity. The farinograph, on the other hand, tests the resistance of dough while it is being mixed to determine whether the amount of gluten makes for optimal mixing performance.

Clearly, proteins play an important—and complicated—role in bread making. Don't worry if you don't understand every detail explained above. The gist of all this is that the protein structure of bread dough is very complex and also an extremely important determinant of the quality of the final loaf. Time, temperature, movement, hydration, and interactions with other ingredients, such as enzymes, all contribute to the performance of those all-important proteins during the bread making process.

The Germ

The germ, or nucleus of a seed, is comparable to the yolk of an egg. It is where new life begins and thus is filled with nutrients essential for a healthy start. Wheat germ is particularly high in tocopherols (vitamin E), phytic acid (phytate or inositol hexaphosphate), and folate, or folic acid. It also contains fatty acids and lipids, the building blocks of fats.

The fatty acids and other oils in the germ put whole grain flours at risk of rancidity. From a purely functional standpoint, flour from which the germ has been removed has a much longer, almost indefinite, shelf life. But it also has been relieved of some of its most important nutrients.

The germ represents about 3% of the total wheat kernel. It is encased in a sac that can be sifted out from the flour during the early milling cycles in much the same way as bran is sifted out. Wheat germ can be purchased in this separated state at natural foods stores and supermarkets. It is often used as a dietary supplement or added to bread dough or cereal, but it will always be at its most beneficial when eaten in its natural state, as part of the whole wheat kernel, in combination with its own bran and endosperm.

• • •

Technical as the above information is, it is actually a simplified explanation of what is going on inside flour and dough. As we connect the dots of the intricate patterns and roles these ingredients play, we can see how their various aspects and properties participate in the great dance of bread baking. How they are handled during the process becomes crucial in the final outcome.

THE TWELVE STAGES OF BREAD REVISITED

Now that we have a sense of the properties of the grain, let's see how this knowledge is put into action. When I teach bread baking to the culinary students at our school, Johnson and Wales University, I tell them in the very first lecture, "Your mission in this class will be to learn how to evoke the full potential of flavor trapped in the grain, and you will accomplish this by understanding the twelve stages of bread."

The twelve stages not only contain useful information, they also provide structure for both the learning process and the baking process. They are the framework that defines the transition from wheat to eat. These stages, however, are not my own invention. Every bread teacher has his

CLASSIFICATIONS OF WHEAT

Professional bakers are vitally concerned about gradations, extractions, and types of flour and become obsessed with subtle nuances in their search for the perfect loaf. Here are some important facts to help get you up to speed at the beginning of *your* obsession.

There are two classifications of commercial wheat: hard and soft; the higher the protein content, the harder the wheat.

Within those classifications there are two subcategories: winter wheat and spring wheat, based on the planting and growing season.

Within those two subcategories there are three more divisions: red and white, which are the main types, plus a third type, durum.

Different combinations of all these variables result in wheat with different characteristics. As you might expect, hard winter red wheat is very different from soft spring white wheat. But it is also quite different from hard winter white wheat or hard spring red wheat. Each type, in fact, has its own performance qualities, and the flour that is derived from these various types of wheat can also be categorized in different ways. Of the various possible combinations, six predominate:

Hard winter red wheat: Mostly grown in the Plains states as well as the northern states and Canada, this variety is moderately high in protein (averaging about 10.5%) and therefore is used in all-purpose flour, as well as bread flour. About 40% of all wheat grown in the United States is hard winter red wheat.

Hard spring red wheat: Mostly grown in the northern states and Canada, this is one of the hardest wheats, and thus one of the highest in protein (averaging about 13.5%). About 24% of the wheat grown in the United States is hard spring red wheat.

Hard winter white wheat: This variety is sweeter and lighter in color than red wheat, with a protein profile similar to hard winter red wheat. Only about 1% of the wheat grown in the United States is hard winter white wheat, but this number is increasing rapidly.

Soft winter red wheat: Ohio is especially famed for this wheat, which is primarily grown in the eastern states. It is low in protein, making it appropriate for pastries, cakes, crackers. About 25% of the wheat grown in the United States is soft winter red wheat.

Soft spring white wheat: Generally grown in a few eastern states and in the Pacific Northwest and California,

or her own way of explaining the twelve-stage process. The stages may be described under different names in some systems, and the emphasis on certain terms or steps may vary, but fundamentally, every bread baker is aware that there are distinct, defined stages within which we and our dough operate. At each stage, choices are made that affect the final outcome. The better we understand this, the more power we have over the process.

Each of the twelve stages of bread is affected by the grain just as the grain is affected by each stage, as you will see as we delve deeper into the subject of wheat and flour. However, the underpinnings of the process hold true whether you are baking whole grain breads with the delayed fermentation method or using more traditional recipes. No matter what type of bread you are making, understanding the twelve stages described below will enhance your success. (Note: I have

this variety is similar to soft winter red wheat, but its flavor is slightly sweeter. About 7% of the wheat grown in the United States is soft spring white wheat.

Durum wheat: The hardest of the wheat strains, durum has a protein content ranging from 12.5% to as high as 17%. About 5% of the wheat grown worldwide is durum, but only about 3% of U.S. wheat is durum, mostly grown in North Dakota.

Within these six classifications there are many varieties and substrains, so these categories offer a seemingly infinite realm of possibilities for millers and bakers. Beyond the inherent differences between various strains of wheat, the specific milling techniques used to create flour from the wheat introduce a new level of variations. This is where the skill of the miller becomes important.

The art of milling includes not only grinding the grain but also blending various types of wheat to achieve specifications, or specs, desired by bakers. As a result, bakers and consumers can choose between soft, low-protein cake and pastry flours, medium-protein all-purpose flours, and various degrees of hard, higher-protein bread flours. Millers have terminologies to differentiate such categories of flour: straight, patent, clear, and whole wheat, for example. They also designate degrees of grind, such as coarse, medium, and fine, and also use terms like grits, groats, chops, cracked, and meal to describe coarseness. These terms are all defined in the glossary (see page 299). (There are also other types of wheat that are not as common, such as spelt and Kamut, two ancient strains that are popular again. See page 49 for a discussion of these other wheat types.)

From left to right: hard winter white wheat flour, hard spring red wheat flour (sifted to 85% extraction for the formula on page 164), and hard winter red wheat flour.

revised the stages somewhat from my explanations in *The Bread Baker's Apprentice* to bring them up to date with how I currently teach them. The stages, like formulas, are tools for understanding and are thus flexible, always tweakable.)

Stage 1: Mise en Place

Mise en place may be the most often used term in any culinary school. It means "everything in its place," and it is the first stage not only of bread baking but of all cooking and, arguably, of successful activity of any kind. In the context of bread, it means to weigh or measure the ingredients (bakers call this scaling), read the instructions, and get organized both externally and internally. I consider it the single most important of the stages because without organization and correct scaling, the chances of success are greatly reduced.

The basic tools for bread making (counterclockwise): strong mixing spoon, instant read food thermometers (dial or digital), rubber spatulas, plastic bowl scraper, *lame* (scoring blade), electronic scale, stand mixer hook and paddle attachments, water mister, and metal pastry bench blade.

Stage 2: Mixing

There are three objectives that must be accomplished during the mixing stage: even distribution of ingredients; activation of the yeast (thus initiating fermentation); and development of the gluten. Mixing can be done in any number of ways; for home baking, the primary methods are by hand, with a countertop stand mixer, or in a food processor. Each method has its advantages, disadvantages, and special requirements, but all must accomplish those three critical objectives.

Stage 3: Fermentation

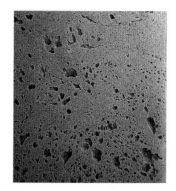

This is what I referred to earlier as the first transformation, when the leavening begins to manifest as growth, transforming inert ingredients into living dough. Fermentation is also when most of the flavor develops. When making large batches of bread, what will become the dough for many loaves starts out in one bulk ferment. Proper bulk fermentation at this stage is necessary for all subsequent fermentation through the succeeding stages. Fermentation may also include degassing the dough by punching it down one or more times. This allows the dough to develop more character in flavor and texture.

Stage 4: Dividing

From stage 4 through stage 9, fermentation continues, but in individuated units—either intermediary units (which will later be further divided) or individual pieces for each loaf of bread. Sometimes these six stages happen very quickly, one right after the other, and sometimes there are resting periods between them; it depends on the dough. Of course, in small, single-loaf batches, as in the recipes in this book, the bulk fermented dough is often the same piece as the final unit.

Stage 5: Rounding

Dough pieces are not always formed into rounds, but this stage is still called rounding (although some people refer to it as preshaping, which is probably the better term). Sometimes the dough is formed into torpedo or oblong shapes. Whatever the shape, the point of this stage is to give the dough the first semblance of its final shape.

Stage 6: Bench Rest

In this stage, sometimes called benching or intermediate proofing, the dough is allowed to rest. The gluten becomes very elastic and tight when the dough is handled during the rounding stage; resting gives it a chance to relax and become more extensible. Sometimes this rest lasts just a few seconds, and sometimes it lasts for an hour or longer, allowing the dough to ferment, or proof, and develop new gas bubbles.

Stage 7: Final Shaping

The dough may or may not be easily formed into its final shape. Two or three resting periods may be required, as in the case of long baguettes, before the dough will hold the desired shape. Depending on the dough, this shaping stage may be performed gently in order to preserve some of the gas from the prior fermentation; this will yield larger, irregular holes, which is desired in many hearth breads. Alternatively, shaping may involve thoroughly degassing the dough so that it will develop smaller, even-sized holes.

Stage 8: **Panning**

This stage usually takes only a few seconds. The dough is placed either on a baking pan, in a prepared loaf pan, or in some type of form, such as a proofing basket (for example, a *banneton*, made from bent willow wood) or a *couche* (a type of linen cloth used for baguettes and other hearth breads).

Stage 9: **Final Proofing**

In this stage, the dough continues to ferment and "proves" that it is still alive as it grows to its final size in preparation for baking. This can take place in a proof box (a warm, humid cabinet) or at room temperature. Duration of proofing may be short or long, depending on the dough and the temperature.

Stage 10: **Baking**

Baking can be defined as the application of heat to a product in a closed environment for the purpose of driving off moisture. This is the second transformation, in which living dough dies in the oven in order to become finished bread. ("Goes in alive comes out dead; goes in dough, comes out bread.") Technically, three oven reactions take place: the proteins coagulate (at about 160°F to 165°F); the starches gelatinize (at about 180°F), and the sugars in the crust caramelize (beginning at approximately 325°F; the crust is the only part of the dough that gets hot enough for the sugars to caramelize).

Stage 11: **Cooling**

The dough continues to bake as it cools down, driving off additional moisture. When a loaf is still hot from the oven, its structure is not fully set. If you cut into it, the loaf will seem underbaked. The proteins need to cool down and firm up in order to provide a strong structure for the bread.

Stage 12: **Packaging or Storage**

The textbooks call it packaging or storage, but many of us prefer to call it eating.

・ ・ ・

Bakers understand that dough fermentation is the key to world-class bread. This has been the artisan baking community's primary focus during the past twenty years of the American bread revolution. The next frontier now facing bread bakers is enzymes.

ENZYMES

Enzyme activity is the underpinning of fermentation. Enzymes are far more subtle and complex than yeast, pre-ferments, and the other ingredients that we associate with fermentation. The amount and variety of enzymes found in whole grain flour is also one of the main reasons why baking with 100% whole grain flour is very different from baking with white flour.

Enzymes can affect how bread tastes and feels in your mouth, as well as how it is broken down by your body after you eat it. Some professional bakeries, mostly the large-volume producers, are now using customized enzyme blends to create textures and unique flavor profiles previously impossible to achieve through standard fermentation methods. These enzyme blends can be directed to affect the starches or the proteins, as well as the extensibility, elasticity, and workability of dough.

Enyzmes themselves are complex proteins that catalyze biochemical reactions. One of the primary functions of enzymes in food (and, again, this is a simplified explanation; there are many other functions and actions of enzymes not related to this) is to break larger molecules into smaller ones so they can be digested and converted into energy. For example, when you chew food, your saliva introduces enzymes produced by your own body to the food in your mouth. These enzymes give the food a head start toward digestion; this is also the reason why some foods change in flavor the more you chew them. Whether in the body or in dough, enzymes that break down starches are known as amylases, and those that break down proteins are known as proteases.

Think of enzymes as small wedges that attach to a molecule and open it up, splitting it into smaller pieces. Another analogy is that they fit, like a key in a lock, into the molecular structure of their corresponding food targets. Thus, a protease enzyme does not fit into a carbohydrate molecule and an amylase enzyme does not attack a protein molecule. Through the gift of nature, most foods come with their own built-in complement of enzymes that facilitate breaking them down into nutrients that can be assimilated.

Enzymes do their job at various rates of speed. While they are not living organisms in their own right but, rather, small proteins or protein fragments, they are, like yeast and bacteria, affected by temperature. Different enzymes function faster and more efficiently at different temperatures.

Again, to keep it simple, when starch enzymes are activated, usually as a result of hydration or increased temperature, they free up smaller threads of sugar from the starch so that the sugar can be converted to energy. In the case of flour, the enzymes alpha- and beta-amylase trigger a reaction that releases threads of various chains of sugar into the dough, making all sorts of new flavors and functions possible. Other enzymes attack smaller sugar chains, such as maltase, which breaks down maltose into its constituent units of glucose. Invertase, an enzyme that exists in yeast, can break sucrose into its component parts, glucose and fructose, thus freeing glucose for the yeast to eat and convert into carbon dioxide and alcohol, while the fructose provides sweetness.

Without enzymes to break it down, starch remains fairly tasteless to us because its molecules are sufficiently complex as to slide right over our taste buds—too complex for us to be able to taste the various threads of glucose, dextrose, fructose, maltose, lactose, and other sugars that may be part of its intricate fabric. Starch is like a woven tapestry composed of threads of these various sugars.

Milling, as already noted, damages a small percentage of starch, but another way to open up food starches, to damage them, is to gelatinize them; that is, to heat them up in liquid until they expand and absorb all the moisture they can—until they simply explode, spewing sugar threads into the surrounding area to absorb even more liquid. We see this action most clearly in gravies and starch-thickened sauces. Gelatinization has nothing to do with enzyme activity, per se; it is strictly a function of the interaction of heat, water, and starch. It not only thickens sauces but also bread dough, while the loaf is baking, transforming its structure from inedible dough into delicious bread. But as we will see later when we discuss mashes, partially gelatinizing starches at lower temperatures can also affect taste and texture of bread by making starch chains vulnerable to enzymes early in the bread making process.

Enzymes, as we have seen, break out the sugar threads from the starch so that we can taste them (because our taste buds can access the flavor of simple sugars but not of complex starches). These freed sugars also become available to yeast and bacteria as food, thus enhancing fermentation. So, once the enzyme activity begins, all sorts of new opportunities become possible in terms of flavor development, increased fermentation activity, and caramelizing of the freed sugars to induce crust coloration.

For example, consider French bread, which consists of only white flour, water, salt, and yeast. If, in making it, we let it rise once, shape it, let it rise again, and then bake it, we get a so-so loaf of bread with a crust that is usually a yellowish gold in color. However, if we make the exact same bread dough and punch it down after the first rise and then let it rise a second time before shaping it, or if we throw a piece of old dough or a pre-ferment, such as a *poolish* or *biga,* into it when we first mix it, the color of the crust is completely different, more of a reddish gold. This is the result of the release of smaller sugar chains as well as a particular kind of browning, the Maillard reaction, in which proteins and sugars, affected by various enzymes, brown up in a different manner than sugars alone. Holding dough overnight in the refrigerator before baking it is another way to induce freeing of sugar from the starches, allowing the enzymes ample time to do their work. Regardless of method, these outcomes are affected by the length of fermentation and by how much time and under what conditions the enzymes and microorganisms have operated in order to complete their work.

Fermentation, Microorganisms, and Enzymes

From a functional standpoint, the job of the yeast is to leaven and slightly acidify the dough via the production of carbon dioxide and ethyl alcohol, while the function of the bacteria is to

FALLING NUMBERS AND MALT

Professional bakers rely on their flour suppliers to test the falling numbers of their flour and adjust the wheat blend accordingly. You may wonder what a "falling number" is. Let me explain: While all flour has plenty of enzymes, not all flour has the same amount of enzyme activity. This activity is determined by a number of factors, including how long the wheat was in the field before it was harvested, how long it was tempered before it was milled into flour, and how much starch damage it incurred during milling. In starch that has been bruised, exposed sugar chains are more vulnerable to early enzyme activity.

As a rule, bakers believe that too much starch damage is not a good thing, that it weakens the structure and yields gummy bread. Too little starch damage has the opposite effect, making it difficult for enzymes to go to work on sugar chains, which leads to a lack of flavor and crust color. A typical range for damaged starch is 7% to 9% of the total flour. Flour with more than 10% damaged starch is considered substandard, as it too easily breaks down, either during the mixing cycle, after it is shaped, or while it is in the oven. The starch converts too quickly to sugar due to amylase enzyme activity, and even the protease enzymes run amok.

Millers use a process called the falling number test to determine the extent of starch damage and alpha-amylase activity. A small amount of flour mixed with hot water to make a slurry is placed in a tube. Then a rod is dropped into it and timed as it works its way to the bottom of the tube. The more enzyme activity in the flour, the less viscosity the slurry has because the enzymes are converting starches to sugars. The faster the rod drops, the lower the falling number.

Most white flour registers somewhere around 227 seconds, plus or minus. Whole wheat flour, on the other hand, especially if it is stone-ground, has higher numbers than this, reflecting less starch damage and, thus, slower enzyme action upon the starch. For this reason, some bakers feel that adding malted wheat or barley flour, which is loaded with diastase (a variety pack of amylase enzymes), is helpful in unlocking some of the bound-up flavor. As we will see, there are other ways to unlock flavor as well, such as time, soakers, and mashes that enable enzymatic sugar breakout.

With the delayed fermentation method, falling number tests, though very important to professional bakers, are less critical to the home baker who has access to consistently reliable flour or wheat berries. By its very nature, the delayed fermentation method obviates some of the reasons for these tests. The long, delayed fermentation allows the enzymes in the soaker plenty of time to do their work, and because there is no yeast in the soaker, those sugars won't be consumed by yeast. The enzymes are later controlled by the high percentage of pre-ferment (either *biga* or starter).

So, while diastatic (enzyme-active) malted flour is often used as a dough improver, it will usually not be necessary in the formulas in this book. If, however, you discover that your starter or final dough does not perform to expectations, perhaps rising too slowly or not caramelizing as described, it is acceptable to add about .5% to 1% diastatic malt to the soaker. This will translate to approximately 1 teaspoon.

acidify and flavor the dough and, to a lesser degree, create some carbon dioxide. I have referred to this as a symbiotic relationship because the organisms harmoniously share the same environment and food supply, and supplement each other's work without, usually (but not always), harming each other.

In a best-case scenario, the acidifying work of the bacteria lowers the pH level of the dough to create an environment ideal for the growth of the desired strains of wild yeast. I use *strains*, the plural form, because wild yeast is not just a specific strain, such as *Saccharomyces cerevisiae*, but an indeterminate variety of strains under the general name *Saccharomyces exiguus* (*exiguus* means "wild"), including lesser-known strains of yeast sometimes included in the umbrella *exiguus* category. Of all the mysteries in bread making, this symbiotic relationship between yeast and bacteria is perhaps the most fascinating. As the pH of the dough becomes more acidic, commercial strains of yeast do not thrive, while wild strains do. Meanwhile, lactic acid bacteria also react to the very acid they helped create and begin to slow down their own activities. It all gets very complex but, fortunately, when properly carried out, this complexity manifests delightfully in the final flavor, as it also does in cheese, beer, or wine.

The starter is merely a medium in which the microorganisms live, grow, and create their important by-products: alcohol, carbon dioxide, and acid. The baker then builds the starter to a size that it is capable of raising the dough or otherwise affecting it. The amount of the starter in the final dough can be anywhere from 10% to, in some instances, 100% or more of the new flour weight. In most bakeries, the amount of starter to fresh flour in the final dough is usually in the 20% to 33% range. Since commercial yeast, with a few exceptions, is only 1% to 3% of the flour weight, there is obviously a much smaller concentration of functioning yeast cells in a starter than in commercial yeast.

You will notice that many of the breads in this book are made with a combination of commercial yeast and either a wild yeast starter or a pre-fermented *biga*. There are reasons for this, but first it must be said that there are many ways to leaven and ferment dough that can bring about a satisfying result, including exclusive use of natural or wild yeast starters and no commercial yeast; exclusive use of commercial yeast and no wild yeast starters; various combinations of the two; and various types of wild yeast starters made in any number of ways. The formulas in this book are just one way to accomplish making excellent bread, based on a method that I am calling delayed fermentation.

You will also notice that the amount of commercial yeast is relatively high in many of the breads in this book even though I have previously advocated, in earlier books, using less yeast and longer fermentation periods. There are reasons for this as well, one of which is that traditional slow rise doughs, made with combinations of white flour, pre-ferments, soakers, and only a small amount of yeast, need to ferment slowly in order for the enzymes to have as much time as possible to complete their flavor development mission before the yeast completes its leavening mission. However, in the delayed fermentation method used here, most of the dough (both the soaker and the starter or *biga*) has already accomplished its enzyme mission by the time the yeast is introduced, so there is no need for a long fermentation. The starch-to-sugar conversion that fuels flavor development has already been accomplished during the Day 1 pre-dough stage, so the only task remaining on Day 2 is to leaven the dough and bake it.

The uniquely satisfying flavor profile of excellent breads (and this has been tested in controlled blind tasting studies) is based on the fact that our taste buds desire not only the taste of sweetness but also acidity—just a touch of sour—and even bitter. Most people do not like an overly sour flavor in their bread, unless they have been raised on it, like those who live in the San Francisco area, where a particular bacteria, *Lactobacillus sanfrancisco*, is prevalent. Even regular French bread (classic baguettes, *bâtards*, and *boules* made with commercial yeast, not wild yeast starters) always contain a measurable amount of acidity brought about by the long, slow yeast fermentation (sometimes by using pre-ferments like *poolishes* or *bigas*). This acidity is an important part of the flavor experience, as well as a protection against early staling (acidity tends to slow down water migration and starch retrogradation, and serves as a humectant and antimolding agent). Acidity, then, is as important as sugar breakout when it comes to flavor; sweet and sour are very synergistic together, magnifying the complexity and overall flavor impression beyond the sum of their parts.

Some acidity is created by yeast fermentation, as yeast itself generates a small amount of acid while it ferments sugar. This is one of the many reasons that pre-ferments improve the flavor of bread. But far more acid is created by a second type of fermentation, bacterial, in which various strains of bacteria also eat sugar, converting it into lactic acid or acetic acid. This part of the fermentation process is responsible for the amazingly complex flavor profiles of naturally leavened, wild yeast breads (also known as sourdough). While many types of bacteria contribute to positive flavor development, there are some that may contribute negatively and create less desirable flavors, depending on the fermentation temperature. Therefore, between the yeast, whether wild or commercial, and the various strains of bacteria, there are all sorts of flavors that can be developed, some of them determined by the fermentation temperature and some by the types of microorganisms.

Enzymes are crucial players in this drama as they perform a number of tasks that influence the final outcome. For example, protease enzymes go after protein molecules, which are even more complex than starch molecules, and break apart peptide bonds between amino acids. This tends to weaken the dough structure or make it more extensible (not necessarily a bad thing), but over time it can also destroy the gluten bonds (not a good thing when trying to make bread). Phytase releases various minerals that are bound to phytate groups, making them nutritionally accessible. And amylases break down starches by various mechanisms. Alpha-amylases can break the saccharide bonds at any point in the starch molecule, whereas beta-amylase can only work from one end of the molecule, removing disaccharide maltose units one at a time. As the various sugar chains are broken free from the larger starch chains, they become available to both the yeast and the bacteria as food. As mentioned earlier, yeast itself contains an enzyme, invertase, which breaks out simple sugars like glucose or dextrose from starch, ultimately leading to the release of carbon dioxide and ethyl alcohol as the yeast feeds on those sugars. In yet another plot twist, yeast also contains its own protease enzymes, which also affect the structure of dough.

In dough, we have a situation where, if the enzymes keep going and going, knocking sugars off of starch chains or breaking apart protein chains, it could create a problem. But if the enzyme activity is properly controlled, the starch only partially breaks down, creating food for the microorganisms, offering sweetness for our taste buds, commingled with the flavors of various acid by-products created by the bacteria and yeast, yet leaving enough starch and protein intact to support the structure of the bread. Whew! It is as much a tightrope walk as it is a dance.

This begs the question: How much of this breakdown can a starch molecule bear before it crumbles apart and loses its ability to provide substance and structure to the bread? At what point will it simply just melt or dissolve into sugar, leaving us with a sticky, gummy loaf?

Controlling Enzyme Activity

When I first learned about this enzyme dimension of bread making, I wondered how far the effects could be pushed. How much sugar can we appropriately break out of the starch, and why does the entire starch molecule not completely unwind into its various sugars and fall apart? The answer is that we control the enzyme activity by using acidity, which slows down enzymes; salt, which also slows enzyme activity; and refrigeration (in some instances), to slow down both yeast activity and enzyme activity in our *bigas* and wild yeast starters.

The method in the demonstration master formula on page 78 captures and controls all of this internal drama in a way that maximizes fermentation, microorganism activity, flavor development, and structural integrity to deliver a loaf that achieves its full potential.

Although we have already examined some of the effects of enzyme activity on flavor, it will be worthwhile to take a more in-depth look at this topic. Some of the most exciting benefits of controlled enzyme activity are in creating flavors that are complex, subtle, and nuanced. As already noted, flavor is more than sweetness. It is a combination of tastes resonating on the palate as sweet, bitter, salty, sour, and rich (also called *umami*), and is also influenced by our olfactory sense working in concert with our taste zones, adding a depth of flavor not experienced by the tongue alone.

Some of the flavor of bread is a direct result of specific ingredients, such as salt, sugar, milk, butter, oil, honey, milk, or different varieties of flour. Other aspects of the flavor result from these ingredients working in concert with each other; for example, oil or fat can enhance or magnify the flavor notes of sugar or salt. But enzyme activity unlocks the door to an entirely new world, triggering a series of actions that allow other flavors to emerge, flavors not inherent in the original ingredients. Examples include the citrus, buttery, or vinegar tones of particular acids, or the release of bitter hops-like flavors from the bran fiber as it mingles with malt sugar. Much of this flavor release is a result of microorganisms feeding upon various sugars and in the process creating by-products such as lactic acid, acetic acid, and various other flavor compounds—both volatile and stable—composed of amino acids. Each strain of bacteria creates different flavors and aromas, which explains why breads made in various parts of the world may have different flavors even if made using the same formula.

The interactions between ingredients, enzymes, microorganisms, and acids are very symbiotic; that is, they rely on each other to bring out qualities that would not occur if one link in the chain were missing. Moreover, some acids not only enhance the flavor but also contribute to better (or worse) leavening. Many strains of bacteria work better together than they do alone to create desirable flavors, while others work better alone. Some strains create too much acid, while others create not enough. Certain bacteria work beautifully in conjunction with commercial yeast but create too much sourness when used with wild yeast, while other bacteria do not work at all well with commercial yeast but are fine when there is none. Some bacteria create clean flavors at low temperatures but musty flavors at higher temperatures, while others do just the opposite.

Some of these interactions are difficult to control in home environments, but most are not. For instance, it is possible to control the fermentation temperature in a home to some degree, perhaps not as easily as in a bakeshop with climate-controlled proofing boxes, but within tolerable ranges. You can do this by adjusting room temperature with the thermostat, or by putting the dough in an improvised proof box, such as a briefly warmed oven or the microwave (don't turn the microwave on; instead use a cup of boiling water to provide warmth). I have even used the dishwasher as a proof box. Home bakers do not have as much control over their choice of flour as commercial bakers; however, it is now possible to buy flour via mail order from reputable suppliers, or go to a favorite bakery and ask to buy some flour from their bulk supply. Home bakers rarely have access to specification sheets on flour that spell out how much mixing at so many rotations is appropriate to match up with the farinograph or alveograph dough tolerance and peak mixing readings, but they generally have a good idea how their favorite brand responds to the type of mixer they use.

Every choice a baker makes has an effect on the final outcome, but by its very methodology the delayed fermentation method helps even out results. The overnight method provides more room for deviation in certain areas of technique, such as mixing time, the feeding schedule for the starter, and even the brand of flour or type of wheat (red or white, spring or winter). While there may still be differences in outcome based on some of these choices, the results will nevertheless be excellent because the tolerance of the dough is broadened. For example, whether you mix the Day 1 soaker or *biga* at 9 P.M. or 11 P.M. makes little difference, nor will it matter whether the Day 2 mixing is at 7 A.M. or 10 A.M., or even in the afternoon, or two days later. In all cases, the product will turn out wonderfully, assuming the Day 1 pre-doughs are properly made and stored. If the soaker, starter, or *biga* is ready before the final mixing is scheduled to begin, it can be kept in the refrigerator without diminishing the quality.

THE SECRET LIFE OF DOUGH

As you've gathered by now, there is a lot of drama going on inside bread dough. Some of it is microbial and some of it is biochemical. Many excellent professional bakers are unaware of the scientific details of this drama, but they are keen witnesses to its outcomes. Bakers know intuitively that slow fermentation usually makes better bread, and they know that temperature affects fermentation. This guides them in how long to mix dough and how to properly ferment, shape, and bake the dough, and this is more than enough to make outstanding, award-winning bread. However, in the never-ending striving for the perfect loaf, the esoteric and poorly understood realm of enzyme activity is the next frontier.

The delayed fermentation method used in this book capitalizes on enzyme activity while also incorporating the parallel drama of the living microorganisms: yeast and bacteria. It uses a new approach to draw out the full flavor potential of the grain, delaying much of the fermentation until after the enzymes have done their work. (Conventionally, fermentation begins right away, so enzyme activity happens concurrently with fermentation.) This new approach addresses the whole grain baking puzzle by combining several distinct entities to create a dough that performs well and yields a loaf of bread with wonderful flavor. These entities, which you'll come to know well as you use the formulas in this book, are soakers, starters, and, sometimes, mashes.

Pre-fermented Doughs

We will be using two types of pre-fermented doughs in most of the formulas in this book: wild yeast starter (also known as sourdough starter) and commercially yeasted *biga*. The most common misperception about wild yeast or sourdough starters is that the wild yeast is what causes the sour flavor. In reality, various strains of bacteria that live side by side with the yeast create these sour flavor tones as they metabolize available sugars and convert them into lactic or acetic acid.

As noted, many of the breads in this book require a large percentage of either wild yeast or *biga* starter, yet they also call for a large amount of commercial yeast (*Saccharomyces cerevisiae*). The acidity from the starter (or *biga*) is important for both flavor development and for controlling enzymatic activity, while the commercial yeast in the final dough ensures a quick, timely rise and prevents adverse souring of the dough. This is very different from the method taught in my previous books and for artisan breads in general, in which long, slow rises are preferable and relatively small amounts of yeast and starter are used.

WILD YEAST (SOURDOUGH) STARTERS

Bigas are relatively simple to grasp, so let's focus instead on wild yeast or sourdough starters because they are much more complex. Wild yeast breads have a number of appealing qualities that draw us to them. Some of this appeal has to do with flavor and some is of a romantic nature.

Capturing and cultivating wild yeast and bacteria to leaven bread dough is satisfyingly compelling and is a craft. The flavor of the breads they yield is often superior to commercially yeasted breads because of the natural pre-ferment (the wild yeast starter, which can go by any number of names, including *levain*, chef, mother, *madre*, barm, *desum*, or sour sponge). In terms of flavor enhancement, this is very similar to the role played by a *poolish*, *biga*, or any other type of pre-fermented dough. Wild yeast starters carry some leavening responsibility, but as you will see reflected in most of the breads in this book, they primarily serve to enhance flavor, though they do provide a leavening boost.

Another important role of wild yeast starters is to control the enzymes that we have activated through various techniques. While we need those enzymes to release maximum flavor, if they are not controlled, they can ruin the bread by reducing too much of the starch to sugar and too much of the protein to amino acids.

There are many ways to make a starter, some more effective than others. Numerous systems and loads of information, misinformation, and folklore are now available online. Many people obsess over their starters, coddling them like newly born infants, keeping them on regular feeding cycles, and fretting when they do not bubble up the way they should. In previous books I gave three different methods for establishing a starter. But after perfecting what I thought was the simplest, most foolproof method in *The Bread Baker's Apprentice*, I discovered that it did not always work the way I said it would.

A team of amateur sleuths and passionate home bakers, led by Debra Wink of Columbia, Missouri, tackled the problem in the Baking Circle discussion group on the King Arthur Flour website. Debra, who is a chemist, put some of the troublesome starter under a microscope and came up with the plausible theory that the problem was caused by leuconostoc, a strain of lactic acid bacteria that generates a lot of carbon dioxide (like yeast) but also interferes with wild yeast growth and development. The interrelationship between yeast and bacteria is a complex subject. (For more on this subject, see the resources on page 304 for a link to Debra's essay on solving the problems caused by leuconostoc.)

Soakers and Sprouted Grains

Many traditional whole grain and multigrain bread formulas call for soakers. The primary function of a soaker is to soften uncooked coarsely ground grains by soaking them first in water. These grains are often too coarse to fully hydrate and soften during the regular mixing and fermentation cycles, so an overnight soaking in water (or milk) not only softens them but also activates the dormant enzymes nestled in the grain, and thus initiates the processes described above.

With unmilled grains (whole kernels such as wheat berries, whole barley, rye berries, and the like), soaking them in water not only initiates enzyme action but also starts the germination process. That is, the seeds come to life as the embryo in the germ begins dividing and growing. The nutrients in the germ and the endosperm become food for the growing seed. As the seed sprouts and begins to grow what looks like a tail, it becomes more like a plant or vegetable and has softened considerably. With some seeds, such as barley and wheat, this early sprouting stage is also part of the process of malting, a name that arose because one of the main sugars released by enzymes during sprouting is maltose. Barley, especially, contains a lot of maltose, which is why it is such a useful grain for making beer and whiskey.

When grain is milled, it can no longer germinate because the germ has been crushed, destroying the embryo. However, when soaked it will still break down and release its sugar threads as the enzymes go to work. So, while one purpose of soakers is to soften the grain, an equally important purpose is to release flavor and introduce enzyme activity. When added to dough, soakers, whether made with whole or milled grains, change the way the dough performs, usually sweetening it and creating a richer, more golden crust.

Finely ground flour is rarely used in traditional soakers because it does not need much time to hydrate, but in the delayed fermentation method we will be soaking flour, regardless of the grind. The main reason, in keeping with our guiding vision, is to release the maximum flavor from the flour. But there is another important reason specific to our whole grain mission: because of the large amount of fiber in whole grain flour, the gluten threads are constantly at risk of getting cut by the sharp edges of the bran. Soaking the flour helps soften the fiber, reducing the damaging effects it has on the structure of the loaf.

Top: Wheat kernels that have just begun sprouting.

Middle: Sprouted wheat dough.

Right: Crumb of sprouted wheat bread.

OTHER WHEATS AND MULTIGRAIN OPTIONS

As you learned earlier in this chapter, wheat is not a monolithic single entity. There are many varieties of just plain wheat (*Triticum aestivum* or *Triticum turgidum*). And beyond standard wheat lies a diverse world of other strains of wheat and other cereal grains. Some of them were once more common than wheat, and some of them remain more common in other parts of the world. In an exciting reversal of the twentieth-century trend toward monoculture, there is now increased interest in diversity in all sorts of agricultural crops—including grains.

OTHER WHEATS

Durum wheat: The hardest of the wheat strains, durum has a protein content ranging from 12.5% to as high as 17%. It is also high in beta-carotene, which accounts for its golden color (and as a result, the name amber durum; there is also a red durum, which is rarely used for human food but, rather, for livestock). About 5% of the wheat grown worldwide is durum, but only about 3% of U.S. wheat is durum, mostly grown in North Dakota. Semolina is the name given to fine durum meal, which is almost sandy in texture and is often used in Italian cooking as well as couscous. When ground into flour it is called fancy durum. This is the flour used to make the finest pastas. *Grano* is the name of a dish made from polished durum kernels that are soaked, boiled, seasoned, and served as a chewy side dish similar to *farro* (which is made from emmer). In the Puglia region of Italy, durum flour is used in the famous pugliese breads, sometimes at 100% and sometimes blended with bread flour.

Einkorn (*Triticum monococcum*): This is the oldest strain of cultivated wheat, dating back as far as 10,000 B.C.E. It is considered the ancestor of all subsequent strains. Einkorn isn't widely cultivated anymore because of its low productivity (each spikelet head yields only one kernel) and the difficulty of separating the kernel from the spikelet, but it is still grown in parts of eastern and western Europe, as well as in India. It is significantly higher in protein than modern red and white wheat.

Emmer (*Triticum dicoccum*): One of the most ancient of all wheats, emmer replaced einkorn as the wheat of choice in about 4,000 B.C.E. Emmer itself was gradually replaced by other strains that were easier to harvest. (Unlike later strains, in einkorn, emmer, and ancient spelt the seeds are covered up in the spikelets, making them more difficult to harvest.) Emmer is still grown in Italy, Ethiopia, and in India and is now being cultivated in Montana and North Dakota as a spring wheat. It is high in protein and has excellent flavor, but it yields low-quality gluten, so it isn't a popular wheat for bread. Boiled, the whole kernels are an excellent grain to add to bread dough.

Kamut (*Triticum turgidum* subsp. *turanicum*): Kamut, thought to be an ancestor of durum wheat, has kernels that are amber in color and nearly twice the size of most wheat kernels. The name Kamut is actually a trade name coined by T. Mack Quinn and his son Bob, Montana wheat farmers who in 1977 obtained the last remaining jar of "King Tut's Wheat" seeds, grown from thirty-six kernels originally brought to the United States by an airman who claimed to have taken them from a box found near an ancient tomb in Egypt. The Quinns believed that the ancient name for wheat was *kamut*, meaning "soul of the earth," and so they adopted this name when they began growing it. Like spelt, it is high in protein (possibly 20% higher than regular wheat) but not high in gluten. Because it can be tolerated by some people who cannot eat wheat, it is now grown in abundance and is used in hundreds of products (450 and counting).

Spelt (*Triticum spelta*): This variety of wheat may have originated in the region of present-day Iran or south-eastern Europe from a crossbreeding of emmer with other local wild grasses. Its seeds are covered and thus not easy to thresh, but each spikelet carries two kernels rather than the one of einkorn and emmer. It is higher in protein, but not specifically gluten, than red and white wheat and has a thicker pericarp than other varieties of wheat. Spelt may also be easier to digest than other forms of wheat, and some people with gluten intolerance (such as those with celiac disease) don't react to spelt. Gliadin is the portion of gluten that people with celiac disease can't digest. One theory is that spelt contains a different, more tolerable, type of gliadin (as do Kamut, emmer, and einkorn). The gliadin in bread flour (from both red and white wheat) seems to be the most difficult to tolerate.

BEYOND WHEAT

Amaranth (*Amaranthus* spp.): This grain was impor-tant to many indigenous cultures in the New World, most famously the Aztecs, who called it "seed sent by God" and used it not just for food but in religious ceremonies. The grain is small enough that it can be added directly to dough or to a soaker. Although rich in protein, amaranth is gluten free. And because it contains all of the essential amino acids, it is one of the few grains to contain complete protein.

Barley (*Hordeum vulgare*): The ancient Egyptians valued barley so much that they buried their dead with neck-laces made from it. In the modern world it is used primarily as animal fodder. Its second most common use is to make malt (sprouted grain), which has a wonderful, rich flavor and is an essential ingredient for making beer and whiskey. Barley is underappreci-ated as an eating grain, probably because it is some-what chewy even when thoroughly cooked. Barley fiber, along with oat bran, is now considered a major asset in cholesterol control. Barley greens, harvested while still in the grassy stage and then dried into a chlorophyll-rich powder, is a very popular item in health food stores for its concentrated nutritional con-tent. In bread baking, diastatic (enzyme-active) barley malt is added to white flour to promote fermentation and crust development. Nondiastatic malt, in which enzymes have been denatured by heat, is used as a flavoring ingredient in many products, including bagels, beverages, and candies.

Buckwheat (*Fagopyrum esculentum*): Buckwheat is not a type of wheat at all; technically it is not even a grain, but a plant related to rhubarb. But its seeds look like grain and function like grain, and so it is used like a grain. Buckwheat flour has no gluten, so it makes very tender pancakes (known as *blini* in Russia); it's also used in Asian noodles (soba). Buckwheat can be added to multigrain breads for both flavor and nutrition, either as flour or as cooked grain. Like amaranth and quinoa, it has a well-rounded amino acid profile, making it one of the few vegetable sources of complete protein. It contains large amounts of rutin, an antioxidant nutrient that helps fight cholesterol.

Cassava (*Manihot esculenta*): Known by many other names, including manioc and tapioca, this is an important food crop throughout the equatorial world, where it is used in many forms, including as a flour. It is not a grain but rather a shrubby plant, sometimes called yuca, that has a long tuberous root loaded with starch, calcium, phosphorous, and vitamin C, but very low in protein. Raw cassava can be poisonous, but cooking in water eliminates the toxins, and this is done when processing the tubers to make flour or tapioca. In the United States, we most often use it as a thickener, but it is also used as a flour for flatbreads and, especially, in gluten-free breads.

Corn (*Zea mays*): The most versatile of all grains, corn (also known as maize) is high in natural starch sugars and thus a source for fructose and other derivatives, which are usually freed up through forced enzyme action. It is also high in niacin and in antioxidants. Ancestors of modern corn were a dietary mainstay in Native American cultures. Seek out whole grain cornmeal, which should have flecks of brown; if the label says "degerminated," it isn't a whole grain product. Corn, in itself, is not a source of quality protein, but when combined with beans, as it often is in Native American cuisine, the combined amino acid profile constitutes complete protein.

Millet (*Panicum miliaceum*): In the United States only birds eat millet on a regular basis, but in China, India, and Africa, it is a staple. Approximately 100 million acres are currently under millet cultivation worldwide. Millet flour is used in some versions of *roti* (see page 281), and it also makes an excellent hot breakfast cereal. Many bakers use uncooked whole millet in their multigrain breads, but it will not completely soften in the dough. Plus, it is better to cook it first in order to access its full range of nutrients; it is particularly high in B vitamins and minerals. Although its protein content is similar to wheat, it is gluten free.

Oats (*Avena sativa*): This is one of the truly great whole grains of the world, and one of the few that everyone eats without realizing that it is a whole grain. The pericarp is high in beta-glucans, a form of fiber that is water soluble and widely believed to be helpful in lowering LDL cholesterol (the bad kind). Oats are usually found as flakes, which are whole oats that have been briefly steamed and then rolled and flattened. Steel-cut oats are a type of groat—oat kernels cut or cracked into bits—which can be boiled for the very best oatmeal. Oats have been used for centuries to make bread in Europe, especially in the British Isles, mainly because they are easy to grow and plentiful, not because they make wonderful bread. But their nutritional value and flavor do lend a lot of value to multigrain breads.

Potato starch: While potatoes (*Solanum tuberosum*) are not grains, potato starch is often used in bread to soften the texture. Potato starch is extracted from the tuber in a variety of ways, including by boiling (which is why potato water makes a nice contribution to bread dough). Commercially, this is sometimes done with the help of sulfur dioxide gas or other chemicals. For bread making purposes, potatoes and potato starch are used for their sweet flavor (which develops as the starch releases its sugars) and also for the thickening and tenderizing properties of the starch.

Quinoa (*Chenopodium quinoa*): Originally grown high in the Andes by the Incas, who considered it to be sacred, quinoa is one of the few grains to be a complete protein, with a full range of amino acids. It is technically not a grain, as its seeds hail not from a grass, but rather from a vegetable; it is related to beets and Swiss chard. Although there are many colors of quinoa (pronounced keen-wah), most of it is yellowish in color, similar to millet. It is important to wash it before you use it, as it is coated with saponins, natural alkaloids that are slightly bitter. As with millet, it is best to cook quinoa before adding it to bread.

Rice (*Oryza sativa*): A major food staple throughout the word, rice is both beloved and extremely functional. Brown rice is the whole grain version, though the pericarp of a grain of rice is very thin and contains less fiber than other grains. Nevertheless, it is far healthier to eat rice in its whole state rather than as white rice, which is mostly starch and, ultimately, sugar. Because it contains no gluten (though some people erroneously confuse the stickiness of rice with gluten), it is the primary grain of choice for gluten-free bread products, usually supplemented with cassava, potato starch, and buckwheat flour. Probably contributing to its universal appeal is that it is easily digested and converts quickly to bodily energy. Brown rice, again showing its superiority over white rice, is converted more slowly, so it doesn't spike blood sugar levels. There are many types of rice, of many colors, flavors, and culinary properties: some are chewy, some fall apart easily, and some are gummy and

sweet, while others are firm and nutty and even have a perfumed scent. You can use any type of rice or rice flour in bread, but stick with whole grain rice, whether brown, black, red, or golden.

Rye (*Secale cereale*): Evidenced by its presence in many a front yard as a lawn grass, rye's greatest value is its ability to survive just about anywhere. Even during growing seasons too harsh for good wheat production, rye almost always manages to produce a decent crop. One thing that makes rye flour unique is that even the endosperm of rye contains fiber, which probably accounts for why so many European immigrants have such a strong taste memory of rye bread; it not only tasted good but also filled them up more effectively than wheat breads. Overall, rye contains a higher percentage of dietary fiber, and some studies suggest a better quality fiber, than either wheat or oats. This is due to lignins in the bran, which create a favorable environment for beneficial bifidobacteria in the gut, as well as its fermentation products, butyric and propionic acid, which lower the pH of the colon and function as a kind of natural antibiotic. Rye does contain gluten but only about half as much as wheat, and of a different quality (instead of glutenin, it has another protein of the glutelin family—similar but not as extensible). Rye is also vulnerable to ergot, a fungus that has been known to cause hallucinations and even death. Rye flour can be dark or white (also known as light). White rye flour is like white flour from wheat, devoid of the bran and germ, and even though it is used in many rye breads, we will not use it here. Dark rye is mostly pericarp with a little endosperm—a good supplement to wheat bread but not the same as whole grain rye flour. What we want is labeled either "whole rye flour" or "pumpernickel rye flour" (more coarsely milled). Rye meal and rye chops are other whole rye products that can be used in some of the breads.

Sorghum (*Sorghum* spp.): Mostly known in the United States for the molasses-type syrup that it yields, sorghum is a cereal grain related to millet, as well as a relative of sugarcane. It is also called milo, milo-maize, or guinea corn. It originally came to the United States from West Africa during the days of slave trading. It is naturally high in carbohydrates that can be converted to sugars (and thus sorghum syrup). The syrup is more buttery and smooth than molasses and can be used interchangeably with sugarcane molasses. Sorghum flour is now available through specialty mills and can be added to dough for flavor and tenderness. It can also be used in gluten-free breads, similar to cassava flour.

Teff (*Eragrostis tef*): Teff is the national grain of Ethiopia and Eritrea, where it is used to make, among other things, their famous *injera* bread (see page 283). This very small grain related to millet is naturally sweet and loaded with iron and calcium. Because of its small size, the grain is easily lost during harvest and threshing. But this small size has also been a virtue for seminomadic people; just a handful of seeds will sow an entire field.

Triticale (*Triticosecale*): A hybrid of durum wheat and rye (*Triticum* is the genus of wheat and *Secale* the genus of rye). A few years ago, there was great hope that this hearty grain might be the next miracle grain: easy to grow and good for baking. But it never really caught on, and these days it is mostly grown for animal feed and as a cover crop to be plowed back in for soil revitalization. However, it is a good-tasting grain, especially when rolled like oats into flakes, and makes an excellent addition to multigrain breads. Its protein is more easily assimilated than wheat protein.

Wild rice (*Zizania* spp.): Just as buckwheat is not wheat, wild rice is not rice but rather the seed of a grass that grows in lakes. Originally, it was found in the Minnesota Great Lakes regions, but it is now also grown in California. Wild rice is usually longer than rice and is ebony black. It is very expensive but can be bought in broken pieces or as a blend with brown rice for a fraction of the cost. It is lower in minerals than traditional rice but is much higher in protein and fiber. And, importantly, there is no other grain that tastes like wild rice, with its nutty flavor and tealike aroma.

Mashes and Scalds

If the two most important pieces of the whole grain bread puzzle are the starter, or pre-ferment, and the soaker, the third piece of the puzzle, in some of the breads, is a mash, a concoction made of scalded, partially gelatinized grain. Historically, grain mashes were used in both baking and brewing as a medium for growing yeast and also for extracting flavor from the grain. When starches are gelatinized by scalding, they are much more welcoming to enzymes. Brewers have made use of this knowledge to make their sweet wort, the grain-based tea that later becomes beer. The problem with scalding the grains, from the bread making perspective, is that most enzymes cannot survive temperatures in excess of 170°F, and some enzymes become denatured at even cooler temperatures.

To grow yeast in the mash, whether for bread or beer, barm (a foamy, yeasty froth atop fermenting malt liquor) was sometimes added to new batches of mash, along with diastatic malt. Before long, an entire new batch of barm would form, teeming with large quantities of yeast. This was called the Parisian mash method. Another technique, called the Virgin method, was made by not exceeding 170°F in the mash, thus allowing more enzymes to survive. With this method, added malt was not required to convert the starch to sugar.

There were many variations of these barm and mash methods, each with its own temperature, timing, and proportions of grain and water. Each version yielded different flavors and

Controlling the temperature is critical when making mashes.

potencies, but in all cases the purpose was the same: to create a medium in which microorganisms, especially yeast, could thrive and propagate. When these mashes were used as the starters for breads, they introduced a large proportion of gelatinized starch to the final dough, and this is the unique flavor and texture that I want to capture in the mash breads in this book. (For a more detailed history of mashes and barms, refer to John Kirkland's *The Modern Baker: Confectioner and Caterer* and William Jago's *The Technology of Bread Making*, listed in the bibliography.)

The mash technique used here, as explained on page 71, is very different from the Monica Spiller mash method that I learned at Camp Bread, as described in the previous chapter. The water will not be heated above 165°F, and the mash will be the consistency of gravy, not thick bread dough. This allows alpha-amylase enzymes to function but denatures the beta-amylase, which will help prevent gumminess. The ratio of water to flour is 2.5 parts water to 1 part flour (a 250% water-to-flour ratio, using the baker's percentage system). This high percentage of water will be compensated for in the final dough.

Breads made using this mash have a denser crumb, but they also have a flavor and texture unlike any other: sweeter, moister, and creamier. In some of our early tests there were complaints about the gumminess of the breads. Many of the testers reported that they enjoyed the flavor but not the texture (and hated cleaning their gummed-up knives after slicing the bread). Our new understanding of enzymes and their effect on dough would indicate that this was probably due to too much enzyme activity during the baking stage, breaking down more of the starch into sugar than the loaf could sustain. To correct this, and as part of the ongoing journey in figuring out how to funnel all of our experimentation into a successful system of baking, we increased the amount of starter (pre-ferment), which serves as the primary controlling agent during baking, to prevent late enzyme attacks on the starches.

. . .

There is nothing quite like a taste memory, in which a flavor, aroma, or texture instantly transports you back to a cherished time or experience. Many of the testers with strong European roots said that the resulting mash bread reminded them of the breads of their childhood. In my case, it reminded me of that seven-grain bread we served at the Root One Café thirty-five years ago—the bread that started me on my own bread odyssey. I know that those great European bread masters did not use the method I am presenting here, nor did the long-haired countercultural bakers in Boston. They had their own methods and tricks for creating similar results, including the use of long fermentation and baking cycles, creating breads so striking that a vivid memory of them is seared into the minds of those who grew up on them. As we discover repeatedly in our study of historical and traditional bread making, there are many ways to achieve similar results, to bring together various techniques and knowledge in creative ways, and to use what we have learned to control the outcomes and achieve our desired goal.

The Theory and Process of Delayed Fermentation

N ow that we have examined the history and chemistry of wheat and grains and laid out the dynamics of what is going on in the dough, it is time to apply that knowledge by creating our method and bread formulas. The procedures introduced in this chapter are not difficult, and once you have made a loaf or two, they will actually seem easier than the more conventional methods because the mixing times are shorter. Most of the formulas in chapter 4 will refer back to the instructional pages and photos that follow in this chapter should you need them.

But first, here are some key points to remember:

- Most of the formulas in this book are made by following a two-day process. On Day 1 we mix the pre-doughs; then, on Day 2 we combine the pre-doughs, add additional yeast and other ingredients specific to the recipe, and mix them together to make the final dough. Unlike conventional bread methods, this delayed fermentation technique initiates enzyme action in some of the dough in order to maximize flavor development *before* inducing yeast fermentation.

- We will use three types of pre-doughs to initiate enzyme activity and release sugars from complex starch molecules:

  Pre-fermented doughs (wild yeast starters or commercially yeasted *bigas*)

  Soakers (hydrated grains with salt but no yeast)

  Mashes (hydrated, partially gelatinized, enzyme-active grain)

- Pre-fermented dough, whether in the form of wild yeast starter or commercially yeasted *biga*, provides both flavor development and acidity to control the enzymes. When baking 100% whole grain breads, a higher percentage of these acidic pre-ferments is required than in white flour breads because of increased enzyme activity (many of the enzymes are brought into the flour via the bran and germ). Late enzyme attacks on the starches and proteins during both the fermentation and baking stages can cause the dough to collapse into a gummy substance.

- The soaker serves to precondition some of the grain to begin its enzyme activity, thus releasing sugars but without the risk of overfermentation, since there is no yeast in the soaker. The addition of salt to the soaker controls the enzyme activity to an extent, so the soaker can be left at room temperature instead being of placed in the refrigerator, thus reducing fermentation time on Day 2.

- Mashes, made from partially gelatinized grain, maximize flavor development but also weaken overall structure, so they generally must be used with caution or in specific applications. They are also ideal mediums for yeast growth, so they are excellent nutrient bases for wild yeast seed cultures and mother starters (see page 71 for how to make a starter with mash).

- The challenge for a baker is to maximize the flavor development without compromising the structural integrity of the loaf. Both starch and protein are necessary for structure, yet they are both affected, positively and negatively, by enzymes. The positive side of enzymes is that they release flavor and help with dough extensibility. The negative side is that, if left uncontrolled, they can cause the dough to break down and lose its internal structure.

- Because the two pieces of pre-dough (the soaker and the starter or *biga*) have had plenty of time to develop flavor, they require less time for fermentation when they are combined in the final dough. Fermentation and proofing times on Day 2 are much shorter than in conventional bread making. The result is a whole grain or multigrain bread that has maximum flavor development and excellent cell structure and mouthfeel.

- We add a relatively high percentage of commercial yeast to the final mix in many of these formulas. Instant yeast, regardless of brand (SAF-Instant, Perfect Rise, Rapid Rise/Highly Active, Bread Machine Yeast, and so on), is recommended because it can be added directly to the dough. Active dry yeast (also called dry active yeast) will also work, but it must be hydrated in warm water before it is added. Fresh yeast (also known as compressed or cake yeast) can also be used, at a ratio of three times the amount of instant yeast by weight.

MAKING THE PRE-DOUGHS

The process for making each of these pre-doughs is easy, but it does take some planning ahead. Once you have become familiar with the steps, using pre-doughs will actually simplify and shorten your overall production time. Most of the breads will utilize two pre-doughs, either a soaker or a mash and either a starter or a *biga*. Soakers are easy to make: grain, liquid, and a small amount of salt are combined until hydrated. They're not leavened and are thus stable at room temperature for up to two days. Pre-fermented doughs, however, require the added ingredients of wild or commercial yeast and time, so the following pages will focus on the details of these two pre-fermented doughs, and then we will take a close look at mashes.

Making Pre-fermented Doughs

A wild yeast starter (also known as a sourdough starter) is the golden child of bread making, full of folklore, myth, and mystery. *Bigas*, as we refer to them here, differ in that they use commercial rather than wild yeast. (In Italy, where the name originates, a *biga* may refer to any type of pre-fermented dough—wild yeast or commercial yeast, wet or firm sponge—but we will use it here specifically to refer to a firm, commercially yeasted pre-dough.) Because a wild yeast starter is much more complicated, we will discuss it first.

MAKING A WILD YEAST STARTER

Making a wild yeast starter involves two preliminary steps: preparing a seed culture and then converting that seed culture into a mother starter. The seed culture cultivates enough microorganisms to get the ball rolling and is then used to make another starter, the mother starter. The mother starter will be the starter that you keep in your refrigerator perpetually. It is kept at 75% hydration; that is, 75% water to 100% flour. This is firmer than the wet sponge starters that many bakers prefer to keep—it feels more like a piece of bread dough than a wet sponge—but this hydration is very close to the final dough hydration, which makes it easier to use in our dough calculations.

From a portion of the mother starter, you'll then build what we'll call a wild yeast starter (often shortened to just "starter" in chapter 4 formulas), only to differentiate it from the mother starter, as it's essentially the same thing. The wild yeast starter will then be combined with a soaker or a mash for your final dough. The actual preparation of the wild yeast starter will be described in more detail on page 80 in the master formula for a whole wheat sandwich loaf.

Making a Seed Culture

A seed culture is an initial colony of microorganisms that will subsequently be elaborated into a permanent mother starter. There are many ways to grow this seed. The simplest is with just flour and water. This does work but, frankly, not always on a predictable schedule. I have seen methods on the Internet calling for the addition of onion skins, wine grapes, plums, potatoes, milk, buttermilk, and yogurt. These can all serve as fuel for the microorganisms, and all will work to make a seed culture, but in the end, a starter (and bread itself) is really about properly fermented flour containing only desirable microorganisms—not ones that create moldy or off flavors.

The following two methods, the pineapple juice solution and the mash-based seed culture, both produce versatile starters that may be used to make breads that can be leavened totally by the starter alone, as in a classic sourdough bread, as well as mixed method breads (that is, breads leavened by a combination of wild yeast starter and commercial yeast, as we will be doing in this book). If you already have a healthy starter or prefer a method of making a starter that is different than the two offered here, feel free to swap in your starter; as long as it's healthy and tastes good, the recipes will still work.

Whole grain starters can be made from either whole wheat flour or whole rye flour. Serious rye bread devotees tend to keep a 100% rye starter in addition to their regular wheat starter, but I have found that wheat starter works just as well in rye breads and can easily be elaborated into a rye starter when one is truly needed. If you already have a starter that you have been nurturing, even if made with white flour, it can be easily converted to a whole wheat or rye starter; within a few feedings only traces of the white flour will remain.

SEED CULTURE: THE PINEAPPLE JUICE SOLUTION

In honor of the efforts made by Debra Wink and her many cohorts on the King Arthur Baking Circle to avoid leuconostoc bacteria problems, I now call this method the pineapple juice solution. Pineapple juice is not the only acid that thwarts the dastardly leuconostoc, but it has proven itself to be reliable, so why tamper with success? However, if you are the mad scientist type, as so many bread baking enthusiasts are, feel free to experiment with ascorbic acid powder (see page 198) or citric acid as found in juices such as lemon or orange juice. And remember, too, that if the seed culture does not respond in exactly the way described or on the exact schedule predicted, just give it more time. In most instances, the good microbial organisms will prevail and the seed will survive to fulfill its mission.

PHASE 1 (DAY 1)

VOLUME	OUNCES	GRAMS	INGREDIENT	%
3½ tablespoons	1	28.5	whole wheat or whole rye flour, any grind	100
¼ cup	2	56.5	unsweetened pineapple juice or filtered or spring water, at room temperature (about 70°F/21°C)	200
½ teaspoon	.03	1	diastatic malt powder or sprouted wheat flour (optional)	3
TOTAL	3.03	86		303

In a small bowl, stir together the flour, juice, and malt powder with a spoon or whisk to make a paste (the liquid can be cold or at room temperature—it doesn't matter). It should be like pancake batter or a thin sponge. (After mixing, transfer the remaining juice from the can to a clean container and refrigerate or go ahead and drink it; acidic juices tend to oxidize in cans once opened and pick up a metallic taste.) Be sure to stir until all of the flour is hydrated. Cover loosely with plastic wrap and leave at room temperature for approximately 48 hours. Two or three times a day, aerate by stirring for 1 minute with a wet spoon or whisk (the dough won't stick as easily to a wet tool). There will be little or no sign of fermentation activity during the first 24 hours; bubbles may begin to appear, however, within the 48-hour time frame. If not, 2 days after the initial mixing proceed to Phase 2 anyway (in other words, on Day 3).

It all begins with whole grain flour and pineapple juice (or water), whisked together to make a sponge.

COMMENTARY

If making a rye starter, use whole rye flour; any grind will do, including pumpernickel flour, which is simply whole rye flour that is somewhat coarsely milled. If you decide to keep both a wheat and a rye starter, be sure to label them, as they may be hard to tell apart.

If you do not have pineapple juice or want to try using water, use filtered or spring water. You can also substitute orange juice or even lemon juice. The starter may or may not stay on the predicted feeding schedule, depending on the presence or absence of the leuconostoc bacteria in your flour. About 30% to 40% of starters end up with a leuconostoc problem, depending on the growing conditions in wheat and rye fields that year. However, if you aerate the starter a few times each day, the starter will eventually overcome any leuconostoc even without pineapple juice.

The optional diastatic malt powder or sprouted wheat flour serves as a catalyst to release sugars from the flour. The yeast and bacteria then feed upon those sugars. Use it if you have it, as it serves as a kind of vitamin pill and speeds along the process, but the starter will work with or without it.

Because the growth of the starter provides an important visual cue to its readiness, I always raise and store my starter in a container or bowl rather than in an oiled plastic bag (as I often do with my *biga* pre-ferment) so I can more easily see how much it has grown.

All tools and bowls should be cleaned and sanitized before use, either by hand in very hot water or in the dishwasher, to remove bacteria they may have accumulated during storage.

Opinions are divided as to whether the pineapple juice is really necessary after Phase 1. It probably is not, but it won't hurt to use it during Phase 2 and may, in some instances, serve as insurance against the appearance of leuconostoc bacteria.

Aeration is very helpful in stimulating the growth of wild yeast, as yeast cells bud more rapidly in the presence of oxygen. Yeast companies actually pump air into their vats of yeast-inoculated liquid nutrients to rapidly stimulate budding (yeast multiplication, or mitosis) for their commercial yeast. And during the testing phase for this book, it was discovered that slow-moving starters came to life much faster when they were stirred

PHASE 2 (DAY 3)

VOLUME	OUNCES	GRAMS	INGREDIENT	%
2 scant tablespoons	.5	14	whole wheat or whole rye flour	100
2 tablespoons	1	28.5	unsweetened pineapple juice or filtered or spring water, at room temperature (about 70°F/21°C)	200
Use all	3	86	Phase 1 sponge	600
TOTAL	4.5	128.5		900

Add the new ingredients to the Phase 1 sponge and mix with a spoon or whisk to distribute and fully hydrate the new flour. Cover loosely with plastic wrap and leave at room temperature for 24 to 48 hours. Stir with a wet spoon or whisk to aerate at least two or three times each day, as before. There should be signs of fermentation (bubbling and growth) during this period. When the dough becomes very bubbly or foamy or at the end of 48 hours, whichever comes first, move on to Phase 3.

In Phase 2, more flour and liquid are added to the Phase 1 sponge.

PHASE 3 (DAY 4 OR 5)

VOLUME	OUNCES	GRAMS	INGREDIENT	%
5¼ tablespoons	1.5	42.5	whole wheat or whole rye flour	100
3 tablespoons	1.5	42.5	filtered or spring water, at room temperature (about 70°F/21°C)	100
Use all	4.5	128	Phase 2 sponge	300
TOTAL	7.5	213		500

Add the new ingredients to the Phase 2 sponge and stir with a spoon or whisk as before. The sponge will be thicker as we reduce the percentage of water, but it will still be very wet, spongy, and sticky. Cover loosely with plastic wrap and leave at room temperature for 24 to 48 hours, stirring with a wet spoon or whisk to aerate at least two to three times each day, as on the previous days. Within 48 hours it should be very bubbly and expanded. If not, wait another day or two, aerating as before, until it becomes active. (If the sponge was active and bubbly prior to this phase, it could become active and bubbly in less than 24 hours. If so, proceed to the next phase.)

PHASE 4 (DAY 5 OR LATER)

VOLUME	OUNCES	GRAMS	INGREDIENT	%
7 tablespoons	2	56.5	whole wheat or whole rye flour	100
3 tablespoons	1.5	42.5	filtered or spring water, at room temperature (about 70°F/21°C)	75
Use half	3.75	106	Phase 3 sponge	187
TOTAL	7.25	205		362

Discard or give away half of the Phase 3 sponge. Add the new ingredients to the other half and mix as before. Cover the bowl loosely and leave at room temperature until the sponge becomes bubbly and foamy. It should swell and nearly double in size, but it will fall when jostled due to its high hydration. This can take anywhere from 4 to 24 hours. If there is little sign of fermentation after 24 hours, continue to aerate as before and leave at room temperature until it becomes very active. The seed culture should register between 3.5 and 4.0 if tested with pH paper (see page 77 for how to use pH paper). You can now proceed to the next step, making the mother starter, or you can cover and refrigerate the seed culture for up to 2 days before making the mother starter.

or kneaded (and thus aerated) two or three times each day. Aeration also minimizes the possibility of contamination by unwanted spores or molds. It has been argued that the real benefit of kneading the seed culture is to reconnect the organisms to their food source. Regardless of the reason, it seems to work.

Though the instructions give a time range between stages, this can only be, at best, an estimate. The timing is greatly affected by the time of year, the ambient temperature, weather conditions (barometric pressure and humidity), the number of times you aerate the dough, and the type or brand of flour. In the winter it may take twice as long for the seed culture to activate; in the summer it may happen very quickly. Ultimately, the fermentation activity itself will dictate when a stage has been fulfilled. If the seed seems to be taking longer than predicted, do not abandon it but continue on, increasing the number of times you aerate the seed and giving it more time between stages. If necessary, you can repeat the Phase 4 step or simply extend the waiting period between phases by a day or two.

Before the Fleischmann Brothers and other yeast experts figured out how to grow commercial yeast, bakers had to cultivate their own. One method, used by brewers as well as bakers, was to grow their own yeast in a mash, as described on page 54. The following method uses this medium—mash—which is ideal for the cultivation of yeast and lactobacillus because the organisms thrive in partially gelatinized, enzyme-rich starches. I have found that this method can produce an active seed culture even faster than the pineapple juice method. Since it only takes a little mash to feed this seed culture, my suggestion is to make a batch of mash as described on page 71, take off what you need for the seed culture (2 ounces in the recipes below; 1 ounce for each of the first two phases), and then refrigerate or freeze the rest and use it in one of the breads calling for mash (pages 195–201). Mash will keep up to 1 week in the refrigerator or for 3 months in the freezer. For comparative purposes, you may want to make both this mash-based seed culture and the pineapple juice version to determine which you prefer. I have used them interchangeably and both produce great breads.

PHASE 1 (DAY 1)

VOLUME	OUNCES	GRAMS	INGREDIENT	%
3 tablespoons	1	28.5	mash (page 72)	100
3 1/2 tablespoons	1	28.5	whole wheat or whole rye flour, any grind	100
1/4 cup	2	56.5	filtered or spring water, at room temperature (about 70°F/21°C)	200
1/2 teaspoon	.03	1	diastatic malt powder or sprouted wheat flour (optional)	3
TOTAL	4.03	114.5		403

In a small bowl, stir together all of the ingredients with a spoon or whisk to make a paste like pancake batter or a thin sponge. Be sure all of the flour is hydrated. You can leave it in the bowl or transfer it to a 2-cup measuring cup. Cover loosely with plastic wrap and leave at room temperature for approximately 48 hours. Two or three times a day, aerate by stirring for 1 minute with a wet spoon or whisk (the dough won't stick as easily to a wet tool). There will be little or no sign of fermentation activity during the first 24 hours; bubbles may begin to appear during the second 24 hours. Regardless, proceed to Phase 2.

PHASE 2 (DAY 3)

VOLUME	OUNCES	GRAMS	INGREDIENT	%
3 tablespoons	1	28.5	mash	100
3½ tablespoons	1	28.5	whole wheat or whole rye flour	100
2 tablespoons	1	28.5	filtered or spring water, at room temperature (about 70°F/21°C)	100
Use all	4	113	Phase 1 sponge	400
TOTAL	7	198.5		700

Add the new ingredients to the Phase 1 sponge and mix with a spoon or whisk to distribute and fully hydrate the new flour. Cover loosely with plastic wrap and leave at room temperature for 24 to 48 hours. Stir with a wet spoon or whisk to aerate two or three times each day, as before. There should be signs of fermentation (bubbling and growth) during this period. When the dough becomes very bubbly or foamy or at the end of 48 hours, whichever comes first, move on to Phase 3.

PHASE 3 (DAY 4 OR 5)

VOLUME	OUNCES	GRAMS	INGREDIENT	%
5¼ tablespoons	1.5	42.5	whole wheat or whole rye flour	100
2 tablespoons	1	28.5	filtered or spring water, at room temperature (about 70°F/21°C)	66
Use half	3.5	99	Phase 2 sponge	233
TOTAL	6	170		399

Discard or give away half of the Phase 2 sponge. Add the new ingredients to the other half and mix as before. The sponge will be thicker as we reduce the percentage of water, but it will still be wet, spongy, and sticky. Cover loosely with plastic wrap and leave at room temperature for 24 to 48 hours, stirring with a wet spoon or whisk to aerate at least twice each day, as on the previous days. Within 48 hours, and probably sooner, it should be very bubbly and expanded. If not, wait another day or two, aerating as before, until it becomes active. (If the sponge was active and bubbly prior to this phase, it could become active and bubbly in less than 24 hours. If so, proceed to the next phase.)

A little starter goes a long way, so the following instructions call for you to discard or give away half of your seed culture. Alternatively, you may wish to save it as backup for a day or two, until your mother starter is established. If you would prefer to keep a larger mother starter on hand, especially if you bake often or prefer to bake larger batches, you can convert the entire seed culture into a mother starter and increase the other ingredients in proportion. This will give you over 3 pounds of starter.

PHASE 4 (DAY 5 OR LATER)

VOLUME	OUNCES	GRAMS	INGREDIENT	%
²/₃ cup	3	85	whole wheat or whole rye flour	100
¹/₄ cup	2	56.5	filtered or spring water, at room temperature (about 70°F/21°C)	66
Use half	3	85	Phase 3 sponge	100
TOTAL	8	226.5		266

Discard or give away half of the Phase 3 sponge. Add the new ingredients to the other half and mix as before. Cover the bowl and leave at room temperature until the sponge becomes bubbly and foamy. It should swell and nearly double in size, but could fall when jostled. This can take anywhere from 4 to 24 hours. If there is little sign of fermentation after 24 hours, continue to aerate as before and leave at room temperature until it becomes very active. The seed culture should register between 3.5 and 4.0 if tested with pH paper (see page 77 for how to use pH paper). You can now proceed to the next step, making the mother starter, or you can cover and refrigerate the seed culture for up to 2 days before making the mother starter.

Making the Mother Starter

Once you have established a seed culture, whether using the pineapple juice solution or the mash-based method, you need to convert it to a mother starter. This is the starter you will keep perpetually in your refrigerator—the permanent starter from which you will build your various breads.

In previous books I also referred to this starter as a *barm*. I have since learned that the term *barm* is more properly used for starters made using mashes as the growth medium. For the sake of clarity and unity, we will refer to our perpetual starter as the mother starter.

To convert a seed culture into a mother starter, you will use the seed culture to inoculate a larger batch of flour and water to make a firm piece of dough. The mature seed culture is full of wild yeast and bacteria, but its structure has been weakened by a buildup of acids and ongoing action by both starch and protein enzymes. To make the mother starter strong and healthy, we will build it with three times the amount of flour as of the seed. We will also hydrate it at 75% the weight of the new flour. The first time you make this feeding (also referred to as a refreshment or an elaboration), the mother starter will be a little wetter than 75% hydration because the seed culture was made at a higher hydration. But within a few feedings the mother starter will settle in at 75% hydration, as will most subsequent elaborations that you make for specific bread formulas.

MOTHER STARTER

VOLUME	OUNCES	GRAMS	INGREDIENT	%
2 1/3 cups	10.5	298	whole wheat or whole rye flour, any grind	100
1 cup	8	227	filtered or spring water (probably more for whole rye flour), at room temperature (about 70°F/21°C)	76
2/3 cup	3.5	99	about half of the seed culture	33.3
TOTAL	22	624		208

1. **Combine all of the ingredients** in a bowl or in the bowl of a stand mixer with the paddle attachment. Mix with a large spoon or your hands or on slow speed for about 1 minute, until the ingredients form a ball of slightly sticky dough. Let the dough rest for 5 minutes, then knead by hand for 1 minute (in the bowl, using wet hands), or until the dough is fairly smooth and all of the ingredients are evenly distributed. The starter need not be developed as much as a final dough (don't worry about developing the gluten).

2. **Transfer the starter to a clean bowl or container** large enough to hold it once doubled in size. Cover loosely with plastic wrap and leave at room temperature for 4 to 8 hours, until it doubles in size; the length of time will depend on the potency of the seed culture and the ambient temperature. It should register between 3.5 and 4.0 if tested with pH paper (see page 77 for how to use pH paper).

3. **Degas the mother starter by kneading** it for a few seconds, then form it back into a ball, cover tightly (to prevent absorption of refrigerator odors or moisture), and refrigerate. After a few hours, vent any carbon dioxide buildup by opening the lid briefly, then reseal it. The mother starter is ready to use now or for up to 3 days.

The mother starter has the same structure and hydration as the final dough.

The fermentation time and sourness may vary between firm and wet starters; some say firm are more sour, some say the opposite. Many factors contribute to flavor and the propagation of microorganisms, including temperature and organisms in the flour. My advice is to use this 75% hydration formula, which fosters a moderate acidic tang and complexity. If you have had success with a wetter or drier starter, use what has worked for you. Just don't forget to adjust the water in the final dough.

If the flour seems to need more water as sometimes happens with coarsely ground rye, add more to achieve the described consistency. Always let the dough dictate what it needs.

Acidity is caused by bacteria and provides an environment in which wild yeast can thrive, but acidity alone does not guarantee yeast activity. You must also see growth in your starter to indicate that the yeast population is replenishing itself. In a healthy starter, yeast and bacteria have learned to cohabitate, and the mix of strains of bacteria and yeast is largely determined during the seed culture stage. However, temperature variations and long dormant periods can adversely affect the wild yeast population, so it may be necessary to wait longer than indicated.

REFRESHING THE MOTHER STARTER

Whenever the mother starter gets low—between 4 days and 2 weeks old—rebuild it by discarding all but 3.5 ounces. Use the retained portion as a new seed culture and follow the instructions above once again. You can also refresh a larger portion, using the same ingredient ratios, if you would prefer to build it into a larger mother starter. If you are planning to make one loaf of bread, in many cases you will take a 2.25-ounce piece of the refreshed starter and add it to 6.75 ounces of flour and 5 ounces of water, or in others, a 2.5-ounce piece and add it to 7.5 ounces of flour and up to 6 ounces of water (these amounts may vary depending on the particular bread you are making). After fermenting this new piece of starter, you will have a starter for a final dough that requires 14 ounces, as many of the recipes in this book do.

Any mother starter that's older than 2 weeks or that has lost all its gluten strength due to protease activity (it will have the structural consistency of potato soup), should be built back in increments from 1 ounce. To do this, add 1 ounce of mother starter to 3 ounces of whole wheat or rye flour and 2.25 ounces of water. This will produce 6.25 ounces of starter within 4 to 8 hours. You can then build all or part of that into a larger amount by using the same ratios: 100% flour, 75% water, and 33.3% starter. So if you were to build upon all 6.25 ounces, you would add 18.75 ounces of flour (6.25 multiplied by 3) and 14 ounces of water (18.75 ounces of flour multiplied by .75). In very little time at all, you will have built a tiny, 1-ounce piece of starter into a large, 39-ounce piece. Personally, I rarely keep more than 16 ounces of mother starter on hand because it takes so little of it to elaborate a final starter.

HOW TO CONVERT A WHOLE WHEAT MOTHER STARTER INTO A WHITE SOURDOUGH STARTER, OR VICE VERSA

The same rules apply for converting a whole wheat starter to a white flour starter, or a white starter into a whole wheat starter. The difference with white flour is that 75% hydration creates wet, rustic doughs such as ciabatta dough, while 75% hydration with whole wheat flour creates a dough similar in feel to white flour baguette dough. That said, the 3-to-1 ratio of new flour to mother starter still holds, but the amount of water will be determined by the type of flour you are using. If converting a whole wheat starter to a white flour starter, you need to add only 63% water to new flour. If converting a wet sponge starter to a firmer, doughlike starter, you will have to feel your way into the proper hydration. Again, let the dough dictate what it needs and adjust accordingly.

HOW TO CONVERT A WHOLE WHEAT MOTHER STARTER INTO A RYE STARTER

Unless you are a rye bread fanatic and make it often, there is no need to keep a separate rye starter. Your whole wheat mother starter can be used in some recipes as is, and it can also be used to build a predominantly rye starter for specific applications. Should you want to keep a rye mother starter for future breads, you can either convert your whole wheat mother starter by elaborating it with whole rye flour instead of whole wheat, or you can make a whole rye seed culture from scratch and build into a 100% rye starter. If converting a whole wheat starter, the amount of residual whole wheat flour will gradually dwindle as you continue to refresh the starter with rye.

If you are going to convert a whole wheat mother starter, my suggestion is to start your rye bread baking with a *meteil*-style loaf (that is, one with less rye than wheat). As you refresh your converted starter, it will soon be almost 100% rye and suitable for *seigle*-style breads (which have more rye than wheat), and even 100% rye breads.

Simple math shows that as you elaborate following the 3-to-1 ratio, one elaboration will immediately convert a 100% whole wheat starter into a predominantly rye starter. In 2.25 ounces of starter there is about 1.25 ounces of flour and 1 ounce of water. If you add 6.75 ounces of rye flour and 5 ounces of water to that (a typical 3-to-1 elaboration at 75% hydration), the new starter will contain 8 ounces of flour, of which 6.75 ounces is rye, or 84%. You can see how quickly the starter can be converted. If you take 2.25 ounces of the newly converted starter and elaborate it with rye flour once again, the resulting starter would contain about 95% rye.

As already noted, 75% hydration is a guideline for making a starter that feels like a piece of bread dough as opposed to a wet sponge. If the particular grind of flour you use requires additional water or flour to achieve this texture, let the dough determine what it needs, not the formula. If you happen to make the starter a little too wet or firm, you can always adjust when you make the final dough.

Converting one kind of starter, such as whole wheat, to another kind, such as rye or white, requires only following the correct starter/flour/water ratios.

MAKING A BIGA

A *biga*, as we will make it for the breads in this book, consists of flour, liquid (usually water but sometimes milk, buttermilk, yogurt, or even eggs), and a small amount of yeast to initiate fermentation. It is mixed briefly to form a piece of dough, and then it is covered and placed in the refrigerator for a long, slow fermentation to develop flavor and acidity. There is no salt in this pre-ferment as salt slows down fermentation; in this instance, we will use refrigeration to accomplish the same task and add the required salt during the final mixing on Day 2.

Because biga uses commercial yeast (*Saccharomyces cerevisiae*) rather than wild yeast (*Saccaramyces exiguus* and other strains), it will not achieve the lower pH ranges of wild yeast starters and will not be as acidic. In some instances, we may provide additional acidity by using buttermilk or yogurt, but a *biga*-type bread will typically have less acidity and less sourness than a bread made with wild yeast starter. Many of the breads in this book can be made with either type of pre-ferment, so if you prefer a less acidic or sour flavor, you can often replace a wild yeast starter with an equal amount of *biga*. In rye breads, however, which rely on acidity to help control the enzymatic activity and protect against starch attacks, buttermilk or yogurt is suggested in place of water for hydrating the *biga*. Conversely, most of the breads that call for *biga* can also be made with an equal amount of wild yeast starter. In these instances, if there is acidified dairy product in the dough, you can replace it with water, as the starter will generate its own acidity. Instructions for making the various *bigas* are included with each formula.

Making a Soaker

Soakers are usually made of coarsely milled grains soaked overnight in liquid to soften them. But in this book, we will make soakers with either coarse or finely milled flour and use them to draw out more flavor from the grain. Since a soaker is nonfermented dough, consisting only of grain, liquid, and (optionally) salt, it is very easy to make. The objective is to hydrate the grains in advance in order to precondition and soften them, and to activate amylase enzyme activity without initiating the leavening transformations that occur during fermentation. This action allows some of the sugar threads to break out of the starch without being converted to carbon dioxide and alcohol. Of course, if a soaker is left for a long period of time, the natural yeast and bacteria inherent in the grain will slowly turn the soaker into a starter, but this will not happen if soaking is limited to 8 to 24 hours, as suggested in these formulas. If for some reason it becomes necessary to hold a soaker longer than 24 hours, you can refrigerate it for up to 3 days without adversely affecting the dough.

The method of preparation is simple and will be described in more detail on page 79 in the master formula for a whole wheat sandwich loaf. The only action necessary is to stir the ingredients together until the grain is fully hydrated. It does not need to be mixed for gluten development, as that will take place when the soaker is combined with the other ingredients during the final mixing stage. Simply cover the bowl of soaked grain with plastic wrap and set it aside at

The *biga* (left) and soaker (right) are very similar in structure and feel, even though only one has yeast (the *biga*) while the other has salt (the soaker). They are both soft and supple and feel like final dough.

room temperature; it doesn't matter whether you cover it tightly or loosely. Because it remains at room temperature, the soaker can be mixed into the final dough just as it is. However, if you have to chill it in order to hold it longer than 24 hours, remove it from the refrigerator about 2 hours before the final mixing stage to take off the chill. Otherwise it will delay the fermentation schedule.

Making a Mash

It bears repeating: The only reason to use any culinary technique is to make a better-tasting product. Mashes are a minor hassle to make because they require an extra step in the overall process, but they contribute a flavor not easily achieved by any other method and they also help to soften the texture, which is particularly important when making 100% whole grain breads. Mash is also an ideal medium for the cultivation of wild yeast, and it is used for this purpose in one of the suggested methods for making a wild yeast starter (see page 64).

A mash is similar to what has historically also been called a scald; that is, grain or flour scalded by hot or boiling water. It can be fully or partially cooked, but for our purposes, we do not heat the grain above 165°F (74°C). What distinguishes our mash from a conventional scald is this attention to temperature, which keeps the natural alpha-amylase enzymes intact, allowing them to break smaller sugar chains out of the more complex starch. The hot water partially gelatinizes the starches and also denatures the beta-amylase enzymes, which have a lower threshold for heat. The beta-amylase enzymes are the ones that can reduce a dough to mush as they break off double glucose units, or maltose. The most noticeable aspect of a mash is that it tastes much sweeter after 3 hours than it did when the ingredients were first combined. This is the enzymatic conversion in action.

There are many ways to make a mash, and the flour-to-water ratio can vary. At one extreme is the very stiff, thick mash preferred by Monica Spiller—about 1.3 parts water to 1 part flour. This allows for the greatest amount of gelatinized grain to be incorporated into the dough. There are also methods that use a smaller amount of flour, such as the Chinese soup seed technique referred to in the introduction, which is used as a thickener and flavor enhancer for soups and sauces. With a ratio of 5 parts water to 1 part flour, its consistency is like thin gravy. It is much easier to make than the thick mash.

After a great deal of experimentation, I have decided upon an intermediate mash that combines the benefits of both. This will be the version called for in the recipes beginning on page 195. It is not difficult to make and adds a great deal of flavor to bread.

You will need the following:

- An ovenproof saucepan or small pot with a lid. Aluminum foil can be used if a lid is not available.

- An instant-read thermometer to determine when the water reaches 165°F. If you do not have a thermometer or want to do it by feel, shoot for a temperature at which the water's hot, but you can keep a finger in it for about 2 seconds. It should not be bubbling or simmering.

- A whisk or large spoon.

- A spatula or plastic pastry scraper (also called a bowl scraper in bakeshops).

- A bowl of room-temperature water in which to dip the spatula or scraper. (Mash is very sticky.)

The mash should be made in advance of making the final dough, preferably the day before you need it, on what we will call Day 1. The following version is scaled to work in most of the recipes found in this book, but it can be made in larger batches, keeping all of the temperatures and ratios the same.

MASH

VOLUME	OUNCES	GRAMS	INGREDIENT	%
1¼ cups plus 1 tablespoon	10.6	300	water, at 165°F (74°C)	236
1 cup	4.5	128	whole wheat flour, any grind (or other whole grains, as indicated in each formula)	100
1 teaspoon	.07	2	diastatic malt powder or sprouted wheat flour (optional)	1.6
TOTAL	15.17	430		336.5

1. **Preheat the oven to 200°F (93°C).**

2. **Heat the water to 165°F (74°C)** in an ovenproof saucepan, then remove the pan from the heat and whisk or stir in the flour (or other grain) and malt until the flour is fully hydrated

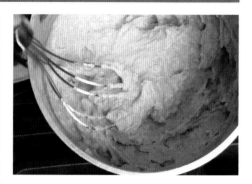

When the temperature of the water is 165°F (74°C), the addition of flour will cool to 150°F (66°C), partially gelatinizing the starches. It will make a mash that looks like gravy, thin pudding, or cream of wheat.

and makes a paste similar to a thin pudding or gravy. Using a spatula or plastic pastry scraper dipped in water, scrape the spoon or whisk and the walls of the pan to get all of the dough back into the pan and off the inside walls. (The mash temperature will drop to about 150°F/66°C during the stirring.) Immediately cover the pan and place it in the oven.

3. **Turn the oven down to warm/150°F (66°C),** if it has this setting, and leave the mash in the oven for at least 1 hour (it can stay in the oven for up to 3 hours). If the oven can't be turned down this low, turn the oven off and 10 minutes later turn it back on to the lowest setting (typically 200°F/93°C) for about 10 minutes; continue alternating between on and off at 10-minute intervals for the first hour, then turn the oven off and leave it off. If possible, leave the mash in the warm oven for the full 3 hours. However, you can also remove it from the oven after the first hour and leave it at room temperature, covered, if you need to use the oven for other purposes.

4. **After 3 hours, refrigerate the mash** until you are ready to use it. You can also leave it out overnight at room temperature if you plan to use it within 24 hours. The mash can also be stored in a sealed container in the freezer for up to 3 months. Whether frozen or refrigerated, remove the mash far enough in advance to bring it back to room temperature—a few hours if refrigerated, and overnight or about 12 hours if frozen.

work if not. "Diastatic" means that the diastase enzymes have not been destroyed or denatured. Do not use barley malt syrup; having been heated, it is nondiastatic and thus is used strictly for flavor and sweetness (such as in bagels), not for its enzymes.

The first hour in the oven is critical, as most of the starch conversion takes place then. The second and third hours can be done either in the oven or at room temperature. The starch-to-sugar conversion will be complete at the end of the third hour. Taste the mash at the beginning and the end to experience the difference.

The final weight of the mash will be less than the total weight of the ingredients due to evaporation. It will weigh approximately 14 ounces when finished.

MIXING AND THE AUTOLYSE METHOD

Mixing is a critical step in all methods of bread making and the mixing time is usually crucial to the final outcome. In a professional bakery, each type of bread and flour requires its own very specific mixing time and intensity. These mixing times are also based on the type of mixing machine used and the number of beater revolutions per minute. Dough with a lot of enrichments, such as butter, sugar, or eggs, generally requires intensive mixing because it takes longer for the gluten to develop. The longer the mixing time, the more organized the gluten gets. A well-organized gluten structure is important in certain types of bread, like brioche, soft sandwich bread, challah, dinner rolls, and the like. Lean hearth-style dough, on the other hand, usually performs and tastes better when it is mixed for a short time, so that the gluten develops but does not become overly organized. This promotes large, irregular holes rather than the regular, even-sized holes found in soft sandwich breads.

No matter how intensively the dough is mixed, it typically takes at least 6 to 8 minutes for the gluten to develop, that is, for the gliadin and glutenin proteins to link up and create the new protein chain that we call gluten. It can even take up to 15 minutes in large spiral or fork mixers that only work on small sections of dough at a time. For this reason, artisan bakers sometimes employ a method in which the dough is allowed to rest after just a few minutes of mixing. This resting period, which the French refer to as *autolyse*, allows gluten to develop without becoming overorganized. Typically, only flour and water are mixed for a few minutes and the dough then rests, usually for 5 to 20 minutes, but sometimes as long as overnight. The remaining ingredients, such as salt, yeast, and pre-ferments, are added after the autolyse.

This resting period, among its other virtues, minimizes friction, and thus keeps the dough cool, slowing down fermentation. The short mixing time and less gluten organization promote large, irregular holes. The short mixing time also reduces mixer oxidation, that is, bringing oxygen into dough through the action of mixing. Oxidation of this type tends to bleach out the beta-carotene pigments in flour, diminishing the aroma and flavor of the baked bread. Some oxidation is necessary to develop the various chemical bonds, but too much can affect color, flavor, and dough strength.

While the dough is in the autolyse phase, the gluten continues to develop even without mixing, as some of the glutenin and gliadin molecules bond to each other as they hydrate. When the mixing resumes, the gluten is poised and ready to strengthen and organize after just a few turns of the mixer, or a few strokes of kneading by hand. We take advantage of this in the delayed fermentation method, where pre-doughs are mixed for only a short time before going into an overnight autolyse period. The gluten develops overnight and is then organized during the Day 2 final mix, when the remaining yeast, salt, and other ingredients are also introduced to the dough. Conventional whole grain dough usually requires longer mixing than white flour hearth dough because of its high fiber content and other nongluten ingredients, such as dairy, sweeteners, and other grains, but with the delayed fermentation method, only a few minutes of final mixing is required to accomplish proper gluten development. If you were mixing the dough all in one step, as in conventional techniques, it might take 15 to 18 minutes to get the same development you will achieve in just 3 to 5 minutes using the overnight delayed fermentation method.

Combining the pre-doughs ("epoxy-style," as I like to think of it) with the final ingredients transforms the parts into a greater whole.

INCORPORATING THE YEAST AND SALT

It takes a minimum of 2 minutes of vigorous mixing to properly hydrate and distribute the salt and yeast when they are added on Day 2 of the process. In most instances the dough will require about 3 to 4 minutes of final mixing, so incorporation should not be a problem. With the *biga* pre-ferments, a small amount of yeast is added on Day 1 and the dough is then immediately chilled to slow down the yeast fermentation and enzyme activity. Soaker pre-doughs, on the other hand, will have some salt in them, but no yeast. The salt serves as a regulator of enzyme activity, ensuring that sugars are freed from the starch slowly, rather than at a runaway speed.

While most of the recipes in this book call for the majority of yeast to be added on Day 2, there are exceptions. For instance, when making soft, wet, sticky dough (the category I call rustic bread), less yeast is required than in firmer dough. Completing all the mixing on Day 1, then immediately refrigerating the dough so that it will not overferment, means that it will be ready on the following day for shaping, final proofing, and baking without a second mixing (in the style of the *pain à l'ancienne* in *The Bread Baker's Apprentice*). This is especially appropriate for focaccia, as well as for ciabatta and pugliese-type breads. But with firmer, standard whole grain and multigrain breads, the *struans* and such, the dough performs much more reliably when the yeast is mixed in on Day 2, after the enzyme action is completed.

Instant yeast (including Rapid Rise, Perfect Rise, Bread Machine Yeast, and other brand names) is added straight into the final dough on Day 2 without hydrating it (except when making bagels), while active dry yeast, because the grains are coarser, must be hydrated in a small amount of lukewarm water before adding it to the dough.

MAKING THE FINAL DOUGH

As we embrace the difficult challenge of working mainly with 100% whole grains (with the inclusion of a dozen or so "transitional" breads that incorporate some white flour), we need to revisit some of the details of bread baking, especially since the delayed fermentation method is so different from more conventional methods of baking. For example, in conventional whole grain recipes, the dough requires longer kneading than white flour dough. One of my favorite whole grain bread books, *The Laurel's Kitchen Bread Book*, contains pages and pages of useful information, but the thing I remember most from it is the instruction to knead dough for at least six hundred strokes. As the authors say, "This is the most amazing and outrageous requirement, but after many hundreds of loaves, we are convinced that thorough kneading makes the critical difference."

However, with the delayed fermentation method this long kneading is no longer required. I have tried kneading for six hundred strokes and it takes a while, about 12 to 15 minutes, and is pretty exhausting (although it is a good upper body workout). In a small stand mixer like a KitchenAid, that much mixing will burn out the motor. The good news is that the delayed fermentation method significantly decreases the kneading time because the long overnight resting period (the autolyse) allows both the gluten and the flavor to develop in advance.

Here are a few important and useful principles, tips, and tricks for making whole grain breads utilizing the delayed fermentation method:

- The instructions will give you the general steps, but it is always a good idea to write out your own checklist of all the steps you need to perform, especially a baking schedule with predicted time targets for each stage. In other words, create a worksheet so you have a fair idea when you need to check on the dough in order to move to the next step. You can always refer back to the book, but writing a worksheet is an effective way to internalize the process or, as I tell my freshman baking students, *own* the process.

- In many of the bread recipes in this book you will be making 2 pieces of pre-dough on Day 1, resting them overnight, and then mixing them together with additional ingredients on Day 2. Most of the flavor has already been brought forth from the flour during the overnight resting period, so the final fermentation cycles are relatively short. Typically, the breads will be ready to bake within 2 to 2^1/$_2$ hours of mixing and are out of the oven approximately 3 to 3^1/$_2$ hours from mixing. The flavors will be more complex than found in most bread, especially if you allow the breads to cool thoroughly before eating them, which gives the flavors a chance to permeate the entire loaf. The flavors are always more noticeable when the bread is served at room temperature.

- These whole grain dough recipes will be more hydrated than white flour dough and must be handled as such. Use generous amounts of dusting flour to keep the dough from sticking to your hands and work surfaces, or use the wet hands method (see the first commentary note on page 83).

- Preheat the oven at least 50°F to 100°F (10°C to 38°C) hotter than the actual desired baking temperature so that your oven will not have a long recovery period when you open the door. But remember to reset the oven to the correct temperature after you put the dough in the oven! (Each set of instructions will provide a reminder about this.)

- For steaming, use a heavy-gauge metal pan; don't use a tempered glass dish like Pyrex, as it may crack. Place the pan in the oven on a shelf either above or below the baking shelf and pour in hot water, not ice cubes; that's old school and will cause the oven temperature to plummet. This will create steam and moist vapor, which helps with oven spring. (Be careful to cover any glass oven windows with a cloth towel to protect them from backsplash—the hot glass could crack if water hits it.) You can also use a mister or even a power steamer, such as the Conair SC10 or SC20, but do so with caution.

- Remember to pull your starter or *biga* from the refrigerator 1 or 2 hours prior to mixing the final dough so it will be closer to room temperature. If it is still cold to the touch, which means it is probably below 78°F (26°C), you may have to increase the fermentation time by as much as 45 to 60 minutes when you mix the final dough. If the final dough seems cold from the pre-ferment, you can also warm it by mixing it longer—every minute of vigorous kneading will add about 2°F (1°C) of warmth. For those who work away from home, one option is to take your pre-ferment to work with you and keep in a refrigerator there, then remove it 2 hours before you anticipate arriving home.

The actual method for preparing the final dough is described in the master formula that follows.

WHAT IS pH AND WHY AND HOW DO WE MEASURE IT?

The technical definition of pH is a logarithmic measure of hydrogen ion concentration. But what makes this esoteric definition useful to us is that it identifies the acid versus alkalinity of a substance on a scale of 1 to 14. Litmus paper can be used to measure this, with 7 being neutral and anything under 7 being acid. All measurements above 7 indicate alkalinity. Because the potency of a starter often correlates to its acidity (as the microorganisms multiply and feed they release various types of acids), testing the pH of a starter can be a good indicator, along with growth or expansion of the dough, of its readiness. The typical pH range of a healthy starter is between 3.5 and 4.0. Doughs made without wild yeast starters but with *bigas* or without any pre-ferments, will register mostly between 4.5 and 6.0 on the scale because they generate less acid. Litmus or pH paper can be acquired from bakery mail order catalogs, some pharmacies, beer making supply houses, and swimming pool maintenance companies. To use it, cut off a small piece of dough and smear it on a small strip of pH paper. The paper will change color, depending on the acidity level. Match the color against the guide that comes with the paper.

MASTER FORMULA

The following pages show how to make the pre-doughs and final dough for a basic enriched 100% whole wheat sandwich loaf, though with much more detail on each of the steps involved, including instructional photos, than will be provided in the formulas in chapter 4. Other breads will require different combinations of ingredients, including other grains or mashes or different liquids, but you can always refer back to this master formula (and "Making a Mash" above) if questions arise later, as the extra information here applies to all formulas.

This particular recipe was chosen as the master formula because it is a basic, versatile loaf that can be made in many shapes and can be made with either a *biga* or wild yeast starter (instructions for both appear below). The *biga* version will be milder and less acidic, whereas the starter version will be more complex, with a slight sourdough flavor. Some people prefer the milder flavor, while others love the full gusto of the starter version. To make the final dough, we will combine two pre-doughs—the starter or *biga* and a soaker—and then add additional ingredients.

Day 2, just before mixing: the epoxy method brings the pre-doughs and remaining ingredients together into a stronger final dough.

SOAKER

VOLUME	OUNCES	GRAMS	INGREDIENT	%
1¾ cups	8	227	whole wheat flour, preferably fine grind, or a mix of fine and medium or coarse	100
½ teaspoon	.14	4	salt	1.8
¾ cup plus 2 tablespoons	7	198	milk, scalded and cooled to room temperature (about 70°F/21°C), or soy milk or rice milk; or buttermilk or yogurt if using a *biga* instead of a wild yeast starter	87
TOTAL	15.14	429		188.8

1. **Using a large spoon, stir together** all of the ingredients for about 1 minute, until all of the flour is hydrated and the ingredients form a ball of dough. You can also make this in a stand mixer with the paddle attachment, mixing on low speed for 1 minute.

2. **Cover the bowl with plastic wrap** and leave at room temperature overnight or anywhere between 12 and 24 hours. (If it will be more than 24 hours until you mix the final dough, place the soaker in the refrigerator; it will be good for up to 3 days. Remove it 2 hours before mixing the final dough to take off the chill.)

MAKING A SOAKER

The soaker comes together quickly. The goal is simply to hydrate the grain, sometimes with water and, as here, sometimes with milk.

COMMENTARY

When hydrating the flour with milk in a soaker, we sometimes use a higher percentage of liquid (about 87.5%) than if we were using water (75%) because of the milk solids and other nonliquid components in the milk. Also, note that scalding and cooling the milk is optional; this is explained in greater depth on page 237.

〜

You can use either liquid milk or nonfat dry milk, called DMS (for dry milk solids) in professional bakeshops, though it does have a distinctive powdered milk flavor. I prefer using fresh whole milk for its flavor and richness. Regardless of which type you use, the texture of the bread will be the same.

〜

If using a *biga*, you may substitute buttermilk or yogurt for the milk. Cultured buttermilk and yogurt are very similar, as both are acidified by various strains of lactic acid bacteria. Though yogurt tends to be thicker, they are interchangeable by weight, as the thickness is due to the method of bacterial fermentation, not the amount of solid material in the product. If you use buttermilk or yogurt, feel free to add a small amount of water or liquid milk until the dough feels the way the instructions indicate.

WILD YEAST STARTER

VOLUME	OUNCES	GRAMS	INGREDIENT	%
5 tablespoons	2.25	64	mother starter (page 67)	33.3
1½ cups	6.75	191	whole wheat flour, any grind	100
½ cup plus 2 tablespoons	5	142	filtered or spring water, at room temperature (about 70°F/21°C)	75
TOTAL	14	397		208.3

COMMENTARY

If you have a recently refreshed mother starter, you can simply weigh off 14 ounces and use it in the final dough and then rebuild your mother starter. Otherwise, you can elaborate a small piece of your mother starter and make 14 ounces of final starter specifically for the recipe at hand.

To prepare a clean, lightly oiled bowl for the new starter's rising period (or for any pre-dough or dough for that matter), the bowl should be cleaned either in hot water or in the dishwasher to make sure no undesirable microorganisms are present. To oil the bowl, wipe it with a lightly oiled paper towel or mist it lightly with pan spray.

1. **Using a large spoon, combine** all of the ingredients together in a bowl to form a ball of dough (this is easily done by hand but can also be done using a stand mixer with the paddle attachment or dough hook). Using wet hands, knead the dough in the bowl for about 2 minutes to be sure all of the ingredients are evenly distributed and the flour is fully hydrated. The dough should feel very tacky. Let the dough rest for about 5 minutes, then knead it again with wet hands for 1 minute. The dough will become smoother but still be tacky.

2. **Transfer the dough** to a clean, lightly oiled bowl (oiling the bowl is optional). Cover the bowl loosely with plastic wrap and leave at room temperature for approximately 4 to 6 hours, until the dough is nearly double in size. The dough should register between 3.5 and 4.0 if tested with pH paper (see page 77) and have a pleasant aroma similar to apple cider vinegar. If the starter has not doubled or acidified properly, allow it to continue to develop at room temperature. It could take up to 8 hours or even longer, depending on conditions such as the ambient temperature or the strength of the original piece of starter, but 4 to 6 hours is typical.

3. **When the starter has fully developed, knead** it for a few seconds to degas it, return it to the bowl, cover the bowl tightly with plastic wrap, and refrigerate. The starter will be ready to use anytime, and it will be usable for 3 to 4 days.

BIGA

VOLUME	OUNCES	GRAMS	INGREDIENT	%
1¾ cups	8	227	whole wheat flour, any grind	100
¼ teaspoon	.03	1	instant yeast	.4
¾ cup	6	170	filtered or spring water, at room temperature (about 70°F/21°C)	75
TOTAL	14.03	398		175.4

1. **Using a large spoon, stir** all of the ingredients together in a bowl to form a ball of dough (this is easily done by hand but can also be done in a stand mixer with the paddle attachment or dough hook). Using wet hands, knead the dough in the bowl for about 2 minutes to be sure all of the ingredients are evenly distributed and the flour is fully hydrated. The dough should feel very tacky. Let the dough rest for about 5 minutes, then knead it again, either in the bowl or on a lightly floured work surface, with wet hands for 1 minute. The dough will become smoother but still be tacky.

2. **Transfer the dough** to a clean, lightly oiled bowl (oiling the bowl is optional), cover the bowl loosely with plastic wrap, and immediately refrigerate; alternatively, you can put the dough in a plastic bag that has been misted with pan spray. The *biga* will ferment even as it is cooling down. It will be ready to use after 8 hours, and will remain usable for up to 3 days.

3. **Approximately 2 hours before** you plan to mix the final dough, remove the *biga* from the refrigerator to take off the chill. It will have risen slightly but probably will not be double in size. It need not have risen significantly in order to use it in the final dough.

MAKING A BIGA

The *biga* will be coarse at first, but then will smooth out after a short resting period and 1 minute of additional kneading.

COMMENTARY

You may use a variety of types of salt, but its measurement by weight will always be the same regardless of type or grind. Volume measurements will vary based on the size of the crystals. Kosher salt is much lighter than table grind, for instance, and different brands have different volume measurements. The salt volume measurements in this book are based on table grind.

Every formula requires extra flour because the amount necessary to adjust the final dough varies depending on the flour you use. Sometimes none may be needed; sometimes you may use as much as a cup. Use the descriptions in the instructions to give you an idea as to how the dough should feel. The more often you make bread, the better your sense of feel for the dough will become.

Keep a separate bowl of flour to use solely for adjustments. It will not only help you gauge how much extra flour you're using, it's also just good *mise en place* practice. It also prevents contaminating your entire bag or container of flour by reaching into it often with a wet hand or spoon. Any leftover flour can go back in the bag if still in good shape, or you can just leave it out if you will be baking again soon.

VOLUME	OUNCES	GRAMS	INGREDIENT
Use all	15.14	429	soaker
Use all	14	397	starter (or *biga*)
7 tablespoons	2	56.5	whole wheat flour, any grind
⁵⁄₈ teaspoon	.18	5	salt
2¼ teaspoons	.25	7	instant yeast
2¼ tablespoons	1.5	42.5	honey or agave nectar
or 3 tablespoons	1.5	42.5	or sugar or brown sugar
2 tablespoons	1	28.5	unsalted butter, melted, or vegetable oil
			extra whole wheat flour for adjustments
TOTAL	34.07	965.5	

1. **Using a metal pastry scraper, chop** the soaker and the starter or *biga* into 12 smaller pieces each (sprinkle some of the extra flour over the pre-doughs to keep the pieces from sticking back to each other).

HAND MIXING

Whether mixing by hand or machine, the objective is the same: a soft, pliable dough.

MACHINE MIXING

With an electric mixer, start with the paddle and then switch to the hook.

It's always a good idea to keep a bowl of room temperature water on the counter for your hands and your mixing tools. Wet dough won't stick to wet hands (or wet tools), so I find it easier to work with dough if I frequently dip my hands in water. The wetness also makes the dough less sticky on the surface, which surprisingly makes it easier to knead.

2. **If mixing by hand,** combine the soaker and starter pieces in a bowl with all of the other ingredients except the extra flour and stir vigorously with a mixing spoon or knead with wet hands for about 2 minutes, until all of the ingredients are evenly distributed and integrated into the dough. The dough should be soft and slightly sticky; if not, add some of the extra flour or more water as needed. **If using a stand mixer,** put the pre-dough pieces and all of the other ingredients except the extra flour into the mixer with the paddle attachment (preferable) or dough hook. Mix on slow speed for 1 minute to bring the ingredients together into a ball, adding some of the extra flour or additional water as needed until soft and slightly sticky. Switch to the dough hook if need be, increase the speed to medium-low, and mix for 2 to 3 minutes; you may have to scrape down the bowl a couple of times with a rubber spatula or plastic pastry scraper. The pieces of soaker and starter should become cohesive and assimilated into each other.

If using a stand mixer with the dough hook, the mixing time may actually be longer than if mixing by hand. The dough hook doesn't always grab the entire mass of dough, so additional mixing time is necessary to ensure that the ingredients are thoroughly incorporated, with no dry or lumpy spots.

3. **Dust a work surface with flour,** then roll the dough in the flour to coat. Knead by hand for 3 to 4 minutes. Incorporate only as much extra flour as needed. The dough should feel soft and tacky but not sticky. If the dough becomes too sticky to knead, dip your hands in a bowl of water (sticky dough will not stick to wet hands) and mist the work surface lightly with water to prevent sticking. You can also use a pastry scraper to move aside any loose flour and clean the surface to keep the dough from sticking to it, or dab the surface with vegetable oil or a light misting of pan spray. Form the dough into a ball and let it rest on the work surface for 5 minutes while you prepare a clean, lightly oiled bowl.

While the dough is resting, prepare a clean, lightly oiled bowl. After 1 minute of additional hand mixing, the dough will be smooth, tacky, and supple. Place the dough in the prepared bowl and cover loosely.

4. **Resume kneading the dough by hand for 1 minute.** This will strengthen the gluten and allow for any final adjustments with additional flour or water. The dough should have strength and substance when fully kneaded and pass the windowpane test (see below), yet still feel soft, supple, and very tacky. Form the dough into a ball and place it in the prepared bowl, rolling to coat with oil. Cover the bowl loosely with plastic wrap and let the dough rise (ferment) at room temperature for approximately 45 minutes to 1 hour, until it is about $1^{1}/_{2}$ times its original size.

5. **Transfer the risen dough** to a lightly floured work surface and form it into a loaf pan shape or a freestanding *bâtard*, or torpedo-shaped loaf (see pages 87–91 for shaping instructions).

WINDOWPANE TEST

The most reliable method to determine when gluten development is sufficient is called the windowpane test. This is performed by cutting off a small piece of dough and gently stretching, pulling, and turning it to see if it will hold a paper-thin, translucent membrane. If the

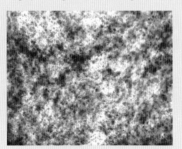

dough falls apart, continue mixing for another minute or two and then test again. It is very difficult to overmix bread dough, even when using a stand mixer; if you are hand kneading, you will probably cramp up well before your dough breaks down. (Because of all the fiber in whole wheat flour, it is more difficult to achieve the windowpane membrane, but if you follow the mixing instructions in the formulas, the gluten will be properly developed.)

HEARTH BAKING

Many professional bakeries use hearth or thick-stoned deck ovens to create their beautiful crusty loaves. Home bakers are at a disadvantage because most household ovens do not get as hot or hold heat as well as professional ovens. Fortunately, there are some things we can do to improve the performance of a home oven for hearth baking. The most obvious is to use a baking stone (the thicker the better), ceramic tiles, or an insert like the Hearth Kit, which replicates brick oven baking. These materials serve as thermal masses, absorbing heat and then radiating it back into the bread, and need at least 1 hour to preheat, even if the oven appears to have reached the desired preheating temperature. They also act as insulators, reducing the recovery time an oven needs to return to the set-point after the door has been opened. (Loaves baked in loaf pans do not need to be baked on a stone, because the crust should be softer than that of a hearth bread.)

If you do not have a baking stone, tiles, or an insert, use an inverted sheet pan as a shelf; it may not hold as much heat but will provide a hotter baking platform. Do not use a nonstick pan for this purpose, as Teflon is not rated for hearth baking temperatures and the coating may volatize and turn into gas or go into the bread. Dough can also be raised and then baked on the sheet pan (covered with baking parchment or a silicon pad) but it will take longer for the heat to penetrate through the bottom of the pan into the dough, so oven spring may be reduced.

To create steam (enhances oven spring and crisps the crust), place a cast iron baking pan or rimmed sheet pan on the shelf immediately above or below the baking shelf (the type and size of the oven will dictate where to best place the steam pan) *before* preheating the oven. Just after the dough is placed on the baking shelf (or stone), pour 1 cup of hot water into the pan, being careful to avoid getting splashed or steamed yourself. It is also a good idea to cover the oven window with a towel to protect it from backsplash, which can cause the glass to crack. As soon as the water hits the pan it will begin to turn to steam and should all evaporate within the first 5 to 10 minutes of baking. If the steam pan is located under the baking shelf, carefully remove it after the water has evaporated. You can also mist the oven walls with water from a plant mister or spray bottle at 1 minute intervals (3 times), but avoid misting the glass window or oven's light bulb. Minimize the number of times you go in and out of the oven.

Use a flour-dusted peel, either wooden or metal, to load the dough onto the baking shelf. If you do not have a peel, use the back of a sheet pan, dusted generously with flour, to serve as the peel. Flour actually works better than cornmeal or semolina because it does not burn and smoke as easily. When done baking and the oven has cooled, sweep the pan or stone of all loose flour with a wire brush or cloth rag into an extra pan and discard.

You will have to do some practice baking to determine where best to place the baking shelf to achieve a balanced bake, but the center shelf, or perhaps one notch lower, is usually reliable. Convection ovens can also be used for hearth baking, but remember to lower the temperature anywhere from 25 to 50 degrees, as the breads will bake much faster. Also, no oven bakes perfectly evenly, so rotate the loaves 180 degrees at least once about mid-way through the bake. Sometimes it will take two or three rotations to achieve even browning of the crust.

These are just a few basic tips for how to do hearth baking in a home oven. As you do it more often, I'm sure you will come up with any tricks of your own.

(A) Preheat the oven with a baking stone and steam plan in place. Slide the shaped dough onto the preheated baking stone. (B) Lay a kitchen towel over the oven's glass window to protect it from any potential backsplash, and then pour approximately 1 cup of hot water into the preheated steam pan (I like using a watering can because of the control the spout provides). (C) Using a plant mister, spritz the oven walls a couple of times to create additional steam.

For loaf pan bread, place the dough in a greased 4 by 8^1/$_2$-inch bread pan (a 4^1/$_2$ by 9-inch pan will also work). For a *bâtard*, place it on a proofing cloth or on a sheet pan covered with parchment paper and dusted with a little whole wheat flour if you like. Mist the top of the dough with pan spray (this is optional; it just makes it easier to remove the plastic wrap later), cover the dough loosely with plastic wrap, and let rise at room temperature for approximately 45 minutes to 1 hour, until it has grown to 1^1/$_2$ times its original size. In a loaf pan, the dough should rise to about 1^1/$_2$ inches above the rim.

6. **Preheat the oven to 425°F (218°C)** and, if baking a freestanding loaf, prepare it for hearth baking (see above), including a steam pan (steaming is optional for a sandwich loaf). When the dough is ready to bake, place it in the oven (either with a peel or in the loaf pan), pour 1 cup of hot water into the steam pan, lower the temperature to 350°F (177°C), and bake for 20 minutes. Rotate the loaf 180 degrees and continue baking for another 20 to 30 minutes, until the loaf is a rich, reddish brown on all sides (you can lift the loaf from its pan to check the sides and bottom), sounds hollow when thumped on the bottom, and registers at least 195°F (91°C) in the center of the loaf.

7. **Remove the bread from the pan immediately,** transfer to a cooling rack, and cool for at least 1 hour before serving.

• • •

You are now ready to begin making whole grain breads using the delayed fermentation method. Revisit this background information as needed until you have internalized the method; it will only take a few loaves before you have it mastered. Happy baking!

TECHNIQUES FOR FORMING TRADITIONAL BREAD SHAPES

SANDWICH LOAF

(A) Flatten the dough into a 5 by 8-inch rectangle and roll up the length of the dough.

(B) Pinch the final seam closed using your fingertips or the back edge of your hand.

(C) Rock the loaf to even it out; do not taper the ends. Keep the top surface of the loaf even.

(D) Place the loaf in an oiled pan for proofing.

BÂTARD (TORPEDO)

(A) Gently pat the risen dough into a thick rectangle. (B) Fold the bottom half to the center and press with your fingertips to hold in place and create a seam. (C) Fold the top half to the center and again, press with your fingertips to seal and seam. (D) Roll the top half over the seam to create a new seam on the bottom of the loaf. Pinch it closed with your fingertips or the edge of your hand to create surface tension on the outer skin, making a tight loaf.

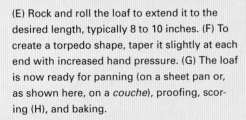
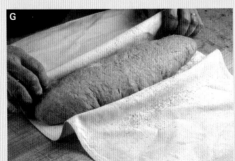

(E) Rock and roll the loaf to extend it to the desired length, typically 8 to 10 inches. (F) To create a torpedo shape, taper it slightly at each end with increased hand pressure. (G) The loaf is now ready for panning (on a sheet pan or, as shown here, on a *couche*), proofing, scoring (H), and baking.

BOULE (BALL)

(A) Gently pat the dough into a rectangle, and then bring all four corners to the center into a common point. Squeeze the corners to seal them together, tightening the skin of the dough to create surface tension. (B) Use your hands to rotate the dough on the counter to make a tight, round ball. (C) Prepare a floured proofing basket or a baking pan with parchment and dusted with flour, semolina, or cornmeal. (D) Transfer the dough to a floured proofing basket (upside down) or place it on a baking pan (top side up) to proof.

When ready to bake, gently turn the dough out of the proofing form onto a floured peel and score the top with either a blade (*lame*) or a sharp knife (preferably serrated).

Start by making a bâtard (page 88) and then let it rest for 5 to 10 minutes. (A) Repeat the folding process: top to center, bottom to center, and pinch to create a seam. (B) Seal the new seam with your fingers, thumbs, or the heel of your hand. It should create a tight surface tension. (C) With the seam side under, gently rock and roll the loaf from the center with each hand moving out toward the ends, increasing the pressure to slightly taper the loaf. It should be the length of the baking pan or baking stone. (D) Transfer the shaped loaf to a pan or *couche* (proofing cloth), cover, and proof. When the dough is ready to bake, score it and place it in the oven.

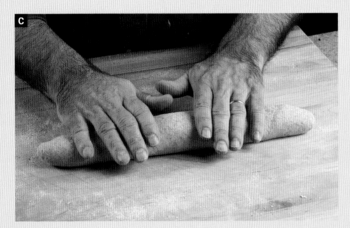

ÉPI—Shape and pan any hearth bread dough as for a baguette. Just prior to baking, use a scissors to make the cuts. Start about 2½ inches from one of the ends, cutting down through the top of the loaf, and snip back toward the end at a 45-degree angle, cutting almost all the way through the dough. Turn the inside portion of the cut piece (the pointed end) to either the right or left, facing the point away from the loaf. Move down another 2½ inches and repeat, turning the next piece in the opposite direction, until you reach the end of the loaf. Bake as you would a baguette.

KNOTTED AND ROUND ROLLS

(A) Extend a 2-ounce dough ball into a strand about 10-inches long. (B) Tie it into a single loop knot, leaving enough dough (about 2 inches at each end) for one additional wrap-around. (C) Bring one end around and down and the other end around and up through the center. (D) There should be a nub of dough poking up in the center on both the top and underside of the roll. Place the nicest side up, pan, proof, brush with egg wash, garnish with seeds, and bake.

ROUND ROLLS—Cup your hand around a 2-ounce piece of dough and rotate the dough rapidly in a circular motion, as if trying to push it through the work surface. If needed, wipe the work surface with a damp towel to add traction to the dough as you round it into a tight, smooth ball. Pan, proof, brush with egg wash, garnish with seeds, and bake.

· IV ·

The Breads

Most of the formulas that follow use the delayed fermentation method. There are many versions of these breads in other books, but you will not find these exact formulas or this method specifically designed for whole grain and transitional breads anywhere else. For all of the reasons explained in the previous chapters, I believe these are the best-tasting versions of whole grain breads you will ever find. At first glance, the formulas may seem complicated, but most of the nearly 350 recipe testers reported that they actually found the method relatively easy once they established a pattern and rhythm for the two-day process and had a sense of how the final dough should feel. I believe it will take you only one or two baking sessions to arrive at this comfort level.

Before you embark on any of these formulas, it is important that you read the previous chapter, in which the fundamentals are explained and illustrated. It would also help to read chapter 2, in order to understand the science of delayed fermentation. This method represents a radical departure from conventional baking, even from what is called artisan baking, though it is based on many artisan principles. If you approach these formulas with the mind-set that you already know how to bake bread and try to impose your previous ideas on these techniques, you will confuse yourself. After making a few of these breads, you will indeed figure out techniques of your own that work perfectly well and improve upon what I have written. That would be fantastic and it is certainly one of my hopes for you. But it is important to first integrate these new methods into your repertoire by following them as written.

Every home baking situation is unique, whether due to the oven, the mixing tools, or the ambient temperatures, or other factors, so you will have to adjust accordingly, and the instructions do give leeway for that. But the broad strokes of the method are solid, even if unconventional. There is more yeast in these breads than in many I have previously developed, and the fermentation times of the final dough are shorter due to the length of time the overnight pre-doughs develop. Combining two pre-doughs ("epoxy-style," as I like to think of it) to make the final dough is uncommon, though not unheard of, and it is a logical progression of technique when viewed through the lens of dough science as outlined in chapters 2 and 3. So please do refer to the previous chapters before attempting your first loaves.

Many of the breads offer the option of using either a *biga* (a commercially yeasted preferment) or a wild yeast starter. If you do not already have a whole wheat starter or a white flour starter that can easily be converted to whole wheat, you will want to start that process as soon as possible, as it will take approximately 1 week before a new starter will be ready to use in breads. For complete instructions for making a wild yeast starter, see page 59. In the meanwhile, you can immediately begin with the *biga* versions. My suggestion is to start with one of the breads that I refer to as transitional breads (part whole grain, part white flour) or the 100% whole wheat bread on the facing page (also featured in the previous chapter, on pages 78–86). Once you have made these basic breads, you should be able to easily leap into some of the more challenging formulas and variations.

As you examine the formulas, you will notice in many instances that the breads are simply variations on a theme. Many elements may vary—the amount of hydration, the type of flour and grains, the hydrating liquid, whether water, milk, yogurt, soy milk, or rice milk—but the technique is the common thread. Once this technique is mastered, you can create countless variations of your own.

∾ ENRICHED BREADS ∾

We distinguish enriched from lean breads by the amount of fat, sugar, and/or dairy they include. These ingredients soften and sweeten bread beyond the effects of flour alone. Lean dough is usually baked into crusty hearth loaves, while enriched dough is often used as sandwich bread because it is softer. However, enriched dough can also be baked as freestanding, hearth-style loaves, though at a lower temperature than lean dough in order to prevent premature caramelization of the crust. As always, understanding the balancing act between time and temperature is crucial and the general rule is, the more sugar and other enrichments in the dough, the lower the baking temperature.

100% Whole Wheat Sandwich Bread

Makes 1 large loaf

This is the foundational loaf for all the 100% whole grain breads in this book, and as such, the method for making it is presented in more detail in the master formula in chapter 3 (see page 78). The essentials are repeated here for use once you're comfortable with the epoxy method and just want to make this bread without all the extra info and page flipping. It is versatile enough to be baked in any shape or form, whether as a sandwich loaf, a freestanding hearth bread, or rolls. I suggest that you make this bread first before moving on to other, more complex formulas.

BREAD PROFILE

Enriched, medium soft dough; delayed fermentation method; commercial yeast

DAYS TO MAKE: 2

Day 1: Soaker and *biga*, 20 minutes set up and mix; overnight autolyse
Day 2: 2 hours to de-chill *biga*; 12 to 15 minutes mixing; 2 to 3 hours fermentation, shaping, proofing; 40 to 60 minutes baking

If you use pasteurized milk in the soaker, the final loaf may not benefit from scalding the milk, but the general feedback from many of the recipe testers was that scalded and cooled milk outperformed unscalded milk. The best way to find out if it makes a difference in your situation is to try it and see.

You can substitute an equal amount of wild yeast starter (page 80) for the *biga*.

SOAKER

VOLUME	OUNCES	GRAMS	INGREDIENT	%
1³/₄ cups	8	227	whole wheat flour	100
¹/₂ teaspoon	.14	4	salt	1.75
³/₄ cup plus 2 tablespoons	7	198	milk, buttermilk, yogurt, soy milk, or rice milk	87.5
TOTAL	15.14	429		189.5

1. **Mix all of the soaker ingredients together** in a bowl for about 1 minute, until all of the flour is hydrated and the ingredients form a ball of dough.

2. **Cover loosely with plastic wrap** and leave at room temperature for 12 to 24 hours. (If it will be more than 24 hours, place the soaker in the refrigerator; it will be good for up to 3 days. Remove it 2 hours before mixing the final dough to take off the chill.)

BIGA

VOLUME	OUNCES	GRAMS	INGREDIENT	%
1³/₄ cups	8	227	whole wheat flour	100
¹/₄ teaspoon	.03	1	instant yeast	.4
³/₄ cup	6	170	filtered or spring water, at room temperature (about 70°F/21°C)	75
TOTAL	14. 03	398		175.4

1. **Mix all of the *biga* ingredients together** in a bowl to form a ball of dough. Using wet hands, knead the dough in the bowl for 2 minutes to be sure all of the ingredients are evenly distributed and the flour is fully hydrated. The dough should feel very tacky. Let the dough rest for 5 minutes, then knead it again with wet hands for 1 minute. The dough will become smoother but still be tacky.

2. **Transfer the dough to a clean bowl, cover** tightly with plastic wrap, and refrigerate for at least 8 hours and up to 3 days.

3. **About 2 hours before mixing the final dough, remove** the *biga* from the refrigerator to take off the chill. It will have risen slightly but need not have risen significantly in order to use it in the final dough.

FINAL DOUGH

VOLUME	OUNCES	GRAMS	INGREDIENT
Use all	15.14	429	soaker
Use all	14.03	398	*biga*
7 tablespoons	2	56.5	whole wheat flour
⁵⁄₈ teaspoon	.18	5	salt
2¹⁄₄ teaspoons	.25	7	instant yeast
2¹⁄₄ tablespoons	1.5	42.5	honey or agave nectar
or 3 tablespoons	1.5	42.5	or sugar or brown sugar
1 tablespoon	.5	14	unsalted butter, melted, or vegetable oil
			extra whole wheat flour for adjustments
TOTAL	33.6	952	

Recipe tester Michael Arnoldi came up with a shortcut when chopping and re-combining his pre-doughs for the final mixing. He stacks one on top of the other and then chops them up together. Makes sense and saves a whole step—wish I'd thought of it. Thankfully Michael did and told me about it just in time to make it into the book!

1. **Using a metal pastry scraper, chop** the soaker and the *biga* into 12 smaller pieces each (sprinkle some of the extra flour over the pre-doughs to keep the pieces from sticking back to each other).

2. **If mixing by hand,** combine the soaker and *biga* pieces in a bowl with all of the other ingredients except the extra flour and stir vigorously with a mixing spoon or knead with wet hands until all of the ingredients are evenly integrated and distributed into the dough. It should be soft and slightly sticky; if not, add more flour or water as needed. **If using a stand mixer,** put the pre-dough pieces and all of the other ingredients except the extra flour into the mixer with the paddle attachment (preferable) or dough hook. Mix on slow speed for 1 minute to bring the ingredients together into a ball. Switch to the dough hook and mix on medium-low speed, occasionally scraping down the bowl, for 2 to 3 minutes, until the pre-doughs become cohesive and assimilated into each other. Add more flour or water as needed until the dough is soft and slightly sticky.

3. **Dust a work surface with flour,** then toss the dough in the flour to coat. Knead by hand for 3 to 4 minutes, incorporating only as much extra flour as needed, until the dough feels soft and tacky, but not sticky. Form the dough into a ball and let it rest on the work surface for 5 minutes while you prepare a clean, lightly oiled bowl.

4. **Resume kneading the dough for 1 minute** to strengthen the gluten and make any final flour or water adjustments. The dough should have strength and pass the windowpane test (see page 84), yet still feel soft, supple, and very tacky. Form the dough into a ball and place it in the prepared bowl, rolling to coat with oil. Cover loosely with plastic wrap and let rise

BAKER'S FORMULA	%
Whole wheat flour	100
Salt	1.8
Instant yeast	1.5
Milk	39
Water	33
Honey	8.5
Unsalted butter or oil	3
Total	186.8

NUTRITION FACTS	
Calories (kcal)	92.93
Protein (g)	3.54
Carbohydrates (g)	18.38
Dietary fiber (g)	2.84
Total sugars (g)	1.91
Fat (g)	1.23
Saturated fat (g)	.56
Trans fatty acid (g)	.02
Cholesterol (mg)	2.22
Sodium (mg)	16.33

at room temperature for approximately 45 to 60 minutes, until it is about 1$^1/_2$ times its original size.

5. **Transfer the dough to a lightly floured work surface** and form it into either a loaf pan shape or a freestanding *bâtard* (see pages 87–91 for shaping instructions). For loaf pan bread, place the dough in a greased 4 by 8$^1/_2$-inch bread pan. For a *bâtard*, place it on a proofing cloth or on a sheet pan lined with parchment paper and, if you like, dusted with flour. Mist the top of the dough with pan spray (optional), cover loosely with plastic wrap, and let rise at room temperature for approximately 45 to 60 minutes, until it is about 1$^1/_2$ times its original size.

6. **Preheat the oven to 425°F (218°C),** and, if baking a freestanding loaf, prepare the oven for hearth baking (see page 86), including a steam pan (steaming is optional for a sandwich loaf). When the dough is ready to bake, place it in the oven, pour 1 cup of hot water into the steam pan, lower the temperature to 350°F (177°C), and bake for 20 minutes. Rotate the loaf 180 degrees and continue baking for another 20 to 30 minutes, until the loaf is a rich brown on all sides, sounds hollow when thumped on the bottom, and registers at least 195°F (91°C) in the center.

7. **Transfer the bread to a cooling rack** and allow it to cool for at least 1 hour before serving.

FAQ ∽ *Do you have any other baking tips before I start making these breads?*

Yes! I learned some by trial and error and some from recipe tester suggestions. Here are a few:

- If a recipe calls for oil and honey (or agave nectar, molasses, or sorghum syrup), it will be easier to first measure the oil and then use the oiled measuring container for the honey.

- Use a plastic bowl scraper. This inexpensive tool will be the single most used item in your tool kit. The same goes for a metal pastry scraper.

- Invest in a scale; it is by far the most accurate way to bake. Look for one that gives both imperial and metric readings, and that measures in increments at least as small as $^1/_4$ ounce.

- When making pizzas or any hearth breads that need to be peeled into the oven, consider using parchment paper under the dough and sliding the dough into the oven from the peel, parchment and all. After a few minutes, once the dough has set, you can remove the parchment paper and discard it.

- Give yourself two or three attempts at making a particular bread before you give up on it. As you figure out what adjustments you need to make in your situation, the entire process will become very easy and will actually be less time-consuming than conventional methods.

- Active dry yeast contains a small amount of glutathione, which causes gluten to relax. In side-by-side test bakes, it definitely enhances extensibility; however, I still prefer instant yeast because of the simplicity of adding it directly to the flour. If you use active dry yeast, hydrate it in a small amount of lukewarm water (about 100°F/38°C) for a minute or two to dissolve the grains and activate the yeast.

Transitional Whole Wheat Sandwich Bread

Makes 1 large loaf

This is a wonderful, all-purpose sandwich bread that can also be baked as a freestanding loaf or be divided into smaller pieces for mini loaves, dinner rolls, or sandwich rolls. It is made with a 50-50 blend of white flour and whole wheat flour, producing a loaf that is lighter than 100% whole wheat yet still high in fiber. This bread is especially good for helping family members make the switch to whole grain breads. You can gradually increase the amount of whole wheat flour by substituting it, little by little, in the *biga*. For every ounce of white flour that you replace with whole wheat flour, increase the amount of water by about 1 or 2 teaspoons.

BREAD PROFILE

Enriched, medium soft dough; delayed fermentation method; commercial yeast

DAYS TO MAKE: 2

Day 1: Soaker and *biga*, 20 minutes set up and mix; overnight autolyse
Day 2: 2 hours to de-chill *biga*; 12 to 15 minutes mixing; 2 to 3 hours fermentation, shaping, proofing; 40 to 60 minutes baking

You will notice that the hydration of the *biga* is only 62.5% compared to 87.2% hydration in the soaker, yet both of these pre-doughs will feel similarly soft and supple. There are two reasons for this: The white bread flour, which is pure endosperm, requires less hydration than whole wheat flour because it does not contain any bran or germ, both of which absorb more liquid than endosperm. Also, milk contains milk solids, such as minerals and proteins, so it does not provide the same hydration as water. If you decide to make the soaker with water instead of milk, reduce the amount to 6 ounces (170 grams).

SOAKER

VOLUME	OUNCES	GRAMS	INGREDIENT	%
1³/₄ cups	8	227	whole wheat flour	100
¹/₂ teaspoon	.14	4	salt	1.75
³/₄ cup plus 2 tablespoons	7	198	milk, buttermilk, yogurt, soy milk, or rice milk	87.5
TOTAL	15.14	429		189.25

1. **Mix all of the soaker ingredients together** in a bowl for about 1 minute, until all of the flour is hydrated and the ingredients form a ball of dough.

2. **Cover loosely with plastic wrap** and leave at room temperature for 12 to 24 hours. (If it will be more than 24 hours, place the soaker in the refrigerator; it will be good for up to 3 days. Remove it 2 hours before mixing the final dough to take off the chill.)

BIGA

VOLUME	OUNCES	GRAMS	INGREDIENT	%
1³/₄ cups	8	227	unbleached bread flour	100
¹/₄ teaspoon	.03	1	instant yeast	.4
¹/₂ cup plus 2 tablespoons	5	142	filtered or spring water, at room temperature (about 70°F/21°C)	62.5
TOTAL	13.03	370		162.9

1. **Mix all of the *biga* ingredients together** in a bowl to form a ball of dough. Using wet hands, knead the dough in the bowl for 2 minutes to be sure all of the ingredients are evenly distributed and the flour is fully hydrated. The dough should feel very tacky. Let the dough rest for 5 minutes, then knead it again with wet hands for 1 minute. The dough will become smoother but still be tacky.

2. **Transfer the dough to a clean bowl, cover** tightly with plastic wrap, and refrigerate for at least 8 hours and up to 3 days.

3. **About 2 hours before mixing the final dough,** remove the *biga* from the refrigerator to take off the chill. It will have risen slightly but need not have risen significantly in order to use it in the final dough.

FINAL DOUGH

VOLUME	OUNCES	GRAMS	INGREDIENT
Use all	15.14	429	soaker
Use all	13.03	370	*biga*
3 1/2 tablespoons	1	28.5	whole wheat flour
5/8 teaspoon	.18	5	salt
2 1/4 teaspoons	.25	7	instant yeast
2 1/4 tablespoons	1.5	42.5	honey or agave nectar
or 3 tablespoons	1.5	42.5	or sugar or brown sugar
1 tablespoon	.5	14	unsalted butter, melted, or vegetable oil
3 1/2 tablespoons	1	28	extra whole wheat flour for adjustments
TOTAL	32.6	924	

BAKER'S FORMULA	%
Whole wheat flour	56
Bread flour	44
Salt	1.8
Instant yeast	1.5
Milk	39
Water	28
Honey	8
Unsalted butter or oil	2.8
Total	181.1

NUTRITION FACTS	
Calories (kcal)	98.05
Protein (g)	3.47
Carbohydrates (g)	18.94
Dietary fiber (g)	1.92
Total sugars (g)	1.96
Fat (g)	1.25
Saturated fat (g)	.57
Trans fatty acid (g)	.02
Cholesterol (mg)	2.29
Sodium (mg)	164.91

1. **Using a metal pastry scraper, chop** the soaker and the *biga* into 12 smaller pieces each (sprinkle with some of the extra flour to keep the pieces from sticking back to each other).

2. **If mixing by hand,** combine the soaker and *biga* pieces in a bowl with all of the other ingredients except the extra flour and stir vigorously with a mixing spoon or knead with wet hands for about 2 minutes, until all of the ingredients are evenly integrated and distributed into the dough. The dough should be soft and slightly sticky; if not, add more flour or water as needed. **If using a stand mixer,** put the pre-dough pieces and all of the other ingredients except the extra flour into the mixer with the paddle attachment (preferable) or dough hook. Mix on slow speed for 1 minute to bring the ingredients together into a ball. Switch to the dough hook if need be and mix on medium-low speed, occasionally scraping down the bowl, for 2 to 3 minutes, until the pre-doughs become cohesive and assimilated into each other. Add more flour or water as needed until the dough is soft and slightly sticky.

3. **Proceed as in steps 3 through 7** in the whole wheat sandwich bread on page 97.

FAQ ∾ *What are transitional breads?*

Breads that use a combination of whole grain flour and unbleached white bread flour, making the dough easier to work with. The goal of this book is to help people make the move to 100% whole grain breads, and these transitional breads are offered as bridges toward that goal. A major difference between transitional and 100% whole grain formulas is the hydration; the bran component in whole grains absorbs more water than the starches and proteins of the endosperm.

Multigrain Struan

Makes 1 large loaf

BREAD PROFILE

Enriched, medium soft dough; delayed fermentation method; commercial yeast

DAYS TO MAKE: 2

Day 1: Soaker and *biga*, 20 minutes set up and mix; overnight autolyse

Day 2: 2 hours to de-chill *biga*; 12 to 15 minutes mixing; 2 to 3 hours fermentation, shaping, proofing; 40 to 60 minutes baking

COMMENTARY

The total weight of the grains in the soaker, including any cooked grains, should be 6 ounces (excluding the 2 ounces of whole wheat flour listed as the first ingredient, which is needed to provide sufficient gluten to support the structure of the bread). It is especially important to measure these grains by weight, not volume. The volume needed can vary substantially depending on the grains used, how coarsely they are milled, and whether they are cooked. If you do not have a scale, a volume approximation is provided, but this is really dependent on which grains you choose. After you have made a loaf or two you will be able to discern whether you should increase or decrease the grain amounts.

Struan is the bread that truly launched my bread baking career. In Gaelic, *struan* means "the convergence or confluence of streams," and what better way to describe multigrain breads. Since there is no official, traditional recipe for *struan* other than to use whatever is available at harvest time, we are all free to create our own *struans*. The following new version is made from 100% whole grains in various combinations; from it, you should be able to create dozens of variations of your own.

SOAKER				
VOLUME	OUNCES	GRAMS	INGREDIENT	%
7 tablespoons	2	56.5	whole wheat flour	25
1⅓ cups (approx.)	6	170	any combination of cooked and uncooked grains (see Commentary)	75
½ teaspoon	.14	4	salt	1.75
¾ cup	6	170	milk, buttermilk, yogurt, soy milk, or rice milk	75
TOTAL	14.14	400.5		176.75

1. **Mix all of the soaker ingredients together** in a bowl for about 1 minute, until all of the flour is hydrated and the ingredients form a thick, porridge-like dough.

2. **Cover loosely with plastic wrap** and leave at room temperature for 12 to 24 hours. (If it will be more than 24 hours, place the soaker in the refrigerator; it will be good for up to 3 days. Remove it 2 hours before mixing the final dough to take off the chill.)

FAQ ∽ *Should I use cooked or uncooked grains in the multigrain breads?*

It is up to you, but I like a blend. Large kernels, like brown rice and steel-cut oats, should always be cooked to the point of softness. In volume measurements, most grains require 2½ parts water to 1 part grain (but wild rice requires 4 parts water to 1 part grain). Simmer the grain in a covered pot until the water is completely absorbed. Medium-size grains, like millet and quinoa, will remain crunchy or chewy if not precooked, but they are also small enough to soften in the soaker without cooking. I prefer to cook them, using equal parts water to grain (by volume). Again, simmer in a covered pot until the water is completely absorbed. When making a grain mash, remember that it is more akin to a soaker than it is to fully cooked grain. Whole rice or wheat kernels, for instance, will not soften sufficiently in a mash, though rye chops and flaxseeds will.

Smaller or softer grains may be used uncooked, such as amaranth, rolled oats, oat or wheat bran, triticale flakes, multigrain cereal mixes, flaxseeds, and any type of flour or meal (for example, cornmeal). Precook larger or harder grains, such as barley, buckwheat, bulgur, couscous, cracked wheat, grits, millet, quinoa, rice, steel-cut oats, and whole wheat berries or rye berries. See page 102 for cooking instructions.

If you use bran in the soaker, a little goes a long way; don't use more than 1 tablespoon.

You can substitute an equal amount of wild yeast starter (page 80) for the *biga*.

BIGA

VOLUME	OUNCES	GRAMS	INGREDIENT	%
1³/₄ cups	8	227	whole wheat flour	100
¹/₄ teaspoon	.03	1	instant yeast	.4
³/₄ cup	6	170	filtered or spring water, at room temperature (about 70°F/21°C)	75
TOTAL	14.03	398		175.4

1. **Mix all of the *biga* ingredients together** in a bowl to form a ball of dough. Using wet hands, knead the dough in the bowl for 2 minutes to be sure all of the ingredients are evenly distributed and the flour is fully hydrated. The dough should feel very tacky. Let the dough rest for 5 minutes, then knead it again with wet hands for 1 minute. The dough will become smoother but still be tacky.

2. **Transfer the dough to a clean bowl, cover** tightly with plastic wrap, and refrigerate for at least 8 hours and up to 3 days.

3. **About 2 hours before mixing the final dough, remove** the *biga* from the refrigerator to take off the chill. It will have risen slightly but need not have risen significantly in order to use it in the final dough.

A poppy seed or sesame seed topping complements this loaf nicely. To top with seeds, after shaping the loaf, brush with water or beaten egg white, sprinkle generously with seeds, then allow to rise, as usual.

FINAL DOUGH

VOLUME	OUNCES	GRAMS	INGREDIENT
Use all	14.14	400.5	soaker
Use all	14.03	398	*biga*
7 tablespoons	2	56.5	whole wheat flour
⁵/₈ teaspoon	.18	5	salt
2¹/₄ teaspoons	.25	7	instant yeast
3 tablespoons or ¹/₄ cup	2 2	56.5 56.5	honey or agave nectar or sugar or brown sugar
1 tablespoon	.5	14	unsalted butter, melted, or vegetable oil
			extra whole wheat flour for adjustments
TOTAL	33.1	937.5	

Multigrain *biga* and soaker.

BAKER'S FORMULA	%
Whole wheat flour	67
Multigrain blend	33
Salt	1.8
Instant yeast	1.6
Milk	33
Water	33
Honey	11
Unsalted butter or oil	2.8
Total	183.2

NUTRITION FACTS	
Fat (g)	1.42
Saturated fat (g)	.24
Trans fatty acid (g)	0
Cholesterol (mg)	.30
Sodium (mg)	201.33
Calories (kcal)	97.05
Protein (g)	3.41
Carbohydrates (g)	18.97
Dietary fiber (g)	2.52
Total sugars (g)	2.39

1. **Using a metal pastry scraper, chop** the soaker and the *biga* into 12 smaller pieces each (sprinkle some of the extra flour over the pre-doughs to keep the pieces from sticking back to each other).

2. **If mixing by hand,** combine the soaker and *biga* pieces in a bowl with all of the other ingredients except the extra flour and stir vigorously with a mixing spoon or knead with wet hands for about 2 minutes, until all of the ingredients are evenly integrated and distributed into the dough. The dough should be soft and slightly sticky; if not, add more flour or water as needed. **If using a stand mixer,** put the pre-dough pieces and all of the other ingredients except the extra flour into the mixer with the paddle attachment (preferable) or dough hook. Mix on slow speed for 1 minute to bring the ingredients together into a ball. Switch to the dough hook if need be and mix on medium-low speed, occasionally scraping down the bowl, for 2 to 3 minutes, until the pre-doughs become cohesive and assimilated into each other. Add more flour or water as needed until the dough is soft and slightly sticky.

3. **Proceed as in steps 3 through 7** in the whole wheat sandwich bread on page 97.

Proceed as in steps 3 through 7 in the whole wheat sandwich bread on page 97.

FAQ ∽ *What is the difference between a formula and a recipe?*

Most cooks do not differentiate between them, but bakers do. A formula is more about the ratio between the ingredients and the overall method, rather than its application in a specific size (the recipe). What you will see in this book are both recipes and formulas: the recipe, in most instances, is for one large loaf or a few smaller units, about 2 pounds of bread. The formula, expressed in the baker's formula column, shows how much of each ingredient to use as a percentage of the total flour. (Flour is always the 100% ingredient, and everything else is considered in relationship to it.)

Transitional Multigrain Sandwich Bread

Makes 1 large loaf

BREAD PROFILE

Enriched, medium soft dough; delayed fermentation method; commercial yeast

DAYS TO MAKE: 2

Day 1: Soaker and *biga*, 20 minutes set up and mix; overnight autolyse
Day 2: 2 hours to de-chill *biga*; 12 to 15 minutes mixing; 2 to 3 hours fermentation, shaping, proofing; 40 to 60 minutes baking

COMMENTARY

The total weight of the grains should be 6 ounces (excluding the 2 ounces of whole wheat flour). The volume needed can vary substantially depending on the grains used. For that reason, the volume measure provided is an approximation, but one that will get you pretty close if you don't have a scale. As you make this bread again, you can increase or decrease the grain amounts, as determined from the first batch.

Smaller or softer grains may be used uncooked, such as amaranth, rolled oats, oat bran, triticale flakes, multigrain cereal mixes, flaxseeds, and any type of flour or meal. It is best to precook larger or harder grains, such as barley, buckwheat, couscous, cracked wheat, grits, millet, quinoa, rice, steel-cut oats, and whole wheat berries or rye berries. See page 102 for cooking instructions.

This is a multigrain variation of the transitional whole wheat bread on page 99. As such, it is a type of *struan* bread, lighter in texture than the 100% whole grain *struan* on page 102.

SOAKER

VOLUME	OUNCES	GRAMS	INGREDIENT	%
7 tablespoons	2	56.5	whole wheat flour or unbleached bread flour	25
7 tablespoons	2	56.5	cornmeal, coarse grind	25
1/2 cup	2	56.5	rolled oats	25
5 tablespoons	1.5	42.5	cooked brown rice or other cooked grain	18.8
1 tablespoon	.25	7	oat bran	3.1
or 2 tablespoons	.25	7	or wheat bran	
2 1/4 teaspoons	.25	7	flaxseeds, whole or ground (optional)	3.1
1/2 teaspoon	.14	4	salt	1.75
3/4 cup plus 2 tablespoons	6	170	milk, buttermilk, yogurt, soy milk, or rice milk	75
TOTAL	14.14	400		176.75

1. **Mix all of the soaker ingredients together** in a bowl for about 1 minute, until all of the flour is hydrated and the ingredients form a thick, porridge-like dough.

2. **Cover loosely with plastic wrap** and leave at room temperature for 12 to 24 hours. (If it will be more than 24 hours, place the soaker in the refrigerator; it will be good for up to 3 days. Remove it 2 hours before mixing the final dough to take off the chill.)

FAQ ∞ *This is a lot of work for just one loaf. Can I make larger batches so as to make better use of my time?*

Yes, you can double or triple these recipes; simply keep all of the ingredients in the same proportion. Your mixer may not be large enough, but it is very easy to mix the dough by hand. As always, read through the instructions carefully before you weigh or measure your ingredients. And most important of all: Write down the ingredients and do the math on each one if you are increasing the size. Do not try to keep it in your head. This is the single most common cause of mistakes and failure.

BIGA

VOLUME	OUNCES	GRAMS	INGREDIENT	%
1³/₄ cups	8	227	unbleached bread flour or high-gluten flour	100
¹/₄ teaspoon	.03	1	instant yeast	.4
¹/₂ cup plus 2 tablespoons	5	142	filtered or spring water, at room temperature (about 70°F/21°C)	62.5
TOTAL	13.03	370		162.9

1. **Mix all of the *biga* ingredients together** in a bowl to form a ball of dough. Using wet hands, knead the dough in the bowl for 2 minutes to be sure all of the ingredients are evenly distributed and the flour is fully hydrated. The dough should feel very tacky. Let the dough rest for 5 minutes, then knead it again with wet hands for 1 minute. The dough will become smoother but still be tacky.

2. **Transfer the dough to a clean bowl, cover** tightly with plastic wrap, and refrigerate for at least 8 hours and up to 3 days.

3. **About 2 hours before mixing the final dough, remove** the *biga* from the refrigerator to take off the chill. It will have risen slightly but need not have risen significantly in order to use it in the final dough.

FINAL DOUGH

VOLUME	OUNCES	GRAMS	INGREDIENT
Use all	14.14	400	soaker
Use all	13.03	370	*biga*
3¹/₂ tablespoons	1	28.5	whole wheat flour
⁵/₈ teaspoon	.18	5	salt
2¹/₄ teaspoons	.25	7	instant yeast
2¹/₄ tablespoons or 3 tablespoons	1.5 1.5	42.5 42.5	honey or agave nectar or sugar or brown sugar
1 tablespoon	.5	14	unsalted butter, melted, or vegetable oil
			extra whole wheat flour for adjustments
TOTAL	30.6	867	

A poppy seed or sesame seed topping complements this loaf nicely. To top with seeds, after shaping the loaf, brush with water or beaten egg white, sprinkle generously with seeds, then allow to rise, as usual.

1. **Using a metal pastry scraper, chop** the soaker and the *biga* into 12 smaller pieces each (sprinkle some of the extra flour over the pre-doughs to keep the pieces from sticking back to each other).

BAKER'S FORMULA	%
Whole wheat flour	17.5
Bread flour	47
Multigrain mix	29.5
Salt	1.9
Instant yeast	1.6
Milk	35
Water	29.5
Honey	9
Unsalted butter or oil	3
Total	174

NUTRITION FACTS	
Calories (kcal)	96.30
Protein (g)	3.43
Carbohydrates (g)	18.93
Dietary fiber (g)	1.49
Total sugars (g)	2.03
Fat (g)	1.37
Saturated fat (g)	.21
Trans fatty acid (g)	0
Cholesterol (mg)	.32
Sodium (mg)	174.23

2. **If mixing by hand,** combine the soaker and *biga* pieces in a bowl with the all of the other ingredients except the extra flour and stir vigorously with a mixing spoon or knead with wet hands for about 2 minutes, until all of the ingredients are evenly integrated and distributed into the dough. The dough should be soft and slightly sticky; if not, add more flour or water as needed. **If using a stand mixer,** put the pre-dough pieces and all of the other ingredients except the extra flour into the mixer with the paddle attachment (preferable) or dough hook. Mix on slow speed for 1 minute to bring the ingredients together into a ball. Switch to the dough hook if need be and mix on medium-low speed, occasionally scraping down the bowl, for 2 to 3 minutes, until the pre-doughs become cohesive and assimilated into each other. Add more flour or water as needed until the dough is soft and slightly sticky.

3. **Proceed as in steps 3 through 7** in the whole wheat sandwich bread on page 97.

FAQ ∾ *Which is better, measuring by weight or by volume, and why are you listing metric and Celsius conversions? How do you make these conversions?*

Weight measurements are always more accurate. Inaccuracies creep into volume measurements because of differences in measuring techniques, measuring tools, how dense a particular ingredient is, and how tightly or loosely packed it is. This assumes that the scale is accurate and has been zeroed out before using it. (This zero point is called tare, so bakers often say, "Tare your scale before measuring anything.") Metric weights, such as grams and kilograms, are used almost everywhere except here in the United States, and even most home bakers in the United States agree that metrics are far more accurate, logical, and easy to use than the imperial system of pounds and ounces. More and more professional and home bakers are converting over to metrics, especially as scales are now available that give readings in both systems.

There are 28.35 grams in 1 ounce, so to convert from ounces to grams, multiply the number of ounces by 28.35. To go from grams to ounces, divide by 28.35. As the decimals, whether in ounces or grams, are difficult to measure, you will notice that I often round the number to a measurable figure. The exception is with very small units, such as with instant yeast and salt, where rounding might throw off the amount too much. These instances of very small amounts of an ingredient are the one time I suggest using teaspoons and tablespoons.

Celsius temperatures are provided because some readers of this book use the Celsius (C) rather than Fahrenheit (F) system. To convert from Fahrenheit to Celsius, take the temperature in Fahrenheit (for instance 212°F, the boiling point) and subtract 32. Then multiply by $5/9$ (or .556). So $212 - 32 = 180 \times .556 = 100$. Thus, the boiling point in Fahrenheit is 212°F, while in Celsius it is 100°C. To convert from Celsius to Fahrenheit, reverse the process: Take the Celsius number and multiply it by $9/5$ (1.8), then add 32 ($100 \times 1.8 = 180 + 32 = 212$). (Note: you can also use conversion programs easily found on the Internet if you don't want to do the math yourself.)

Oat Bran Broom Bread

Makes 1 large loaf

All whole grain breads are high in fiber, but this one is a super-fiber loaf, loaded with both water soluble fiber (from the oat bran and flax) and insoluble fiber (from the wheat bran), as well as healthful omega-3 fatty acids from the flaxseeds. I call it "broom bread" because it really cleans out the colon as it works its way through your system. As with all high-fiber foods, be sure to drink plenty of water to keep it moving and to get the full health value from it.

BREAD PROFILE

Enriched, medium soft dough; delayed fermentation method; commercial yeast

DAYS TO MAKE: 2

Day 1: Soaker and *biga*, 20 minutes set up and mix; overnight autolyse
Day 2: 2 hours to de-chill *biga*; 12 to 15 minutes mixing; 2 to 3 hours fermentation, shaping, proofing; 40 to 60 minutes baking

SOAKER

VOLUME	OUNCES	GRAMS	INGREDIENT	%
1⅓ cups plus 1 tablespoon	6.5	184	whole wheat flour, preferably fine grind	100
4 tablespoons	1	28	oat bran	16.7
1½ tablespoons	.5	14	flaxseeds	7.7
½ teaspoon	.14	4	salt	2.2
¾ cup plus 2 tablespoons	7	198	water	108
TOTAL	15.14	428		234.6

1. **Mix all of the soaker ingredients together** in a bowl for about 1 minute, until all of the flour is hydrated and the ingredients form a ball of dough.

2. **Cover loosely with plastic wrap** and leave at room temperature for 12 to 24 hours. (If it will be more than 24 hours, place the soaker in the refrigerator; it will be good for up to 3 days. Remove it 2 hours before mixing the final dough to take off the chill.)

BIGA

VOLUME	OUNCES	GRAMS	INGREDIENT	%
1¾ cups	8	227	whole wheat flour	100
¼ teaspoon	.03	1	instant yeast	.4
¾ cup	6	170	filtered or spring water, at room temperature (about 70°F/21°C)	75
TOTAL	14.03	398		175.4

1. **Mix all of the *biga* ingredients together** in a bowl to form a ball of dough. Using wet hands, knead the dough in the bowl for 2 minutes to be sure all of the ingredients are evenly distributed and the flour is fully hydrated. The dough should feel very tacky. Let the dough rest for 5 minutes, then knead it again with wet hands for 1 minute. The dough will become smoother but still be tacky.

2. **Transfer the dough to a clean bowl, cover** tightly with plastic wrap, and refrigerate for at least 8 hours and up to 3 days.

3. **About 2 hours before mixing the final dough,** remove the *biga* from the refrigerator to take off the chill. It will have risen slightly but need not have risen significantly in order to use it in the final dough.

FINAL DOUGH

VOLUME	OUNCES	GRAMS	INGREDIENT
Use all	15.14	429	soaker
Use all	14.03	398	*biga*
7 tablespoons	2	56.5	whole wheat flour
⁵⁄₈ teaspoon	.18	5	salt
2¼ teaspoons	.25	7	instant yeast
2¼ tablespoons	1.5	42.5	honey or agave nectar
or 3 tablespoons	1.5	42.5	or sugar or brown sugar
1 tablespoon	.5	14	olive oil or vegetable oil
			extra whole wheat flour for adjustments
TOTAL	33.6	952	

BAKER'S FORMULA	%
Whole wheat flour	100
Oat bran	6
Flaxseeds	3
Salt	1.9
Instant yeast	1.7
Water	79
Honey	9
Olive oil	3
Total	203.6

NUTRITION FACTS	
Calories (kcal)	91.73
Protein (g)	3.44
Carbohydrates (g)	18.27
Dietary fiber (g)	3.05
Total sugars (g)	1.56
Fat (g)	1.37
Saturated fat (g)	.21
Trans fatty acid (g)	0
Cholesterol (mg)	0
Sodium (mg)	161.68

1. **Using a metal pastry scraper, chop** the soaker and the *biga* into 12 smaller pieces each (sprinkle some of the extra flour over the pre-doughs to keep the pieces from sticking back to each other).

2. **If mixing by hand,** combine the soaker and *biga* pieces in a bowl with all of the other ingredients except the extra flour and stir vigorously with a mixing spoon or knead with wet hands for about 2 minutes, until all of the ingredients are evenly integrated and distributed into the dough. The dough should be soft and slightly sticky; if not, add more flour or water as needed. **If using a stand mixer,** put the pre-dough pieces and all of the other ingredients except the extra flour into the mixer with the paddle attachment (preferable) or dough hook. Mix on slow speed for 1 minute to bring the ingredients together into a ball. Switch to the dough hook if need be and mix on medium-low speed, occasionally scraping down the bowl, for 2 to 3 minutes, until the pre-doughs become cohesive and assimilated into each other. Add more flour or water as needed until the dough is soft and slightly sticky.

3. **Proceed as in steps 3 through 7** in the whole wheat sandwich bread on page 97.

You can further the protein level in this bread by adding 4 ounces (³⁄₄ cup) of lightly toasted seeds or nuts during the final mixing.

An oat bran topping complements this loaf nicely. After shaping the loaf, spray or brush with water, sprinkle generously with oat bran, then allow to rise, as usual.

Rye Sandwich Meteil

Makes 1 large loaf

Meteil refers to rye breads with less than 50% rye flour. The best tasting rye breads usually require the acidity of a wild yeast starter to control the enzymes during the baking stage, preventing them from attacking the starches and breaking down the loaf. (This is especially true when the amount of rye flour exceeds that of wheat flour—as in the rye *seigle* on page 116—as rye flour is loaded with enzymes.) However, when testing this recipe, we discovered that buttermilk (or yogurt) also provides enough acidity to protect the integrity of the dough, so we use it in the soaker. This makes it possible to use a *biga* instead of a starter for this bread (see Commentary).

SOAKER

VOLUME	OUNCES	GRAMS	INGREDIENT	%
1³/₄ cups	8	227	whole wheat flour, preferably fine grind	100
¹/₂ teaspoon	.14	4	salt	1.75
³/₄ cup	6	170	milk, buttermilk, yogurt, soy milk, or rice milk	75
1 tablespoon	.25	7	vital wheat gluten (optional; see Commentary)	3
TOTAL	14.39	408		179.75

1. **Mix all of the soaker ingredients together** in a bowl for about 1 minute, until all of the flour is hydrated and the ingredients form a ball of dough.

2. **Cover loosely with plastic wrap** and leave at room temperature for 12 to 24 hours. (If it will be more than 24 hours, place the soaker in the refrigerator; it will be good for up to 3 days. Remove it 2 hours before mixing the final dough to take off the chill.)

STARTER

VOLUME	OUNCES	GRAMS	INGREDIENT	%
¹/₃ cup	2.5	71	whole wheat mother starter (page 67)	33.3
1²/₃ cups	7.5	213	whole rye flour	100
³/₄ cup	6	170	filtered or spring water, at room temperature (about 70°F/21°C)	80
TOTAL	16	454		213.3

1. **Mix all of the starter ingredients together** in a bowl to form a ball of dough. Using wet hands, knead the dough in the bowl for about 2 minutes to be sure all of the ingredients are evenly distributed and the flour is fully hydrated. The dough should feel very tacky. Let the dough rest for about 5 minutes, then knead it again with wet hands for 1 minute. The dough will become smoother but still be tacky.

2. **Transfer the dough to a clean bowl, cover** loosely with plastic wrap, and leave at room temperature for approximately 4 to 6 hours, until the dough is nearly double in size. The dough should register between 3.5 and 4.0 if tested with pH paper (see page 77) and have a pleasant aroma similar to apple cider vinegar. If the starter has not doubled or acidified properly, allow it to continue to develop at room temperature. It could take up to 8 hours or even longer.

3. **When the starter has fully developed, knead** it for a few seconds to degas it. The starter is now ready for mixing into the final dough; however, if necessary to coordinate timing with

COMMENTARY

Now that we are moving into hearty yet gluten-challenged breads, the option of using vital wheat gluten enters the picture. I prefer not to use it, as I find it adds a chewy, rubbery quality and a scratchy taste in the back of my throat. But not everybody feels that way, and many people like to use it because it strengthens the dough and guarantees a higher rise and lighter loaf. It is listed here as an optional ingredient, as this formula works with or without it.

If you do not have a starter, you can make this with a *biga* instead; however, because a *biga* does not have the degree of acidity necessary to fully control the enzymes, the loaf may not rise as tall, and it may even shrink a little in the oven, though it will still taste quite good. If this happens, consider adding ¹/₄ teaspoon of ascorbic acid next time.

The starter in this version is made from a whole wheat mother starter that is elaborated with rye flour. The wheat starter provides just enough total whole wheat flour to tip this over to the *meteil* side of the equation. If you already have a 100% rye mother starter, you can use it instead for a bread with a 50-50 balance of rye and wheat.

Enriched Breads   113

the soaker, cover tightly with plastic wrap and refrigerate overnight (or up to 3 days). About 2 hours before mixing the final dough, remove the starter from the refrigerator to take off the chill.

FINAL DOUGH

VOLUME	OUNCES	GRAMS	INGREDIENT
Use all	14.39	408	soaker
Use all	16	454	starter
7 tablespoons	2	56.5	whole wheat flour
5/8 teaspoon	.18	5	salt
2 1/4 teaspoons	.25	7	instant yeast
1 1/2 tablespoons	1	28.5	molasses, sorghum syrup, or cane syrup
2 1/4 teaspoons	.5	14	honey or agave nectar
or 1 tablespoon	.5	14	or sugar or brown sugar
2 tablespoons	1	28.5	unsalted butter, melted, or vegetable oil
1 small onion	4	113	fresh onion, diced
or 2 tablespoons	.5	14	or minced dried onion (optional)
2 teaspoons	.2	7	caraway seeds, nigella seeds, or anise seeds (optional)
			extra whole wheat flour for adjustments
TOTAL	39.52	1121.5	

1. **Using a metal pastry scraper, chop** the soaker and the starter into 12 smaller pieces each (sprinkle some of the extra flour over the pre-doughs to keep the pieces from sticking back to each other).

2. **If mixing by hand,** combine the soaker and starter pieces in a bowl with all of the other ingredients except the extra flour and stir vigorously with a mixing spoon or knead with wet hands for about 2 minutes, until all of the ingredients are evenly integrated and distributed into the dough. The dough should be soft and slightly sticky; if not, add more flour or water as needed. **If using a stand mixer,** put the pre-dough pieces and all of the other ingredients except the extra flour into the mixer with the paddle attachment (preferable) or dough hook. Mix on slow speed for 1 minute to bring the ingredients together into a ball. Switch to the dough hook if need be and mix on medium-low speed, occasionally scraping down the bowl, for 2 to 3 minutes, until the pre-doughs become cohesive and assimilated into each other. Add more flour or water as needed until the dough is soft and slightly sticky.

3. **Dust a work surface with flour,** then roll the dough in the flour to coat. Knead by hand for 3 to 4 minutes, until the dough has completely assimilated all of the ingredients into a single, cohesive unit. Use only as much of the extra flour as needed, until the dough feels soft and tacky, but not sticky. Form the dough into a ball and let it rest on the work surface for 5 minutes while you prepare a clean, lightly oiled bowl.

4. **Resume kneading the dough for 1 minute** to strengthen the gluten and make any final flour or water adjustments. The dough should have strength and pass the windowpane test (see page 84), yet still feel soft, supple, and very tacky. Form the dough into a ball and place it in the prepared bowl, rolling to coat with oil. Cover loosely with plastic wrap and let rise at room temperature for approximately 45 to 60 minutes, or until it is about $1^1/_2$ times its original size.

5. **Transfer the dough to a lightly floured work surface** and form it into either a loaf pan shape or a freestanding *bâtard* (see pages 87–91 for shaping instructions). For loaf pan bread, place the dough in a greased 4 by $8^1/_2$ -inch bread pan. For a *bâtard*, place it on a proofing cloth or on a sheet pan lined with parchment paper and, if you like, dusted with flour. Mist the top of the dough with pan spray (optional), cover loosely with plastic wrap, and let rise at room temperature for approximately 45 to 60 minutes, until it is about $1^1/_2$ times its original size.

6. **Preheat the oven to 425°F (218°C)** and, if baking a freestanding loaf, prepare the oven for hearth baking (see page 86), including a steam pan (steaming is optional for a sandwich loaf). When the dough is ready to bake, place it in the oven, pour 1 cup of hot water into the steam pan, lower the temperature to 350°F (177°C), and bake for 20 minutes. Rotate the loaf 180 degrees and continue baking for another 20 to 30 minutes, until the loaf is a rich brown on all sides, sounds hollow when thumped on the bottom, and registers at least 195°F (91°C) in the center.

7. **Transfer the bread to a cooling rack** and allow it to cool for at least 1 hour before serving.

BAKER'S FORMULA	%
Whole wheat flour	60.5
Whole rye flour	39.5
Salt	1.7
Instant yeast	1.5
Vital wheat gluten	1.3
Milk	31.5
Water	28
Molasses	5
Honey	2.5
Unsalted butter or oil	5
Onion	21
Total	197.5

NUTRITION FACTS	
Calories (kcal)	93.65
Protein (g)	3.10
Carbohydrates (g)	17.67
Dietary fiber (g)	2.78
Total sugars (g)	1.58
Fat (g)	1.55
Saturated fat (g)	.20
Trans fatty acid (g)	0
Cholesterol (mg)	.26
Sodium (mg)	144.39

FAQ ∾ *What does ascorbic acid do, and should I use it in my dough?*

If you find that your dough is breaking down (that is, it feels good and strong when you mix it and then later, when you shape it, or even later, while it is rising or baking, it seems to slacken or lose its liveliness), the gluten may be losing strength because it is under attack from protease enzymes. Ascorbic acid will help counteract this, in some instances, as it combines with another enzyme to form dehydroascorbic acid, which ultimately interferes with the function of protease enzymes. In other words, it helps preserve the gluten bonds and the structural integrity of the dough, and it may improve oven spring. During testing, we were not able to discern a pattern of whether ascorbic acid makes a difference, because its effectiveness is closely tied to the quality of the flour. Try adding 250 mg ($1/_4$ teaspoon) if you find your dough noticeably weakening or shrinking in the oven.

Rye Sandwich Seigle

Makes 1 large loaf

BREAD PROFILE

Enriched, medium soft dough; delayed fermentation method; mixed leavening method

DAYS TO MAKE: 2

Day 1: Soaker and starter, 20 minutes set up and mix, 4 to 6 hours starter fermentation; overnight autolyse

Day 2: 2 hours to de-chill starter; 12 to 15 minutes mixing; 2 to 3 hours fermentation, shaping, proofing; 40 to 60 minutes baking

COMMENTARY

You can increase the amount of rye in the soaker to your liking, as long as the total flour adds up to 8 ounces.

If you do not have a starter, you can make this with a *biga* (page 81) instead; however, because a *biga* does not have the degree of acidity necessary to fully control the enzymes, the loaf may not rise as tall, and it may even shrink a little in the oven, though it will still taste quite good. If this happens, consider adding ¼ teaspoon of ascorbic acid next time.

In this bread, the percentage of rye tips over to more than 50% of the total flour, placing it in the *seigle* category. Depending on the protein strength of the flour you use, as well as your personal taste preference, you may want to make this bread with vital wheat gluten. I am listing it as an optional ingredient, but it is by no means required.

SOAKER

VOLUME	OUNCES	GRAMS	INGREDIENT	%
7 tablespoons	2	56.5	whole rye flour, preferably fine grind	50
1⅓ cups	6	170	whole wheat flour, preferably fine grind	50
½ teaspoon	.14	4	salt	1.75
¾ cup	6	170	milk, soy milk, or rice milk	87.5
1 tablespoon	.25	7	vital wheat gluten (optional)	3
TOTAL	14.39	408		192.25

1. **Mix all of the soaker ingredients together** in a bowl for about 1 minute, until all of the flour is hydrated and the ingredients form a ball of dough.

2. **Cover loosely with plastic wrap** and leave at room temperature for 12 to 24 hours. (If it will be more than 24 hours, place the soaker in the refrigerator; it will be good for up to 3 days. Remove it 2 hours before mixing the final dough to take off the chill.)

STARTER

VOLUME	OUNCES	GRAMS	INGREDIENT	%
⅓ cup	2.5	71	whole wheat mother starter (page 67)	33.3
1⅔ cups	7.5	213	whole rye flour, preferably fine grind	100
¾ cup	6	170	filtered or spring water, at room temperature (about 70°F/21°C)	80
TOTAL	16	454		213.3

1. **Mix all of the starter ingredients together** in a bowl to form a ball of dough. Using wet hands, knead the dough in the bowl for about 2 minutes to be sure all of the ingredients are evenly distributed and the flour is fully hydrated. The dough should feel very tacky. Let the dough rest for about 5 minutes, then knead it again with wet hands for 1 minute. The dough will become smoother but still be tacky.

2. **Transfer the dough to a clean bowl, cover** loosely with plastic wrap, and leave at room temperature for approximately 4 to 6 hours, until the dough is nearly double in size. The dough should register between 3.5 and 4.0 if tested with pH paper (see page 77) and have a pleasant aroma similar to apple cider vinegar. If the starter has not doubled or acidified properly, allow it to continue to develop at room temperature. It could take up to 8 hours or even longer.

3. **When the starter has fully developed,** knead it for a few seconds to degas it. The starter is now ready for mixing into the final dough; however, if necessary to coordinate timing with the soaker, cover tightly with plastic wrap and refrigerate overnight (or up to 3 days). About 2 hours before mixing the final dough, remove the starter from the refrigerator to take off the chill.

The starter in this version is made from a whole wheat mother starter that is elaborated with rye flour. The wheat starter provides just enough total whole wheat flour to tip this over to the *meteil* side of the equation. If you already have a 100% rye mother starter, you can use it instead for a bread with a 50-50 balance of rye and wheat.

FINAL DOUGH

You may add onions to the final dough as described in the rye *meteil* recipe on page 114.

VOLUME	OUNCES	GRAMS	INGREDIENT
Use all	14.39	408	soaker
Use all	16	454	starter
7 tablespoons	2	56.5	whole rye flour
5/8 teaspoon	.18	5	salt
2 1/4 teaspoons	.25	7	instant yeast
1 1/2 tablespoons	1	28.5	molasses, sorghum syrup, or cane syrup
2 1/4 teaspoons	.5	14	honey or agave nectar
or 1 tablespoon	.5	14	or sugar or brown sugar
2 tablespoons	1	28.5	unsalted butter, melted, or vegetable oil
2 teaspoons	.2	7	caraway seeds, nigella seeds, anise seeds, or dried minced onions (optional)
			extra whole rye flour for adjustments
TOTAL	35.52	1008.5	

BAKER'S FORMULA	%
Whole wheat flour	40
Whole rye flour	60
Salt	1.7
Instant yeast	1.5
Milk	33
Water	33
Molasses	5
Honey	2.5
Unsalted butter or oil	2.5
Total	179.2

NUTRITION FACTS	
Calories (kcal)	10.46
Protein (g)	2.84
Carbohydrates (g)	19.12
Dietary fiber (g)	3.11
Total sugars (g)	1.19
Fat (g)	1.66
Saturated fat (g)	.17
Trans fatty acid (g)	0
Cholesterol (mg)	0
Sodium (mg)	154.38

1. **Using a metal pastry scraper, chop** the soaker and the starter into 12 smaller pieces each (sprinkle some of the extra flour over the pre-doughs to keep the pieces from sticking back to each other).

2. **If mixing by hand,** combine the soaker and starter pieces in a bowl with all of the other ingredients except the extra flour and stir vigorously with a mixing spoon or knead with wet hands for about 2 minutes, until all of the ingredients are evenly integrated and distributed into the dough. The dough should be soft and slightly sticky; if not, add more flour or water as needed. **If using a stand mixer,** put the pre-dough pieces and all of the other ingredients except the extra flour into the mixer with the paddle attachment (preferable) or dough hook. Mix on slow speed for 1 minute to bring the ingredients together into a ball. Switch to the dough hook if need be and mix on medium-low speed, occasionally scraping down the bowl, for 2 to 3 minutes, until the pre-doughs become cohesive and assimilated into each other. Add more flour or water as needed until the dough is soft and slightly sticky.

3. **Proceed as in steps 3 through 7** in the rye *meteil* on page 115.

FAQ ∽ *Why is there so much variation and approximation in fermentation times, baking times, and ingredients by volume?*

There are many variables in whole grain breads, not least of which is the type of wheat, how it was milled, and its hydration capacity. Add to that other choices the baker makes—scalded versus unscalded milk, the blend of grains, using ascorbic acid or malt, room and refrigerator temperatures—and, well, it becomes difficult to predict exact times in which ingredients will perform in certain ways. In addition, volume measurements can vary widely depending on how tightly packed or accurately scooped the ingredients are, so can only properly be expressed as estimates. You'll quickly learn that the dough ultimately dictates what adjustments it needs: sometimes this means more water, sometimes more flour, but bread is forgiving and allows for such tweaking.

Transitional Rye Sandwich Bread

Makes 1 large loaf

This is the transitional version of the rye *meteil* introduced on page 112. It is a soft rye bread, with approximately 60% wheat and 40% rye flour, and very easy to make.

SOAKER

VOLUME	OUNCES	GRAMS	INGREDIENT	%
1¹⁄₃ cups	6	170	whole rye flour	75
7 tablespoons	2	56.5	whole wheat flour	25
¹⁄₂ teaspoon	.14	4	salt	1.75
³⁄₄ cup	6	170	buttermilk or yogurt	75
TOTAL	14.14	401		176.75

1. **Mix all of the soaker ingredients together** in a bowl for about 1 minute, until all of the flour is hydrated and the ingredients form a ball of dough.

2. **Cover loosely with plastic wrap** and leave at room temperature for 12 to 24 hours. (If it will be more than 24 hours, place the soaker in the refrigerator; it will be good for up to 3 days. Remove it 2 hours before mixing the final dough to take off the chill.)

BIGA

VOLUME	OUNCES	GRAMS	INGREDIENT	%
1³⁄₄ cups	8	227	unbleached bread flour or high-gluten flour	100
¹⁄₄ teaspoon	.03	1	instant yeast	.4
¹⁄₂ cup plus 2 tablespoons	5	142	filtered or spring water, at room temperature (about 70°F/21°C)	62.5
TOTAL	13.03	370		162.9

1. **Mix all of the *biga* ingredients together** in a bowl to form a ball of dough. Using wet hands, knead the dough in the bowl for 2 minutes to be sure all of the ingredients are evenly distributed and the flour is fully hydrated. The dough should feel very tacky. Let the dough rest for 5 minutes, then knead it again with wet hands for 1 minute. The dough will become smoother but still be tacky.

Enriched, medium soft dough; delayed fermentation method; commercial yeast

DAYS TO MAKE: 2

Day 1: Soaker and *biga*, 20 minutes set up and mix; overnight autolyse
Day 2: 2 hours to de-chill *biga*; 12 to 15 minutes mixing; 2 to 3 hours fermentation, shaping, proofing; 40 to 60 minutes baking

COMMENTARY

If you already have a white flour sourdough starter, you can use it in place of the *biga*, at 62.5% hydration (see page 178 for an example of a white starter). If using a wild yeast starter, you can use any type of regular milk in place of the buttermilk in the soaker, as the starter will provide ample acidity to control the enzymes.

2. **Transfer the dough to a clean bowl, cover** tightly with plastic wrap, and refrigerate for at least 8 hours and up to 3 days.

3. **About 2 hours before mixing the final dough,** remove the *biga* from the refrigerator to take off the chill. It will have risen slightly but need not have risen significantly in order to use it in the final dough.

FINAL DOUGH

VOLUME	OUNCES	GRAMS	INGREDIENT
Use all	14.14	401	soaker
Use all	13.03	370	*biga*
3½ tablespoons	1	28.5	whole rye flour
⅝ teaspoon	.18	5	salt
2¼ teaspoons	.25	7	instant yeast
1½ tablespoons	1	28.5	molasses, sorghum syrup, or cane syrup
2¼ teaspoons	.5	14	honey or agave nectar
or 1 tablespoon	.5	14	or sugar or brown sugar
1 tablespoon	.5	14	vegetable oil (optional)
2 teaspoons	.2	7	caraway seeds (optional)
			extra whole rye flour for adjustments
TOTAL	30.8	875	

1. **Using a metal pastry scraper, chop** the soaker and the *biga* into 12 smaller pieces each (sprinkle some of the extra flour over the pre-doughs to keep the pieces from sticking back to each other).

2. **If mixing by hand,** combine the soaker and *biga* pieces in a bowl with all of the other ingredients except the extra flour and stir vigorously with a mixing spoon or knead with wet hands for about 2 minutes, until all of the ingredients are evenly integrated and distributed into the dough. The dough should be soft and slightly sticky; if not, add more flour or water as needed. **If using a stand mixer,** put the pre-dough pieces and all of the other ingredients except the extra flour into the mixer with the paddle attachment (preferable) or dough hook. Mix on slow speed for 1 minute to bring the ingredients together into a ball. Switch to the dough hook if need be and mix on medium-low speed, occasionally scraping down the bowl,

for 2 to 3 minutes, until the pre-doughs become cohesive and assimilated into each other. Add more flour or water as needed until the dough is soft and slightly sticky.

3. **Proceed as in steps 3 through 7** in the rye *meteil* on page 115.

BAKER'S FORMULA	%
Whole wheat flour	12
Whole rye flour	41
Bread flour	47
Salt	1.9
Instant yeast	1.6
Water	29.5
Molasses	6
Honey	3
Oil	3
Total	145

NUTRITION FACTS	
Calories (kcal)	97.57
Protein (g)	3
Carbohydrates (g)	18.84
Dietary fiber (g)	1.92
Total sugars (g)	1.67
Fat (g)	1.14
Saturated fat (g)	.16
Trans fatty acid (g)	0
Cholesterol (mg)	.32
Sodium (mg)	174.66

FAQ ✺ *Does it matter what type or brand of flour I use?*

Yes and no. You can make these breads with virtually any brand of whole wheat or whole rye flour. Usually, finely ground whole wheat flour is preferred because it has the ability to develop into the strongest, most extensible dough. Coarser flours have larger bits of bran and germ that act like razors upon gluten strands. However, coarsely ground flour is wonderful for texture and can also be blended into finely ground flour if desired, or used purposely for denser breads. If you have only coarsely ground flour on hand, you can still make breads that specifically call for finely ground flour; the bread may not rise as much, but it will have a wonderful, chewy texture.

Most commercial whole wheat flour is milled from hard red wheat and is high in protein (however, flours from hard white wheat are now more readily available). If for some reason the package indicates soft wheat, perhaps a whole wheat pastry flour, it will not contain enough protein for these breads. Whenever possible, try to find a brand that specifies what it is best used for, or what kind of wheat it contains (such as hard red winter wheat). But if this isn't indicated, you can probably assume that its protein content is comparable to bread flour.

If you are grinding your own flour, be sure to use hard wheat, whether red or white, and keep notes as you make your breads. Every type of flour will absorb a different amount of liquid and have slightly different performance qualities. With the delayed fermentation method, mixing times will be relatively short, but the dough will dictate whether it needs more or less hydration and also whether it requires longer mixing or kneading. The ingredients listed in each recipe, especially the liquid, can only be an approximation, at best. You may find that white wheat absorbs less water than red wheat: you will know this if you have to add more flour to achieve the proper texture, or feel. Keep track of how your different flours perform, and also which ones you enjoy the best.

Many people (and even the large commercial bakeries) have switched to hard white wheat because it has a sweeter taste than red wheat, mainly because the pericarp layers are thinner and less bitter. You will be seeing more white wheat on the shelves as more growers plant it. It does have different performance characteristics than red wheat, such as the aforementioned tendency to absorb less liquid, but it will perform well in these breads.

One final note: Many of our European recipe testers reported that the formulas worked very differently with their flour and that they had to reduce the amount of water significantly. This is another example of how important it is to let the dough dictate what it needs rather than adhering strictly to the written recipe. Wheat grown in Europe tends to have different specifications, often being lower in protein or having a different quality of protein. Regardless, let the instructions serve as a guide, and if you are using European flour, be prepared to reduce the amount of liquid. When you determine how much hydration your particular flour requires, make a note of it in the book for future reference.

Potato Onion Rye Meteil

Makes 2 loaves or 20 rolls

This light rye bread combines the classic flavor of onion rye with the soft texture of potato rosemary bread (page 125). It is especially nice served with meat or poultry dishes as a dinner roll.

BREAD PROFILE

Enriched, medium soft dough; delayed fermentation method; mixed leavening method

DAYS TO MAKE: 2

Day 1: Soaker and starter, 20 minutes set up and mix, 4 to 6 hours starter fermentation; overnight autolyse

Day 2: 2 hours to de-chill starter; 12 to 15 minutes mixing; 2 to 3 hours fermentation, shaping, proofing; 40 to 60 minutes baking

COMMENTARY

If you prefer more rye flavor, you can adjust the amount of rye flour in the soaker, keeping the total amount of flour in the soaker at 8 ounces. Or you can use a rye starter instead of a wheat starter, or substitute rye flour when elaborating a wheat starter, or both.

On Day 1 consider preparing the cooked potatoes that are required on Day 2 by boiling 1 large or 2 small, coarsely chopped potatoes in 2 cups of water until soft. You can leave the skin on or peel it, but my preference is to leave the skin on. Strain out the potato pieces and set them aside to cool. Let the water cool to room temperature before assembling the soaker. Mash the cooked potato with a fork until coarse or smooth (depending on preference), then refrigerate until added during the final mix on Day 2.

SOAKER

VOLUME	OUNCES	GRAMS	INGREDIENT	%
1 cup plus 2 tablespoons	5	142	whole rye flour	62.5
2/3 cup	3	85	whole wheat flour	37.5
1/2 teaspoon	.14	4	salt	1.75
3/4 cup	6	170	potato water, cooled to room temperature (about 70°F/21°C)	75
1 tablespoon	.25	7	vital wheat gluten (optional)	3
TOTAL	14.39	408		179.75

1. **Mix all of the soaker ingredients together** in a bowl for about 1 minute, until all of the flour is hydrated and the ingredients form a ball of dough.

2. **Cover loosely with plastic wrap** and leave at room temperature for 12 to 24 hours. (If it will be more than 24 hours, place the soaker in the refrigerator; it will be good for up to 3 days. Remove it 2 hours before mixing the final dough to take off the chill.)

STARTER

VOLUME	OUNCES	GRAMS	INGREDIENT	%
1/3 cup	2.5	71	whole wheat mother starter (see page 67)	33.3
1 2/3 cups	7.5	213	whole wheat flour, whole rye flour, or a combination of the two	100
3/4 cup	6	170	filtered or spring water, at room temperature (about 70°F/21°C)	75
TOTAL	16	454		208.3

1. **Mix all of the starter ingredients together** in a bowl to form a ball of dough. Using wet hands, knead the dough in the bowl for about 2 minutes to be sure all of the ingredients are

evenly distributed and the flour is fully hydrated. The dough should feel very tacky. Let the dough rest for about 5 minutes, then knead it again with wet hands for 1 minute. The dough will become smoother but still be tacky.

2. **Transfer the dough to a clean bowl, cover** loosely with plastic wrap, and leave at room temperature for approximately 4 to 6 hours, until the dough is nearly double in size. The dough should register between 3.5 and 4.0 if tested with pH paper (see page 77) and have a pleasant aroma similar to apple cider vinegar. If the starter has not doubled or acidified properly, allow it to continue to develop at room temperature. It could take up to 8 hours or even longer.

3. **When the starter has fully developed, knead** it for a few seconds to degas it. The starter is now ready for mixing into the final dough; however, if necessary to coordinate timing with the soaker, cover tightly with plastic wrap and refrigerate overnight (or up to 3 days). About 2 hours before mixing the final dough, remove the starter from the refrigerator to take off the chill.

Rather than boiling a potato for this bread, feel free to use leftover mashed potatoes, or even mashed potato flakes.

If you do not have potato water (often the case when using leftover mashed potatoes, or potato flakes), you can use plain water in the soaker, but the potato water really makes a noticeable contribution to flavor and texture. If you have potato starch on hand, you can achieve a similar effect by dissolving 1 teaspoon of potato starch in the soaker water.

Instructions are given for both hand and machine mixing, but this voluminous dough will not fit in all machines. It is not difficult to mix by hand, and the dough has such a nice feel to it that it might win some of you away from machine mixing and back to kneading by hand.

FINAL DOUGH

VOLUME	OUNCES	GRAMS	INGREDIENT
Use all	14.39	408	soaker
Use all	16	454	starter
1 cup	4.5	128	whole wheat or whole rye flour, or a combination
1¼ teaspoons	.35	10	salt
1 tablespoon	.32	9	instant yeast
1 large or 2 small	8	227	cooked potatoes (see Commentary)
or 1 cup	7.5	213	or leftover mashed potatoes
1 small	4	113	fresh onion, diced
2¼ teaspoons	.5	14	honey, molasses, sorghum syrup, or agave nectar
1 tablespoon	.32	9	caraway seeds
or 1 tablespoon	.11	3	or fresh rosemary (optional)
			extra whole wheat or rye flour for adjustments
TOTAL	48.38	1372	

1. **Using a metal pastry scraper, chop** the soaker and the starter into 12 smaller pieces each (sprinkle some of the extra flour over the pre-doughs to keep the pieces from sticking back to each other).

BAKER'S FORMULA	%
Whole wheat flour	76
Whole rye flour	24
Vital wheat gluten	1.2
Salt	2.4
Instant yeast	1.5
Water	57
Potato	38
Onion	19
Honey	2.4
Caraway seeds	1.5
Total	223

NUTRITION FACTS	
Calories (kcal)	79.24
Protein (g)	2.99
Carbohydrates (g)	16.80
Dietary fiber (g)	2.78
Total sugars (g)	.68
Fat (g)	.43
Saturated fat (g)	.06
Trans fatty acid (g)	0
Cholesterol (mg)	0
Sodium (mg)	117.87

Rather than hearth baking with steam, another option with potato breads is to brush the loaves with an egg white wash, made by whipping 1 egg white with 1 tablespoon of water and a pinch of salt. Brush the tops of the loaves or rolls with the wash before baking.

2. **If mixing by hand,** combine the soaker and starter pieces in a bowl with all of the other ingredients except the extra flour and stir vigorously with a mixing spoon or knead with wet hands for about 2 minutes, until all of the ingredients are evenly integrated and distributed into the dough. The dough should be soft and slightly sticky; if not, add more flour or water as needed. **If using a stand mixer,** put the pre-dough pieces and all of the other ingredients except the extra flour into the mixer with the paddle attachment (preferable) or dough hook. Mix on slow speed for 1 minute to bring the ingredients together into a ball. Switch to the dough hook if need be and mix on medium-low speed, occasionally scraping down the bowl, for 2 to 3 minutes, until the pre-doughs become cohesive and assimilated into each other. Add more flour or water as needed until the dough is soft and slightly sticky.

3. **Dust a work surface with flour,** then roll the dough in the flour to coat. Knead for 4 minutes, incorporating only as much extra flour as needed, until the dough feels soft and tacky, but not sticky. Form the dough into a ball and let it rest on the work surface for 5 minutes while you prepare a clean, lightly oiled bowl.

4. **Resume kneading the dough for 1 minute** to strengthen the gluten and make any final flour or water adjustments. The dough should have strength and pass the windowpane test (see page 84), yet still feel soft, supple, and very tacky. Form the dough into a ball and place it in the prepared bowl, rolling to coat with oil. Cover loosely with plastic wrap and let rise at room temperature for approximately 45 to 60 minutes, until it is about 1¹/₂ times its original size.

5. **Transfer the dough to a lightly floured work surface** and form it into 2 loaves—whether loaf pan shapes, *boules*, or *bâtards*—or into dinner rolls (see pages 87–91 for shaping instructions). For loaf pan bread, place the dough in greased 4 by 8¹/₂-inch bread pans. *Boules* can be proofed in *bannetons* or prepared proofing bowls. For *bâtards* and dinner rolls, raise the loaves on a proofing cloth or on a sheet pan lined with parchment paper and, if you like, dusted with flour. Mist the top of the dough with pan spray (optional), cover loosely with plastic wrap, and let rise at room temperature for approximately 45 to 60 minutes, until it is about 1¹/₂ times its original size.

6. **Preheat the oven to 425°F (218°C)** and, if baking a freestanding loaf, prepare it for hearth baking (see page 86), including a steam pan (steaming is optional for a sandwich loaf) or brush it with an egg white wash (see Commentary). When the dough is ready to bake, place the loaves in the oven, pour 1 cup of hot water into the steam pan, lower the temperature to 350°F (177°C), and bake for 20 minutes. Rotate the loaves 180 degrees and continue baking for another 20 to 30 minutes, until the loaves are a rich brown on all sides, sound hollow when thumped on the bottom, and register at least 195°F (91°C) in the center.

7. **Transfer the bread to a cooling rack** and cool for at least 1 hour before serving.

Potato Rosemary Bread

Makes 2 loaves or 20 rolls

This bread is popular because of its flavor and also for the soft texture provided by the starch in the potato water. Using potato water is a favorite baker's trick, and I suggest that whenever you boil potatoes, you save the water and plan to make bread soon thereafter. You can refrigerate the potato water for about 5 days, or freeze it for up to 6 months. You can actually use potato water in place of water in most of the recipes in this book; the dissolved starches contribute a unique sweetness to the flavor and a pillowy softness to the crumb.

BREAD PROFILE

Slightly enriched, medium soft dough; delayed fermentation method; commercial yeast

DAYS TO MAKE: 2

Day 1: Soaker and *biga*, 20 minutes set up and mix; overnight autolyse
Day 2: 2 hours to de-chill *biga*; 12 to 15 minutes mixing; 2 to 3 hours fermentation, shaping, proofing; 40 to 60 minutes baking

COMMENTARY

The final dough calls for fresh rosemary. If only dried rosemary is available, use 1 tablespoon and put it in the soaker.

On Day 1 you will need to cut up 1 medium-size potato (weighing 6 ounces or more) and boil it in 2 cups of water until soft. You can leave the skin on or peel it, but my preference is to leave the skin on. Strain out the potato pieces and set them aside to cool. Let the water cool to room temperature before assembling the soaker and *biga*. Mash the cooked potato with a fork until coarse or smooth (depending on your preference), then refrigerate until added during the final mix on Day 2.

You can substitute an equal amount of wild yeast starter (page 80) for the *biga*.

SOAKER

VOLUME	OUNCES	GRAMS	INGREDIENT	%
1³/₄ cups	8	227	whole wheat flour, preferably fine grind	100
¹/₂ teaspoon	.14	4	salt	1.75
³/₄ cup	6	170	potato water, cooled to room temperature (about 70°F/21°C)	75
TOTAL	14.14	401		176.75

1. **Mix all of the soaker ingredients together** in a bowl for about 1 minute, until all of the flour is hydrated and the ingredients form a ball of dough.

2. **Cover loosely with plastic wrap** and leave at room temperature for 12 to 24 hours. (If it will be more than 24 hours, place the soaker in the refrigerator; it will be good for up to 3 days. Remove it 2 hours before mixing the final dough to take off the chill.)

BIGA

VOLUME	OUNCES	GRAMS	INGREDIENT	%
1³/₄ cups	8	227	whole wheat flour, preferably fine grind	100
¹/₄ teaspoon	.03	1	instant yeast	.4
³/₄ cup plus 2 tablespoons	7	198	potato water, cooled to room temperature (about 70°F/21°C)	75
TOTAL	15.03	426		175.4

1. **Mix all of the *biga* ingredients together** in a bowl to form a ball of dough. Using wet hands, knead the dough in the bowl for 2 minutes to be sure all of the ingredients are evenly distributed and the flour is fully hydrated. The dough should feel very tacky. Let the dough rest for 5 minutes, then knead it again with wet hands for 1 minute. The dough will become smoother but still be tacky.

2. **Transfer the dough to a clean bowl, cover** tightly with plastic wrap, and refrigerate for at least 8 hours and up to 3 days.

3. **About 2 hours before mixing the final dough,** remove the *biga* from the refrigerator to take off the chill. It will have risen slightly but need not have risen significantly in order to use it in the final dough.

FINAL DOUGH

VOLUME	OUNCES	GRAMS	INGREDIENT
Use all	14.14	401	soaker
Use all	15.03	426	*biga*
7 tablespoons	2	56.5	whole wheat flour
1¹/₈ teaspoons	.32	9	salt
2¹/₄ teaspoons	.25	7	instant yeast
1 medium	6	170	cooked potato (see Commentary)
1 tablespoon	.5	14	olive oil
2 tablespoons	.2	5.5	fresh rosemary (see Commentary)
¹/₄ cup	1	28.5	roasted garlic (optional)
¹/₄ teaspoon	.03	1	black pepper, coarsely ground (optional)
			extra whole wheat flour for adjustments
TOTAL	39.47	1118.5	

The optional addition of roasted garlic and black pepper gives the bread yet another flavor dimension, one that many fans of this bread love, similar to the wonderfulness of garlic mashed potatoes.

1. **Using a metal pastry scraper, chop** the soaker and the *biga* into 12 smaller pieces each (sprinkle some of the extra flour over the pre-doughs to keep the pieces from sticking back to each other).

2. **If mixing by hand,** combine the soaker and *biga* pieces in a bowl with all of the other ingredients except the extra flour and stir vigorously with a mixing spoon or knead with wet hands for about 2 minutes, until all of the ingredients are evenly integrated and distributed into the dough. The dough should be soft and slightly sticky; if not, add more flour or water as needed. **If using a stand mixer,** put the pre-dough pieces and all of the other ingredients except the extra flour into the mixer with the paddle attachment (preferable) or dough hook. Mix on slow speed for 1 minute to bring the ingredients together into a ball. Switch to the dough hook if need be and mix on medium-low speed, occasionally scraping down the bowl, for 2 to 3 minutes, until the pre-doughs become cohesive and assimilated into each other. Add more flour or water as needed until the dough is soft and slightly sticky.

3. **Dust a work surface,** then roll the dough in the flour to coat. Knead for 3 to 4 minutes, incorporating only as much extra flour as needed, until the dough feels soft and tacky, but not sticky. Form the dough into a ball and let it rest on the work surface for 5 minutes while you prepare a clean, lightly oiled bowl.

BAKER'S FORMULA	%
Whole wheat flour	100
Salt	2.5
Instant yeast	1.5
Water	67
Potato	33
Olive oil	2.8
Rosemary	1
Garlic	5.5
Total	213.3

NUTRITION FACTS	
Calories (kcal)	82.22
Protein (g)	3.12
Carbohydrates (g)	16.48
Dietary fiber (g)	2.71
Total sugars (g)	.18
Fat (g)	.99
Saturated fat (g)	.16
Trans fatty acid (g)	0
Cholesterol (mg)	0
Sodium (mg)	204.22

In addition to hearth baking with steam, another option with potato breads is to brush the loaves with an egg white wash, made by whipping 1 egg white with 1 tablespoon of water and a pinch of salt. Brush the tops of the loaves or rolls with the wash before baking.

4. **Resume kneading the dough for 1 minute** to strengthen the gluten and make any final flour or water adjustments. The dough should have strength and pass the windowpane test (see page 84), yet still feel soft, supple, and very tacky. Form the dough into a ball and place it in the prepared bowl, rolling to coat with oil. Cover loosely with plastic wrap and let rise at room temperature for approximately 45 to 60 minutes, until it is about 1¹/₂ times its original size.

5. **Transfer the dough to a lightly floured work surface** and form it into 2 freestanding *boules* or *bâtards*, or 20 dinner rolls (see pages 87–91 for shaping instructions). A *boule* can be proofed in a *banneton* or another prepared proofing bowl. For a *bâtard*, place it on a proofing cloth or on a sheet pan lined with parchment paper and, if you like, dusted with flour. Mist the top of the dough with pan spray (optional), cover loosely with plastic wrap, and let rise at room temperature for approximately 45 to 60 minutes, until 1¹/₂ times its original size.

6. **Preheat the oven to 425°F (218°C)** and prepare it for hearth baking (see page 86), including a steam pan, or brush it with an egg white wash (see Commentary). When the loaves are ready to bake, place them in the oven (scoring is optional), pour 1 cup of hot water into the steam pan, lower the temperature to 350°F (177°C), and bake for 20 minutes. Rotate the loaves 180 degrees and continue baking for another 20 to 30 minutes, until the loaves are a rich brown on all sides, sound hollow when thumped on the bottom, and register at least 195°F (91°C) in the center.

7. **Transfer the bread to a cooling rack** and allow to cool for at least 1 hour before serving.

Potatoes soften the texture of this very popular table bread, while the rosemary should provide a noticeable but subtle presence.

Anadama Bread

Makes 1 large loaf

The original version of this bread, apocryphally created in Rockport, Massachusetts, could be considered a New England version of *struan*, as it seems very much in the spirit of the harvest with its strong cornmeal presence and molasses richness. It is usually made with white flour in order to give it an open lightness, but with the delayed fermentation method we can make an equally light yet healthier version using whole wheat flour.

BREAD PROFILE

Enriched, medium soft dough; delayed fermentation method; commercial yeast

DAYS TO MAKE: 2

Day 1: Soaker and *biga*, 20 minutes set up and mix; overnight autolyse
Day 2: 2 hours to de-chill *biga*; 12 to 15 minutes mixing; 2 to 3 hours fermentation, shaping, proofing; 40 to 50 minutes baking

SOAKER

VOLUME	OUNCES	GRAMS	INGREDIENT	%
³/₄ cup plus 2 tablespoons	4	113	cornmeal	66.5
7 tablespoons	2	56.5	whole wheat flour, preferably fine grind	33.5
¹/₂ teaspoon	.14	4	salt	2.3
¹/₂ cup plus 2 tablespoons	5	142	water	83.3
TOTAL	11.14	316		185.6

1. **Mix all of the soaker ingredients together** in a bowl for about 1 minute, until all of the flour is hydrated and the ingredients form a ball of dough.

2. **Cover loosely with plastic wrap** and leave at room temperature for 12 to 24 hours. (If it will be more than 24 hours, place the soaker in the refrigerator; it will be good for up to 3 days. Remove it 2 hours before mixing the final dough to take off the chill.)

FAQ ∾ *What are the advantages of using oil or other fats in these breads?*

The function of fats and oil in bread is mainly to soften it and slow down staling. Some studies indicate that it also may help trap carbon dioxide by strengthening the walls of gas cells in the crumb and thus make a taller, airier loaf. On the downside, fat, even in heart-healthy forms like olive oil, contributes more calories—9 calories per gram as opposed to 4 calories per gram for carbohydrates and protein. Where fat is listed as an optional ingredient, you will find that the bread will probably show these airier characteristics more in versions with the fat than without it. However, the bread will be excellent either way. If you omit the fat, you may need to increase the amount of liquid slightly, but this will vary depending on the type of flour you are using.

You can substitute an equal
amount of wild yeast starter
(page 80) for the *biga*.

BIGA

VOLUME	OUNCES	GRAMS	INGREDIENT	%
1³/₄ cups	8	227	whole wheat flour, preferably fine grind	100
¹/₄ teaspoon	.03	1	instant yeast	.4
³/₄ cup	6	170	filtered or spring water, at room temperature (about 70°F/21°C)	75
TOTAL	14.03	398		175.4

1. **Mix all of the *biga* ingredients together** in a bowl to form a ball of dough. Using wet hands, knead the dough in the bowl for 2 minutes to be sure all of the ingredients are evenly distributed and the flour is fully hydrated. The dough should feel very tacky. Let the dough rest for 5 minutes, then knead it again with wet hands for 1 minute. The dough will become smoother but still be tacky.

2. **Transfer the dough to a clean bowl, cover** tightly with plastic wrap, and refrigerate for at least 8 hours and up to 3 days.

3. **About 2 hours before mixing the final dough,** remove the *biga* from the refrigerator to take off the chill. It will have risen slightly but need not have risen significantly in order to use it in the final dough.

As an alternative to molasses,
try sorghum syrup, a lighter,
golden cousin of molasses,
with a smooth, buttery flavor.

FINAL DOUGH

VOLUME	OUNCES	GRAMS	INGREDIENT
Use all	11.14	316	soaker
Use all	14.03	398	*biga*
1 cup	4.5	128	whole wheat flour
⁵/₈ teaspoon	.18	5	salt
2¹/₄ teaspoons	.25	7	instant yeast
3 tablespoons	2	56.5	molasses or sorghum syrup
2 tablespoons	1	28.5	unsalted butter, melted, or vegetable oil
			extra whole wheat flour for adjustments
TOTAL	33.1	939	

1. **Using a metal pastry scraper, chop** the soaker and the *biga* into 12 smaller pieces each (sprinkle some of the extra flour over the pre-doughs to keep the pieces from sticking back to each other).

2. **If mixing by hand,** combine the soaker and *biga* pieces in a bowl with all of the other ingredients except the extra flour and stir vigorously with a mixing spoon or knead with wet hands for about 2 minutes, until all of the ingredients are evenly integrated and distributed into the dough. The dough should be soft and slightly sticky; if not, add more flour or water as needed. **If using a stand mixer,** put the pre-dough pieces and all of the other ingredients except the extra flour into the mixer with the paddle attachment (preferable) or dough hook. Mix on slow speed for 1 minute to bring the ingredients together into a ball. Switch to the dough hook if need be and mix on medium-low speed, occasionally scraping down the bowl, for 2 to 3 minutes, until the pre-doughs become cohesive and assimilated into each other. Add more flour or water as needed until the dough is soft and slightly sticky.

3. **Dust a work surface with flour,** then roll the dough in the flour to coat. Knead for 3 to 4 minutes, incorporating only as much extra flour as needed, until the dough feels soft and tacky, but not sticky. Form the dough into a ball and let it rest on the work surface for 5 minutes while you prepare a clean, lightly oiled bowl.

4. **Resume kneading the dough for 1 minute** to strengthen the gluten and make any final flour or water adjustments. The dough should have strength and pass the windowpane test (see page 84), yet still feel soft, supple, and very tacky. Form the dough into a ball and place it in the prepared bowl, rolling to coat with oil. Cover loosely with plastic wrap and let rise at room temperature for approximately 45 to 60 minutes, until it is about $1^1/_2$ times its original size.

5. **Transfer the dough to a lightly floured work surface** and form it into a loaf pan shape. Place the dough into a greased 4 by $8^1/_2$-inch bread pan. Mist the top of the dough with pan spray (optional), cover loosely with plastic wrap, and let rise at room temperature for approximately 45 to 60 minutes, until it is about $1^1/_2$ times its original size.

6. **Preheat the oven to 425°F (218°C).** Place the pan on the middle shelf, lower the temperature to 350°F (177°C), and bake for 20 minutes. Rotate the pan 180 degrees and continue baking for another 20 to 30 minutes, until the loaf is a rich brown on all sides, sounds hollow when thumped on the bottom, and registers at least 195°F (91°C) in the center.

7. **Transfer the bread to a cooling rack** and allow it to cool for at least 1 hour before serving.

BAKER'S FORMULA	%
Whole wheat flour	78
Cornmeal	22
Salt	1.7
Instant yeast	1.5
Water	59.5
Molasses	11
Unsalted butter or oil	5.5
Total	179.2

NUTRITION FACTS	
Calories (kcal)	94.46
Protein (g)	2.99
Carbohydrates (g)	18.83
Dietary fiber (g)	2.55
Total sugars (g)	1.49
Fat (g)	1.44
Saturated fat (g)	.72
Trans fatty acid (g)	.03
Cholesterol (mg)	2.65
Sodium (mg)	155.53

Whole Wheat Cinnamon Raisin Bread

Makes 1 large loaf

BREAD PROFILE

Enriched, medium soft dough;
delayed fermentation method;
commercial yeast

DAYS TO MAKE: 2

Day 1: Soaker and *biga*, 20 minutes
set up and mix; overnight autolyse
Day 2: 2 hours to de-chill *biga*;
12 to 15 minutes mixing; 2 to 3
hours fermentation, shaping, proofing; 40 to 60 minutes baking

Cinnamon is one of those feel-good spices that nearly everyone loves, and now it is being touted for its heart-healthy, cholesterol-fighting properties. Adding toasted nuts, usually walnuts or pecans, is optional, but highly recommended (and walnuts, too, are an excellent heart-healthy food). The nuts combine wonderfully with the classic flavors of cinnamon and raisins and make eating a couple of toasted slices of this bread like enjoying a bowl of your favorite breakfast cereal.

SOAKER

VOLUME	OUNCES	GRAMS	INGREDIENT	%
1⅓ cups	6	170	whole wheat flour	100
⅜ teaspoon	.11	3	salt	1.8
¾ cup	6	170	milk, buttermilk, yogurt, soy milk, or rice milk	100
1 cup	6	170	raisins or other dried fruit (see Commentary)	100
TOTAL	18.11	513		301.8

COMMENTARY

You can make a multigrain version of this bread by using the multigrain soaker on page 102 instead of the whole wheat version given here.

To use this dough for cinnamon buns (if you'd like a version that is less rich than the following recipe), omit the raisins here in the soaker, and then after letting this final dough rise, proceed as in steps 5 through 7 on page 139.

1. **Combine the flour, salt, and milk** in a bowl and mix for about 1 minute, until all of the flour is hydrated and the ingredients form a ball of dough. Add the raisins and use wet hands to knead the dough until evenly incorporated.

2. **Cover loosely with plastic wrap** and leave at room temperature for 12 to 24 hours. (If it will be more than 24 hours, place the soaker in the refrigerator; it will be good for up to 3 days. Remove it 2 hours before mixing the final dough to take off the chill.)

BIGA

VOLUME	OUNCES	GRAMS	INGREDIENT	%
1⅓ cups	6	170	whole wheat flour	100
¼ teaspoon	.03	1	instant yeast	.5
6 tablespoons	3	85	milk, buttermilk, yogurt, soy milk, or rice milk, at room temperature (about 70°F/21°C)	50
¼ cup	2	56.5	unsalted butter, melted, or vegetable oil	33.3
1 large	1.65	47	egg, slightly beaten	27.5
TOTAL	12.68	359.5		211.3

1. **Mix all of the _biga_ ingredients together** in a bowl to form a ball of dough. Using wet hands, knead the dough in the bowl for 2 minutes to be sure all of the ingredients are evenly distributed and the flour is fully hydrated. The dough should feel very tacky. Let the dough rest for 5 minutes, then knead it again with wet hands for 1 minute. The dough will become smoother but still be tacky.

2. **Transfer the dough to a clean bowl, cover** tightly with plastic wrap, and refrigerate for at least 8 hours and up to 3 days.

3. **About 2 hours before mixing the final dough,** remove the _biga_ from the refrigerator to

take off the chill. It will have risen slightly but need not have risen significantly in order to use it in the final dough.

FINAL DOUGH

VOLUME	OUNCES	GRAMS	INGREDIENT
Use all	18.11	513	soaker
Use all	12.68	359.5	*biga*
7 tablespoons	2	56.5	whole wheat flour
⅝ teaspoon	.18	5	salt
2¼ teaspoons	.25	7	instant yeast
1½ tablespoons	1	28.5	honey or agave nectar
or 2 tablespoons	1	28.5	or sugar or brown sugar
½ teaspoon	.14	4	ground cinnamon
¾ cup	3	85	walnuts or pecans, lightly toasted and coarsely chopped (optional)
¼ cup	2	56.5	cinnamon sugar (3 generous tablespoons granulated sugar plus 2 teaspoons ground cinnamon) for spiral swirl (optional)
			extra whole wheat flour for adjustments
TOTAL	39.36	1115	

1. **Using a metal pastry scraper, chop** the soaker and the *biga* into 12 smaller pieces each (sprinkle some of the extra flour over the pre-doughs to keep the pieces from sticking back to each other).

2. **If mixing by hand,** combine the soaker and *biga* pieces in a bowl with the 7 tablespoons flour and the salt, yeast, honey, and cinnamon. Stir vigorously with a large spoon or knead with wet hands for about 2 minutes, until all of the ingredients are evenly integrated and distributed into the dough. The dough should be soft and slightly sticky; if not, add more flour or water as needed. **If using a stand mixer,** put the pre-dough pieces in the bowl along with the 7 tablespoons flour and the salt, yeast, honey, and cinnamon. Mix with the paddle attachment (preferable) or dough hook on slow speed for 1 minute to bring the ingredients together into a ball. Switch to the dough hook if need be and mix on medium-low speed, occasionally scraping down the bowl, for 2 to 3 minutes, until the pre-doughs become cohesive and assimilated into each other. Add more flour or water as needed until the dough is soft and slightly sticky.

3. **Dust a work surface with flour,** then roll the dough in the flour to coat. Sprinkle the walnuts over the surface of the dough and knead by hand for 3 to 4 minutes, incorporating only as much extra flour as needed, until the dough feels soft and tacky, but not sticky. Form the dough into a ball and let it rest on the work surface for 5 minutes while you prepare a clean, lightly oiled bowl.

4. **Resume kneading the dough for 1 minute** to strengthen the gluten and make any final flour or water adjustments. The dough should have strength and pass the windowpane test (see page 84), yet still feel soft, supple, and very tacky. Form the dough into a ball and place it in the prepared bowl, rolling to coat with oil. Cover loosely with plastic wrap and let rise at room temperature for approximately 45 to 60 minutes, until it is about $1^1/2$ times its original size.

5. **When the dough has risen,** dust the work surface with about 1 tablespoon of the extra flour and gently transfer the dough to the floured work surface with a plastic bowl scraper (try not to rip or tear the dough). Roll the dough out to an 8-inch square approximately $1/2$ inch thick, as shown on page 139. Sprinkle the cinnamon sugar over the surface and roll it up into a tight loaf. Place the dough into a greased $4^1/2$ by 9-inch bread pan (it can also be baked as a freestanding loaf on a sheet pan). Mist the top of the dough with pan spray, cover loosely with plastic wrap, and let rise at room temperature for approximately 45 to 60 minutes, until the loaf crests above the pan.

6. **Preheat the oven to 400°F (204°C).** Place the pan on the middle shelf, lower the temperature to 325°F (163°C), and bake for 20 minutes. Rotate the pan 180 degrees and continue baking for another 25 to 40 minutes, until the loaf is a rich brown on all sides, sounds hollow when thumped on the bottom, and registers at least 195°F (91°C) in the center.

7. **Transfer the bread to a cooling rack** and allow it to cool for at least 1 hour before serving.

BAKER'S FORMULA	%
Whole wheat flour	100
Salt	2.3
Instant yeast	2
Milk	64
Egg	12
Honey	7
Raisins	43
Unsalted butter or oil	14
Walnuts	21
Total	265.3

NUTRITION FACTS	
Calories (kcal)	115.21
Protein (g)	3.36
Carbohydrates (g)	17.47
Dietary fiber (g)	2.47
Total sugars (g)	5.85
Fat (g)	4.29
Saturated fat (g)	1.42
Trans fatty acid (g)	.05
Cholesterol (mg)	12.10
Sodium (mg)	143.43

For a delicious crunchy cinnamon crust, when the loaf comes out of the oven, immediately brush the top with 1 tablespoon of melted butter, then roll the buttered top in additional cinnamon sugar, made with 5 parts sugar to 1 part cinnamon.

FAQ ∾ *Why do these breads taste better after they have thoroughly cooled down?*

The complexity of flavors generated by the various microorganisms in the dough is difficult to discern when the bread is still warm, as the warmth obscures the subtle flavor tones. Ideally, bread should be eaten at room temperature in order to taste the full range of flavors. Also, the migration of moisture out of the baked bread begins to settle down as it cools, and eventually the flavors even out. While it is difficult to maintain a crisp crust for more than a few hours, the taste of the bread actually intensifies as it dries out. The denser, moister breads actually taste better two or three days after baking.

Whole Wheat Cinnamon Buns

Makes 8 to 10 buns

BREAD PROFILE

Enriched, medium soft dough;
delayed fermentation method;
commercial yeast

DAYS TO MAKE: 2

Day 1: Soaker and *biga*, 20 minutes
set up and mix; overnight autolyse
Day 2: 2 hours to de-chill *biga*; 12
to 15 minutes mixing; 2 to 3 hours
fermentation, shaping, proofing;
20 to 35 minutes baking

This is slightly different from the preceding recipe for cinnamon raisin bread. Because it is specifically for cinnamon buns—the ultimate comfort food—the dough is enriched with more honey in the final dough to produce a sweeter, more tender finished product.

VOLUME	OUNCES	GRAMS	INGREDIENT	%
1³/₄ cups	8	227	whole wheat flour	100
¹/₂ teaspoon	.14	4	salt	1.75
³/₄ cup	6	170	milk, buttermilk, yogurt, soy milk, or rice milk	75
TOTAL	14.14	401		176.75

Adding raisins to the dough is not recommended for cinnamon buns because too many are exposed to direct heat during baking, and they tend to burn.

1. **Mix all of the soaker ingredients together** in a bowl for about 1 minute, until all of the flour is hydrated and the ingredients form a ball of dough.

2. **Cover loosely with plastic wrap** and leave at room temperature for 12 to 24 hours. (If it will be more than 24 hours, place the soaker in the refrigerator; it will be good for up to 3 days. Remove it 2 hours before mixing the final dough to take off the chill.)

BIGA

VOLUME	OUNCES	GRAMS	INGREDIENT	%
1³/₄ cups	8	227	whole wheat flour	100
¹/₄ teaspoon	.03	1	instant yeast	.4
¹/₂ cup plus 2 tablespoons	5	142	milk, buttermilk, yogurt, soy milk, or rice milk, at room temperature (about 70°F/21°C)	62.5
1 large	1.65	47	egg, slightly beaten	20.5
TOTAL	14.68	417		183.4

1. **Mix all of the *biga* ingredients together** in a bowl to form a ball of dough. Using wet hands, knead the dough in the bowl for 2 minutes to be sure all of the ingredients are evenly distributed and the flour is fully hydrated. The dough should feel very tacky. Let the dough rest for 5 minutes, then knead it again with wet hands for 1 minute. The dough will become smoother but still be tacky.

2. **Transfer the dough to a clean bowl, cover** tightly with plastic wrap, and refrigerate for at least 8 hours and up to 3 days.

3. **About 2 hours before mixing the final dough,** remove the *biga* from the refrigerator to take off the chill. It will have risen slightly but need not have risen significantly in order to use it in the final dough.

To make a fondant glaze, sift 1 cup of confectioners' sugar into a bowl. Add 2 tablespoons of milk, 1 teaspoon of corn syrup (optional), and ½ teaspoon of either vanilla, lemon, orange, or almond extract (all optional). Whisk until smooth. Add more sifted sugar or milk as needed to make a thick but drizzly fondant paste.

To make a cream cheese and honey glaze, using a mixer with the paddle attachment or a large mixing spoon, combine 4 ounces of cream cheese, 3 tablespoons of honey, 2 tablespoons of milk, and 1 teaspoon of vanilla extract. Mix until the ingredients form a smooth paste. Adjust the flavor by adding more honey or vanilla. If too thick, add a small amount of milk.

FINAL DOUGH

VOLUME	OUNCES	GRAMS	INGREDIENT
Use all	14.14	401	soaker
Use all	14.68	417	*biga*
7 tablespoons	2	56.5	whole wheat flour
⅝ teaspoon	.18	5	salt
2¼ teaspoons	.25	7	instant yeast
3 tablespoons	2	56.5	honey or agave nectar
or 4 tablespoons	2	56.5	or sugar or brown sugar
¼ cup	2	56.5	unsalted butter, melted, or vegetable oil
½ cup	4	113	cinnamon sugar (6½ tablespoons granulated sugar plus 1½ tablespoons ground cinnamon)
			extra whole wheat flour for adjustments
			fondant or cream cheese and honey glaze (see Commentary)
TOTAL	39.25	1112.5	

1. **Using a metal pastry scraper, chop** the soaker and the *biga* into 12 smaller pieces each (sprinkle some of the extra flour over the pre-doughs to keep the pieces from sticking back to each other).

2. **If mixing by hand,** combine the soaker and *biga* pieces in a bowl with the 7 tablespoons flour and the salt, yeast, honey, and butter. Stir vigorously with a large spoon or knead with wet hands for about 2 minutes, until all of the ingredients are evenly integrated and distributed into the dough. The dough should be soft and slightly sticky; if not add more flour or water as needed. **If using a stand mixer,** put the pre-dough pieces in the bowl along with the 7 tablespoons flour and the salt, yeast, honey, and butter. Mix on slow speed with the paddle attachment (preferable) or dough hook for 1 minute to bring the ingredients together into a ball. Switch to the dough hook if need be and mix on medium-low speed, occasionally scraping down the bowl, for 2 to 3 minutes, until the pre-doughs become cohesive and assimilated into each other. Add more flour or water as needed until the dough is soft and slightly sticky.

3. **Dust a work surface with flour,** then roll the dough in the flour to coat. Knead by hand for 3 to 4 minutes, incorporating only as much extra flour as needed, until the dough feels soft and tacky, but not sticky. Form the dough into a ball and let it rest on the work surface for 5 minutes while you prepare a clean, lightly oiled bowl.

4. **Resume kneading the dough for 1 minute** to strengthen the gluten and make any final flour or water adjustments. The dough should have strength and pass the windowpane test (see page 87), yet still feel soft, and very tacky. Form the dough into a ball and place it in the prepared bowl, rolling it to coat it with oil. Cover loosely with plastic wrap and let rise at room temperature for approximately 45 to 60 minutes, until it is about 1¹/₂ times its original size.

5. **When the dough has risen,** dust the work surface with about 1 tablespoon of the extra flour and gently transfer the dough to the floured work surface with a plastic bowl scraper (try not to rip or tear the dough). Roll the dough out to a 9-inch square approximately ¹/₂ inch thick. Sprinkle the cinnamon sugar over the surface and roll it up into a tight loaf. Slice the dough into 1-inch-thick slices and lay them out, 1 inch apart, on a sheet pan lined with parchment paper or a silicon mat. Mist the top of the buns with pan spray, cover loosely with plastic wrap, and let rise at room temperature for approximately 45 to 60 minutes, until the buns are nearly double in size.

BAKER'S FORMULA	%
Whole wheat flour	100
Salt	1.8
Instant yeast	1.5
Milk	61
Egg	9
Honey	11
Unsalted butter or oil	11
Total	184.3

NUTRITION FACTS	
Calories (kcal)	268.94
Protein (g)	9.84
Carbohydrates (g)	58.70
Dietary fiber (g)	7.74
Total sugars (g)	17.19
Fat (g)	1.95
Saturated fat (g)	.56
Trans fatty acid (g)	0
Cholesterol (mg)	23.27
Sodium (mg)	406.39

SHAPING CINNAMON BUNS

(A) Once dough is rolled out, sprinkle the cinnamon sugar over the surface. (B) Roll the dough into a tight loaf. (C) With the seam side down, cut the dough into 8 to 10 pieces each 1 inch thick.

6. **Preheat the oven to 400°F (204°C).** Place the pan on the middle shelf, lower the temperature to 350°F (177°C), and bake for 15 minutes. Rotate the pan 180 degrees and continue baking for another 10 to 15 minutes. While the buns are baking, make one of the glazes on page 138. The buns will be a rich brown and very springy when poked in the center. If they still seem doughy, continue baking.

7. **Remove the pan from the oven** and cool the buns for 5 minutes before glazing.

Transitional Cinnamon Raisin Bread (and Buns)

Makes 2 loaves or 9 to 12 buns

BREAD PROFILE

Enriched, medium soft dough;
delayed fermentation method;
commercial yeast

DAYS TO MAKE: 2

Day 1: Soaker and *biga*, 20 minutes
set up and mix; overnight autolyse
Day 2: 2 hours to de-chill *biga*; 12
to 15 minutes mixing; 2 to 3 hours
fermentation, shaping, proofing;
20 to 35 minutes baking for buns,
40 to 60 minutes baking for loaves

COMMENTARY

The raisins in the soaker are for
loaf bread only. Adding raisins
to the dough is not recommended for cinnamon buns
because too many are exposed
to direct heat during baking,
and they tend to burn. But for
loaf bread, putting the raisins
in the soaker helps plump and
soften them.

The main difference between this transitional formula and the 100% whole wheat version cinnamon raisin bread on page 132 is the use of unbleached bread flour which absorbs more liquid than whole wheat flour. This versatile dough can be used for either loaf pan cinnamon raisin bread, which makes delicious breakfast toast, or, without the raisins, cinnamon buns.

SOAKER

VOLUME	OUNCES	GRAMS	INGREDIENT	%
2¼ cups	10	283	whole wheat flour	100
⅝ teaspoon	.18	5	salt	1.8
¾ cup plus 2 tablespoons	7	198	milk, buttermilk, yogurt, soy milk, or rice milk	70
1⅓ cups	8	227	raisins (optional)	80
TOTAL	25.18	713		251.8

1. **Combine the flour, salt, and milk** in a bowl and mix for about 1 minute, until all of the flour is hydrated and the ingredients form a ball of dough. If making bread, add the raisins and use wet hands to knead them into the dough until evenly incorporated; if, however, you are making cinnamon buns, they should be omitted from the soaker.

2. **Cover loosely with plastic wrap** and leave at room temperature for 12 to 24 hours. (If it will be more than 24 hours, place the soaker in the refrigerator; it will be good for up to 3 days. Remove it 2 hours before mixing the final dough to take off the chill.)

BIGA

VOLUME	OUNCES	GRAMS	INGREDIENT	%
2¼ cups	10	283	unbleached bread flour	100
¼ teaspoon	.03	1	instant yeast	.3
¾ cup	6	170	milk, buttermilk, yogurt, soy milk, or rice milk, at room temperature (about 70°F/21°C)	60
1 large	1.65	47	egg, slightly beaten	16.5
TOTAL	17.68	501		176.5

1. **Mix all of the *biga* ingredients together** in a bowl to form a ball of dough. Using wet hands, knead the dough in the bowl for 2 minutes to be sure all of the ingredients are evenly distributed and the flour is fully hydrated. The dough should feel very tacky. Let the dough rest for 5 minutes, then knead it again with wet hands for 1 minute. The dough will become smoother but still be tacky.

2. **Transfer the dough to a clean bowl, cover** tightly with plastic wrap, and refrigerate for at least 8 hours and up to 3 days.

3. **About 2 hours before mixing the final dough,** remove the *biga* from the refrigerator to take off the chill. It will have risen slightly but need not have risen significantly in order to use it in the final dough.

FINAL DOUGH

VOLUME	OUNCES	GRAMS	INGREDIENT
Use all	25.18	713	soaker
Use all	17.68	501	*biga*
3/4 cup plus 2 tablespoons	4	113	whole wheat flour
5/8 teaspoon	.18	5	salt
2 1/4 teaspoons	.25	7	instant yeast
1 tablespoon	.67	19	honey or agave nectar
or 4 teaspoons	.67	19	or sugar or brown sugar
1/4 cup	2	56.5	unsalted butter, melted, or vegetable oil
1 teaspoon	.25	7	ground cinnamon
			extra whole wheat flour for adjustments
1/4 cup	2	56.5	cinnamon sugar (3 generous tablespoons granulated sugar plus 2 teaspoons ground cinnamon)
			fondant or cream cheese and honey glaze (optional; see Commentary page 138)
TOTAL	52.21	1478	

1. **Using a metal pastry scraper, chop** the soaker and the *biga* into 12 smaller pieces each (sprinkle some of the extra flour over the pre-doughs to keep the pieces from sticking back to each other).

2. **If mixing by hand,** combine the soaker and *biga* pieces with the 4 ounces of whole wheat flour and the salt, yeast, honey, butter, and cinnamon. Stir vigorously with a large spoon or knead with wet hands for about 2 minutes, until all of the ingredients are evenly integrated and distributed into the dough. It should be soft and slightly sticky; if not, add more flour or water as needed. **If using a stand mixer,** put the pre-dough pieces in the bowl along with the 4 ounces of whole wheat flour and the salt, yeast, honey, butter, and cinnamon. Mix on slow speed with the paddle attachment (preferable) or dough hook for 1 minute to bring the ingredients together into a ball. Switch to the dough hook if need be and mix on medium-low speed, occasionally scraping down the bowl, for 2 to 3 minutes, until the pre-doughs become cohesive and assimilated into each other. Add more flour or water as needed until the dough is soft and slightly sticky.

3. **Dust a work surface with flour,** then roll the dough in the flour to coat. Knead the dough by hand for 3 to 4 minutes, incorporating only as much extra flour as needed, until the dough feels soft and tacky, but not sticky. Form the dough into a ball and let it rest on the work surface for 5 minutes while you prepare a clean, lightly oiled bowl.

4. **Resume kneading the dough for 1 minute** to strengthen the gluten and make any final flour or water adjustments. The dough should have strength and pass the windowpane test (see page 84), yet still feel soft, supple, and very tacky. Form the dough into a ball and place it in the prepared bowl, rolling to coat with oil. Cover loosely with plastic wrap and let rise at room temperature for approximately 45 to 60 minutes, until it is about $1^1/_2$ times its original size.

5. **When the dough has risen,** dust the work surface with about 1 tablespoon of the extra flour and gently transfer the dough to the floured work surface with a plastic bowl scraper (try not to rip or tear the dough). For loaf pan bread, first divide the dough in half, then roll it out into two 8-inch squares approximately $1/_2$ inch thick, as shown on page 139; for buns, roll the entire dough out to a 9 by 12-inch rectangle, approximately $1/_2$ inch thick. In either case, sprinkle the cinnamon sugar over the surface and roll the dough up tightly. **For loaf pan bread,** oil two $4^1/_2$ by 8-inch bread pans and place the loaves into them (you may also bake them as freestanding loaves on a sheet pan). **For cinnamon buns,** slice the rolled dough into 1-inch-thick slices and lay them out, 1 inch apart, on a sheet pan lined with parchment paper or a silicon mat.

6. **Mist the top of the loaves or the buns with pan spray,** cover loosely with plastic wrap, and let rise at room temperature for approximately 1 hour, until the loaves crest above the pans or the buns are nearly double in size.

7. **Preheat the oven to 400°F (204°C).** Bake the loaves or buns on the middle shelf and, **for loaf bread,** lower the temperature to 325°F (163°C); **for cinnamon buns,** lower the temperature to 350°F (177°C). While the buns are baking, make one of the glazes on page 138. Rotate the loaves or pan 180 degrees after 15 minutes (20 minutes for loaves) and bake for another 10 to 15 minutes (for cinnamon buns) or 25 to 40 minutes (loaves). The buns will be golden and very springy when poked in the center. If they still seem doughy, continue baking. The loaves will be a rich brown on all sides, sound hollow when thumped on the bottom, and register above 195°F (91°C) in the center. Allow the loaves to cool for at least 1 hour before serving.

8. **For cinnamon buns, allow them to cool** for 5 minutes before drizzling or brushing the glaze over the top.

BAKER'S FORMULA	%
Whole wheat flour	58
Bread flour	42
Salt	1.3
Instant yeast	1.2
Milk	62.5
Egg	7
Honey	2.8
Unsalted butter or oil	8
Ground cinnamon	1
Raisins	33
Total	216.8

NUTRITION FACTS	
Calories (kcal)	112.58
Protein (g)	3.32
Carbohydrates (g)	21.21
Dietary fiber (g)	2.11
Total sugars (g)	6.83
Fat (g)	2.17
Saturated fat (g)	.34
Trans fatty acid (g)	0
Cholesterol (mg)	6.11
Sodium (mg)	105.84

FAQ *Why do you list the baker's percentage of each ingredient?*

These recipes are for individual loaves, but production bakeries need to make larger batches of varying sizes. Formulas allow them to do this easily. By looking at the ratio of other ingredients to the flour, bakers can tell how the bread will taste, feel, and look. They can tweak the percentages to change aspects of the final product, and they can create any size batch by using the mathematics of the baker's percentage system. The percentages are, in essence, the formula. They immediately show bakers everything they need to know about that bread. As you begin to refer to the percentages, you will begin to think like a professional baker.

In this book, the percentages of each ingredient in the pre-doughs (soakers, mashes, *bigas*, and starters) are listed with them, but because these then become part of a larger final dough, you will find the percentage break-out of all the ingredients of the total dough in a separate chart. This total consolidates all the flour, liquid, salt, yeast and other ingredients into one formula so that you can see the ratio of every ingredient, whether in a pre-dough or the final dough, against the total flour. This formula reveals not only the relationship of ingredients, but provides a blueprint for understanding the type of dough (lean, enriched, rich, firm, rustic, etc.) and how it should perform.

For a delicious crunchy cinnamon crust, when the loaf comes out of the oven, brush the top with 1 tablespoon of melted butter, then roll the buttered top in additional cinnamon sugar, made with 5 parts sugar to 1 part cinnamon.

FAQ *How were the nutrition facts calculated?*

All ingredients were entered into ESHA Research's nutritional SQL database program called The Food Processor. With the exception of four breads (see below), the nutrition facts were based on a 1¹/₂-ounce serving (42 grams). Note that the serving size of commercial breads is often slightly less, at 1 ounce (28 grams), as they typically contain more air and are sliced thinner than homemade breads. The nutrition facts of the following formulas were based on a different serving size: 1 bagel (4 ounces/113.5 grams); ¹/₂ naan (3 ounces/85 grams); 1 pita (4 ounces/113.5 grams); and 1 cinnamon bun (4 ounces/113.5 grams). Because there is no single diet that is right for everyone, this book does not suggest daily dietary intakes.

Whole Wheat Challah

Makes 1 large or 2 small loaves

BREAD PROFILE

Enriched, medium soft dough; delayed fermentation method; commercial yeast

DAYS TO MAKE: 2

Day 1: Soaker and *biga*, 20 minutes set up and mix; overnight autolyse
Day 2: 2 hours to de-chill *biga*; 12 to 15 minutes mixing; 2 to 3 hours fermentation, shaping, proofing; 40 to 60 minutes baking

Challah, the traditional Jewish Sabbath and celebration bread, is made from a rich dough that incorporates both whole eggs and additional yolks. There are many versions, all with their own egg specifications. In addition to contributing flavor and sweetness, the eggs add structural strength to the dough. The more yolks, the more golden the crumb; some versions even use spices such as saffron or turmeric to boost the golden color, but the yolks provide lecithin as well as color, which makes them a very important functional ingredient for structure.

Challah has many symbolic as well as culinary purposes and is best known in its braided form. But all braided breads are not challah, and not every challah is braided. It can be made into rounded coils (which symbolize the cyclical and eternal nature of creation), rolls, and even sandwich loaves. Most versions are made with white flour, but there is no rule that demands the use of only white flour, and there is no reason that it cannot be made as a 100% whole wheat or multigrain loaf, provided that you adjust your expectations of a bright yellow loaf. It is the eggs that define challah, not the flour, and the eggs and egg yolks, along with the vegetable oil, help tenderize the dough in this whole grain version.

SOAKER

VOLUME	OUNCES	GRAMS	INGREDIENT	%
1³/₄ cups	8	227	whole wheat flour, preferably fine grind	100
¹/₂ teaspoon	.14	4	salt	1.75
³/₄ cup	6	170	water	75
TOTAL	14.14	401		176.75

1. **Mix all of the soaker ingredients together** in a bowl for about 1 minute, until all of the flour is hydrated and the ingredients form a ball of dough.

2. **Cover loosely with plastic wrap** and leave at room temperature for 12 to 24 hours. (If it will be more than 24 hours, place the soaker in the refrigerator; it will be good for up to 3 days. Remove it 2 hours before mixing the final dough to take off the chill.)

BIGA

VOLUME	OUNCES	GRAMS	INGREDIENT	%
1³/₄ cups	8	227	whole wheat flour, preferably fine grind	100
¹/₄ teaspoon	.03	1	instant yeast	.4
¹/₂ cup	4	113	filtered or spring water, at room temperature (about 70°F/21°C)	50
2 tablespoons	1	28.5	vegetable oil	12.5
1 large	1.65	47	egg, slightly beaten	20.6
4	2	56	egg yolks	25
TOTAL	16.68	472.5		208.5

1. **Mix all of the *biga* ingredients together** in a bowl to form a ball of dough. Using wet hands, knead the dough in the bowl for 2 minutes to be sure all of the ingredients are evenly distributed and the flour is fully hydrated. The dough should feel very tacky. Let the dough rest for 5 minutes, then knead it again with wet hands for 1 minute. The dough will become smoother but still be tacky.

2. **Transfer the dough to a clean bowl, cover** tightly with plastic wrap, and refrigerate for at least 8 hours and up to 3 days.

3. **About 2 hours before mixing the final dough,** remove the *biga* from the refrigerator to take off the chill. It will have risen slightly but need not have risen significantly in order to use it in the final dough.

FINAL DOUGH

VOLUME	OUNCES	GRAMS	INGREDIENT
Use all	14.14	401	soaker
Use all	16.68	472.5	*biga*
7 tablespoons	2	56.5	whole wheat flour
⁵/₈ teaspoon	.18	5	salt
2¹/₄ teaspoons	.25	7	instant yeast
2 tablespoons	1	28.5	sugar or brown sugar
or 1¹/₂ tablespoons	1	28.5	or honey or agave nectar
2 tablespoons	1	28.5	vegetable oil
			extra whole wheat flour for adjustments
			1 egg beaten with 1 tablespoon water and a pinch of salt for egg wash
			poppy seeds or sesame seeds for topping (optional)
TOTAL	35.25	999	

1. **Using a metal pastry scraper, chop** the soaker and the *biga* into 12 smaller pieces each (sprinkle some of the extra flour over the pre-doughs to keep the pieces from sticking back to each other).

2. **If mixing by hand,** combine the soaker and *biga* pieces in a bowl with the 7 tablespoons flour and the salt, yeast, sugar, and vegetable oil. Stir vigorously with a mixing spoon or knead with wet hands for about 2 minutes, until all of the ingredients are evenly integrated and distributed into the dough. The dough should be soft and slightly sticky; if not, add more flour or water as needed. **If using a stand mixer,** put the pre-dough pieces in the bowl along with the 7 tablespoons flour and the salt, yeast, sugar, and vegetable oil. Mix on slow speed with the paddle attachment (preferable) or dough hook for 1 minute to bring the ingredients together into a ball. Switch to the dough hook if need be and mix on medium-low speed, occasionally scraping down the bowl, for 2 to 3 minutes, until the pre-doughs become cohesive and assimilated into each other. Add more flour or water as needed until the dough is soft and slightly sticky.

3. **Dust a work surface with flour,** then roll the dough in the flour to coat. Knead the dough by hand for 3 to 4 minutes, incorporating only as much extra flour as needed, until the dough feels soft and tacky, but not sticky. Form the dough into a ball and let it rest on the work surface for 5 minutes while you prepare a clean, lightly oiled bowl.

4. **Resume kneading the dough for 1 minute** to strengthen the gluten and make any final flour or water adjustments. The dough should have strength and pass the windowpane test (see page 84), yet still feel soft, supple, and very tacky. Form the dough into a ball and place it in the prepared bowl, rolling to coat with oil. Cover loosely with plastic wrap and let rise at room temperature for approximately 45 to 60 minutes, until it is about $1^1/_2$ times its original size.

5. **Gently transfer the dough to a lightly floured work surface** with a plastic bowl scraper (try not to rip or tear the dough). You can make 1 large braided loaf or 2 smaller loaves, or you can cut as many as 16 smaller pieces for dinner rolls. For braided challah, use a metal pastry scraper to cut the dough into 3, 4, 5, or 6 equal pieces, depending on the type of braid you want to make; do not rip the dough—make clean cuts. Roll the pieces into short ropes about 3 inches long. Cover loosely with a cloth towel or plastic wrap, let rest for 5 minutes, then roll each piece into a longer rope, about 10 inches long. Braid the ropes as shown below for 3-braid, or on the next page for 4-, 5-, or 6-braid loaves.

SHAPING 3-BRAID CHALLAH

This is the only braid that begins in the middle. (A) Lay three equal strands side by side. Start by overlapping one of the outside strands over the middle strand. Take the opposite outside strand and lay it over the new middle strand. (B) Continue this pattern until you run out of dough. Pinch the end closed. (C) Rotate the loaf 180 degrees and repeat the pattern. The loaf is now ready to pan and proof.

6. **Place the braided loaf on a sheet pan** lined with parchment paper or a silicon mat. Brush the egg wash on the loaf, mist the top of the dough with pan spray (optional), and cover loosely with plastic wrap, or place the pan in a plastic bag. Let the dough rise at room temperature for 30 minutes.

BAKER'S FORMULA	%
Whole wheat flour	100
Salt	1.8
Instant yeast	1.5
Water	56
Egg	9
Egg yolk	11
Sugar	5.5
Oil	11
Total	195.8

NUTRITION FACTS	
Calories (kcal)	102.99
Protein (g)	3.51
Carbohydrates (g)	16.08
Dietary fiber (g)	2.56
Total sugars (g)	1.24
Fat (g)	3.43
Saturated fat (g)	.59
Trans fatty acid (g)	0
Cholesterol (mg)	35.70
Sodium (mg)	145.17

SHAPING 6-BRAID CHALLAH

(A) Connect six equal strands at one end. Number the strands 1 through 6 and bring strand 6 over strand 1 to build up the end of the loaf. Strand 5 has now become the new strand 6, and the old strand 6 is now strand 1. Now follow this pattern: 2 over 6, 1 over 3, 5 over 1, and 6 over 4. (B) Repeat the pattern until you run out of dough. (C) Pinch off the ends, place the prettiest side up, pan, and proof. Challah requires two applications of egg wash. After the second, sprinkle with poppy or sesame seeds. (D) Challah requires two egg washes, one after shaping and one just before baking. (E) After the second egg wash, you can apply poppy or sesame seeds (the egg wash is required even if you don't use the seeds).

SHAPING 4-BRAID CHALLAH PATTERN: 4 over 2, 1 over 3, and 2 over 3.

SHAPING 5-BRAID CHALLAH PATTERN: 1 over 3, 2 over 3, and 5 over 2.

COMMENTARY

If you make smaller breads or rolls from this dough, increase the oven temperature by 25°F (14°C). Larger loaves take longer and need to bake more slowly, but because rolls and mini loaves bake quickly, they can be baked at a higher temperature.

7. **Brush the dough with egg wash** a second time, then top with poppy seeds or sesame seeds. Leave the dough uncovered to continue rising for 15 more minutes. Preheat the oven to 400°F (204°C).

8. **Place the challah on the middle shelf,** reduce the heat to 325°F (163°C), and bake for 20 minutes. Rotate the loaf 180 degrees and bake for another 20 minutes. Check the bread and rotate again if it is baking unevenly. Continue baking for an additional 10 to 15 minutes, until the bread is a rich brown all around, sounds hollow when thumped on the bottom, and registers at least 195°F (91°C) in the center.

9. **Transfer the bread to a cooling rack** and let it cool for at least 1 hour before serving.

Transitional Challah

Makes 1 large loaf, 2 small loaves, or up to 16 dinner rolls

This is the transitional version of the 100% whole wheat challah presented on page 144. The only difference is the percentage of hydration and, of course, the use of a blend of whole wheat and white flours. Challah does not have to be braided. It can be rolled out into a long strand and then coiled like a snail, or it can be used to make soft rolls of any shape or size.

BREAD PROFILE

Enriched, medium soft dough; delayed fermentation method; commercial yeast

DAYS TO MAKE: 2

Day 1: Soaker and *biga*, 20 minutes set up and mix; overnight autolyse
Day 2: 2 hours to de-chill *biga*; 12 to 15 minutes mixing; 2 to 3 hours fermentation, shaping, proofing; 40 to 60 minutes baking

SOAKER

VOLUME	OUNCES	GRAMS	INGREDIENT	%
1³/₄ cups	8	227	whole wheat flour, preferably fine grind	100
¹/₂ teaspoon	.14	4	salt	1.75
³/₄ cup	6	170	water	75
TOTAL	14.14	401		176.75

1. **Mix all of the soaker ingredients together** in a bowl for about 1 minute, until all of the flour is hydrated and the ingredients form a ball of dough.

2. **Cover loosely with plastic wrap** and leave at room temperature for 12 to 24 hours. (If it will be more than 24 hours, place the soaker in the refrigerator; it will be good for up to 3 days. Remove it 2 hours before mixing the final dough to take off the chill.)

FAQ ∾ *How important is the temperature of the liquids used in these formulas?*

In almost every formula, unless otherwise stipulated, the temperature should be about room temperature, around 70°F (21°C). The predicted fermentation times of the starters and *bigas*, as well as the overnight development of the soakers, are based on this moderate temperature range. If you use scalded milk instead of unscalded, be sure to allow the milk enough time to cool down to room temperature. If using refrigerated milk to make a soaker, you can add the cold milk without waiting for it to warm up (the soaker will have plenty of time to come to room temperature during the overnight development). But if you are using unscalded milk in a *biga*, do not use it directly from the refrigerator, as it will chill the *biga* too much, preventing the small amount of yeast from acidifying the dough. Even though the *biga* goes directly into the refrigerator, the yeast does activate and stays active until the *biga* completely cools down, which takes an hour or two; the delayed fermentation method counts on this time line. Either warm the milk to room temperature in a saucepan, or pull it from the refrigerator an hour or two before you make the dough.

The *biga* is a little different in this bread than usual, as it contains eggs and egg yolks. It is necessary to add these to the *biga* because the eggs are an important part of the hydration for this dough (eggs are about 80% water). If we wait until mixing the final dough to add them, it will be necessary to add a great deal of additional flour.

BIGA

VOLUME	OUNCES	GRAMS	INGREDIENT	%
1³/₄ cups	8	227	unbleached bread flour	100
¹/₄ teaspoon	.03	1	instant yeast	.4
7 tablespoons	3.5	99	filtered or spring water, at room temperature (about 70°F/21°C)	44
1 large	1.65	47	egg, slightly beaten	20.6
4	2	56	egg yolks	25
TOTAL	15.18	430		190

1. **Mix all of the *biga* ingredients together** in a bowl to form a ball of dough. Using wet hands, knead the dough in the bowl for 2 minutes to be sure all of the ingredients are evenly distributed and the flour is fully hydrated. The dough should feel very tacky. Let the dough rest for 5 minutes, then knead it again with wet hands for 1 minute. The dough will become smoother but still be tacky.

2. **Transfer the dough to a clean bowl, cover** tightly with plastic wrap, and refrigerate for at least 8 hours and up to 3 days.

3. **About 2 hours before mixing the final dough,** remove the *biga* from the refrigerator to take off the chill. It will have risen slightly but need not have risen significantly in order to use it in the final dough.

FAQ ∾ *Does it matter whether I use a stand mixer or mix by hand? And can I use a bread machine or a food processor?*

There are three objectives that must be achieved during mixing: even distribution of ingredients, activation of the yeast to initiate fermentation, and the development of gluten. Any method of mixing can accomplish these as long you honor these requirements. **Hand mixing** and **stand mixers** are addressed in the instructions in each recipe. You may find it surprising that some recipes call for longer mixing with a stand mixer and dough hook than by hand. However, the dough hook doesn't always grab the entire mass of dough, so additional mixing time is necessary to ensure that the ingredients are thoroughly incorporated, with no dry or lumpy spots. **Food processors** are powerful and generate a great deal of friction, so the rule of thumb is to pulse the ingredients at first, and then mix for no longer than 45 seconds. Next, let the dough rest for 5 minutes, and then finish mixing for 30 to 45 seconds. **Bread machines** are not designed for delayed fermentation, but some models are programmable, and could be used for the mixing cycle only, whether for a *biga* or starter, or for mixing and fermenting a final dough. A bread machine could also be used for the final dough, from start to finish, for enriched sandwich-style breads. The recipes are given in single-loaf batches so many can work in a bread machine.

FINAL DOUGH

VOLUME	OUNCES	GRAMS	INGREDIENT
Use all	14.14	401	soaker
Use all	15.18	430	*biga*
7 tablespoons	2	56.5	whole wheat flour
½ teaspoon	.14	4	salt
2¼ teaspoons	.25	7	instant yeast
1½ tablespoons	1	28.5	honey or agave nectar
or 2 tablespoons	1	28.5	or sugar or brown sugar
2 tablespoons	1	28.5	vegetable oil
			extra whole wheat flour for adjustments
			1 egg beaten with 1 tablespoon water plus a pinch of salt for egg wash
			poppy seeds or sesame seeds for topping (optional)
TOTAL	33.71	955.5	

BAKER'S FORMULA	%
Whole wheat flour	55.5
Bread flour	44.5
Salt	1.8
Instant yeast	1.6
Water	53
Egg	9
Egg yolk	11
Sugar	5.5
Oil	5.6
Total	187.5

NUTRITION FACTS	
Calories (kcal)	95.37
Protein (g)	3.58
Carbohydrates (g)	16.59
Dietary fiber (g)	1.66
Total sugars (g)	1.23
Fat (g)	2.20
Saturated fat (g)	.45
Trans fatty acid (g)	0
Cholesterol (mg)	36.68
Sodium (mg)	148.71

1. **Using a metal pastry scraper, chop** the soaker and the *biga* into 12 smaller pieces each (sprinkle some of the extra flour over the pre-doughs to keep the pieces from sticking back to each other).

2. **If mixing by hand,** combine the soaker and *biga* pieces in a bowl with the 7 tablespoons flour and the salt, yeast, honey, and vegetable oil. Stir vigorously with a mixing spoon or knead with wet hands for about 2 minutes, until all of the ingredients are evenly integrated and distributed into the dough. The dough should be soft and slightly sticky; if not, add more flour or water as needed. **If using a stand mixer,** put the pre-dough pieces in the bowl along with the 7 tablespoons flour and the salt, yeast, sugar, and vegetable oil. Mix on slow speed with the paddle attachment (preferable) or dough hook for 1 minute to bring the ingredients together into a ball. Switch to the dough hook if need be and mix on medium-low speed, occasionally scraping down the bowl, for 2 to 3 minutes, until the pre-doughs become cohesive and assimilated into each other. Add more flour or water as needed until the dough is soft and slightly sticky.

3. **Proceed as in steps 3 through 9** in the whole wheat challah on page 146.

⌘ HEARTH BREADS ⌘

We use the term hearth bread for freestanding, crusty, chewy loaves that are usually baked at high temperatures, oftentimes with steam. With some leaner doughs, it is not unusual to bake at 500°F (260°C), but since so much natural sugar has been released from the flour during delayed fermentation, it is necessary to often reduce the temperature a bit to prevent the crust from overbrowning. In addition, some of the formulas suggest small amounts of honey, sugar, or oil as optional ingredients (to help tenderize the bread), so if using these, a lower oven temperature is advised, the amount based on the type of oven you have (typically about 25°F/14°C). Hearth breads, with their crisp, crackly crusts, are often characterized by a nutlike crust flavor (often compared to toasted hazelnuts) and a toothsome but creamy interior crumb.

Whole Wheat Hearth Bread

Makes 1 loaf

This is the foundational formula for crusty 100% whole wheat hearth bread (shown opposite). It can be formed into many different shapes, including baguettes, *boules*, *bâtards*, *épis*, and rolls. See pages 87–91 for shaping instructions. Because this is a lean bread (that is, no fats have been added to tenderize it), the dough should be baked at a high temperature with steam during the first 5 minutes in order to caramelize the crust. As the bread cools, it will soften slightly as the moisture works its way to the surface. This formula makes a hearty, crispy loaf that can be used for many applications. You may be surprised that this formula does not conform to typical recipes for artisan breads, which use very little yeast. The approach here is a completely different way of accomplishing the same goal.

See pages 87–91 for shaping instructions.

BREAD PROFILE

Lean dough; delayed fermentation method; commercial yeast

DAYS TO MAKE: 2

Day 1: Soaker and *biga*, 20 minutes set up and mix; overnight autolyse
Day 2: 2 hours to de-chill *biga*; 12 to 15 minutes mixing; 2 to 3 hours fermentation, shaping, proofing; 40 to 60 minutes baking

COMMENTARY

You can replace the *biga* with 14 ounces of wild yeast starter (page 80) for a *pain au levain* variation. If you want a non-yeasted version, a true sourdough bread, omit the yeast from the final dough and use only starter as the leaven.

SOAKER

VOLUME	OUNCES	GRAMS	INGREDIENT	%
1³/₄ cups	8	227	whole wheat flour	100
¹/₂ teaspoon	.14	4	salt	1.75
³/₄ cup	6	170	water	75
TOTAL	14.14	401		176.75

1. **Mix all of the soaker ingredients together** in a bowl for about 1 minute, until all of the flour is hydrated and the ingredients form a ball of dough.

2. **Cover loosely with plastic wrap** and leave at room temperature for 12 to 24 hours. (If it will be more than 24 hours, place the soaker in the refrigerator; it will be good for up to 3 days. Remove it 2 hours before mixing the final dough to take off the chill.)

BIGA

VOLUME	OUNCES	GRAMS	INGREDIENT	%
1³/₄ cups	8	227	whole wheat flour	100
¹/₄ teaspoon	.03	1	instant yeast	.4
³/₄ cup	6	170	filtered or spring water, at room temperature (about 70°F/21°C)	75
TOTAL	14.03	398		175.4

1. **Mix all of the *biga* ingredients together** in a bowl to form a ball of dough. Using wet hands, knead the dough in the bowl for 2 minutes to be sure all of the ingredients are evenly distributed and the flour is fully hydrated. The dough should feel very tacky. Let the dough rest for 5 minutes, then knead it again with wet hands for 1 minute. The dough will become smoother but still be tacky.

2. **Transfer the dough to a clean bowl, cover** tightly with plastic wrap, and refrigerate for at least 8 hours and up to 3 days.

3. **About 2 hours before mixing the final dough,** remove the *biga* from the refrigerator to take off the chill. It will have risen slightly but need not have risen significantly in order to use it in the final dough.

Feel free to tweak the dough with the honey and melted butter options; both of these ingredients will tenderize the dough, soften the crust (for hoagies and hero sandwiches), and also cause it to brown faster while baking.

It is difficult to make great baguettes in a home oven because it is impossible to replicate the intense steam of a commercial hearth oven. Also, home ovens cannot accommodate the full length of a baguette. For this reason, it is best to make mini baguettes (see page 263), no longer than your baking stone or sheet pan, of no more than 8 ounces in weight. The smaller loaves have a much better chance of good oven spring, an even bake, and a crisper crust.

The key to a great baguette crumb is gentle shaping, preserving some of the gas already generated during the first rise and building on it in the final rise. Be firm but gentle.

FINAL DOUGH

VOLUME	OUNCES	GRAMS	INGREDIENT
Use all	14.14	401	soaker
Use all	14.03	398	*biga*
3½ tablespoons	1	28.5	whole wheat flour
⅝ teaspoon	.18	5	salt
2¼ teaspoons	.25	7	instant yeast
2¼ teaspoons or 1 tablespoon	.5 .5	14 14	honey or agave nectar or sugar or brown sugar (optional)
1 tablespoon	.5	14	unsalted butter, melted, vegetable oil, or olive oil (optional)
			extra whole wheat flour for adjustments
TOTAL	30.6	867.5	

1. **Using a metal pastry scraper, chop** the soaker and the *biga* into 12 smaller pieces each (sprinkle some of the extra flour over the pre-doughs to keep the pieces from sticking back to each other).

2. **If mixing by hand,** combine the soaker and *biga* pieces in a bowl with all of the other ingredients except the extra flour and stir vigorously with a mixing spoon or knead with wet hands for about 2 minutes, until all of the ingredients are evenly integrated and distributed into the dough. The dough should be soft and slightly sticky; if not, add more flour or water as needed. **If using a stand mixer,** put the pre-dough pieces and all of the other ingredients

except the extra flour into the mixer with the paddle attachment (preferable) or dough hook. Mix on slow speed for 1 minute to bring the ingredients together into a ball. Switch to the dough hook if need be and mix on medium-low speed, occasionally scraping down the bowl, for 2 to 3 minutes, until the pre-doughs become cohesive and assimilated into each other. Add more flour or water as needed until the dough is soft and slightly sticky.

3. **Dust a work surface with flour,** then roll the dough in the flour to coat. Knead the dough by hand for 3 to 4 minutes, incorporating only as much extra flour as needed, until the dough feels soft and tacky, but not sticky. Form the dough into a ball and let it rest on the work surface for 5 minutes while you prepare a clean, lightly oiled bowl.

4. **Resume kneading the dough for 1 minute** to strengthen the gluten and make any final flour or water adjustments. The dough should have strength and pass the windowpane test (see page 84), yet still feel soft, supple, and very tacky. Form the dough into a ball and place it in the prepared bowl, rolling to coat with oil. Cover loosely with plastic wrap and let rise at room temperature for approximately 45 to 60 minutes, until it is about $1^1/_2$ times its original size.

5. **Gently transfer the dough to a lightly floured work surface** with a plastic bowl scraper (try not to rip or tear the dough). Form the dough into a large *boule* or 2 to 4 *bâtards* (see pages 87–91 for shaping instructions) or 4 mini baguettes (see page 263), being careful to degas the dough as little as possible when shaping it. A *boule* can be proofed in a *banneton* or another prepared proofing bowl. For baguettes or *bâtards*, raise the loaves on a proofing cloth or on a sheet pan lined with parchment paper and, if you like, dusted with flour. Mist the top of the dough with pan spray (optional), cover loosely with plastic wrap or a cloth towel, and let rise at room temperature for approximately 45 minutes, until nearly $1^1/_2$ times its original size.

6. **Preheat the oven to 500°F (260°C)** and prepare it for hearth baking (see page 86), including a steam pan. When the dough is ready to bake, place it in the oven (either with a peel or on a sheet pan), and pour 1 cup of hot water into the steam pan (or mist the oven three times at 1-minute intervals). Lower the temperature to 450°F (232°C) and bake for 20 minutes (15 minutes for mini baguettes). Rotate the bread 180 degrees and continue baking for another 15 to 30 minutes, until the bread is a rich brown on all sides, sounds hollow when thumped on the bottom, and registers at least 200°F (93°C) in the center. The crust should be hard (though it will soften somewhat as it cools). If the crust is dark but the bread still feels soft, turn off the oven and leave the bread in for another 5 to 10 minutes. You can also cover the bread loosely with aluminum foil to prevent it from burning.

7. **Transfer the bread to a cooling rack** and cool for at least 1 hour before serving.

BAKER'S FORMULA	%
Whole wheat flour	100
Salt	1.9
Instant yeast	1.6
Water	70.5
Honey	3
Unsalted butter or oil	3
Total	180

NUTRITION FACTS	
Calories (kcal)	87.45
Protein (g)	3.38
Carbohydrates (g)	17.64
Dietary fiber (g)	2.95
Total sugars (g)	.62
Fat (g)	1.01
Saturated fat (g)	.43
Trans fatty acid (g)	.02
Cholesterol (mg)	1.48
Sodium (mg)	172.26

Transitional Country Hearth Bread

Makes 1 loaf

BREAD PROFILE

Lean dough; delayed fermentation
method; commercial yeast

DAYS TO MAKE: 2

Day 1: Soaker and *biga*, 20 minutes
set up and mix; overnight autolyse
Day 2: 2 hours to de-chill *biga*; 12
to 15 minutes mixing; 2 to 3 hours
fermentation, shaping, proofing;
40 to 60 minutes baking

The term *country bread*, or *pain de campagne*, has come to mean a combination of mostly white flour and a little whole wheat flour or other whole grain flour. Usually, the percentage of whole grain is perhaps 10% to 20% of the total flour. The transitional version here contains about half whole wheat and half white flour, which makes it healthier and lends it a more complex flavor than conventional *campagne*-style breads. It bakes up into a beautiful, crusty hearth loaf of any shape you choose.

SOAKER

VOLUME	OUNCES	GRAMS	INGREDIENT	%
1³/₄ cups	8	227	whole wheat flour	100
¹/₂ teaspoon	.14	4	salt	1.75
³/₄ cup	6	170	water	75
TOTAL	14.14	401		176.75

1. **Mix all of the soaker ingredients together** in a bowl for about 1 minute, until all of the flour is hydrated and the ingredients form a ball of dough.

2. **Cover loosely with plastic wrap** and leave at room temperature for 12 to 24 hours. (If it will be more than 24 hours, place the soaker in the refrigerator; it will be good for up to 3 days. Remove it 2 hours before mixing the final dough to take off the chill.)

BIGA

VOLUME	OUNCES	GRAMS	INGREDIENT	%
1³/₄ cups	8	227	unbleached bread flour	100
¹/₄ teaspoon	.03	1	instant yeast	.4
¹/₂ cup plus 2 tablespoons	5	142	filtered or spring water, at room temperature (about 70°F/21°C)	62.5
TOTAL	13.03	370		162.9

1. **Mix all of the *biga* ingredients together** in a bowl to form a ball of dough. Using wet hands, knead the dough in the bowl for 2 minutes to be sure all of the ingredients are evenly

distributed and the flour is fully hydrated. The dough should feel very tacky. Let the dough rest for 5 minutes, then knead it again with wet hands for 1 minute. The dough will become smoother but still be tacky.

2. **Transfer the dough to a clean bowl, cover** tightly with plastic wrap, and refrigerate for at least 8 hours and up to 3 days.

3. **About 2 hours before mixing the final dough,** remove the *biga* from the refrigerator to take off the chill. It will have risen slightly but need not have risen significantly in order to use it in the final dough.

BAKER'S FORMULA	%
Whole wheat flour	53
Bread flour	47
Salt	1.9
Instant yeast	1.6
Water	65
Total	168.5

NUTRITION FACTS	
Calories (kcal)	88.66
Protein (g)	3.40
Carbohydrates (g)	18.28
Dietary fiber (g)	2.01
Total sugars (g)	.09
Fat (g)	.46
Saturated fat (g)	.08
Trans fatty acid (g)	0
Cholesterol (mg)	0
Sodium (mg)	183.82

FINAL DOUGH

VOLUME	OUNCES	GRAMS	INGREDIENT
Use all	14.14	401	soaker
Use all	13.03	370	*biga*
3¹/₂ tablespoons	1	28.5	whole wheat flour
⁵/₈ teaspoon	.18	5	salt
2¹/₄ teaspoons	.25	7	instant yeast
			extra whole wheat or bread flour for adjustments
TOTAL	28.6	811.5	

1. **Using a metal pastry scraper, chop** the soaker and the *biga* into 12 smaller pieces each (sprinkle some of the extra flour over the pre-doughs to keep the pieces from sticking back to each other).

2. **If mixing by hand,** combine the soaker and *biga* pieces in a bowl with all of the other ingredients except the extra flour and stir vigorously with a mixing spoon or knead with wet hands for about 2 minutes, until all of the ingredients are evenly integrated and distributed into the dough. The dough should be soft and slightly sticky; if not, add more flour or water as needed. **If using a stand mixer,** put the pre-dough pieces and all of the other ingredients except the extra flour into the mixer with the paddle attachment (preferable) or dough hook. Mix on slow speed for 1 minute to bring the ingredients together into a ball. Switch to the dough hook if need be and mix on medium-low speed, occasionally scraping down the bowl, for 2 to 3 minutes, until the pre-doughs become cohesive and assimilated into each other. Add more flour or water as needed until the dough is soft and slightly sticky.

3. **Proceed as in steps 3 through 7** in the whole wheat hearth bread on page 155.

Multigrain Hearth Bread

Makes 1 loaf

BREAD PROFILE

Lean dough; delayed fermentation method; commercial yeast

DAYS TO MAKE: 2

Day 1: Soaker and *biga*, 20 minutes set up and mix; overnight autolyse
Day 2: 2 hours to de-chill *biga*; 12 to 15 minutes mixing; 2 to 3 hours fermentation, shaping, proofing; 40 to 60 minutes baking

The method here is the same as for whole wheat hearth bread, but the soaker allows you to introduce some of your other favorites grains. You might say that these are the crusty hearth bread variations of the *struan* bread, as described on page 102. As in all of the multigrain breads in this book, the golden mean for these breads is two-thirds whole wheat flour and one-third multigrain blend.

SOAKER

VOLUME	OUNCES	GRAMS	INGREDIENT	%
7 tablespoons	2	56.5	whole wheat flour	25
1 1/3 cup (approx.)	6	170	any combination of cooked and uncooked grains (see Commentary)	75
1/2 teaspoon	.14	4	salt	1.75
3/4 cup	6	170	water	75
TOTAL	14.14	401		176.75

1. **Mix all of the soaker ingredients together** in a bowl for about 1 minute, until all of the flour is hydrated and the ingredients form a thick, porridge-like dough.

2. **Cover loosely with plastic wrap** and leave at room temperature for 12 to 24 hours. (If it will be more than 24 hours, place the soaker in the refrigerator; it will be good for up to 3 days. Remove it 2 hours before mixing the final dough to take off the chill.)

BIGA

VOLUME	OUNCES	GRAMS	INGREDIENT	%
1 3/4 cups	8	227	whole wheat flour	100
1/4 teaspoon	.03	1	instant yeast	.4
3/4 cup	6	170	filtered or spring water, at room temperature (about 70°F/21°C)	75
TOTAL	14.03	398		175.4

1. **Mix all of the *biga* ingredients together** in a bowl to form a ball of dough. Using wet hands, knead the dough in the bowl for 2 minutes to be sure all of the ingredients are evenly distributed and the flour is fully hydrated. The dough should feel very tacky. Let the dough rest for 5 minutes, then knead it again with wet hands for 1 minute. The dough will become smoother but still be tacky.

2. **Transfer the dough to a clean bowl, cover** tightly with plastic wrap, and refrigerate for at least 8 hours and up to 3 days.

3. **About 2 hours before mixing the final dough, remove** the *biga* from the refrigerator to take off the chill. It will have risen slightly but need not have risen significantly in order to use it in the final dough.

COMMENTARY

The total weight of the grains in the soaker, including any cooked grains, should be 6 ounces (excluding the 2 ounces of whole wheat flour, which is needed to provide sufficient gluten to support the structure of the bread). It is especially important to weigh these grains as the volume can vary substantially depending on the grains used. The volume measure provided is an approximation, but one that will get you pretty close if you don't have a scale. As you make this bread again, you can increase or decrease the grain amounts, as determined from the first batch.

Smaller or softer grains may be used uncooked, such as amaranth, rolled oats, oat bran, triticale flakes, multigrain cereal mixes, flaxseeds, and any type of flour or meal. It is best to precook larger or harder grains, such as barley, buckwheat, bulgur, couscous, cracked wheat, grits, millet, quinoa, rice, steel-cut oats, and whole wheat or rye berries. See page 102 for cooking instructions.

You can substitute an equal amount of wild yeast starter (page 80) for the *biga*.

BAKER'S FORMULA	%
Whole wheat flour	67
Multigrain mix	33
Salt	1.8
Instant yeast	1.6
Water	67
Honey	2.8
Unsalted butter or oil	2.8
Total	176

NUTRITION FACTS	
Calories (kcal)	92.03
Protein (g)	3.16
Carbohydrates (g)	18.36
Dietary fiber (g)	2.66
Total sugars (g)	.61
Fat (g)	1.15
Saturated fat (g)	.46
Trans fatty acid (g)	.02
Cholesterol (mg)	1.43
Sodium (mg)	166.75

FINAL DOUGH

VOLUME	OUNCES	GRAMS	INGREDIENT
Use all	14.14	401	soaker
Use all	14.03	398	*biga*
7 tablespoons	2	56.5	whole wheat flour
⁵⁄₈ teaspoon	.18	5	salt
2¹⁄₄ teaspoons	.25	7	instant yeast
2¹⁄₄ teaspoons	.5	14	honey or agave nectar
or 1 tablespoon	.5	14	or sugar or brown sugar (optional)
1 tablespoon	.5	14	unsalted butter, melted, or vegetable oil (optional)
			extra whole wheat flour for adjustments
TOTAL	31.6	895.5	

1. **Using a metal pastry scraper, chop** the soaker and the *biga* into 12 smaller pieces each (sprinkle some of the extra flour over the pre-doughs to keep the pieces from sticking back to each other).

2. **If mixing by hand,** combine the soaker and *biga* pieces in a bowl with all of the other ingredients except the extra flour and stir vigorously with a mixing spoon or knead with wet hands for about 2 minutes, until all of the ingredients are evenly integrated and distributed into the dough. The dough should be soft and slightly sticky; if not, add more flour or water as needed. **If using a stand mixer,** put the pre-dough pieces and all of the other ingredients except the extra flour into the mixer with the paddle attachment (preferable) or dough hook. Mix on slow speed for 1 minute to bring the ingredients together into a ball. Switch to the dough hook if need be and mix on medium-low speed, occasionally scraping down the bowl, for 2 to 3 minutes, until the pre-doughs become cohesive and assimilated into each other. Add more flour or water as needed until the dough is soft and slightly sticky.

3. **Proceed as in steps 3 through 7** in the whole wheat hearth bread on page 155.

Transitional Multigrain Hearth Bread

Makes 1 loaf

This is a variation on basic country hearth bread (*pain de campagne*) with a wonderful flavor. Because it contains a fair amount of bread flour, it bakes up a little taller and airier than the 100% version, and is a good way to introduce newcomers to whole grains.

SOAKER

VOLUME	OUNCES	GRAMS	INGREDIENT	%
7 tablespoons	2	56.5	whole wheat flour	25
1/2 cup	2	56.5	rolled oats	25
7 tablespoons	2	56.5	cornmeal	25
5 1/4 tablespoons	1.5	42.5	whole rye flour	19
2 1/4 teaspoons	.25	7	flaxseeds, whole or ground	3
1 tablespoon	.25	7	oat bran	3
or 2 tablespoons	.25	7	or wheat bran	
1/2 teaspoon	.14	4	salt	1.75
3/4 cup	6	170	water	75
TOTAL	14.14	400		176.75

1. **Mix all of the soaker ingredients together** in a bowl for about 1 minute, until all of the flour is hydrated and the ingredients form a thick, porridge-like dough.

2. **Cover loosely with plastic wrap** and leave at room temperature for 12 to 24 hours. (If it will be more than 24 hours, place the soaker in the refrigerator; it will be good for up to 3 days. Remove it 2 hours before mixing the final dough to take off the chill.)

BREAD PROFILE

Lean dough; delayed fermentation method; commercial yeast

DAYS TO MAKE: 2

Day 1: Soaker and *biga*, 20 minutes set up and mix; overnight autolyse
Day 2: 2 hours to de-chill *biga*; 12 to 15 minutes mixing; 2 to 3 hours fermentation, shaping, proofing; 40 to 60 minutes baking

COMMENTARY

The total weight of the grains in the soaker, including any cooked grains, should be 6 ounces (excluding the 2 ounces of whole wheat flour, which is needed to provide sufficient gluten to support the structure of the bread). It is especially important to weigh these grains as the volume needed can vary substantially depending on the grains used. The volume measure provided is an approximation, but one that will get you pretty close if you don't have a scale. As you make this bread again, you can increase or decrease the grain amounts, as determined from the first batch.

Smaller or softer grains may be used uncooked, such as amaranth, rolled oats, oat bran, triticale flakes, multigrain cereal blends, and any type of flour or meal. It is best to precook larger or harder grains, such as barley, buckwheat, bulgur, couscous, cracked wheat, grits, millet, quinoa, rice, steel-cut oats, and whole wheat berries or rye berries. See page 102 for cooking instructions.

BIGA

VOLUME	OUNCES	GRAMS	INGREDIENT	%
1³/₄ cups	8	227	unbleached bread flour	100
¹/₄ teaspoon	.03	1	instant yeast	.4
¹/₂ cup plus 2 tablespoons	5	142	filtered or spring water, at room temperature (about 70°F/21°C)	62.5
TOTAL	13.03	370		162.9

1. **Mix all of the *biga* ingredients together** in a bowl to form a ball of dough. Using wet hands, knead the dough in the bowl for 2 minutes to be sure all of the ingredients are evenly distributed and the flour is fully hydrated. The dough should feel very tacky. Let the dough rest for 5 minutes, then knead it again with wet hands for 1 minute. The dough will become smoother but still be tacky.

2. **Transfer the dough to a clean bowl, cover** tightly with plastic wrap, and refrigerate for at least 8 hours and up to 3 days.

FAQ ∽ *If a type of grain or flour that I want to use isn't listed in a recipe, can I still use it?*

Usually, yes. Determine whether or not it needs to be precooked, or if it will soften sufficiently in the soaker. Only wheat and rye flour have enough gluten to sustain any kind of lift, so the amount of other grains the dough can contain and still rise nicely is limited. However, some people prefer denser breads. There is no rule that says you have to stay with the ratios suggested in this book. The only rule is that the spirit of the law takes precedent over the letter of the law (Theology 101).

FAQ ∽ *What about spelt and Kamut, can they be used as substitutes for wheat?*

These are both in the wheat family, but they do perform differently than regular red or white wheat. You should be able to substitute these flours, but the breads will, of course, perform differently. The crumb will be tighter and you may need to increase the hydration, but yes, any bread in this book that calls for wheat flour can be made with whole spelt or Kamut, alone or in combination with whole wheat flour. For this reason, I have not written out any specific spelt or Kamut bread formulas. The method is the same and the choice of flour is yours, but remember the mantra: Let the dough tell you what it needs in terms of adjustments to amounts of flour and liquids.

3. **About 2 hours before mixing the final dough, remove** the *biga* from the refrigerator to take off the chill. It will have risen slightly but need not have risen significantly in order to use it in the final dough.

FINAL DOUGH

VOLUME	OUNCES	GRAMS	INGREDIENT
Use all	14.14	400	soaker
Use all	13.03	370	*biga*
7 tablespoons	2	56.5	whole wheat flour
⁵⁄₈ teaspoon	.18	5	salt
2¹⁄₄ teaspoons	.25	7	instant yeast
3 tablespoons	1	28.5	sunflower seeds, toasted (optional)
3 tablespoons	1	28.5	pumpkin seeds, toasted (optional)
3 tablespoons	1	28.5	sesame seeds (optional)
			extra whole wheat flour for adjustments
TOTAL	32.6	924	

BAKER'S FORMULA	%
Whole wheat flour	22
Bread flour	44.5
Multigrain mix	33.5
Salt	1.8
Instant yeast	1.6
Water	61
Seeds	16.5
Total	180.9

NUTRITION FACTS	
Calories (kcal)	104.43
Protein (g)	3.79
Carbohydrates (g)	17.27
Dietary fiber (g)	2.07
Total sugars (g)	.13
Fat (g)	2.50
Saturated fat (g)	.28
Trans fatty acid (g)	0
Cholesterol (mg)	0
Sodium (mg)	159.29

1. **Using a metal pastry scraper, chop** the soaker and the *biga* into 12 smaller pieces each (sprinkle some of the extra flour over the pre-doughs to keep the pieces from sticking back to each other).

2. **If mixing by hand,** combine the soaker and *biga* pieces in a bowl with all of the other ingredients except the extra flour and stir vigorously with a mixing spoon or knead with wet hands for about 2 minutes, until all of the ingredients are evenly integrated and distributed into the dough. The dough should be soft and slightly sticky; if not, add more flour or water as needed. **If using a stand mixer,** put the pre-dough pieces and all of the other ingredients except the extra flour into the mixer with the paddle attachment (preferable) or dough hook. Mix on slow speed for 1 minute to bring the ingredients together into a ball. Switch to the dough hook if need be and mix on medium-low speed, occasionally scraping down the bowl, for 3 to 4 minutes, until the pre-doughs become cohesive and assimilated into each other. Add more flour or water as needed until the dough is soft and slightly sticky.

3. **Proceed as in steps 3 through 7** in the whole wheat hearth bread on page 155.

Adding the optional 3 ounces of seeds to the final dough will enhance the bread's nutritional profile, particularly the protein content.

High-Extraction Flour Miche

Makes 1 large or 2 small loaves

BREAD PROFILE

Lean dough; delayed fermentation method; mixed leavening method

DAYS TO MAKE: 2

Day 1: Soaker and starter, 20 minutes set up and mix, 4 to 6 hours starter fermentation; overnight autolyse

Day 2: 2 hours to de-chill starter; 12 to 15 minutes mixing; 2 to 3 hours fermentation, shaping, proofing; 50 to 75 minutes baking

COMMENTARY

You may have difficulty obtaining high-extraction flour in small quantities. You may, however, be able to coax 5 or 10 pounds of it from a local artisan baker. Otherwise, here are two acceptable substitutions: Try sifting coarse whole wheat flour through a sieve or sifter that filters out about 15% of the total (you can weigh it before and after). Finely milled whole wheat flour will completely pass through most sieves; that's why it is necessary to use a coarse grind. The other option is to blend about 25% bread flour with 75% whole wheat flour (in other words, about 1 part bread flour to 3 parts whole wheat). It may not be an exact match, but in this formula it will perform similarly to the high-extraction flour.

This is a delayed fermentation version of the famous 2-kilo Poilâne breads of France, although our finished loaf, weighing in at 3 pounds, is only about three-fourths the size of a true *pain Poilâne*. Nevertheless, it is still quite impressive looking when it emerges from a home oven. This type of bread is properly made with high-extraction flour, which uses about 85% of the whole wheat kernel (the extraction rate of most white flour is closer to 72% to 75%). High-extraction flour is higher in ash and fiber than white flour is, but not as high as whole wheat flour; thus, it offers an interesting balance of white flour performance and whole grain nutrition.

Our version uses a higher percentage of starter than the true Poilâne versions, and it also uses commercial yeast, something neither Lionel nor his brother Max Poilâne would ever put into their dough. However, because of the delayed fermentation method, it produces a similar result. If you prefer to omit the yeast, the dough will take about three times longer to rise and will develop an intense tang, but feel free to try it this way if you like very sour breads.

SOAKER

VOLUME	OUNCES	GRAMS	INGREDIENT	%
3½ cups	16	454	high-extraction flour (see Commentary)	100
1⅛ teaspoons	.3	8.5	salt	1.9
1¼ cups plus 2 tablespoons	11	312	water	69
TOTAL	27.3	775		170.9

1. **Mix all of the soaker ingredients together** in a bowl for about 1 minute, until all of the flour is hydrated and the ingredients form a ball of dough.

2. **Cover loosely with plastic wrap** and leave at room temperature for 12 to 24 hours. (If it will be more than 24 hours, place the soaker in the refrigerator; it will be good for up to 3 days. Remove it 2 hours before mixing the final dough to take off the chill.)

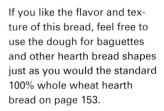

If you like the flavor and texture of this bread, feel free to use the dough for baguettes and other hearth bread shapes just as you would the standard 100% whole wheat hearth bread on page 153.

STARTER

VOLUME	OUNCES	GRAMS	INGREDIENT	%
6½ tablespoons	3	85	whole wheat mother starter (page 67)	33.3
2 cups	9	255	high-extraction flour (see Commentary)	100
¾ cup	6	170	filtered or spring water, at room temperature (about 70°F/21°C)	67
TOTAL	18	510		200.3

1. **Mix all of the starter ingredients together** in a bowl to form a ball of dough. Using wet hands, knead the dough in the bowl for about 2 minutes to be sure all of the ingredients are evenly distributed and the flour is fully hydrated. The dough should feel very tacky. Let the dough rest for about 5 minutes, then knead it again with wet hands for 1 minute. The dough will become smoother but still be tacky.

2. **Transfer the dough to a clean bowl, cover** loosely with plastic wrap, and leave at room temperature for approximately 4 to 6 hours, until the dough is nearly double in size. The dough should register between 3.5 and 4.0 if tested with pH paper (see page 77) and have a pleasant aroma similar to apple cider vinegar. If the starter has not doubled or acidified properly, allow it to continue to develop at room temperature. It could take up to 8 hours or even longer.

3. **When the starter has fully developed, knead** it for a few seconds to degas it. The starter is now ready for mixing into the final dough; however, if necessary to coordinate timing with the soaker, cover tightly with plastic wrap and refrigerate overnight (or up to 3 days). About 2 hours before mixing the final dough, remove the starter from the refrigerator to take off the chill.

This version is too large for most home mixers, so the instructions will be for hand mixing. However, if you have a mixer large enough to handle a 3-pound ball of dough, feel free to use it.

FINAL DOUGH

VOLUME	OUNCES	GRAMS	INGREDIENT
Use all	27.3	775	soaker
Use all	18	510	starter
7 tablespoons	2	56.5	high-extraction flour (see Commentary)
⅞ teaspoon	.25	7	salt
2¼ teaspoons	.25	7	instant yeast
			extra high-extraction flour for adjustments
TOTAL	47.8	1355.5	

1. **Using a metal pastry scraper, chop** the soaker and the starter into 12 smaller pieces each (sprinkle some of the extra flour over the pre-doughs to keep the pieces from sticking back to each other).

2. **Combine the soaker and starter pieces in a bowl** with all of the other ingredients except the extra flour and stir vigorously with a mixing spoon or knead with wet hands for about 2 minutes, until all of the ingredients are evenly integrated and distributed into the dough. The dough should be soft and slightly sticky; if not, add more flour or water as needed.

3. **Dust a work surface with flour,** then roll the dough in the flour to coat. Knead by hand for 3 to 4 minutes, incorporating only as much extra flour as needed, until the dough feels soft and tacky, but not sticky. Form the dough into a ball and let it rest on the work surface for 5 minutes while you prepare a clean, lightly oiled bowl.

4. **Resume kneading the dough for 1 minute** to strengthen the gluten and make any final flour or water adjustments. The dough should have strength and substance when fully kneaded and pass the windowpane test (see page 84), yet still feel soft, supple, and very tacky. Form the dough into a ball and place it in the prepared bowl, rolling to coat with oil. Cover loosely with plastic wrap and let rise at room temperature for approximately 45 to 60 minutes, until it is about $1^1/_2$ times its original size.

5. **Carefully transfer the dough** to a lightly floured work surface with a plastic bowl scraper (try not to rip or tear the dough), then gently form it in into a *boule*, as shown on page 89, being careful to degas the dough as little as possible when shaping it. Transfer the dough, top side down, to a floured *banneton* or a bowl lined with a cloth and dusted with flour. Mist the dough with pan spray or dust it with flour, cover loosely with a cloth towel or plastic wrap, and let rise at room temperature for approximately 45 to 60 minutes, until it has grown to $1^1/_2$ times its original size.

BAKER'S FORMULA	%
High-extraction or sifted whole wheat flour	100
Salt	2
Instant yeast	.9
Water	65
Total	**167.9**

NUTRITION FACTS	
Calories (kcal)	86.77
Protein (g)	3.44
Carbohydrates (g)	18.25
Dietary fiber (g)	2.60
Total sugars (g)	.10
Fat (g)	.47
Saturated fat (g)	.08
Trans fatty acid (g)	0
Cholesterol (mg)	0
Sodium (mg)	199.06

FAQ ∾ *What kind of salt is best?*

Salt (sodium chloride) is essential for most breads (except Tuscan bread and a few others—there are always exceptions to the rules). The type of salt does not matter unless you are measuring it by volume rather than weight. Be aware that 1 teaspoon of table salt is not the same weight as 1 teaspoon of kosher or sea salt, and even the two main brands of kosher salt do not weigh the same. The volume measurement given in these formulas is for table salt grind. If you are using a coarser salt, you may have to increase the amount, but there is no single rule because there are so many types. Make note in the book as to whether your first breads seem properly salted, and adjust accordingly when baking thereafter. Some bakers prefer not to use iodized salt because they feel it is adulterated and affects the flavor of the bread, but I have not found this to be the case.

(A) Just prior to baking, gently transfer the dough from the proofing basket or bowl onto a floured peel or the back of a floured sheet pan. (B) Using a blade (*lame*) or serrated knife, score the loaf about ¹/₂ inch deep. If using a blade, keep the back end up so that it does not drag through and tear the dough. If using a knife, do not exert excessive downward force; let the knife do the work. (C) There are many pattern options when scoring a miche or boule—square, pound sign, asterisk, sunburst, or parallel lines.

6. **Preheat the oven to 500°F (260°C)** and prepare it for hearth baking (see page 86), including a steam pan. When the dough is ready to bake, carefully transfer it, turning it right side up, to a floured peel or other transfer tool, then score it (a square, with the four lines toward the edge of the loaf as shown above, is traditional). Slide the loaf onto the baking surface or bake it on a prepared sheet pan. Pour 1 cup of hot water into the steam pan, lower the oven temperature to 425°F (218°C), and bake for approximately 25 minutes. Rotate the loaf 180 degrees and continue baking for another 25 to 40 minutes, until the dough has reached at least 200°F (93°C) in the center, rotating the loaf as needed to ensure it bakes evenly. The crust should be hard and a rich chestnut brown, and the loaf should sound hollow when thumped on the bottom. If the crust is dark but the loaf still feels soft, turn off the oven and leave the bread in for another 5 to 10 minutes. You can also cover the loaf loosely with aluminum foil to prevent it from burning. If the bottom crust seems to be baking faster than the top crust and is at risk of burning, place an inverted sheet pan under it to serve as a heat buffer.

7. **Transfer the bread to a cooling rack** and allow it to cool for at least 2 hours before serving.

Three Rye Hearth Bread Variations

These breads represent only a fraction of all the rye variations that are possible, especially when you consider adding other types of flour, flavorings, or seeds. You can adjust the ratio of wheat to rye to whatever proportion you wish once you have mastered the basic process. My suggestion is to begin with the 45% (*meteil*) version and work up to the 68% (*seigle*) and, ultimately, to the 100% rye.

BREAD PROFILE

Lean or slightly enriched dough; delayed fermentation method; mixed leavening method

DAYS TO MAKE: 2

Day 1: Soaker and starter, 20 minutes set up and mix, 4 to 6 hours starter fermentation; overnight autolyse

Day 2: 2 hours to de-chill starter; 12 to 15 minutes mixing; 2 to 3 hours fermentation, shaping, proofing; 40 to 60 minutes baking

COMMENTARY

All three variations use a wild yeast starter instead of a *biga*. Rye flour contains more enzymes than wheat, and if unchecked, heightened enzyme activity can damage the structural integrity of the dough. The acidity of the starter will control the enzymes, protecting the starches in the dough from enzyme attacks during the bake.

The amount of water needed may vary depending on the type of rye flour you use. For this reason, the amount of water indicated in these formulas should be considered approximate; be prepared to adjust as needed by adding more flour or water during the final mix.

VARIATION ONE: 45% RYE HEARTH BREAD

Makes 1 loaf

SOAKER

VOLUME	OUNCES	GRAMS	INGREDIENT	%
1³/₄ cups	8	227	whole wheat flour	100
¹/₂ teaspoon	.14	4	salt	1.75
³/₄ cup	6	170	water	75
TOTAL	14.14	401		176.75

1. **Mix all of the soaker ingredients together** in a bowl for about 1 minute, until all of the flour is hydrated and the ingredients form a ball of dough.

2. **Cover loosely with plastic wrap** and leave at room temperature for 12 to 24 hours. (If it will be more than 24 hours, place the soaker in the refrigerator; it will be good for up to 3 days. Remove it 2 hours before mixing the final dough to take off the chill.)

STARTER

VOLUME	OUNCES	GRAMS	INGREDIENT	%
¹/₃ cup	2.5	71	whole wheat or rye mother starter (pages 67 and 69)	33.3
1²/₃ cups	7.5	213	whole rye flour	100
³/₄ cup	6	170	filtered or spring water, at room temperature (about 70°F/21°C)	80
TOTAL	16	454		213.3

1. **Mix all of the starter ingredients together** in a bowl to form a ball of dough. Using wet hands, knead the dough in the bowl for about 2 minutes to be sure all of the ingredients are evenly distributed and the flour is fully hydrated. The dough should feel very tacky. Let the dough rest for about 5 minutes, then knead it again with wet hands for 1 minute. The dough will become smoother but still be tacky.

2. **Transfer the dough to a clean bowl, cover** loosely with plastic wrap, and leave at room temperature for approximately 4 to 6 hours, until the dough is nearly double in size. The dough should register between 3.5 and 4.0 if tested with pH paper (see page 77) and have a pleasant aroma similar to apple cider vinegar. If the starter has not doubled or acidified properly, allow it to continue to develop at room temperature. It could take up to 8 hours or even longer.

3. **When the starter has fully developed, knead** it for a few seconds to degas it. The starter is now ready for mixing into the final dough; however, if necessary to coordinate timing with the soaker, cover tightly with plastic wrap and refrigerate overnight (or up to 3 days). About 2 hours before mixing the final dough, remove the starter from the refrigerator to take off the chill.

FINAL DOUGH

VOLUME	OUNCES	GRAMS	INGREDIENT
Use all	14.14	401	soaker
Use all	16	454	starter
7 tablespoons	2	56.5	whole wheat or whole rye flour, or a combination
5/8 teaspoon	.18	5	salt
2 1/4 teaspoons	.25	7	instant yeast
2 1/4 teaspoons	.5	14	honey, molasses, or sorghum syrup (optional)
1 tablespoon	.5	14	unsalted butter, melted, or vegetable oil (optional)
2 teaspoons	2	7	caraway seeds, nigella seeds, anise seeds, or dried minced onions (optional)
			extra whole wheat or rye flour for adjustments
TOTAL	35.57	958.5	

1. **Using a metal pastry scraper, chop** the soaker and the starter into 12 smaller pieces each (sprinkle some of the extra flour over the pre-doughs to keep the pieces from sticking back to each other).

2. **If mixing by hand,** combine the soaker and starter pieces in a bowl with all of the other ingredients except the extra flour and stir vigorously with a mixing spoon or knead with wet hands for about 2 minutes, until all of the ingredients are evenly integrated and distributed into the dough. The dough should be soft and slightly sticky; if not, add more flour or water as needed. **If using a stand mixer,** put the pre-dough pieces and all of the other ingredients except the extra flour into the mixer with the paddle attachment (preferable) or dough hook. Mix on slow speed for 1 minute to bring the ingredients together into a ball. Switch to the dough hook if need be and mix on medium-low speed, occasionally scraping down the bowl, for 2 to 3 minutes, until the pre-doughs become cohesive and assimilated into each other. Add more flour or water as needed until the dough is soft and slightly sticky.

3. **Dust a work surface with flour,** then roll the dough in the flour to coat. Knead by hand for 3 to 4 minutes, incorporating only as much extra flour as needed, until the dough feels soft

BAKER'S FORMULA	%
Whole wheat flour	55
Whole rye flour	45
Salt	1.7
Instant yeast	1.5
Water	70
Honey	2.7
Unsalted butter or oil	2.7
Total	178.6

NUTRITION FACTS	
Calories (kcal)	93.65
Protein (g)	3.12
Carbohydrates (g)	18.64
Dietary fiber (g)	3.16
Total sugars (g)	.56
Fat (g)	1.11
Saturated fat (g)	.12
Trans fatty acid (g)	0
Cholesterol (mg)	0
Sodium (mg)	163.75

and tacky, but not sticky. Form the dough into a ball and let it rest on the work surface for 5 minutes while you prepare a clean, lightly oiled bowl.

4. **Resume kneading the dough by hand for 1 minute** to strengthen the gluten and make any final flour or water adjustments. The dough should have strength and pass the windowpane test (see page 84), yet still feel soft, supple, and very tacky. Form the dough into a ball and place it in the prepared bowl, rolling to coat with oil. Cover loosely with plastic wrap and let rise at room temperature for approximately 45 to 60 minutes, until it is about 1 1/2 times its original size.

5. **Transfer the dough to a lightly floured work surface** and form it into either 1 or 2 free-standing *bâtards* (see page 88 for shaping instructions). Mist the top of the dough with pan spray (optional), cover loosely with plastic wrap, and let rise at room temperature for approximately 45 to 60 minutes, until it has grown to 1 1/2 times its original size.

6. **Preheat the oven to 475°F (246°C)** and prepare it for hearth baking (page 86), including a steam pan. When the dough is ready to bake, place it in the oven, pour 1 cup of hot water into the steam pan, lower the temperature to 425°F (218°C), and bake for 20 minutes. Rotate the bread 180 degrees and continue baking for another 20 to 30 minutes, until the loaf is a rich brown on all sides, sounds hollow when thumped on the bottom, and registers at least 200°F (93°C) in the center.

7. **Transfer the bread to a cooling rack** and allow it to cool for at least 1 hour before serving.

FAQ ∽ *Can I grind my own flour?*

Absolutely! If you are fortunate enough to have your own mill, you cannot get flour any fresher, and this translates into better flavor. Jennifer Lapidus, for instance, insists that the key to the amazing flavor of her *desem* bread is that she mills the flour the same day she makes the dough. Great Harvest Bread Company built its reputation on milling their flour fresh each day, right in the bakery. Another advantage to milling your own flour is that you can control the coarseness of the grind, giving you a number of options for creating textures in your breads.

The quality of the wheat and any other grains you use is obviously important, and one issue that home millers run into is wheat consistency, especially when buying wheat kernels from a bin at a local market. Every growing season endows the wheat with different qualities, so if you find that the dough is performing differently than it previously did, you may have to make adjustments in hydration or mixing time. Most wheat is performance tested before it is sold to the public, but that does not mean it will always be the same. The falling number could be different if the starch damage was affected by weather or other conditions. The protein quality could be different from season to season. Or the retailer may have switched suppliers. As always, let the dough dictate what it needs as you mix it; most of the time, you will be able to adjust for differences in the wheat.

VARIATION TWO: 68% RYE HEARTH BREAD

Makes 1 loaf

SOAKER

VOLUME	OUNCES	GRAMS	INGREDIENT	%
³/₄ cup plus 2 tablespoons	4	113	whole wheat flour	50
³/₄ cup plus 2 tablespoons	4	113	whole rye flour	50
¹/₂ teaspoon	.14	4	salt	1.75
³/₄ cup	6	170	water	75
1 tablespoon	.25	7	vital wheat gluten (optional)	3
TOTAL	14.39	408		179.75

1. **Mix all of the soaker ingredients together** in a bowl for about 1 minute, until all of the flour is hydrated and the ingredients form a ball of dough.

2. **Cover loosely with plastic wrap** and leave at room temperature for 12 to 24 hours. (If it will be more than 24 hours, place the soaker in the refrigerator; it will be good for up to 3 days. Remove it 2 hours before mixing the final dough to take off the chill.)

STARTER

VOLUME	OUNCES	GRAMS	INGREDIENT	%
¹/₃ cup	2.5	71	whole wheat or rye mother starter (pages 67 and 69)	33.3
1²/₃ cups	7.5	213	whole rye flour	100
³/₄ cup	6	170	filtered or spring water, at room temperature (about 70°F/21°C)	80
TOTAL	16	454		213.3

1. **Mix all of the starter ingredients together** in a bowl to form a ball of dough. Using wet hands, knead the dough in the bowl for about 2 minutes to be sure all of the ingredients are evenly distributed and the flour is fully hydrated. The dough should feel very tacky. Let the dough rest for about 5 minutes, then knead it again with wet hands for 1 minute. The dough will become smoother but still be tacky.

BAKER'S FORMULA	%
Whole rye flour	68
Whole wheat flour	32
Salt	1.7
Instant yeast	1.3
Water	67
Honey	2.5
Unsalted butter or oil	2.5
Vital wheat gluten	1.3
Total	176.3

NUTRITION FACTS	
Fat (g)	1.07
Saturated fat (g)	.10
Trans fatty acid (g)	0
Cholesterol (mg)	0
Sodium (mg)	157.36
Calories (kcal)	97.85
Protein (g)	3.04
Carbohydrates (g)	19.30
Dietary fiber (g)	3.28
Total sugars (g)	.51

2. **Transfer the dough to a clean bowl, cover** loosely with plastic wrap, and leave at room temperature for approximately 4 to 6 hours, until the dough is nearly double in size. The dough should register between 3.5 and 4.0 if tested with pH paper (see page 77) and have a pleasant aroma similar to apple cider vinegar. If the starter has not doubled or acidified properly, allow it to continue to develop at room temperature. It could take up to 8 hours or even longer.

3. **When the starter has fully developed, knead** it for a few seconds to degas it. The starter is now ready for mixing into the final dough; however, if necessary to coordinate timing with the soaker, cover tightly with plastic wrap and refrigerate overnight (or up to 3 days). About 2 hours before mixing the final dough, remove the starter from the refrigerator to take off the chill.

FINAL DOUGH

VOLUME	OUNCES	GRAMS	INGREDIENT
Use all	14.39	408	soaker
Use all	16	454	starter
2/3 cup	3	85	whole wheat or whole rye flour, or a combination
5/8 teaspoon	.18	5	salt
2¼ teaspoons	.25	7	instant yeast
2¼ teaspoons	.5	14	honey, molasses, or sorghum syrup (optional)
1 tablespoon	.5	14	unsalted butter, melted, or vegetable oil (optional)
2 teaspoons	2	7	caraway seeds, nigella seeds, anise seeds, or dried minced onions (optional)
			extra whole wheat or rye flour for adjustments
TOTAL	36.82	994	

1. **Using a metal pastry scraper, chop** the soaker and the starter into 12 smaller pieces each (sprinkle some of the extra flour over the pre-doughs to keep the pieces from sticking back to each other).

2. **If mixing by hand,** combine the soaker and starter pieces in a bowl with all of the other ingredients except the extra flour and stir vigorously with a mixing spoon or knead with wet hands for about 2 minutes, until all of the ingredients are evenly integrated and distributed into the dough. The dough should be soft and slightly sticky; if not, add more flour or water as needed. **If using a stand mixer,** put the pre-dough pieces and all of the other ingredients except the extra flour into the mixer with the paddle attachment (preferable) or dough hook. Mix on slow speed for 1 minute to bring the ingredients together into a ball. Switch to the dough hook

if need be and mix on medium-low speed, occasionally scraping down the bowl, for 2 to 3 minutes, until the pre-doughs become cohesive and assimilated into each other. Add some of the extra flour or more water as needed until the dough is soft and slightly sticky.

3. **Proceed as in steps 3 through 7** in the 45% rye hearth bread on page 171.

VARIATION THREE: 100% RYE HEARTH BREAD

Makes 1 loaf

SOAKER

VOLUME	OUNCES	GRAMS	INGREDIENT	%
1³/₄ cups	8	227	whole rye flour	100
¹/₂ teaspoon	.14	4	salt	1.75
1 cup	8	227	water	100
4 teaspoons	.32	9	vital wheat gluten (optional)	4
TOTAL	16.46	467		205.75

COMMENTARY

It is tricky to make 100% rye breads because rye is low in gluten and has difficulty holding a rise. However, more hydration helps so this soaker has more water than previous rye formulas and other hearth breads. The trick is to use a lot of flour or cornmeal on the work surface during the final shaping, give the dough a short final rise, and start it off in a hotter oven than usual to achieve maximum oven spring.

୧ଓ

Vital wheat gluten will give this bread more lift. It would then, of course, not be a 100% rye bread, but nearly so. I suggest making it first without the gluten to see how you like it.

୧ଓ

The instructions call for a rye mother starter to make this as much a 100% rye bread as possible. You can also begin with a wheat mother starter (page 67) and elaborate it with whole rye flour, and only a very small fraction of whole wheat will remain in the final dough.

1. **Mix all of the soaker ingredients together** in a bowl for about 1 minute, until all of the flour is hydrated and the ingredients form a ball of dough.

2. **Cover loosely with plastic wrap** and leave at room temperature for 12 to 24 hours. (If it will be more than 24 hours, place the soaker in the refrigerator; it will be good for up to 3 days. Remove it 2 hours before mixing the final dough to take off the chill.)

STARTER

VOLUME	OUNCES	GRAMS	INGREDIENT	%
¹/₃ cup	2.5	71	rye mother starter (page 69; see Commentary)	33.3
1²/₃ cups	7.5	213	whole rye flour	100
³/₄ cup	6	170	filtered or spring water, at room temperature (about 70°F/21°C)	80
TOTAL	16	454		213.3

1. **Mix all of the starter ingredients together** in a bowl to form a ball of dough. Using wet hands, knead the dough in the bowl for about 2 minutes to be sure all of the ingredients are evenly distributed and the flour is fully hydrated. The dough should feel very tacky. Let the

dough rest for about 5 minutes, then knead it again with wet hands for 1 minute. The dough will become smoother but still be tacky.

2. **Transfer the dough to a clean bowl,** cover loosely with plastic wrap, and leave at room temperature for approximately 4 to 6 hours, until the dough is nearly double in size. The dough should register between 3.5 and 4.0 if tested with pH paper (see page 77) and have a pleasant aroma similar to apple cider vinegar. If the starter has not doubled or acidified properly, allow it to continue to develop at room temperature. It could take up to 8 hours or even longer.

3. **When the starter has fully developed,** knead it for a few seconds to degas it. The starter is now ready for mixing into the final dough; however, if necessary to coordinate timing with the soaker, cover tightly with plastic wrap and refrigerate overnight (or up to 3 days). About 2 hours before mixing the final dough, remove the starter from the refrigerator to take off the chill.

This dough is soft enough that the paddle attachment can be used from start to finish if you are using a stand mixer. The dough hook will also work, but you will have to stop to scrape down the bowl from time to time.

FINAL DOUGH

VOLUME	OUNCES	GRAMS	INGREDIENT
Use all	16.46	467	soaker
Use all	16	454	starter
3/4 cup plus 2 tablespoons	4	113	whole rye flour
5/8 teaspoon	.18	5	salt
2 1/4 teaspoons	.25	7	instant yeast
2 teaspoons	2	7	caraway seeds, nigella seeds, anise seeds, or dried minced onions (optional)
			extra whole rye flour for adjustments
TOTAL	38.89	1053	

1. **Using a metal pastry scraper, chop** the soaker and the starter into 12 smaller pieces each (sprinkle some of the extra flour over the pre-doughs to keep the pieces from sticking back to each other).

2. **If mixing by hand,** combine the soaker and starter pieces in a bowl with all of the other ingredients except the extra flour and stir vigorously with a mixing spoon or knead with wet hands for about 2 minutes, until all of the ingredients are evenly integrated and distributed into the dough. The dough should be soft and slightly sticky; if not, add more flour or water

as needed. **If using a stand mixer,** put the pre-dough pieces and all of the other ingredients except the extra flour into the mixer with the paddle attachment (preferable) or dough hook. Mix on slow speed for 1 minute to bring the ingredients together into a ball. Switch to the dough hook if need be and mix on medium-low speed, occasionally scraping down the bowl, for 3 minutes, until the pre-doughs become cohesive and assimilated into each other. Add more flour or water as needed until the dough is soft and slightly sticky.

3. **Dust a work surface with flour,** then roll the dough in the flour to coat. Knead the dough by hand for 3 to 4 minutes, incorporating only as much extra flour as needed, until the dough feels very sticky yet lively, like modeling clay. Form the dough into a ball and let it rest on the work surface for 5 minutes while you prepare a clean, lightly oiled bowl.

4. **Resume kneading the dough for 1 minute** to strengthen the gluten and make any final flour or water adjustments. The dough should have strength but it will not necessarily pass the windowpane test (see page 84). It will be slightly sticky. Form the dough into a ball, roll in rye flour to coat, and place in the prepared bowl. Cover loosely with plastic wrap and let rise at room temperature for approximately 45 to 60 minutes, until it is about $1^1/_2$ times its original size.

5. **Prepare a sheet pan** by covering it with either parchment paper or a silicon mat and dusting with a generous portion (about $^1/_4$ cup) of coarse whole rye flour or cornmeal, or a combination of the two. Mist the work surface with water or wipe it with a damp towel, then transfer the dough to the work surface and form it into either 1 or 2 freestanding *bâtards* or *boules* (see pages 87–91 for shaping instructions). Place the dough on the baking sheet and roll them in the flour to coat the entire surface. Mist the top of the dough with pan spray (optional), cover loosely with plastic wrap or a cloth towel, and let rise at room temperature for approximately 30 minutes, until it has swelled in size (but not to $1^1/_2$ times its original size).

6. **Preheat the oven to 500°F (260°C)** and prepare it for hearth baking (see page 86), including a steam pan. When the dough is ready to bake, place the pan in the oven, pour 1 cup of hot water into the steam pan, lower the temperature to 425°F (218°C), and bake for 20 minutes. If the dough blisters and big air pockets form near the surface, poke them with a skewer or knife. Rotate the pan 180 degrees and continue baking for another 20 to 30 minutes, until the bread is a rich brown on all sides, sounds hollow when thumped on the bottom, and registers at least 200°F (93°C) in the center. When the bread appears to be fully baked, turn off the oven and leave it in for another 5 to 10 minutes.

7. **Transfer the bread to a cooling rack** and allow it to cool for at least 2 hours before serving. For the best flavor, wrap the cooled loaves in aluminum foil and serve the next day.

BAKER'S FORMULA	%
Whole rye flour	100
Salt	1.8
Instant yeast	1.4
Water	86
Vital wheat gluten	1.8
Total	191

NUTRITION FACTS	
Calories (kcal)	91.61
Protein (g)	2.82
Carbohydrates (g)	18.83
Dietary fiber (g)	3.32
Total sugars (g)	0
Fat (g)	.42
Saturated fat (g)	.01
Trans fatty acid (g)	0
Cholesterol (mg)	0
Sodium (mg)	172.13

Transitional Rye Hearth Meteil

Makes 1 large or 4 small loaves

BREAD PROFILE

Lean dough; delayed fermentation method; commercial yeast or
mixed leavening method

DAYS TO MAKE: 2

Day 1: Soaker and *biga*, 20 minutes
set up and mix; overnight autolyse
Day 2: 2 hours to de-chill *biga*; 12
to 15 minutes mixing; 2 to 3 hours
fermentation, shaping, proofing;
40 to 60 minutes baking

COMMENTARY

Because it contains less than
50% rye flour, the dough can
be made with a *biga* instead of
a wild yeast starter. However,
feel free to substitute an equal
amount of white sourdough
starter (page 182) in place of
the *biga*, in which case you
should replace the 7 ounces of
buttermilk in the soaker with
6 ounces of water.

This makes a classic farmer-style rye bread, similar to those found throughout eastern Europe. Several optional ingredients are listed for the final dough—seeds, orange or lemon zest, and molasses or sorghum syrup. By experimenting with these options, you can create breads with a wide range of flavors and personalities.

SOAKER

VOLUME	OUNCES	GRAMS	INGREDIENT	%
1 1/3 cups	6	170	whole rye flour	75
7 tablespoons	2	56.5	whole wheat flour	25
1/2 teaspoon	.14	4	salt	1.75
3/4 cup plus 2 tablespoons	7	198	buttermilk or yogurt	87.5
TOTAL	15.14	428.5		189.25

1. **Mix all of the soaker ingredients together** in a bowl for about 1 minute, until all of the flour is hydrated and the ingredients form a ball of dough.

2. **Cover loosely with plastic wrap** and leave at room temperature for 12 to 24 hours. (If it will be more than 24 hours, place the soaker in the refrigerator; it will be good for up to 3 days. Remove it 2 hours before mixing the final dough to take off the chill.)

BIGA

VOLUME	OUNCES	GRAMS	INGREDIENT	%
1 3/4 cups	8	227	unbleached bread flour	100
1/4 teaspoon	.03	1	instant yeast	.4
1/2 cup plus 2 tablespoons	5	142	filtered or spring water, at room temperature (about 70°F/21°C)	62.5
TOTAL	13.03	370		162.9

1. **Mix all of the *biga* ingredients together** in a bowl to form a ball of dough. Using wet hands, knead the dough in the bowl for 2 minutes to be sure all of the ingredients are evenly

distributed and the flour is fully hydrated. The dough should feel very tacky. Let the dough rest for 5 minutes, then knead it again with wet hands for 1 minute. The dough will become smoother but still be tacky.

2. **Transfer the dough to a clean bowl,** cover tightly with plastic wrap, and refrigerate for at least 8 hours and up to 3 days.

3. **About 2 hours before mixing the final dough,** remove the *biga* from the refrigerator to take off the chill. It will have risen slightly but need not have risen significantly in order to use it in the final dough.

FINAL DOUGH

VOLUME	OUNCES	GRAMS	INGREDIENT
Use all	15.14	428.5	soaker
Use all	13.03	370	*biga*
7 tablespoons	2	56.5	whole wheat or whole rye flour, or a combination
5/8 teaspoon	.18	5	salt
2 1/4 teaspoons	.25	7	instant yeast
1 1/2 tablespoons	1	28.5	molasses or sorghum syrup (optional)
1 tablespoon	.32	9	caraway seeds, nigella seeds, or anise seeds
or 1 tablespoon	.12	3.5	or orange or lemon zest (optional)
			extra whole wheat or rye flour for adjustments
TOTAL	31.92	904.5	

Not everyone enjoys the flavor of molasses or sorghum syrup, and not every baker uses it in this type of bread. However, the flavors of molasses and rye complement one another nicely, and they are often used together in bread. If you use either, you will probably have to add extra flour during the final mix.

The suggested amount of seeds or orange or lemon zest in the final dough is just a rough guideline; you may wish to use more or less.

1. **Using a metal pastry scraper, chop** the soaker and the *biga* into 12 smaller pieces each (sprinkle some of the extra flour over the pre-doughs to keep the pieces from sticking back to each other).

2. **If mixing by hand,** combine the soaker and *biga* pieces in a bowl with all of the other ingredients except the extra flour and stir vigorously with a mixing spoon or knead with wet hands for about 2 minutes, until all of the ingredients are evenly integrated and distributed into the dough. The dough should be soft and slightly sticky; if not, add more flour or water as needed. **If using a stand mixer,** put the pre-dough pieces and all of the other ingredients except the extra flour into the mixer with the paddle attachment (preferable) or dough hook. Mix on slow speed for 1 minute to bring the ingredients together into a ball. Switch to the dough hook if need be and mix on medium-low speed, occasionally scraping down the bowl,

BAKER'S FORMULA	%
Bread flour	44.5
Whole wheat flour	22.5
Whole rye flour	33
Salt	1.8
Instant yeast	1.6
Buttermilk	39
Water	28
Molasses	5.5
Total	175.9

NUTRITION FACTS	
Calories (kcal)	94.53
Protein (g)	3.28
Carbohydrates (g)	19.27
Dietary fiber (g)	2.07
Total sugars (g)	1.24
Fat (g)	.51
Saturated fat (g)	.10
Trans fatty acid (g)	0
Cholesterol (mg)	.37
Sodium (mg)	176.14

for 2 to 3 minutes, until the pre-doughs become cohesive and assimilated into each other. Add more flour or water as needed until the dough is soft and slightly sticky.

3. **Dust a work surface with flour,** then roll the dough in the flour to coat. Knead the dough by hand for 3 to 4 minutes, incorporating only as much extra flour as needed, until the dough feels soft and tacky, but not sticky. Form the dough into a ball and let it rest on the work surface for 5 minutes while you prepare a clean, lightly oiled bowl.

4. **Resume kneading the dough for 1 minute** to strengthen the gluten and make any final flour or water adjustments. The dough should have strength and pass the windowpane test (see page 84), yet still feel soft, supple, and very tacky. Form the dough into a ball and place it in the prepared bowl, rolling to coat with oil. Cover loosely with plastic wrap and let rise at room temperature for approximately 45 to 60 minutes, until it is about $1^1/_2$ times its original size.

5. **Gently transfer the dough to a lightly floured work surface** with a plastic bowl scraper (try not to rip or tear the dough). Form the dough into a large *boule* or 2 to 4 *bâtards* (see pages 87–91 for shaping instructions), being careful to degas the dough as little as possible when shaping it. A *boule* can be proofed in a *banneton* or another prepared proofing bowl. For *bâtards,* raise the loaves on a proofing cloth or on a sheet pan lined with parchment paper and, if you like, dusted with flour. Mist the top of the dough with pan spray or dust with flour, cover loosely with a cloth towel or plastic wrap, and let rise at room temperature for approximately 45 minutes, until it has grown to $1^1/_2$ times its original size.

6. **Preheat the oven to 500°F (260°C)** and prepare it for hearth baking (see page 86), including a steam pan. When the dough is ready to bake, score it (as shown at left), place it in the oven (either with a peel or on a sheet pan), and pour 1 cup of hot water into the steam pan. Lower the temperature to 450°F (232°C) and bake for approximately 20 minutes. Rotate the bread 180 degrees and continue baking for another 20 to 30 minutes, until the crust is hard and a rich golden brown, the bread sounds hollow when thumped on the bottom, and the center registers at least 200°F (93°C). If the crust is dark but the bread still feels soft, turn off the oven and leave the bread in for another 5 to 10 minutes. You can also cover the bread loosely with aluminum foil to prevent it from burning.

7. **Transfer the bread to a cooling rack** and allow it to cool for at least 1 hour before serving.

Transitional Hearth Rye Seigle

Makes 1 loaf

A rye bread with more than 50% rye flour is called a *seigle*. In this version, we will use a rye soaker with a white sourdough starter. (On page 175, you will find a 100% rye hearth *seigle* that uses a whole rye starter.) A *biga* will not provide enough acidity to fully protect the starches against enzyme attacks in *seigle*-type breads, so the wild yeast starter is necessary to control the enzymes during baking.

If you want to try making this bread with a *biga* instead of a starter, use buttermilk in the soaker instead of water. The bread will still taste good, but it will probably shrink a little during baking and may have a tighter, gummier crumb. If you try this, consider adding 1/4 teaspoon of ascorbic acid to help prevent shrinking.

If you already have a white flour mother starter, you can use it instead of the converted whole wheat version provided here. However, it should be fairly stiff and low in hydration, about 63% water to flour. Otherwise, you will have to add a fair amount of additional flour during the final mixing, as the dough will be too wet to hold its shape.

SOAKER

VOLUME	OUNCES	GRAMS	INGREDIENT	%
2¼ cups	10	283	whole rye flour	100
⅝ teaspoon	.18	5	salt	1.8
1 cup	8	227	water	80
TOTAL	18.18	515		181.8

1. **Mix all of the soaker ingredients together** in a bowl for about 1 minute, until all of the flour is hydrated and the ingredients form a ball of dough.

2. **Cover loosely with plastic wrap** and leave at room temperature for 12 to 24 hours. (If it will be more than 24 hours, place the soaker in the refrigerator; it will be good for up to 3 days. Remove it 2 hours before mixing the final dough to take off the chill.)

STARTER

VOLUME	OUNCES	GRAMS	INGREDIENT	%
⅓ cup	2.5	71	whole wheat mother starter (page 67)	33
1⅔ cups	7.5	213	unbleached bread flour or high-gluten flour	100
½ cup plus 1½ tablespoons	4.75	135	filtered or spring water, at room temperature (about 70°F/21°C)	63
TOTAL	14.75	419		196

1. **Mix all of the starter ingredients together** in a bowl to form a ball of dough. Using wet hands, knead the dough in the bowl for about 2 minutes to be sure all of the ingredients are evenly distributed and the flour is fully hydrated. The dough should feel very tacky. Let the dough rest for about 5 minutes, then knead it again with wet hands for 1 minute. The dough will become smoother but still be tacky.

2. **Cover loosely with plastic wrap** and leave at room temperature for approximately 4 to 6 hours, until the dough is nearly double in size. The dough should register between 3.5 and 4.0 if tested with pH paper (see page 77) and have a pleasant aroma similar to apple cider vinegar. If the starter has not doubled or acidified properly, allow it to continue to develop at room temperature. It could take up to 8 hours or even longer.

3. **When the starter has fully developed, knead** it for a few seconds to degas it. The starter is now ready for mixing into the final dough; however, if necessary to coordinate timing with the soaker, cover tightly with plastic wrap and refrigerate overnight (or up to 3 days). About

2 hours before mixing the final dough, remove the starter from the refrigerator to take off the chill.

FINAL DOUGH

VOLUME	OUNCES	GRAMS	INGREDIENT
Use all	18.18	515	soaker
Use all	14.75	418	starter
7 tablespoons	2	56.5	whole rye flour
⅝ teaspoon	.18	5	salt
2¼ teaspoons	.25	7	instant yeast
1½ tablespoons	1	28.5	molasses or sorghum syrup (optional)
1 tablespoon	.32	9	caraway seeds, nigella seeds, or anise seeds
or 1 tablespoon	.12	3.5	or orange or lemon zest (optional)
			extra whole rye flour for adjustments
TOTAL	36.68	1039	

BAKER'S FORMULA	%
Whole rye flour	56
Whole wheat flour	9
Bread flour	35
Salt	1.5
Instant yeast	1
Water	65
Molasses	4.5
Total	172

NUTRITION FACTS	
Calories (kcal)	97.76
Protein (g)	2.98
Carbohydrates (g)	2.29
Dietary fiber (g)	2.50
Total sugars (g)	.70
Fat (g)	.45
Saturated fat (g)	.03
Trans fatty acid (g)	0
Cholesterol (mg)	0
Sodium (mg)	149.90

1. **Using a metal pastry scraper, chop** the soaker and the starter into 12 smaller pieces each (sprinkle some of the extra flour over the pre-doughs to keep the pieces from sticking back to each other).

2. **If mixing by hand,** combine the soaker and starter pieces in a bowl with all of the other ingredients except the extra flour and stir vigorously with a mixing spoon or knead with wet hands for about 2 minutes, until all of the ingredients are evenly integrated and distributed into the dough. The dough should be soft and slightly sticky; if not, add more flour or water as needed. **If using a stand mixer,** put the pre-dough pieces and all of the other ingredients except the extra flour into the mixer with the paddle attachment (preferable) or dough hook. Mix on slow speed for 1 minute to bring the ingredients together into a ball. Switch to the dough hook if need be and mix on medium-low speed, occasionally scraping down the bowl, for 2 to 3 minutes, until the pre-doughs become cohesive and assimilated into each other, leaving no streaks of light and dark. Add more flour or water as needed until the dough is soft and slightly sticky. The dough will be soft and will press against the side walls of the mixer, but you will be able to see the strands of gluten as they develop.

3. **Proceed as in steps 3 through 7** in the 45% rye hearth *meteil* on page 171.

This category includes breads that fall outside easy categorization. Yes, they may be lean or enriched, baked on the hearth or in a pan, but they also have something uniquely their own, whether unusual ingredients, such as sprouted grains, partially gelatinized mashed grains, or spent grain from beer makers, or an unusual preparation—chemically leavened and steam-baked in a can, for example. These are fun breads and push the limits of what is possible in the seemingly limitless world of bread baking.

Power Bread

Makes 1 loaf or 8 to 16 rolls

This bread (shown opposite) utilizes a raisin puree and various seeds for both flavor and nutrition. When I go on the road to teach bread baking classes around the country, this is the bread that is requested most often. It follows a different method than most of the formulas in this book. The pre-soaker makes it a three-day process, as the raisins and flaxseeds are hydrated on Day 1 (which takes just a few minutes), the regular soaker and *biga* are made on Day 2, and then the final mixing, shaping, and baking occur on Day 3. The Day 1 pre-soaker takes such a short amount of time that it really shouldn't count, but it does require you to plan three days ahead.

This bread is high in protein and fiber for sustained energy, yet it also offers a quick carbohydrate burst via the raisin puree with its more readily available sugars. The raisins are soaked overnight so they will puree easily in a blender or food processor, almost, but not quite, disappearing in the bread. Sunflower seeds are just plain delicious, as well as nutritionally rich. They give this bread a wonderful nutty flavor and a long, pleasant finish. Oat bran has many documented benefits and is an especially good source of cholesterol-fighting soluble fiber.

Like several other breads in this book, this one contains flaxseeds, one of the real miracle foods that have recently come into their own, especially in breakfast cereals and as a nutritional supplement. Flaxseeds are extremely high in alpha-linolenic acid, an essential omega-3 fatty acid, as well as the best source of lignin fiber (not to be confused with flax's lignans, phytochemicals that also have numerous health benefits). Soaking them in water overnight starts the germination process, which activates enzymes that make the seeds easier to digest.

BREAD PROFILE

Enriched, medium soft dough; delayed fermentation method; commercial yeast

DAYS TO MAKE: 3

Day 1: Pre-soaker, 10 minutes set up
Day 2: Soaker and *biga*, 30 minutes set up and mix; overnight autolyse
Day 3: 2 hours to de-chill *biga*; 12 to 15 minutes mixing; 2 to 3 hours fermentation, shaping, proofing; 20 to 50 minutes baking (rolls or loaves)

COMMENTARY

Make the pre-soaker on Day 1, the soaker and *biga* on Day 2, and the final dough on Day 3.

↩

You can use either regular or golden raisins. Golden raisins will keep the dough lighter in color. For an adventurous variation that will provide an even more healthful nutritional profile, replace half the raisins with dried cranberries, which are rich in antioxidants and other beneficial phytonutrients.

PRE-SOAKER

VOLUME	OUNCES	GRAMS	INGREDIENT	%
6¹/₂ tablespoons	2.5	71	raisins, regular or golden	42
1¹/₂ tablespoons	.5	14	flaxseeds, whole	8
³/₄ cup	6	170	water	100
TOTAL	9	255		150

Combine all of the ingredients in a small bowl, cover with plastic wrap, and leave at room temperature overnight or anywhere between 8 and 24 hours.

SOAKER

VOLUME	OUNCES	GRAMS	INGREDIENT	%
Use all	9	255	pre-soaker	150
1⅓ cups	6	170	whole wheat flour	100
2 tablespoons	.5	14	oat bran	8.2
½ teaspoon	.14	4	salt	2.3
TOTAL	15.64	443		260.5

1. **Puree the pre-soaker** in a blender or food processor (don't worry if the flaxseeds stay whole).

2. **Combine the whole wheat flour, oat bran, and salt in a bowl** and add the raisin puree. Stir for about 1 minute, until all of the flour is hydrated and the ingredients form a ball of dough.

3. **Cover loosely with plastic wrap** and leave at room temperature for 12 to 24 hours. (If it will be more than 24 hours, place the soaker in the refrigerator; it will be good for up to 3 days. Remove it 2 hours before mixing the final dough to take off the chill.)

BIGA

VOLUME	OUNCES	GRAMS	INGREDIENT	%
1⅓ cups	6	170	whole wheat flour, preferably fine grind	100
¼ teaspoon	.03	1	instant yeast	.5
½ cup plus 2 tablespoons	5	142	milk, buttermilk, yogurt, soy milk, or rice milk, at room temperature (about 70°F/21°C)	83.3
TOTAL	11.03	313		183.8

1. **Mix all of the *biga* ingredients together** in a bowl to form a ball of dough. Using wet hands, knead the dough in the bowl for 2 minutes to be sure all of the ingredients are evenly distributed and the flour is fully hydrated. The dough should feel very tacky. Let the dough rest for 5 minutes, then knead it again with wet hands for 1 minute. The dough will become smoother but still be tacky.

2. **Transfer the dough to a clean bowl,** cover tightly with plastic wrap, and refrigerate for at least 8 hours and up to 3 days.

3. **About 2 hours before mixing the final dough,** remove the *biga* from the refrigerator to take off the chill. It will have risen slightly but need not have risen significantly in order to use it in the final dough.

FINAL DOUGH

VOLUME	OUNCES	GRAMS	INGREDIENT
Use all	15.64	443	soaker
Use all	11.03	313	*biga*
6 tablespoons	2	56.5	sunflower seeds, ground into flour (see Commentary)
7 tablespoons	2	56.5	whole wheat flour
3 tablespoons	1	28.5	sesame seeds, whole
1/2 teaspoon	.14	4	salt
2 1/4 teaspoons	.25	7	instant yeast
3 1/2 teaspoons or 1 1/2 tablespoons	.75 .75	21 21	honey or agave nectar or sugar or brown sugar
			extra whole wheat flour for adjustments
			1 egg beaten with 1 tablespoon water and a pinch of salt for egg wash (optional)
TOTAL	32.81	929.5	

1. **Using a metal pastry scraper, chop** the soaker and the *biga* into 12 smaller pieces each (sprinkle some of the extra flour over the pre-doughs to keep the pieces from sticking back to each other).

2. **If mixing by hand,** combine the soaker and *biga* pieces in a bowl with all of the other ingredients except the extra flour and stir vigorously with a mixing spoon or knead with wet hands for about 2 minutes, until all of the ingredients are evenly integrated and distributed into the dough. The dough should be soft and slightly sticky; if not, add more flour or water as needed. **If using a stand mixer,** put the pre-dough pieces and all of the other ingredients except the extra flour into the mixer with the paddle attachment (preferable) or dough hook. Mix on slow speed for 1 minute to bring the ingredients together into a ball. Switch to the dough hook if need be and mix on medium-low speed, occasionally scraping down the bowl, for 2 to 3 minutes, until the pre-doughs become cohesive and assimilated into each other. Add more flour or water as needed until the dough is soft and slightly sticky.

3. **Dust a work surface with flour,** then roll the dough in the flour to coat. Knead the dough by hand for 3 to 4 minutes, incorporating only as much extra flour as needed, until the dough feels firm but tacky. Form the dough into a ball and let it rest on the work surface for 5 minutes while you prepare a clean, lightly oiled bowl.

If measuring the sunflower seeds by volume, use 1/2 cup of seeds *before* grinding, which will yield about 6 tablespoons of ground sunflower seed.

Use a dry food processor, spice grinder, or blender to grind the seeds. But be careful to not generate too much friction, or you'll end up making sunflower seed butter as the oils in the seeds warm up—tasty, but not what we're after. Work in small batches in a blender or use the pulse switch on a food processor. It is okay if the seeds are not too finely ground (a food processor is not likely to grind them to a fine powder, anyway). Toasting the seeds is optional, but if you do so, they should be completely cooled before you grind them; again, so they do not turn into sunflower seed butter.

For portable power bars, add 5 ounces (1 cup) of toasted pumpkin seeds to the dough during the final mixing. Instead of shaping the dough as a loaf or rolls, roll it out into an 8-inch square and then cut it into smaller squares or rectangles. Lay them out on a parchment-lined sheet pan, brush with egg white wash, and proof for 30 minutes. Bake at 350°F (177°C) for about 20 minutes, until brown on the top and bottom.

BAKER'S FORMULA	%
Whole wheat flour	100
Salt	2
Instant yeast	2
Water	43
Milk	35
Honey	5.5
Raisins	18
Flaxseeds	3.5
Oat bran	3.5
Sesame seeds	7
Sunflower seeds	14
Total	233.5

NUTRITION FACTS	
Calories (kcal)	101.94
Protein (g)	3.97
Carbohydrates (g)	17.61
Dietary fiber (g)	2.98
Total sugars (g)	3
Fat (g)	2.56
Saturated fat (g)	.26
Trans fatty acid (g)	0
Cholesterol (mg)	.37
Sodium (mg)	142.60

4. **Resume kneading the dough for 1 minute** to strengthen the gluten and make any final flour or water adjustments. The dough should have strength and pass the windowpane test (see page 84), yet still feel soft, supple, and very tacky (shown at left). Form the dough into a ball and place it in the prepared bowl, rolling to coat with oil. Cover loosely with plastic wrap and let rise at room temperature for approximately 45 to 60 minutes, until it is about $1^1/_2$ times its original size.

5. **Transfer the dough to a lightly floured work surface** and form it into a loaf pan shape or rolls (see pages 87–91 for shaping instructions). For loaf pan bread, place the dough in a greased 4 by $8^1/_2$-inch bread pan. For rolls, place them on one or more sheet pans lined with parchment paper or silicon mats. Mist the top of the dough with pan spray (optional), cover loosely with plastic wrap, and let rise at room temperature for approximately 45 to 60 minutes, until about $1^1/_2$ times its original size.

6. **Preheat the oven to 425°F (218°C)** with a steam pan. If you are making rolls, brush them with egg wash if you wish. When the dough is ready to bake, place it in the oven, pour 1 cup of hot water into the steam pan, lower the temperature to 350°F (177°C), and bake for 20 minutes. Remove the steam pan, rotate the bread or roll pan 180 degrees, and continue baking for another 20 to 30 minutes, until the loaf or rolls are a rich brown on all sides, sound hollow when thumped on the bottom, and register at least 195°F (91°C) in the center.

7. **Transfer the bread or rolls to a cooling rack** and cool for at least 1 hour before serving.

Whole Wheat and Sprouted Grain Bread

Makes 1 loaf

Sprouting grains is a viable alternative to mashing them, and it makes for a nutritious addition. (Instructions for sprouting grains can be found on page 195.) Sprouts contribute a great deal of enzyme activity, so the acidity of either a a *biga* or a starter (even more so) is useful in controlling them. There are recipes for sprouted breads that do not use either a *biga* or a starter, but with the delayed fermentation method the pre-dough is necessary for maximum flavor and performance. The first formula can be used for either sandwich or hearth breads. If baked on the hearth, it will form a hard crust with a soft interior crumb. If baked in a loaf pan, the crust will be softer.

It uses a combination of flour and sprouted grains; the next recipe is for a bread made with 100% sprouted wheat. In both cases, the sprouts are used when young and just beginning to show their tail. They should be ground into a mashlike pulp, using either a food processor or a meat grinder, before they are added to the dough. Because they have been soaked, the sprouts serve the same role as a soaker in this dough.

BREAD PROFILE

Slightly enriched, medium soft dough; delayed fermentation method; commercial yeast

DAYS TO MAKE: 3 TO 4

Days 1 and 2: 5 minutes set up wheat kernels for sprouting
Day 2 or 3: *Biga*, 20 minutes set up and mix; overnight autolyse
Day 3 or 4: 5 to 10 minutes grinding sprouted wheat; 2 hours to de-chill *biga*; 12 to 15 minutes mixing; 2 to 3 hours fermentation, shaping, proofing; 40 to 60 minutes baking

BIGA

VOLUME	OUNCES	GRAMS	INGREDIENT	%
1³/₄ cups	8	227	whole wheat flour	100
¹/₄ teaspoon	.03	1	instant yeast	.4
³/₄ cup	6	170	filtered or spring water, at room temperature (about 70°F/21°C)	75
TOTAL	14.03	398		175.4

COMMENTARY

You can use either a *biga* or an equal amount of wild yeast starter (page 80) in this dough. The starter controls the enzymes better than the *biga*, but some people prefer the *biga* version because the flavor is less acidic.

1. **Mix all of the *biga* ingredients together** in a bowl to form a ball of dough. Using wet hands, knead the dough in the bowl for 2 minutes to be sure all of the ingredients are evenly distributed and the flour is fully hydrated. The dough should feel very tacky. Let the dough rest for 5 minutes, then knead it again with wet hands for 1 minute. The dough will become smoother but still be tacky.

2. **Transfer the dough to a clean bowl,** cover tightly with plastic wrap, and refrigerate for at least 8 hours and up to 3 days.

3. **About 2 hours before mixing the final dough,** remove the *biga* from the refrigerator to take off the chill. It will have risen slightly but need not have risen significantly in order to use it in the final dough.

COMMENTARY

For instructions on how to sprout grains, see page 195. When weighing or measuring grain prior to sprouting it, remember that it will nearly double in weight during the sprouting process. So, for 10 ounces of sprouted grain, I suggest soaking at least 6 ounces of grain and then weighing it again before grinding and adding to the dough. Any leftover sprouts can be cooked and used as a hot or cold breakfast cereal or grown for another day (they will soften as they grow) and used in salads.

Vital wheat gluten, listed as an optional ingredient in the final dough, can be added to increase the strength and potential height of the bread. (Wheat sprouts contain less gluten than wheat flour due to chemical changes in the grain during germination.) If you feel your loaf is too tight or dense, the next time you make this bread add vital wheat gluten to the dough as indicated. But be aware that using too much gluten results in a rubbery texture and a little bit of a harsh flavor.

FINAL DOUGH

VOLUME	OUNCES	GRAMS	INGREDIENT
1²/₃ cups (approx.)	10	283	sprouted wheat kernels, other sprouted grains, or a combination (see Commentary)
Use all	14.03	398	*biga*
7 tablespoons	2	56.5	whole wheat flour
1 teaspoon	.28	8	salt
2¹/₄ teaspoons	.25	7	instant yeast
¹/₄ cup	2	56.5	water, at room temperature (about 70°F/21°C)
3¹/₂ teaspoons or 1¹/₂ tablespoons	.75 .75	21 21	honey or agave nectar or sugar or brown sugar
1 tablespoon	.5	14	unsalted butter, melted, or vegetable oil (optional)
2 tablespoons	.5	14	vital wheat gluten (optional)
			extra whole wheat flour for adjustments
TOTAL	30.31	858	

1. **Grind the sprouted grains** in a food processor or run them through a meat grinder to as fine a pulp as possible, but not to the point of generating a lot of heat, which can create too much enzyme activity. If the pulp begins to feel warm to the touch, stop processing it and let it sit for about 10 minutes to cool off before continuing. If you have a meat grinder, manual or electric, it works even better than a food processor and does not generate heat.

2. **Using a metal pastry scraper, chop** the *biga* into 12 smaller pieces (sprinkle some of the extra flour over the pre-dough to keep the pieces from sticking back to each other).

3. **If mixing by hand,** combine the *biga* pieces in a bowl with all of the other ingredients except the extra flour and stir vigorously with a mixing spoon or knead with wet hands for about 2 minutes, until all of the ingredients are evenly integrated and distributed into the dough. The dough should be soft and slightly sticky; if not, add more flour or water as needed. **If using a stand mixer,** put the pre-dough pieces and all of the other ingredients except the extra flour into the mixer with the paddle attachment (preferable) or dough hook. Mix on slow speed for 1 minute to bring the ingredients together into a ball. Switch to the dough hook if need be and mix on medium-low speed, occasionally scraping down the bowl, for 2 to 3 minutes, until the pulp and the pre-dough become cohesive and assimilated into each other. Add more flour or water as needed until the dough is soft and slightly sticky.

4. **Dust a work surface with flour,** then roll the dough in the flour to coat. Knead by hand for 3 to 4 minutes, incorporating only as much extra flour as needed, until the dough feels soft and tacky, but not sticky (shown on the opposite page). Form the dough into a ball and let it rest on the work surface for 5 minutes while you prepare a clean, lightly oiled bowl.

5. **Resume kneading the dough for 1 minute** to strengthen the gluten and make any final flour or water adjustments. The dough should have strength and pass the windowpane test (see page 84), yet still feel soft, supple, and tacky. Form the dough into a ball and place it in the prepared bowl, rolling to coat with oil. Cover loosely with plastic wrap and let rise at room temperature for approximately 45 to 60 minutes, until it is about $1^1/_2$ times its original size.

6. **Transfer the dough to a lightly floured work surface** and form it into either a loaf pan shape or a freestanding *bâtard* (see pages 87–91 for shaping instructions). For loaf pan bread, place the dough in a greased 4 by $8^1/_2$-inch bread pan. For a *bâtard*, place it on a proofing cloth or on a sheet pan lined with parchment paper and, if you like, dusted with flour. Mist the top of the dough with pan spray (optional), cover loosely with plastic wrap, and let rise at room temperature for approximately 45 to 60 minutes, until it has grown to $1^1/_2$ times its original size.

7. **Preheat the oven to 425°F (218°C)** and, if baking a freestanding loaf, prepare the oven for hearth baking (see page 86), including a steam pan (steaming is optional for a sandwich loaf). When the dough is ready to bake, place it in the oven, pour 1 cup of hot water into the steam pan, lower the temperature to 350°F (177°C), and bake for 20 minutes. Rotate the loaf 180 degrees and continue baking for another 20 to 30 minutes, until the loaf is a rich brown on all sides, sounds hollow when thumped on the bottom, and registers at least 200°F (93°C) in the center.

8. **Transfer the bread to a cooling rack** and allow it to cool for at least 1 hour before serving.

BAKER'S FORMULA	%
Whole wheat flour	100
Salt	1.6
Instant yeast	1.4
Water	54
Honey	4
Unsalted butter or oil	2.5
Sprouted wheat kernels or other sprouted grain	51
Vital wheat gluten	2.5
Total	217

NUTRITION FACTS	
Calories (kcal)	91.37
Protein (g)	3.67
Carbohydrates (g)	18.48
Dietary fiber (g)	2.46
Total sugars (g)	.62
Fat (g)	.96
Saturated fat (g)	.14
Trans fatty acid (g)	0
Cholesterol (mg)	0
Sodium (mg)	121.82

FAQ ∽ *What should I do if the bread seems to be baking too quickly?*

It may take a few test bakes before you figure out the best shelves on which to bake your loaves. If you notice that the top of the bread is baking too fast (common in convection ovens), you may want to bake on a lower shelf the next time. In an immediate situation, cover the top of the bread with aluminum foil to slow down the caramelizing of the top crust. If the bottom is baking too fast, place an inverted sheet pan under the pan in which the bread is baking (or directly under the bread itself if it is baking directly on a stone). This will create an air gap and temperature buffer.

100% Sprouted Grain Bread

Makes 1 loaf

BREAD PROFILE

Lean, slightly sweetened, medium soft dough; straight dough method, commercial yeast.

DAYS TO MAKE: 2 TO 3

Day 1: 5 minutes to set up the wheat kernels for sprouting.
Day 2: 5 minutes to drain and rinse the sprouts
Day 2 or 3: 5 to 10 minutes grinding the sprouted wheat; 12 to 15 minutes mixing; $2^1/_2$ to $3^1/_2$ hours fermentation, shaping, and proofing; 40 to 60 minutes baking

COMMENTARY

For instructions on how to sprout grains, see page 195. When weighing or measuring grain prior to sprouting it, remember that it will nearly double in weight during the sprouting process. So, for 10 ounces of sprouted grain, I suggest soaking at least 6 ounces of grain and then weighing it again before grinding and adding to the dough. Any leftover sprouts can be cooked and used as a hot or cold breakfast cereal or grown for another day (they will soften as they grow) and used in salads.

There are dense, moist breads made with only sprouted grains and no flour, such as Essene bread, and there are lighter versions, such as those made by Alvarado Street Bakery and Food for Life's Ezekiel brand. The main difference between the dense and airy loaves is the use of vital wheat gluten. There are pluses and minuses when it comes to adding gluten to bread, but if you want a tall, light loaf using 100% sprouted grains, you will have to add gluten at a ratio of 1 part gluten to 10 parts wheat pulp to achieve it, as in this recipe (the ratio is based on the weight of the grains after they are soaked and sprouted). There is no *biga*, soaker, or mash for this bread because the sprouted wheat fulfills all of those functions.

FINAL DOUGH

VOLUME	OUNCES	GRAMS	INGREDIENT
4 cups (approx.)	24	680	sprouted wheat kernels, other sprouted grains, or a combination (see Commentary)
$^1/_2$ cup plus 2 tablespoons	2.4	68	vital wheat gluten (optional)
$1^1/_8$ teaspoons	.32	9	salt
$2^1/_4$ teaspoons	.25	7	instant yeast
$1^1/_2$ tablespoons or 2 tablespoons	1 1	28.5 28.5	honey or agave nectar or sugar or brown sugar
$^1/_2$ cup	4	113	water, at room temperature (about 70°F/21°C)
			whole wheat flour for adjustments
TOTAL	31.97	905.5	

1. **Process the sprouted grains** to as fine a pulp as possible, but not to the point of generating a lot of heat. If the pulp begins to feel warm to the touch, stop processing it and let it sit for about 10 minutes to cool off before continuing. If you have a meat grinder, manual or electric, it works even better than a food processor and does not generate heat.

2. **If mixing by hand,** combine the sprout pulp, wheat gluten, salt, yeast, honey, and $^1/_4$ cup of the water in a bowl and stir vigorously with a mixing spoon or knead with wet hands for about 2 minutes, until all of the ingredients are evenly integrated and distributed into the dough. The dough should be soft and slightly sticky; if not, add more of the water to form

Vital wheat gluten, listed as an optional ingredient in the final dough, can be added to increase the strength and potential height of the bread. (Wheat sprouts contain less gluten than wheat flour due to chemical changes in the grain during germination.) If you feel your loaf is too tight or dense, the next time you make this bread add vital wheat gluten to the dough as indicated. But be aware that using too much gluten results in a rubbery texture and a little bit of a harsh flavor.

If mixing by hand, you will need to use wet hands and a wet kneading surface to keep the dough from sticking. The dough will seem quite wet and sticky during the early stages, but it will be easier to handle after it rests. If using a mixer, you will need to use a wet bowl scraper throughout the mixing process to scrape the dough off of the walls of the bowl and back into a ball.

This is a totally flourless bread even though it uses wheat. If you have no objections to including flour in the dough, you can use whole wheat flour during the final hand kneading stages instead of wet hands and a wet surface, as suggested in the instructions. Use only as much flour as you need to achieve the desired texture.

BAKER'S FORMULA	%
Sprouted wheat kernels	100
Vital wheat gluten	10
Salt	1.3
Instant yeast	1
Water	16.5
Honey	4
Total	132.8

NUTRITION FACTS

Calories (kcal)	63.85
Protein (g)	3.42
Carbohydrates (g)	12.52
Dietary fiber (g)	.35
Total sugars (g)	.80
Fat (g)	.33
Saturated fat (g)	.06
Trans fatty acid (g)	0
Cholesterol (mg)	0
Sodium (mg)	134.94

a sticky ball of dough. **If using a stand mixer,** combine the sprout pulp, wheat gluten, salt, yeast, honey, and $1/4$ cup of the water in the bowl. Mix on slow speed with the dough hook for 1 minute to bring the ingredients together into a ball, adding additional water as needed. Continue mixing at medium-low speed for 2 to 3 minutes, occasionally scraping down the bowl. The dough should form a sticky ball.

3. **Mist a work surface with a spray of water,** place the dough on the work surface, and knead with wet hands for 1 to 2 minutes. Although the dough will be sticky on the surface, it should have the strength and feel of normal bread dough. Form the dough into a ball and let it rest on the work surface for 5 minutes while you prepare a clean, lightly oiled bowl.

4. **Resume kneading the dough for 1 minute** with wet hands to strengthen it. The dough should have strength and pass the windowpane test (see page 84), yet still feel soft, supple, and very tacky. Form the dough into a ball and place it in the prepared bowl, rolling to coat with oil. Cover loosely with plastic wrap and let rise at room temperature for approximately 45 to 60 minutes, until it is about $1^1/2$ times its original size.

5. **Transfer the dough to a lightly floured work surface** and form it into either a loaf pan shape or a freestanding *bâtard* (see pages 87–91 for shaping instructions). For loaf pan bread, place the dough in a greased 4 by $8^1/2$-inch bread pan. For a *bâtard*, place it on a proofing cloth or on a sheet pan lined with parchment paper and, if you like, dusted with flour. Mist the top of the dough with pan spray (optional), cover loosely with plastic wrap, and let rise at room temperature for approximately 45 to 60 minutes, until it has grown to $1^1/2$ times its original size.

6. **Preheat the oven to 425°F (218°C)** and, if baking a freestanding loaf, prepare the oven for hearth baking (see page 86), including a steam pan (steaming is optional for a sandwich loaf). When the dough is ready to bake, place it in the oven, pour 1 cup of hot water into the steam pan, lower the temperature to 350°F (177°C), and bake for 20 minutes. Rotate the loaf 180 degrees and continue baking for another 20 to 30 minutes, until the loaf is a rich brown on all sides, sounds hollow when thumped on the bottom, and registers at least 200°F (93°C) in the center.

7. **Transfer the bread to a cooling rack** and allow it to cool for at least 1 hour before serving.

Whole Wheat Mash Bread

Makes 1 loaf

This is the bread that sent me on a long journey of trial and error in search of that tricky balance between flavor and structure. While the ingredients in this bread are no different than those in regular whole wheat hearth bread, the scalded, partially gelatinized grain in the mash creates an unparalleled dense texture and naturally sweet flavor (mashes are discussed in greater depth beginning on page 54). Some of the recipe testers said this was the best whole wheat bread they ever tasted. Try it and see what you think. The following breads are customarily made not with mashes but with soakers, so feel free to substitute a regular soaker where the formula indicates a mash. While there are only a couple mash breads presented here, the method, once mastered, can be applied to any number of international breads, especially dense, moist breads, that would benefit from the use of a mash. There are very few mash bread formulas in publication, so these adaptations are forging into frontier territory.

BREAD PROFILE

Slightly enriched dough; delayed fermentation method; yeast or mixed leavening method

DAYS TO MAKE: 2

Day 1: Mash and starter, 20 minutes set up and mix, 3 hours mash development; overnight autolyse
Day 2: 2 hours to de-chill starter or biga; 12 to 15 minutes mixing; 2 to 3 hours fermentation, shaping, proofing; 40 to 60 minutes baking

FAQ ⁓ *What's the benefit of sprouting grains and how do I do it?*

The nutritional value of sprouted grains is now a well understood fact, but it has taken a number of years for this awareness to reach the public. When seed kernels, such as wheat, rye, alfalfa, and barley, or legumes, like lentils, chick peas, or mung beans, are placed in water, three main chemical changes occur as they germinate: the seeds begin to break down due to increased enzyme activity; elements of the seed begin to move around between the endosperm and the germ; and new molecules are formed. In the process, vitamin content and accessibility is increased, especially of vitamins A, B-complex, and C; minerals like calcium, potassium, and iron are released; and the carbohydrates become more easily digested.

To make sprouted wheat kernels or other grain sprouts, first rinse the grains to eliminate foreign matter (stones and dirt). Place 1 part grains in a covered container, cover with 2 parts filtered or spring water (at room temperature, about 70°F/21°C), and soak for 12 to 24 hours.

Drain the grains and either discard the soaking water, drink it or water your plants with it (it's full of minerals and enzymes), or use it in soups or in the final bread dough. Rinse the soaked grains, then return them to the container, cover, and let sprout at room temperature. You should see the beginning of a tail within 3 to 6 hours. If not, rinse and drain again and wait for the sprouts to show. As soon as a little tail shows itself (and well before it grows into a longer tail), the sprouted grains are ready to use. The final weight of the sprouted grains should be a little more than 1 1/2 times their original; for example, 6 ounces of wheat kernels soaked in 12 ounces of water should yield about 10 ounces of sprouted wheat kernels. Immediately refrigerate the sprouted grains and store in the refrigerator until you are ready to make the final dough.

MASH

VOLUME	OUNCES	GRAMS	INGREDIENT	%
1¹/₄ cups plus 1 tablespoon	10.6	300	water	250
³/₄ cup plus 3 tablespoons	4.25	120	whole wheat flour	100
¹/₂ teaspoon	.03	1	diastatic malt powder or sprouted wheat flour (optional)	.7
TOTAL	14.88	421		350.7

COMMENTARY

Diastatic malt powder is optional. Some of the recipe testers felt that it created more sweetness and an airier loaf, but the formula will work fine with or without it.

The mash used here is somewhat wet: 2¹/₂ parts water to 1 part flour. (There are mash formulas that are both thicker and thinner than this, but the formulas in this book have been created with a medium mash.)

1. **Preheat the oven to 200°F (93°C).**

2. **Heat the water to 165°F (74°C)** in an ovenproof saucepan, then remove the pan from the heat and whisk or stir in the flour and malt until the flour is fully hydrated and makes a paste similar to a thin pudding or gravy. Using a spatula or plastic pastry scraper dipped in water, scrape the spoon or whisk and the walls of the pan to get all of the dough back into the pan and off the inside walls. (The mash temperature will drop to about 150°F/66°C during the stirring). Immediately cover the pan with its lid or aluminum foil and place it in the oven.

3. **Turn the oven down to warm/150°F (66°C),** if it has this setting, and leave the mash in the oven for at least 1 hour and up to 3 hours. If the oven can't be turned down this low, turn it off and 10 minutes later turn it back on to the lowest setting (typically 200°F/93°C) for about 10 minutes; continue alternating between on and off at 10-minute intervals for the first hour, then turn the oven off and leave it off. If possible, leave the mash in the warm oven for the full 3 hours. However, you can also remove it from the oven after the first hour and leave it at room temperature, covered, if you need to use the oven for other purposes. After 3 hours, refrigerate the mash until you are ready to use it. You can also leave it out overnight at room temperature if you plan to use it within the next 24 hours.

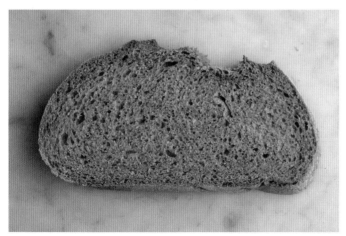

Breads made with mash will have a naturally sweeter taste and a creamier texture.

You can substitute an equal amount of *biga* (page 81) for the starter. The choice between a *biga* and a wild yeast starter is a personal one. A starter is the best way to control the enzyme action, but some of the testers preferred the flavor of the bread when a *biga* made with buttermilk was used (the buttermilk provides acidity, which helps control enzyme activity).

STARTER

VOLUME	OUNCES	GRAMS	INGREDIENT	%
5 tablespoons	2.25	64	whole wheat mother starter (page 67)	33.3
1½ cups	6.75	191	whole wheat flour	100
½ cup plus 2 tablespoons	5	142	filtered or spring water, at room temperature (about 70°F/21°C)	250
TOTAL	14	398		283.3

1. **Mix all of the starter ingredients together** in a bowl to form a ball of dough. Using wet hands, knead the dough in the bowl for about 2 minutes to be sure all of the ingredients are evenly distributed and the flour is fully hydrated. The dough should feel very tacky. Let the dough rest for about 5 minutes, then knead it again with wet hands for 1 minute. The dough will become smoother but still be tacky.

2. **Transfer the dough to a clean bowl,** cover loosely with plastic wrap, and leave at room temperature for approximately 4 to 6 hours, until the dough is nearly double in size. The dough should register between 3.5 and 4.0 if tested with pH paper (see page 77) and have a pleasant aroma similar to apple cider vinegar. If the starter has not doubled or acidified properly, allow it to continue to develop at room temperature. It could take up to 8 hours or even longer.

3. **When the starter has fully developed, knead** it for a few seconds to degas it. The starter is now ready for mixing into the final dough; however, if necessary to coordinate timing with the mash, cover tightly with plastic wrap and refrigerate overnight (or up to 3 days). About 2 hours before mixing the final dough, remove the starter from the refrigerator to take off the chill.

FAQ ∾ *When should I use diastatic malt in these formulas?*

Because it is loaded with diastase enzymes (a collection of amylase enzymes), diastatic malt promotes enzymatic fermentation. The effect of diastatic malt on bread is to promote crust color and release enough sugar from the starch so that fermentation is lively and the dough becomes naturally sweet. Experiments have shown that diastatic malt can make a big difference in the size and flavor of a loaf, especially when the flour is lacking in enzymes or damaged starch. With whole wheat flour the need is usually not as great, as the bran and germ contribute many enzymes on their own. And in the method presented here, the long overnight fermentation of the pre-doughs seems to encourage ample enzyme activity and flavor development. However, for those who mill their own flour, and also for those who find that their dough does not seem to rise in a timely manner nor brown as described, the addition of a small amount of diastatic malt could make a difference. The usual amount is about .5% of the total flour weight, so 16 ounces of flour would require about .08 ounce (½ teaspoon).

FINAL DOUGH

VOLUME	OUNCES	GRAMS	INGREDIENT
Use all	14	398	starter
Use all	14	397	mash
2 cups	9	255	whole wheat flour
1⅛ teaspoons	.3	8.5	salt
2¼ teaspoons	.25	7	instant yeast
2¼ teaspoons	.5	14	honey or agave nectar
or 1 tablespoon	.5	14	or sugar or brown sugar (optional)
1 tablespoon	.5	14	unsalted butter, melted, or vegetable oil (optional)
			extra whole wheat flour for adjustments
TOTAL	38.55	1093.5	

You will discover that the final weight of the finished mash is less than the weight of the ingredients. This is due to evaporation. Not to worry, just use the full amount of mash in the final dough. If you prefer to make large batches of mash for multiple bakes, weigh out 14 ounces for each use. It will keep in the refrigerator for up to a week, or you can freeze preweighed portions in zippered freezer bags; they will keep for up to 3 months in the freezer.

1. **Using a metal pastry scraper, chop** the starter into 12 smaller pieces (sprinkle some of the extra flour over the pre-dough to keep the pieces from sticking back to each other).

2. **If mixing by hand,** combine the pre-dough pieces and the mash in a bowl with all of the other ingredients except the extra flour and stir vigorously with a mixing spoon or knead with wet hands for about 2 minutes, until all of the ingredients are evenly integrated and distributed into the dough. The dough should be soft and slightly sticky; if not, add more flour or water as needed. **If using a stand mixer,** put the pre-dough pieces and all of the other ingredients except the extra flour into the mixer with the paddle attachment (preferable) or dough hook. Mix on slow speed for 1 minute to bring the ingredients together into a ball. Switch to the dough hook if need be and mix on medium-low speed, occasionally scraping down the bowl, for 2 to 3 minutes, until the pre-doughs become cohesive and assimilated into each other. Add more flour or water as needed until the dough is soft and slightly sticky.

3. **Dust a work surface with flour,** then roll the dough in the flour to coat. Knead the dough by hand for 3 to 4 minutes, incorporating only as much extra flour as needed, until the dough feels soft and tacky, but not sticky. Form the dough into a ball and let it rest on the work surface for 5 minutes while you prepare a clean, lightly oiled bowl.

4. **Resume kneading the dough for 1 minute** to strengthen the gluten and make any final flour or water adjustments. The dough should have strength and pass the windowpane test (see page 84), yet still feel soft, supple, and very tacky. Form the dough into a ball and place it in the prepared bowl, rolling to coat with oil. Cover loosely with plastic wrap and let rise at room temperature for approximately 45 to 60 minutes, until it is about 1½ times its original size.

֍

Mash breads, like most whole grain breads, tend to taste better after they have fully cooled. The denser breads almost always taste better one or two days after they come out of the oven. (Store them in aluminum foil or a paper bag.)

5. **Transfer the dough to a lightly floured work surface** and form it into either a loaf pan shape or a freestanding *bâtard* (see pages 87–91 for shaping instructions). For loaf pan bread, place the dough in a greased 4 by 8^1/$_2$-inch bread pan. For a *bâtard*, place it on a proofing cloth or on a sheet pan lined with parchment paper and, if you like, dusted with flour. Mist the top of the dough with pan spray (optional), cover loosely with plastic wrap, and let rise at room temperature for approximately 45 to 60 minutes, until it has grown to 1^1/$_2$ times its original size.

6. **Preheat the oven to 425°F (218°C)** and, if baking a freestanding loaf, prepare the oven for hearth baking (see page 86), including a steam pan (steaming is optional for a sandwich loaf). When the dough is ready to bake, place it in the oven, pour 1 cup of hot water into the steam pan, lower the temperature to 350°F (177°C), and bake for 20 minutes. Rotate the loaf 180 degrees and continue baking for another 20 to 30 minutes, until the loaf is rich brown on all sides, sounds hollow when thumped on the bottom, and registers at least 200°F (93°C) in the center.

7. **Transfer the bread to a cooling rack** and allow it to cool for at least 2 hours before serving, and longer if possible.

FAQ ֍ *How accurate are the listed baking times?*

I wish I could say very accurate, but it's impossible to do so because every oven, even professional ovens or the same brand of ovens, bakes differently. The temperatures and times given can only be considered an estimate; you will have to adjust either the time or the oven setting according to your situation. It should not take more than one or two bakes before you are able to determine what those adjustments should be.

FAQ ֍ *What if I have a convection oven? Are the baking temperatures the same as listed?*

No, convection ovens are much more efficient than conventional ovens. However, many new convection ovens have two speeds of convection, so there is no single rule that assures a proper adjustment. My suggestion is that for convection ovens that offer a low setting, reduce the temperature by 25°F (14°C). If the convection is very powerful, reduce the temperature by 50°F (28°C). The baking time is usually shorter in a convection oven, even with the reduced temperature, so you will have to monitor your oven the first few times you bake until you have a sense of the proper time and temperature adjustments.

Multigrain Mash Bread

Makes 1 loaf

This variation on whole wheat mash bread allows you make a mash from any combination of your favorite grains. Since the amount of grain is relatively small, consider serving cooked grain for a meal and saving some for use in the bread later. This makes moister, denser, and sweeter bread than the *struan*-style multigrain bread on page 102, but it really is, in the spirit of *struan*, a type of harvest bread.

MASH

VOLUME	OUNCES	GRAMS	INGREDIENT	%
1¼ cups plus 1 tablespoon	10.6	300	water	250
1 cup (approx.)	4.25	120	any combination of cooked and uncooked grains (see Commentary page 193)	100
½ teaspoon	.03	1	diastatic malt powder or sprouted wheat flour (optional)	.7
TOTAL	14.88	421		350.7

1. **Preheat the oven to 200°F (93°C).**

2. **Heat the water to 165°F (74°C)** in an ovenproof saucepan, then remove the pan from the heat and stir in the grains and malt. Using a spatula or plastic pastry scraper dipped in water, scrape the spoon or whisk and the walls of the pan to get all of the dough back into the pan and off the inside walls. (The mash temperature will drop to about 150°F/66°C during the stirring). Immediately cover the pan with its lid or aluminum foil and place it in the oven.

3. **Proceed as in step 3** on page 197 and onward in the whole wheat mash bread.

BREAD PROFILE

Slightly enriched dough; delayed fermentation method; yeast or mixed leavening method

DAYS TO MAKE: 2

Day 1: Mash and starter, 20 minutes set up and mix, 3 hours mash development; overnight autolyse

Day 2: 2 hours to de-chill starter or *biga*; 12 to 15 minutes mixing; 2 to 3 hours fermentation, shaping, proofing; 40 to 60 minutes baking

COMMENTARY

Remember, the mash will evaporate down to about 14 ounces.

BAKER'S FORMULA	%
Whole wheat flour	79
Mulitgrain mix	21
Instant yeast	1.3
Salt	1.4
Water	79
Honey	2
Unsalted butter	2
Total	185.7

NUTRITION FACTS	
Calories (kcal)	84.34
Protein (g)	3.04
Carbohydrates (g)	17.14
Dietary fiber (g)	2.69
Total sugars (g)	.51
Fat (g)	.93
Saturated fat (g)	.37
Trans fatty acid (g)	.01
Cholesterol (mg)	1.18
Sodium (mg)	129.69

Steamed Boston Brown Bread

Makes 1 large or 3 small loaves

BREAD PROFILE

Enriched, medium soft dough;
quick bread; chemical leavening
method; commercial yeast

DAYS TO MAKE: 2

Day 1: Soaker, 10 to 20 minutes set
up and mix; overnight autolyse
Day 2: 20 minutes mixing and panning; 3 hours baking

COMMENTARY

Because this is chemically leavened batter bread, the soaker is
wetter than in yeasted breads,
so do not compare this to any
other soaker in the book.

Steamed breads are usually raised not by yeast but by baking powder and/or baking soda; in other words, they are chemically leavened rather than biologically leavened. That places them in the category of quick breads. They are really more like what the English call puddings, as in plum or fig pudding. Steamed breads are dense and sometimes sliced with string rather than a knife.

The most famous American steamed bread is Boston brown bread, the *brown* referring to the color imparted by molasses. Buttermilk is used to react with the baking soda and create carbon dioxide, giving the bread a little aeration, and the sour flavor of the buttermilk is enhanced by the sweet richness of the molasses. There are many versions of this bread, some more heavily sweetened with molasses than others, some with raisins and some without, some with white flour and some with whole wheat. In all instances, a defining characteristic of Boston brown bread is the trilogy of grains: wheat, rye, and corn, usually in equal amounts. The steaming method is especially useful around campfires and probably originated in New England homes that did not have hearth ovens.

SOAKER				
VOLUME	OUNCES	GRAMS	INGREDIENT	%
³/₄ cup plus 2 tablespoons	4	113	whole wheat flour	33.4
³/₄ cup plus 2 tablespoons	4	113	whole rye flour	33.3
³/₄ cup plus 2 tablespoons	4	113	cornmeal	33.3
¹/₂ teaspoon	.14	4	salt	1.2
1¹/₂ cups	12	340	buttermilk or yogurt	100
TOTAL	24.14	683		201.2

1. **Mix all of the soaker ingredients** together in a bowl just until they are evenly distributed and fully hydrated. It will make a thick batter.

2. **Cover loosely with plastic wrap** and leave at room temperature overnight or anywhere between 8 and 24 hours. (If it will be more than 24 hours, place the soaker in the refrigerator; it will be good for up to 3 days. Remove it 2 hours before mixing the final dough to take off the chill.)

Steamed breads can be cooked in cylindrical containers made for this purpose, but they are often made instead in coffee cans (lid off, bottom on), and also in unglazed clay flower pots. Generously greased waxed paper has long been used to line the containers, but oiled parchment paper also works. If using a clay pot, first line it with aluminum foil to prevent any of the water bath from seeping into the dough.

BAKER'S FORMULA	%
Whole wheat flour	38
Whole rye flour	31
Salt	1.1
Buttermilk	92
Cornmeal	31
Baking powder	1
Baking soda	1
Raisins	23
Molasses	46
Total	264.1

NUTRITION FACTS

Calories (kcal)	93.62
Protein (g)	2.30
Carbohydrates (g)	21.20
Dietary fiber (g)	1.81
Total sugars (g)	7.01
Fat (g)	.43
Saturated fat (g)	.13
Trans fatty acid (g)	0
Cholesterol (mg)	.59
Sodium (mg)	141.47

If molasses is not to your liking, you can replace all or part of it with an equal amount (by weight) of sorghum syrup, honey, maple syrup, brown sugar, or white sugar.

You can use other dried fruits, such as apricots, cranberries, prunes, or figs in place of some or all of the raisins.

This formula uses both baking powder and baking soda in the final dough, which together create enough push to raise the bread sufficiently.

FINAL DOUGH

VOLUME	OUNCES	GRAMS	INGREDIENT
1/2 cup	6	170	molasses or sorghum syrup (see Commentary)
1/2 cup	3	85	raisins (optional)
Use all	24.14	683	soaker
3 1/2 tablespoons	1	28.5	whole wheat flour
1/2 teaspoon	.12	3.5	baking soda
1/2 teaspoon	.12	3.5	baking powder
TOTAL	34.38	973.5	

1. **Add the molasses and raisins to the soaker,** stirring only long enough to distribute all of the ingredients evenly. In a separate bowl, sift the flour, baking soda, and baking powder together, then add to the batter. Stir for 1 minute, just until all the ingredients are evenly distributed and fully hydrated. (If using a stand mixer, use the paddle attachment and mix for 20 to 30 seconds).

2. **Prepare a 1 pound coffee can** (or up to 3 small containers) by lining it with a sheet of greased waxed paper or parchment paper large enough to cover the inside walls. Also, cut out a parchment or waxed paper circle to line the bottom of the can. The greased side should face in, toward the interior of the can, and it may be greased with melted butter or vegetable oil or misted with pan spray. Pour 4 inches of water into a soup pot and place a small cooling rack or raised, heat-proof trivet in the pot.

3. **Fill the prepared container with the batter.** It should not be more than three-quarters full, and if it is less than half full, the container is too large. Cover the top of the container with a piece of lightly greased aluminum foil. Place the can in the pot of water and add enough water to come halfway up the side of the can. Cover the pot, bring the water to a boil, then reduce it to a low simmer and steam the bread for 3 hours.

4. **Remove the can from the pot,** put it on a cooling rack, and remove the foil cover. Let the bread cool for about 15 minutes, then carefully remove the bread from the container by turning it on its side and sliding the bread out. Remove the waxed paper from the bread and return the bread to the cooling rack for another 45 minutes before slicing and serving.

Spent-Grain Bread

Makes 1 loaf

Beer has been called "liquid bread" because the processes for making bread and beer are very similar: grain is fermented and develops different flavors determined by starch to sugar conversions. The science of brewing is far more detailed than that of bread because, frankly, bread making is much easier. With beer, the slightest temperature variation or imbalance of grain or hops can quickly develop into a flaw because the fermented liquid does not have the bulk of flour to hide behind. The grains used to make beer, mostly malted barley and wheat but sometimes rye, rice, and corn, are strained out and either discarded or used as animal feed—or, if you are clever, added into bread for flavor and fiber.

Much of the technique used in our mash breads is derived from the mashing methods used by brewers, in which malted grain and hops are steeped in hot water at very precisely controlled temperatures. This allows enzyme activity to bring about the types of changes discussed in chapters 2 and 3. The liquid is strained and cooled, and then yeast is added—either ale yeast or lager yeast. (Ale yeast ferments from the top of the liquid, at warmer temperatures, and works its way down the vat; lager yeast ferments from the bottom of the liquid up, at cooler temperatures.) Of course, brewing is much more complicated than this, but the close relationship between beer and bread is undeniable, and in fact, many historians now believe leavened bread emerged as an outgrowth of beer making in ancient Egypt and the Fertile Crescent of Mesopotamia.

Dave Gonzalez, of my local microbrewery, Rock Bottom Brewery, has been saving some of his used-up, or "spent," grain for me, and I have become enamored of the flavor and texture it imparts to bread. While much of the sugar from these grains goes into the beer, there is still quite a bit of residual flavor remaining. More valuable, though, is that these spent (really, mashed) grains are an ideal medium for yeast growth and also provide additional fiber to the dough. Because the spent grains usually include the husks, they are fibrous and chewy, but they are not hard because of all the mashing they have endured. So, in one fell swoop, the recycling of these spent grains adds flavor, yeast food, and nutritional value, and also recycles a valuable resource—a true win-win situation.

This is a foundational formula from which you can make any number of variations and shapes. For some specific suggestions, see the Commentary.

BREAD PROFILE

Slightly enriched, medium soft dough; delayed fermentation method; commercial yeast (or mixed method optional)

DAYS TO MAKE: 2

Day 1: Soaker and *biga*, 20 minutes set up and mix; overnight autolyse
Day 2: 2 hours to de-chill *biga*; 12 to 15 minutes mixing; 2 to 3 hours fermentation, shaping, proofing; 40 to 60 minutes baking

Spent grain from wheat beer (front) and Irish stout (rear).

SOAKER

VOLUME	OUNCES	GRAMS	INGREDIENT	%
1³/₄ cups	8	227	whole wheat flour	100
¹/₂ teaspoon	.14	4	salt	1.75
³/₄ cup	6	170	water	75
TOTAL	14.14	401		176.75

1. **Mix all of the soaker ingredients** together in a bowl for about 1 minute, until all of the flour is hydrated and the ingredients form a ball of dough.

2. **Cover loosely with plastic wrap** and leave at room temperature for 12 to 24 hours. (If it will be more than 24 hours, place the soaker in the refrigerator; it will be good for up to 3 days. Remove it 2 hours before mixing the final dough to take off the chill.)

BIGA

VOLUME	OUNCES	GRAMS	INGREDIENT	%
1³/₄ cups	8	227	whole wheat flour	100
¹/₄ teaspoon	.03	1	instant yeast	.4
³/₄ cup	6	170	filtered or spring water, at room temperature (about 70°F/21°C)	75
TOTAL	14.03	398		175.4

1. **Mix all of the *biga* ingredients** together in a bowl to form a ball of dough. Using wet hands, knead the dough in the bowl for 2 minutes to be sure all of the ingredients are evenly distributed and the flour is fully hydrated. The dough should feel very tacky. Let the dough rest for 5 minutes, then knead it again with wet hands for 1 minute. The dough will become smoother but still be tacky.

2. **Transfer the dough to a clean bowl,** cover tightly with plastic wrap, and refrigerate for at least 8 hours and up to 3 days.

3. **About 2 hours before mixing** the final dough, remove the *biga* from the refrigerator to take off the chill. It will have risen slightly but need not have risen significantly in order to use it in the final dough.

COMMENTARY

You can make a multigrain variation of this bread by using the master multigrain soaker on page 102 instead of the whole wheat soaker, but by the very nature of the spent grains, this is already a multigrain bread.

For a rye version, use a rye soaker. You can adjust the amount of rye to suit your taste, as long as the total flour in the soaker equals 8 ounces. (For specific formulas according to preference, see the *seigle* variations on pages 173 and 175.) For rye breads, also use a wild yeast starter (page 80) rather than the *biga*; this is necessary to control the enzyme activity, since rye naturally contains more enzymes than wheat.

If you prefer a softer loaf, substitute 7 ounces of milk, buttermilk, yogurt, soy milk, or rice milk for the 6 ounces of water in the soaker.

You can use either a *biga* or a wild yeast starter (page 80) in this recipe.

VOLUME	OUNCES	GRAMS	INGREDIENT
Use all	14.14	401	soaker
Use all	14.03	398	*biga*
³/₄ cup	4	113	spent grain (see Commentary)
7 tablespoons	2	56.5	whole wheat flour
⁵/₈ teaspoon	.18	5	salt
2¼ teaspoons	.25	7	instant yeast
2¼ tablespoons	1.5	42.5	honey or agave nectar
or 3 tablespoons	1.5	42.5	or sugar or brown sugar
1 tablespoon	.5	14	vegetable oil (optional)
			extra whole wheat flour for adjustments
TOTAL	36.6	1037	

You may be able to obtain spent grains from a local microbrewery, or perhaps you know someone who is a home brewer. Make friends with small-scale professional brewers, or check in at brewing supply stores to find local beer makers. Trade them a loaf of bread for a bag of spent grain; it will be the best barter either of you have ever made.

Typically, the amount of spent grain should weigh between 15% and 25% of the flour weight. I prefer the full 25%, but you may wish to use less.

The spent grains are already soaked and mashed, and also loaded with active enzymes, so they should be stored in the refrigerator until they are added during the final mix. Spent grains will keep for up to 1 week in the refrigerator, or for 3 months in the freezer.

The amount of honey or other sweetener can be varied, to taste.

1. **Using a metal pastry scraper, chop** the soaker and the *biga* or starter into 12 smaller pieces each (sprinkle some of the extra flour over the pre-doughs to keep the pieces from sticking back to each other).

2. **If mixing by hand,** combine the soaker and *biga* or starter pieces in a bowl with all of the other ingredients except the extra flour and stir vigorously with a mixing spoon or knead with wet hands for about 2 minutes, until all of the ingredients are evenly integrated and distributed into the dough. The dough should be soft and slightly sticky; if not, add more flour or water as needed. **If using a stand mixer,** put the pre-dough pieces and all of the other ingredients except the extra flour into the mixer with the paddle attachment (preferable) or dough hook. Mix on slow speed for 1 minute to bring the ingredients together into a ball. Switch to the dough hook if need be and mix on medium-low speed, occasionally scraping down the bowl, for 2 to 3 minutes, until the pre-doughs become cohesive and assimilated into each other. Add more flour or water as needed until the dough is soft and slightly sticky.

3. **Dust a work surface with flour,** then roll the dough in the flour to coat. Knead the dough by hand for 3 to 4 minutes, incorporating only as much extra flour as needed, until the dough feels soft and tacky, but not sticky. Form the dough into a ball and let it rest on the work surface for 5 minutes while you prepare a clean, lightly oiled bowl.

4. **Resume kneading the dough for 1 minute** to strengthen the gluten and make any final flour or water adjustments. The dough should have strength and pass the windowpane test (see page 84), yet still feel soft, supple, and very tacky. Form the dough into a ball and place

it in the prepared bowl, rolling to coat with oil. Cover loosely with plastic wrap and let rise at room temperature for approximately 45 to 60 minutes, until it is about 1^1/$_2$ times its original size.

5. **Transfer the dough to a lightly floured work surface** and form it into either a loaf pan shape or a freestanding *bâtard* (see pages 87–91 for shaping instructions). For loaf pan bread, place the dough in a greased 4 by 8^1/$_2$-inch bread pan. For a *bâtard*, place it on a proofing cloth or on a sheet pan lined with parchment paper and, if you like, dusted with flour. Mist the top of the dough with pan spray (optional), cover loosely with plastic wrap, and let rise at room temperature for approximately 45 to 60 minutes, until it has grown to 1^1/$_2$ times its original size.

6. **Preheat the oven to 425°F (218°C)** and, if baking a freestanding loaf, prepare the oven for hearth baking (see page 86), including a steam pan (steaming is optional for a sandwich loaf). When the dough is ready to bake, place it in the oven, pour 1 cup of hot water into the steam pan, lower the temperature to 350°F (177°C), and bake for 20 minutes. Rotate the loaf 180 degrees and continue baking for another 20 to 30 minutes, until the loaf is rich brown on all sides, sounds hollow when thumped on the bottom, and registers at least 200°F (93°C) in the center.

7. **Transfer the bread to a cooling rack** and allow it to cool for at least 1 hour before serving.

BAKER'S FORMULA	%
Whole wheat flour	100
Salt	1.8
Instant yeast	1.6
Water	67
Honey	8
Oil	2.7
Spent grain	22
Total	203.1

NUTRITION FACTS	
Calories (kcal)	96.50
Protein (g)	3.61
Carbohydrates (g)	19.77
Dietary fiber (g)	2.92
Total sugars (g)	1.39
Fat (g)	1.06
Saturated fat (g)	.13
Trans fatty acid (g)	0
Cholesterol (mg)	0
Sodium (mg)	144.05

FAQ ∽ *How do I know if the bread is done if I don't have a probe thermometer?*

The best way to determine if a loaf is fully baked without a thermometer is to thump the bottom of the bread and listen for a hollow sound. In addition, the bread should be caramelized on the sides as well as the bottom, and the side walls should not feel squishy. For crusty hearth breads, the trick is to bake the bread as thoroughly as possible without burning it. For softer, enriched loaves, the crust should be caramelized all around, at which point, if it passes the thump test, remove it immediately from the oven. The hard crust will soften as the loaf cools.

International breads are a subset of specialty breads, with distinctive cultural associations. There are thousands of such breads, some of them already based on whole grains and others made from white flour, presented here in a whole grain adaptation. Using the delayed fermentation method, feel free to adapt family favorites just as we have done.

Transitional German-Style Many Seed Bread

Makes 1 loaf

One of the most popular breads in my repertoire, this seed bread has been served at two James Beard Dinners in Charlotte, North Carolina, to great acclaim. Between the long, delayed fermentation and the toasted seeds, the flavors will stay with you for hours. It can be baked either as a loaf pan bread or as a freestanding loaf. The crust softens as it cools, so the bread makes a wonderful panini-style sandwiches.

BREAD PROFILE

Slightly enriched, medium soft dough; delayed fermentation method; commercial yeast

DAYS TO MAKE: 2

Day 1: Soaker and *biga*, 20 minutes set up and mix; overnight autolyse
Day 2: 2 hours to de-chill *biga*; 12 to 15 minutes mixing; 2 to 3 hours fermentation, shaping, proofing; 40 to 60 minutes baking

SOAKER

VOLUME	OUNCES	GRAMS	INGREDIENT	%
1⅓ cups	6	170	whole wheat flour	75
7 tablespoons	2	56.5	rye flour	25
2¼ teaspoons	.25	7	flaxseeds, ground or whole	3
½ teaspoon	.14	4	salt	1.75
¾ cup	6	170	water	75
Total	14.39	407.5		179.75

COMMENTARY

Normally, flaxseeds must be finely ground for our bodies to be able to access their nutritive omega-3 and omega-6 fatty acids, but because they are held in the soaker overnight, they are softened and even somewhat germinated, so they can be used whole. You can also use ground flaxseeds if you prefer.

1. **Mix all of the soaker ingredients together** in a bowl for about 1 minute, until all of the flour is hydrated and the ingredients form a ball of dough.

2. **Cover loosely with plastic wrap** and leave at room temperature for 12 to 24 hours. (If it will be more than 24 hours, place the soaker in the refrigerator; it will be good for up to 3 days. Remove it 2 hours before mixing the final dough to take off the chill.)

BIGA

VOLUME	OUNCES	GRAMS	INGREDIENT	%
1¾ cups	8	227	unbleached bread flour or high-gluten flour	100
¼ teaspoon	.03	1	instant yeast	.4
½ cup plus 2 tablespoons	5	142	filtered or spring water, at room temperature (about 70°F/21°C)	62.5
Total	13.03	370		162.9

The variety of seeds is what makes this such delicious and distinctive bread. Lightly toasting the large seeds brings forth even more flavor.

1. **Mix all of the *biga* ingredients together** in a bowl to form a ball of dough. Using wet hands, knead the dough in the bowl for 2 minutes to be sure all of the ingredients are evenly distributed and the flour is fully hydrated. The dough should feel very tacky. Let the dough rest for 5 minutes, then knead it again with wet hands for 1 minute. The dough will become smoother but still be tacky.

2. **Transfer the dough to a clean bowl,** cover tightly with plastic wrap, and refrigerate for at least 8 hours and up to 3 days.

3. **About 2 hours before mixing the final dough,** remove the *biga* from the refrigerator to take off the chill. It will have risen slightly but need not have risen significantly in order to use it in the final dough.

FINAL DOUGH

VOLUME	OUNCES	GRAMS	INGREDIENT
Use all	14.39	407.5	soaker
Use all	13.03	370	*biga*
7 tablespoons	2	56.5	whole wheat flour
6 tablespoons	2	56.5	sesame seeds
6 tablespoons	2	56.5	sunflower seeds, lightly toasted
6 tablespoons	2	56.5	pumpkin seeds, lightly toasted
5/8 teaspoon	.18	5	salt
2 1/4 teaspoons	.25	7	instant yeast
1 1/2 tablespoons	1	28.5	honey or agave nectar
or 2 tablespoons	1	28.5	or sugar or brown sugar
			extra whole wheat flour for adjustments
			extra sesame seeds for topping (optional)
Total	36.85	1044	

1. **Using a metal pastry scraper, chop** the soaker and the *biga* into 12 smaller pieces each (sprinkle some of the extra flour over the pre-doughs to keep the pieces from sticking back to each other).

MIXING GERMAN-STYLE MANY SEED BREAD

As you combine the soaker and *biga* with the seeds and other ingredients, it's important to mix long enough to thoroughly distribute the seeds evenly throughout the dough.

2. **If mixing by hand, combine** the soaker and *biga* pieces in a bowl with the 7 tablespoons flour and the seeds, salt, yeast, and honey. Stir vigorously with a mixing spoon or knead with wet hands for about 2 minutes, until all of the ingredients are evenly integrated and distributed into the dough. The dough should be soft and slightly sticky; if not, add more flour or water as needed. **If using a stand mixer,** put the pre-dough pieces in the bowl along with the 7 tablespoons flour and the seeds, salt, yeast, and honey. Mix on slow speed with the paddle attachment (preferable) or dough hook for 1 minute to bring the ingredients together into a ball. Switch to the dough hook if need be and mix on medium-low speed, occasionally scraping down the bowl, for 3 to 4 minutes, until the pre-doughs become cohesive and assimilated into each other. Add more flour or water as needed until the dough is soft and slightly sticky.

3. **Dust a work surface with flour,** then roll the dough in the flour to coat. Knead the dough by hand for 3 to 4 minutes, incorporating only as much extra flour as needed, until the dough feels soft and tacky, but not sticky. Form the dough into a ball and let it rest on the work surface for 5 minutes while you prepare a clean, lightly oiled bowl.

4. **Resume kneading the dough for 1 minute** to strengthen the gluten and make any final flour or water adjustments. The dough should have strength and pass the windowpane test (see page 84), yet still feel soft, supple, and very tacky. Form the dough into a ball and place it in the prepared bowl, rolling to coat with oil. Cover loosely with plastic wrap and let rise at room temperature for approximately 45 to 60 minutes, until it is about $1^1/_2$ times its original size.

5. **Transfer the dough to a lightly floured work surface** and form it into either a loaf pan shape or a freestanding *bâtard* (see pages 87–91 for shaping instructions). For loaf pan bread, place the dough in a greased 4 by $8^1/_2$-inch bread pan. For a *bâtard*, place it on a proofing cloth or on a sheet pan lined with parchment paper and, if you like, dusted with flour. Brush the top of the dough with water and generously sprinkle sesame seeds on top. Cover loosely with plastic wrap and let rise at room temperature for approximately 45 to 60 minutes, until it is about $1^1/_2$ times its original size.

6. **Preheat the oven to 425°F (218°C)** and, if baking a freestanding loaf, prepare the oven for hearth baking (see page 73), including a steam pan. When the dough is ready to bake, score it (for hearth bread) and place it in the oven. Pour 1 cup of hot water into the steam pan, lower the temperature to 375°F (191°C), and bake for 15 minutes. Rotate the loaf 180 degrees and continue baking for another 20 to 30 minutes, until the loaf is a rich brown on all sides, sounds hollow when thumped on the bottom, and registers at least 200°F (93°C) in the center.

7. **Transfer the bread to a cooling rack** and allow it to cool for 1 hour before serving.

BAKER'S FORMULA	%
Whole wheat flour	44.5
Bread flour	44.5
Whole rye flour	11
Salt	1.8
Instant yeast	1.6
Water	61
Honey	5.5
Sesame, pumpkin, and sunflower seeds	33
Flaxseeds	1.4
Total	204.3

NUTRITION FACTS	
Calories (kcal)	118.04
Protein (g)	4.42
Carbohydrates (g)	17.32
Dietary fiber (g)	2.37
Total sugars (g)	1.04
Fat (g)	3.84
Saturated fat (g)	.38
Trans fatty acid (g)	0
Cholesterol (mg)	0
Sodium (mg)	147.96

Whole Wheat Brioche

Makes 1 large or 12 small loaves

BREAD PROFILE

Rich dough; delayed fermentation method; commercial yeast

DAYS TO MAKE: 2

Day 1: Soaker and *biga*, 20 minutes set up and mix; overnight autolyse
Day 2: 12 to 15 minutes mixing; 3¹/₂ hours shaping and proofing; 20 to 50 minutes baking

COMMENTARY

As with most of these whole wheat breads, you can make a multigrain version by substituting the soaker on page 102 in place of the whole wheat soaker.

Brioche can be made with a little butter, or a lot, and still be considered brioche. Our version uses 40% butter to flour, though I have seen and made versions that go up to 100% butter (and down to 25%). The 40% version offers a middle ground from which the greatest number of tasty products can be made.

This soaker is unlike any other because the melted butter makes up most of the liquid. It will firm up overnight in the refrigerator, causing the soaker to feel thicker than others, but that will change when you make the final dough.

This whole wheat version is almost an oxymoron: brioche is, by definition, rich, buttery, *white* flour bread. But there is no reason why we cannot indulge once in a while in rich, buttery, whole grain bread. Brioche is a very versatile bread that can be used for French toast, bread pudding, tea sandwiches, or toast points for appetizers. It can be flavored with vanilla and used for tender pie and tart dough. It can also be wrapped around meats and mousses for Wellingtons, terrines, and *ballotines*.

The name *brioche* derives from the Old French word *broyer*, which means "knead" or "break up," as the dough usually takes a long time to mix because softened butter is added gradually. However, with the delayed fermentation method and the technique of adding melted butter to the soaker, the kneading time is greatly reduced in this version. The classic *brioche à tête* (meaning "brioche with a head") is the most popular presentation, and many home bakers now have small brioche molds in which to make these. Otherwise, a Kugelhopf pan (shown at right) or muffin tins work well. Shaping instructions for *brioche à tête* are on page 217.

			SOAKER	
VOLUME	**OUNCES**	**GRAMS**	**INGREDIENT**	**%**
1³/₄ cups	8	227	whole wheat flour	100
¹/₂ teaspoon	.14	4	salt	1.75
¹/₂ cup	4	113	whole milk, scalded and cooled	50
1 cup	8	227	unsalted butter, melted	100
Total	20.14	571		251.75

1. **Mix all of the soaker ingredients together** in a bowl for about 1 minute, until all of the flour is hydrated and the ingredients form a ball of dough.

2. **Cover tightly with plastic wrap** and refrigerate the soaker overnight or up to 3 days. Leave it in the refrigerator until you are ready to mix the final dough. This is the one soaker that should be chilled, as the butter must be firm when you mix the final dough.

You can even use a bundt pan or kugelhopf mold to make a coffee cake–style brioche (as shown here). Whip 1 tablespoon softened unsalted butter with 1 teaspoon of whole wheat flour. Brush this butter paste on walls of the pan, including the tube. Sprinkle 2 tablespoons of sliced almonds into the pan, turning the pan to distribute the almonds so that they stick to the inside wall of the pan. Form the prepared brioche dough into a round bagel shape and drop it over the tube to fill the pan three-quarters full. Proof and bake at 325°F (163°C) for 45 to 55 minutes.

BIGA

VOLUME	OUNCES	GRAMS	INGREDIENT	%
1³/₄ cups	8	227	whole wheat flour	100
¹/₄ teaspoon	.03	1	instant yeast	.4
4 large	6.5	184	eggs, slightly beaten	81
Total	14.53	412		181.4

1. **Mix all of the *biga* ingredients together** in a bowl to form a ball of dough. Using wet hands, knead the dough in the bowl for 2 minutes to be sure all of the ingredients are evenly distributed and the flour is fully hydrated. The dough should feel very tacky. Let the dough rest for 5 minutes, then knead it again with wet hands for 1 minute. The dough will become smoother but still be tacky.

2. **Transfer the dough to a clean bowl, cover** tightly with plastic wrap, and refrigerate for at least 8 hours and up to 3 days.

3. **Leave the *biga* in the refrigerator** until you are ready to make the final dough (this is the one time it is preferable to work with cold ingredients because of all the butter). It will have risen slightly but need not have risen significantly in order to use it in the final dough.

FINAL DOUGH

VOLUME	OUNCES	GRAMS	INGREDIENT
Use all	20.14	571	soaker
Use all	14.53	412	*biga*
1 cup	4.5	128	whole wheat flour
⁵/₈ teaspoon	.18	5	salt
2¹/₄ teaspoons	.25	7	instant yeast
3 tablespoons	1.5	42.5	sugar
			extra whole wheat flour for adjustments
			1 egg beaten with 1 tablespoon water and a pinch of salt for egg wash
Total	41.1	1165.5	

1. **Using a metal pastry scraper, chop** the chilled soaker and the *biga* into 12 smaller pieces each (sprinkle some of the extra flour over the pre-doughs to keep the pieces from sticking back to each other).

2. **If mixing by hand,** combine the soaker and *biga* pieces with all of the other ingredients except the extra flour and stir vigorously with a mixing spoon or knead with wet hands until all of the ingredients are evenly integrated and distributed into the dough. The dough should soften as the butter warms up and be slightly sticky; if not, add more flour or water as needed. **If using a stand mixer,** put the pre-dough pieces and all of the other ingredients except the extra flour into the mixer with the dough hook. Mix on slow speed for 3 to 4 minutes, occasionally scraping down the bowl, until the pre-doughs become cohesive and assimilated into each other. Add some of the extra flour or more water as needed until the dough is soft and slightly sticky.

3. **Dust a work surface with flour,** then roll the dough in the flour to coat. Knead the dough by hand for 3 to 4 minutes, incorporating only as much extra flour as needed; the dough should feel cold, firm, and slightly tacky. Form the dough into a ball and let it rest on the work surface for 5 minutes.

4. **Divide the dough into 12 equal pieces** (or as many as desired) and round each into a smooth ball. Butter or grease 12 brioche molds or a 12-slot muffin tin. Form each of the pieces into a *brioche à tête* (see below) or whatever shape you prefer; you can also shape the dough into 1 large or 2 smaller sandwich loaves (see page 87 for shaping instructions). Mist the top of the dough with pan spray (optional), cover loosely with plastic wrap, and let rise at room temperature for approximately 3 hours, until it has grown to $1^1/_2$ times its original size.

Because of all the butter, the dough must be cold in order to shape it. This means it will take much longer to rise than the other doughs in this book—about 3 to 4 hours, depending on the ambient temperature.

There is no bulk fermentation stage; after the final mixing the dough is shaped and then proofed right away.

SHAPING BRIOCHE À TÊTE

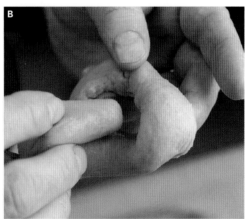

(A) Roll one end of small, brioche dough balls into a cone. (B) Poke a hole in the round, fat half and slip the cone end through it so that a nub of dough comes though to make a "head." (C) Pan the shaped dough in brioche molds.

BAKER'S FORMULA	%
Whole wheat flour	100
Salt	1.6
Instant yeast	1.4
Milk	19.5
Egg	32
Sugar	7.3
Unsalted butter	39
Total	200.8

NUTRITION FACTS	
Calories (kcal)	123.85
Protein (g)	3.38
Carbohydrates (g)	14.31
Dietary fiber (g)	2.20
Total sugars (g)	1.56
Fat (g)	6.55
Saturated fat (g)	3.81
Trans fatty acid (g)	.17
Cholesterol (mg)	38.57
Sodium (mg)	117.28

5. **Preheat the oven to 425°F (218°C).** When the dough is ready to bake, carefully brush the tops with egg wash, place on the middle shelf, lower the temperature to 400°F (204°C), and bake for 10 minutes. Rotate the breads and continue baking for another 10 to 15 minutes, until the breads are a rich, reddish brown all over (lift one from the mold and check the bottom and sides). They should sound hollow when thumped on the bottom and register at least 195°F (91°C) in the center.

6. **Remove the breads from their molds, transfer** them to a cooling rack, and allow to cool for at least 20 minutes before serving.

Vollkornbrot

Makes 1 large loaf

The name *vollkornbrot* means "whole meal bread," and there are many variations in which it can be made. Some versions include oats and even cornmeal, but flaxseeds and sunflower seeds are the most definitive, along with rye in its many grinds: chops, meal, and coarse pumpernickel flour.

This Old World rye bread, sometimes called cocktail rye, is coming back into popularity in this country thanks to artisan bakeries that appreciate its uniqueness and intense flavor. It is made from 100% rye if you have a rye starter; otherwise it is nearly 100% rye. It is dense, moist, and not at all like the soft, open-crumbed breads Americans tend to prefer. But the flavors are so complex and unique that it can easily become an acquired taste and even an obsession. I know people who bring back numerous loaves from Germany in dedicated suitcases. Traditionally, the loaves are about 4 pounds or more in weight and are usually baked in large Pullman-style loaf pans. The smaller version here is easily made at home, and it should last for many days, as it is customarily sliced very thin.

This is definitely one of those breads that tastes better the day after it is baked (some bakers feel two or three days is even better). Because it is dense, it takes a while to bake and holds in a lot of moisture, then releases its complex flavors for days to come.

BREAD PROFILE

Lean or slightly enriched dough; delayed fermentation method; mixed leavening method

DAYS TO MAKE: 2

Day 1: Mash and starter, 20 minutes set up and mix, 3 hours mash development; overnight autolyse
Day 2: 2 hours to de-chill starter; 12 to 15 minutes mixing; 2 to 3 hours fermentation, shaping, proofing; 60 to 80 minutes baking

COMMENTARY

The mash will evaporate down to about 15 ounces, so if you make a large batch of mash to divide out for future baking, measure out 15-ounce portions. The mash will keep for up to 1 week in the refrigerator and up to 3 months in the freezer.

MASH

VOLUME	OUNCES	GRAMS	INGREDIENT	%
1¼ cups plus 1 tablespoon	10.6	300	water	250
¾ cup plus 3 tablespoons	4.25	120	whole rye meal or rye flour, preferably coarse grind, or rye chops (see Commentary)	100
½ teaspoon	.03	1	diastatic malt powder or sprouted wheat flour (optional)	.7
3 tablespoons	1	28.5	flaxseeds	23.5
Total	15.88	449.5		374.2

1. **Preheat the oven to 200°F (93°C).**

2. **Heat the water to 165°F (74°C)** in an ovenproof saucepan, then remove the pan from the heat and whisk or stir in the flour and malt until the flour is fully hydrated and makes a paste similar to a thin pudding or gravy. Using a spatula or plastic pastry scraper dipped in water,

In his book *Bread*, Jeffrey Hamelman offers a good baker's trick for this bread: oil the pan and then dust it generously with rye meal or whole rye flour. This not only helps release the loaf easily, it also gives it an earthy, rustic crust.

scrape the spoon or whisk and the walls of the pan to get all of the dough back into the pan and off the inside walls. (The mash temperature will drop to about 150°F/66°C during the stirring.) Immediately cover the pan with its lid or aluminum foil and place it in the oven.

3. **Turn the oven down to warm/150°F (66°C),** if it has this setting, and leave the mash in the oven for at least 1 hour and up to 3 hours. If the oven can't be turned down this low, turn it off and 10 minutes later turn it back on to the lowest setting (often 200°F/93°C) for about 10 minutes; continue alternating between on and off at 10-minute intervals for the first hour, then turn the oven off and leave it off. If possible, leave the mash in the warm oven for the full 3 hours. However, you can also remove it from the oven after the first hour and leave it at room temperature, covered, if you need to use the oven for other purposes. After 3 hours, stir in the flaxseeds and refrigerate the mash until you are ready to use it. You can also leave it out overnight at room temperature if you plan to use it within the next 24 hours.

STARTER

VOLUME	OUNCES	GRAMS	INGREDIENT	%
1/3 cup	2.5	71	whole wheat or rye mother starter (pages 67 and 69)	33.3
1 2/3 cups	7.5	213	whole rye flour, preferably coarse grind	100
3/4 cup	6	170	filtered or spring water, at room temperature (about 70°F/21°C)	80
Total	16	454		213.3

Whole rye meal and rye chops (similar in size to cracked wheat, steel-cut oats, or buckwheat groats) are coarser grinds than regular rye flour. Rye meal is similar to pumpernickel flour, a coarsely milled whole rye flour. The two are interchangeable in these recipes.

1. **Mix all of the starter ingredients together** in a bowl to form a ball of dough. Using wet hands, knead the dough in the bowl for about 2 minutes to be sure all of the ingredients are evenly distributed and the flour is fully hydrated. The dough should feel very tacky. Let the dough rest for about 5 minutes, then knead it again with wet hands for 1 minute. The dough will become smoother but still be tacky.

2. **Transfer the dough to a clean bowl, cover** loosely with plastic wrap, and leave at room temperature for approximately 4 to 6 hours, until the dough is nearly double in size. The dough should register between 3.5 and 4.0 if tested with pH paper (see page 77) and have a pleasant aroma similar to apple cider vinegar. If the starter has not doubled or acidified properly, allow it to continue to develop at room temperature. It could take up to 8 hours or even longer.

3. **When the starter has fully developed, knead** it for a few seconds to degas it. The starter is now ready for mixing into the final dough; however, if necessary to coordinate timing with the mash, cover tightly with plastic wrap and refrigerate overnight (or up to 3 days). About 2 hours before mixing the final dough, remove the starter from the refrigerator to take off the chill.

The addition of molasses darkens the loaf and gives it a different flavor tone. The molasses variation is sometimes known as *schwartzbrot*, of which there are also many versions, including some with cocoa powder (as here) or caramel coloring. If you add molasses, you will also have to add about 4 tablespoons of additional rye flour.

VOLUME	OUNCES	GRAMS	INGREDIENT
Use all	16	454	starter
Use all	15	425	mash
2 cups	9	255	whole rye flour
1/4 cup	1.5	42.5	sunflower seeds, raw or lightly toasted
1 1/4 teaspoons	.35	10	salt
2 1/4 teaspoons	.25	7	instant yeast
3 tablespoons	2	56.5	molasses (optional; see Commentary)
1 1/2 tablespoons	.5	14	cocoa powder (optional; see Commentary)
			extra whole rye flour for adjustments
Total	44.6	1264	

When *vollkornbrot* is mixed, it makes a dense, clay-like dough that rises very little but develops amazingly complex flavors.

1. **Using a metal pastry scraper, chop** the starter into 12 smaller pieces (sprinkle some of the extra flour over the pre-dough to keep the pieces from sticking back to each other).

2. **If mixing by hand,** combine the starter pieces and the mash in a bowl with all of the other ingredients except the extra flour and stir vigorously with a mixing spoon or knead with wet hands for about 2 minutes, until all of the ingredients are evenly integrated and distributed into the dough. The dough should be soft and slightly sticky; if not, add more flour or water as needed. **If using a stand mixer,** put the pre-dough pieces and all of the other ingredients except the extra flour into the mixer with the paddle attachment (preferable) or dough hook. Mix on slow speed for 1 minute to

bring the ingredients together into a ball. Switch to the dough hook if need be and mix on medium-low speed, occasionally scraping down the bowl, for 2 to 3 minutes, until all of the ingredients become cohesive and assimilated into each other. Add more flour or water as needed until the dough is soft and slightly sticky.

3. **Dust a work surface with flour,** then roll the dough in the flour to coat. Knead the dough by hand for 3 to 4 minutes, incorporating only as much extra flour as needed, until the dough feels soft and slightly sticky. Form the dough into a ball and let it rest on the work surface for 5 minutes while you prepare a clean, lightly oiled bowl.

4. **Resume kneading the dough for 1 minute** to strengthen the gluten and make any final flour or water adjustments. The dough should have strength when fully kneaded, yet still feel soft and supple and be very tacky, verging on sticky. Form the dough into a ball and place it in the prepared bowl, rolling to coat with oil. Cover loosely with plastic wrap and let rise at room temperature for approximately 20 minutes, until it swells and just begins to show signs of growth.

5. **Transfer the dough to a lightly floured work surface** and form it into a loaf pan shape (see page 87 for shaping instructions). Oil a 4 by 8^1/$_2$-inch loaf pan and put 1 tablespoon of whole rye flour in the pan, tossing the flour to evenly coat the inside of the pan. Place the loaf in the pan (it will fill it nearly to the top), sprinkle whole rye flour over the top, then mist the top with pan spray (optional). Cover loosely with plastic wrap and let rise at room temperature for approximately 45 to 60 minutes, until it has grown to the top of the pan (it grows very slowly).

6. **Preheat the oven to 500°F (260°C)** and place a steam pan on one of the shelves. When the dough is ready to bake, place it in the oven, pour 1 cup of hot water into the steam pan, lower the temperature to 375°F (191°C), and bake for 30 minutes, removing the steam pan after the first 10 minutes. Rotate the loaf 180 degrees and continue baking for another 30 minutes, until the loaf is crisp on top and holds its shape when removed from the pan. At this point, remove the bread from the pan, transfer it to a sheet pan, and return it to the oven to bake approximately 40 minutes longer, rotating the loaf every 10 minutes so that a different side of the loaf is face down, including the top. This will bake and crisp the loaf more evenly. Bake until the loaf is caramelized and crisp on all sides, sounds hollow when thumped on the bottom, and registers at least 200°F (93°C) in the center.

7. **Transfer the bread to a cooling rack** and allow it to cool thoroughly before wrapping (about 3 hours). For the first 24 hours, keep it in a paper bag or wrap it in a cloth towel to allow it to continue drying out and developing flavor. After that, it can be packaged in aluminum foil.

BAKER'S FORMULA	%
Whole rye flour	100
Salt	1.6
Instant yeast	1.1
Water	79
Diastatic malt powder	.1
Sunflower seeds	7
Cocoa powder	2.2
Flaxseeds	4.5
Molasses	9
Total	204.5

NUTRITION FACTS	
Calories (kcal)	96.12
Protein (g)	2.77
Carbohydrates (g)	18.09
Dietary fiber (g)	3.28
Total sugars (g)	1.06
Fat (g)	1.81
Saturated fat (g)	.11
Trans fatty acid (g)	0
Cholesterol (mg)	0
Sodium (mg)	126.60

Bavarian Pumpernickel

Makes 1 large loaf

BREAD PROFILE

Lean dough; delayed fermentation method; mixed leavening method

DAYS TO MAKE: 2

Day 1: Mash and starter, 20 minutes set up and mix, 3 hours mash development; overnight autolyse
Day 2: 2 hours to de-chill starter; 12 to 15 minutes mixing; 2 to 3 hours fermentation, shaping, proofing; 60 to 80 minutes baking

This bread, like *vollkornbrot*, is intentionally dense, must be sliced thin, and represents the opposite polarity from light and airy rustic breads. The flavor is intense and the bread is usually served with meats and soups or strong cheeses.

MASH

VOLUME	OUNCES	GRAMS	INGREDIENT	%
1¼ cups plus 1 tablespoon	10.6	300	water	250
¾ cup plus 3 tablespoons	4.25	120	whole rye meal or rye flour, preferably coarse grind	100
Use all	6	170	*altus* (optional; see Commentary)	141
½ teaspoon	.03	1	diastatic malt powder or sprouted wheat flour (optional)	.7
Total	20.88	591		491.7

COMMENTARY

Classic pumpernickel-style breads often use old bread, soaked in water, as an ingredient (it is referred to as *altus* in some books). It is, in a way, yet another type of mash. In our version, this soaked bread is an optional ingredient, but it does add a wonderful layer of flavor and texture.

For *altus* (soaked bread), cover 1 cup of ½-inch bread cubes, crusts on, with just enough hot water to saturate and soften them, about ½ cup. Rye bread is preferable, but you can substitute whole wheat. Let the *altus* sit at room temperature for a minimum of 4 hours, or overnight. You can also use toasted or dried bread, in which case you may need more water. When you are ready to add it to the dough, squeeze out the excess water.

1. **Preheat the oven to 200°F (93°C).**

2. **Heat the water to 165°F (74°C)** in an ovenproof saucepan, then remove the pan from the heat and whisk or stir in the rye flour and malt until the flour is fully hydrated and makes a paste similar to a thin pudding or gravy. Using a spatula or plastic pastry scraper dipped in water, scrape the spoon or whisk and the walls of the pan to get all of the dough back into the pan and off the inside walls. (The mash temperature will drop to about 150°F/66°C during the stirring.) Immediately cover the pan with its lid or aluminum foil and place it in the oven.

3. **Turn the oven down to warm/150°F (66°C),** if it has this setting, and leave the mash in the oven for at least 1 hour and up to 3 hours. If the oven can't be turned down this low, turn it off and 10 minutes later turn it back on to the lowest setting (usually 200°F/93°C for about 10 minutes; continue alternating between on and off at 10-minute intervals for the first hour, then turn the oven off and leave it off. If possible, leave the mash in the warm oven for the full 3 hours. However, you can also remove it from the oven after the first hour and leave it at room temperature, covered, if you need to use the oven for other purposes. After 3 hours, stir in the soaked bread and refrigerate the mash until you are ready to use it. You can also leave it out overnight at room temperature if you plan to use it within the next 24 hours.

STARTER

VOLUME	OUNCES	GRAMS	INGREDIENT	%
⅓ cup	2.5	71	whole wheat or rye mother starter (pages 67 and 69)	33.3
1⅔ cups	7.5	213	rye flour, preferably coarse grind	100
¾ cup	6	170	filtered or spring water, at room temperature (about 70°F/21°C)	80
Total	16	454		213.3

The mash (with the *altus*) will evaporate down to about 20 ounces, so if you make a large batch to divide out for future baking, measure out 20-ounce portions. The mash will keep for up to 1 week in the refrigerator and up to 3 months in the freezer.

Boiled rye berries, like boiled wheat kernels, provide a unique, chewy texture and a wonderfully sweet flavor. You can, of course, substitute other boiled grains, such as barley, brown rice, or wheat. To prepare 1 cup of cooked rye berries, mix ½ cup of rye berries with 1½ cups of water in a saucepan, cover the pan, and bring to a boil (for plumper rye berries, soak them overnight, then boil them in fresh water). Simmer for approximately 1 hour, or until the berries are soft. Drain and cool before using. You can save any leftover water for the soaked bread, if you like. Because the cooked rye berries must be cooled before they are added to the final dough, you may prefer to prepare them on Day 1. Once cooked, they can be kept for up to 24 hours at room temperature or refrigerated.

Cocoa powder is added to darken the bread and provide a touch of bitterness. It is optional, or it can be replaced with caramel coloring, which is just burnt sugar in powdered or liquid form.

1. **Mix all of the starter ingredients together** in a bowl to form a ball of dough. Using wet hands, knead the dough in the bowl for about 2 minutes to be sure all of the ingredients are evenly distributed and the flour is fully hydrated. The dough should feel very tacky. Let the dough rest for about 5 minutes, then knead it again with wet hands for 1 minute. The dough will become smoother but still be tacky.

2. **Transfer the dough to a clean bowl, cover** loosely with plastic wrap, and leave at room temperature for approximately 4 to 6 hours, until the dough is nearly double in size. The dough should register between 3.5 and 4.0 if tested with pH paper (see page 77) and have a pleasant aroma similar to apple cider vinegar. If the starter has not doubled or acidified properly, allow it to continue to develop at room temperature. It could take up to 8 hours or even longer.

3. **When the starter has fully developed, knead** it for a few seconds to degas it. The starter is now ready for mixing into the final dough; however, if necessary to coordinate timing with the mash, cover tightly with plastic wrap and refrigerate overnight (or up to 3 days). About 2 hours before mixing the final dough, remove the starter from the refrigerator to take off the chill.

FINAL DOUGH

VOLUME	OUNCES	GRAMS	INGREDIENT
Use all	16	454	starter
Use all	20	568	mash
2 cups	9	255	whole rye flour
1 cup	6	170	cooked rye berries
1¾ teaspoons	.5	14	salt
2¼ teaspoons	.25	7	instant yeast
1½ tablespoons	.5	14	cocoa powder (optional)
			extra whole rye flour for adjustments
Total	52.25	1482	

1. **Using a metal pastry scraper, chop** the starter into 12 smaller pieces (sprinkle some of the extra flour over the pre-dough to keep the pieces from sticking back to each other).

2. **If mixing by hand,** combine the starter pieces and mash in a bowl with all of the other ingredients except the extra flour and stir vigorously with a mixing spoon or knead with wet hands for about 2 minutes, until all of the ingredients are evenly integrated and distributed into the dough. The dough should be soft and slightly sticky; if not, add more flour or water

as needed. **If using a stand mixer,** put the pre-dough pieces and all of the other ingredients except the extra flour into the mixer with the paddle attachment (preferable) or dough hook. Mix on slow speed for 1 minute to bring the ingredients together into a ball. Switch to the dough hook if need be and mix on medium-low speed, occasionally scraping down the bowl, for 2 to 3 minutes, until all of the ingredients become cohesive and assimilated into each other. Add more flour or water as needed until the dough is soft and slightly sticky.

3. **Dust a work surface with flour,** then roll the dough in the flour to coat. Knead the dough by hand for 3 to 4 minutes, incorporating only as much extra flour as needed, until the dough feels like firm, damp clay. Form the dough into a ball and let it rest on the work surface for 5 minutes while you prepare a clean, lightly oiled bowl.

4. **Resume kneading the dough for 1 minute** to strengthen the gluten and make any final flour or water adjustments. The dough should feel soft and malleable, like modeling clay. Form the dough into a ball and place it in the prepared bowl, rolling to coat with oil. Cover loosely with plastic wrap and let rise at room temperature for approximately 20 minutes, until it swells and just begins to show signs of growth.

5. **Preheat the oven to 400°F (204°C).** Transfer the dough to a lightly floured work surface and form it into a loaf pan shape (see page 87 for shaping instructions). Oil a 4 by 8^1/$_2$-inch loaf pan (or a Pullman pan with a lid) and put 1 tablespoon of whole rye flour in the pan, tossing the flour to evenly coat the inside of the pan (optional). Place the loaf in the pan (it will fill it nearly to the top), sprinkle whole rye flour over the top, mist the top with pan spray, and place an inverted sheet pan over the dough (or use the Pullman lid). Do not proof the bread; bake it immediately.

6. **Place the covered pan on a sheet pan,** put it in the oven, lower the temperature to 375°F (191°C), and bake for 30 minutes. Remove the lid and then, if the loaf holds its shape when removed from the pan, transfer it to the sheet pan. Bake for another 30 to 45 minutes, rotating the loaf every 7 or 8 minutes so that a different side of the loaf is face down, including the top. This will bake and crisp the loaf more evenly. Bake until the loaf is crisp and caramelized on all sides, sounds hollow when thumped on the bottom, and registers at least 200°F (93°C) in the center.

7. **Transfer the bread to a cooling rack** and allow it to cool thoroughly before wrapping (about 3 hours). For the first 24 hours, keep it in a paper bag or wrap it in a cloth towel to allow it to continue drying out and developing flavor. After that, it can be packaged in aluminum foil.

BAKER'S FORMULA	%
Whole rye flour	100
Salt	2.2
Instant yeast	1.1
Water	79
Diastatic malt powder	.1
Altus	27
Whole rye berries	27
Cocoa powder	2.2
Total	238.5

NUTRITION FACTS	
Calories (kcal)	98.23
Protein (g)	3.22
Carbohydrates (g)	19.89
Dietary fiber (g)	3.41
Total sugars (g)	.17
Fat (g)	1
Saturated fat (g)	.02
Trans fatty acid (g)	0
Cholesterol (mg)	0
Sodium (mg)	182.82

This bread is baked Pullman-style; that is, with a lid. If you have a Pullman pan (which is usually longer than a regular loaf pan and comes with its own lid), use it. Otherwise, follow the directions for baking in a regular bread pan with a makeshift lid (an inverted sheet pan).

Hutzelbrot with Dried Fruit

Makes 2 loaves

BREAD PROFILE

Lean dough; delayed fermentation method; mixed leavening method

DAYS TO MAKE: 2

Day 1: Mash and starter, 20 minutes set up and mix, 3 hours mash development; overnight autolyse
Day 2: 2 hours to de-chill starter; 12 to 15 minutes mixing; 2 to 3 hours fermentation, shaping, proofing; 55 to 65 minutes baking

COMMENTARY

For *altus* (soaked bread), cover 1 cup of 1/2-inch bread cubes, crusts on, with just enough hot water to saturate and soften them, about 1/2 cup. Rye bread is preferable, but you can substitute whole wheat. Let the *altus* sit at room temperature for a minimum of 4 hours, or overnight. You can also use toasted or dried bread, in which case you may need more water. When you are ready to add it to the dough, squeeze out the excess water.

This is a dense, freestanding wheat and rye bread with dried fruit, served in Germany mostly at Christmastime. However, the texture of the bread combined with the sweetness of the fruit makes this an excellent bread to serve year-round with cream cheese spreads as well as with marmalades and jams.

MASH

VOLUME	OUNCES	GRAMS	INGREDIENT	%
1 1/4 cups plus 1 tablespoon	10.6	300	water	236
1/2 cup	2.25	64	whole rye meal or rye flour, preferably coarse grind	50
1/2 cup	2.25	64	whole wheat flour	50
1/2 teaspoon	.03	1	diastatic malt powder or sprouted wheat flour (optional)	.66
Use all	6	170	*altus* (see Commentary)	133
Total	21.13	599		469.7

1. **Preheat the oven to 200°F (93°C).**

2. **Heat the water to 165°F (74°C)** in an ovenproof saucepan, then remove the pan from the heat and whisk or stir in the rye flour, whole wheat flour, and malt until the flour is fully hydrated and makes a paste similar to a thin pudding or gravy. Using a spatula or plastic pastry scraper dipped in water, scrape the spoon or whisk and the walls of the pan to get all of the dough back into the pan and off the inside walls. (The mash temperature will drop to about 150°F/66°C during the stirring.) Immediately cover the pan with its lid or aluminum foil and place it in the oven.

3. **Turn the oven down to warm/150°F (66°C),** if it has this setting, and leave the mash in the oven for at least 1 hour and up to 3 hours. If the oven can't be turned down this low, turn it off and 10 minutes later turn it back on to the lowest setting (often 200°F/93°C) for about 10 minutes; continue alternating between on and off at 10-minute intervals for the first hour, then turn the oven off and leave it off. If possible, leave the mash in the warm oven for the full 3 hours. However, you can also remove it from the oven after the first hour and leave it at

room temperature, covered, if you need to use the oven for other purposes. After 3 hours, stir in the soaked bread and refrigerate the mash until you are ready to use it. You can also leave it out overnight at room temperature if you plan to use it within the next 24 hours.

STARTER

VOLUME	OUNCES	GRAMS	INGREDIENT	%
1/3 cup	2.5	71	whole wheat or rye mother starter (pages 67 and 69)	33.3
1 2/3 cups	7.5	213	whole rye flour	100
3/4 cup	6	170	filtered or spring water, at room temperature (about 70°F/21°C)	80
Total	16	454		213.3

1. **Mix all of the starter ingredients together** in a bowl to form a ball of dough. Using wet hands, knead the dough in the bowl for about 2 minutes to be sure all of the ingredients are evenly distributed and the flour is fully hydrated. The dough should feel very tacky. Let the dough rest for about 5 minutes, then knead it again with wet hands for 1 minute. The dough will become smoother but still be tacky.

2. **Transfer the dough to a clean bowl, cover** loosely with plastic wrap, and leave at room temperature for approximately 4 to 6 hours, until the dough is nearly double in size. The dough should register between 3.5 and 4.0 if tested with pH paper (see page 77) and have a pleasant aroma similar to apple cider vinegar. If the starter has not doubled or acidified properly, allow it to continue to develop at room temperature. It could take up to 8 hours or even longer.

3. **When the starter has fully developed, knead** it for a few seconds to degas it. The starter is now ready for mixing into the final dough; however, if necessary to coordinate timing with the mash, cover tightly with plastic wrap and refrigerate overnight (or up to 3 days). About 2 hours before mixing the final dough, remove the starter from the refrigerator to take off the chill.

FINAL DOUGH

VOLUME	OUNCES	GRAMS	INGREDIENT
Use all	16	454	starter
Use all	14	397	mash
3/4 cup	3.5	99	whole wheat flour
3/4 cup	3.5	99	whole rye flour
1 cup	6	170	dried fruit (citron, apricots, figs, plums, cherries, cranberries, golden raisins)
1 3/4 teaspoons	.5	14	salt
2 1/4 teaspoons	.25	7	instant yeast
1 1/2 tablespoons	.5	14	cocoa powder (optional)
			extra whole wheat or whole rye flour for adjustments
			flour paste (see Commentary)
Total	44.25	1254	

The crunchy coating on this bread, similar to mottled coatings used on other regional breads, such as Dutch crunch, is made by mixing 1 cup flour with just enough water to make a thin paste; the amount of water depends on the type of flour used. In his wonderful book *Secrets of a Jewish Baker*, George Greenstein uses rye flour to make *maszda*, which means "paste." Other versions can be made with rice flour, cornstarch, or any low-gluten flour.

1. **Using a metal pastry scraper, chop** the starter into 12 smaller pieces (sprinkle some of the extra flour over the pre-dough to keep the pieces from sticking back to each other).

2. **If mixing by hand,** combine the starter pieces and mash in a bowl with the whole wheat and whole rye flours, dried fruit, salt, yeast, and cocoa. Stir vigorously with a mixing spoon or knead with wet hands for about 2 minutes, until all of the ingredients are evenly integrated and distributed into the dough. The dough should be soft and slightly sticky; if not, add some of the extra flour or more water as needed. **If using a stand mixer,** put the starter pieces and mash in the bowl along with the whole wheat and rye flours, dried fruit, salt, yeast, and cocoa. Mix on slow speed for 1 minute with the paddle attachment (preferable) or dough hook to bring the ingredients together into a ball. Increase the speed to medium-low and continue mixing, occasionally scraping down the bowl, for 2 to 3 minutes, until the ingredients become cohesive and assimilated into each other. You may need to switch to the dough hook at some point if the dough becomes too stiff for the paddle. Add some of the extra flour or more water as needed until the dough is soft and slightly sticky.

3. **Dust a work surface with flour,** then roll the dough in the flour to coat. Knead the dough by hand for 3 to 4 minutes, incorporating only as much extra flour as needed, until the dough feels soft and only slightly sticky. Form the dough into a ball and let it rest on the work surface for 5 minutes while you prepare a clean, lightly oiled bowl.

BAKER'S FORMULA	%
Whole rye flour	65
Whole wheat flour	35
Salt	2.4
Instant yeast	1.2
Water	86
Diastatic malt powder	.1
Altus	29.5
Dried fruit	29.5
Cocoa powder	2.4
Total	251.1

NUTRITION FACTS	
Calories (kcal)	91.64
Protein (g)	2.70
Carbohydrates (g)	19.18
Dietary fiber (g)	2.75
Total sugars (g)	2.47
Fat (g)	.89
Saturated fat (g)	.02
Trans fatty acid (g)	0
Cholesterol (mg)	0
Sodium (mg)	31.51

4. **Resume kneading the dough for 1 minute** to strengthen the gluten and make any final flour or water adjustments. The dough should feel soft, malleable, and very tacky but no longer sticky. Form the dough into a ball and place it in the prepared bowl, rolling to coat with oil. Cover loosely with plastic wrap and let rise at room temperature for approximately 60 minutes, until it is at least 1$^1/_2$ times its original size.

5. **Transfer the dough to a lightly floured work surface** and form it into 2 *bâtards* (see page 88 for shaping instructions). Place them on a sheet pan lined with parchment paper or a silicon mat and dusted with rye or wheat flour. Mist the top of the loaves with pan spray (optional) or dust with flour, cover loosely with plastic wrap or a cloth towel, and let rise at room temperature for approximately 45 to 60 minutes, until 1$^1/_2$ times their original size.

6. **Preheat the oven to 425°F (218°C)** and prepare it for hearth baking (page 86), including a steam pan. When the dough is ready to bake, brush it with the flour paste and score the loaves in a feather, or wheat, pattern (shown at left). First, using a sharp knife or blade, cut a $^1/_2$-inch-deep, horseshoe-shaped border around the top of the loaf. Next, score a 4-inch, slightly doglegged inside line with 4 feather cuts emanating off of each side. Finally, make a deeper cut at the top end of the dogleg; for this cut, try using scissors and cutting straight down, in order to create a deeper and wider space. Place the loaves in the oven, pour 1 cup of hot water into the steam pan, lower the temperature to 375°F (191°C), and bake for 25 minutes. Rotate the loaves 180 degrees and continue baking for another 20 to 35 minutes, until the loaves are a rich brown, sound hollow when thumped on the bottom, and register at least 200°F (93°C) in the center.

Swedish Limpa Rye Bread

Makes 1 loaf

This classic rye bread is distinguished by the use of spices other than caraway seeds, most notably orange zest (or orange oil). It may also include any combination of anise seeds, fennel seeds, powdered cardamom, and even cumin seeds.

SOAKER

VOLUME	OUNCES	GRAMS	INGREDIENT	%
1 cup plus 2 tablespoons	5	142	whole rye flour	62.5
2/3 cup	3	85	whole wheat flour, preferably fine grind	37.5
1/2 teaspoon	.14	4	salt	1.75
3/4 cup	6	170	water	75
Total	14.14	401		176.75

1. **Mix all of the soaker ingredients together** in a bowl for about 1 minute, until all of the flour is hydrated and the ingredients form a ball of dough.

2. **Cover loosely with plastic wrap** and leave at room temperature for 12 to 24 hours. (If it will be more than 24 hours, place the soaker in the refrigerator; it will be good for up to 3 days. Remove it 2 hours before mixing the final dough to take off the chill.)

STARTER

VOLUME	OUNCES	GRAMS	INGREDIENT	%
5 tablespoons	2.25	64	whole wheat mother starter (page 67)	33.3
1 1/2 cups	6.75	191	whole wheat flour	100
1/2 cup plus 2 tablespoons	5	142	filtered or spring water, at room temperature (about 70°F/21°C)	74
Total	14	398		207.3

1. **Mix all of the starter ingredients together** in a bowl to form a ball of dough. Using wet hands, knead the dough in the bowl for about 2 minutes to be sure all of the ingredients are evenly distributed and the flour is fully hydrated. The dough should feel very tacky. Let the

BREAD PROFILE

Enriched dough; delayed fermentation method; mixed leavening method

DAYS TO MAKE: 2

Day 1: Soaker and starter, 20 minutes set up and mix, 4 to 6 hours starter fermentation; overnight autolyse
Day 2: 2 hours to de-chill starter; 12 to 15 minutes mixing; 2 to 3 hours fermentation, shaping, proofing; 40 to 60 minutes baking

COMMENTARY

This dough is lower in rye flour than in wheat, which places it in the *meteil* family, so it can be made with either a *biga* or a wild yeast starter (though I prefer it with the starter, as I do with most rye breads).

If you have a whole rye starter, you can use that instead of the wheat starter. If using a rye starter, then use only whole wheat flour in the soaker instead of the combination of rye and wheat shown in the formula.

If you do use cumin seeds, go light. They can easily dominate and take over the flavor of the bread. Use no more than 1/2 teaspoon.

dough rest for about 5 minutes, then knead it again with wet hands for 1 minute. The dough will become smoother but still be tacky.

2. **Transfer the dough to a clean bowl, cover** loosely with plastic wrap, and leave at room temperature for approximately 4 to 6 hours, until the dough is nearly double in size. The dough should register between 3.5 and 4.0 if tested with pH paper (see page 77) and have a pleasant aroma similar to apple cider vinegar. If the starter has not doubled or acidified properly, allow it to continue to develop at room temperature. It could take up to 8 hours or even longer.

3. **When the starter has fully developed, knead** it for a few seconds to degas it. The starter is now ready for mixing into the final dough; however, if necessary to coordinate timing with the soaker, cover tightly with plastic wrap and refrigerate overnight (or up to 3 days). About 2 hours before mixing the final dough, remove the starter from the refrigerator to take off the chill.

If you use cumin seeds, go light. They can easily dominate and take over the flavor of the bread. Use no more than $1/2$ teaspoon.

FINAL DOUGH

VOLUME	OUNCES	GRAMS	INGREDIENT
Use all	14.14	401	soaker
Use all	14	397	starter
7 tablespoons	2	56.5	whole wheat or whole rye flour, or a combination
$5/8$ teaspoon	.18	5	salt
$2^1/4$ teaspoons	.25	7	instant yeast
3 tablespoons	2	56.5	molasses or sorghum syrup
1 tablespoon	.5	14	vegetable oil
1 tablespoon	.32	9	any combination of anise seeds, fennel seeds, ground cardamom, and cumin seeds
2 tablespoons or 1 teaspoon	.25	7	orange zest or orange oil
			extra whole wheat or rye flour for adjustments
Total	33.64	953	

1. **Using a metal pastry scraper, chop** the soaker and the starter into 12 smaller pieces each (sprinkle some of the extra flour over the pre-doughs to keep the pieces from sticking back to each other).

2. **If mixing by hand,** combine the soaker and starter pieces in a bowl with all of the other ingredients except the extra flour and stir vigorously with a mixing spoon or knead with wet hands for about 2 minutes, until all of the ingredients are evenly integrated and distributed into the dough. The dough should be soft and slightly sticky; if not, add more flour or water as needed. **If using a stand mixer,** put the pre-dough pieces and all of the other ingredients except the extra flour into the mixer with the paddle attachment (preferable) or dough hook. Mix on slow speed for 1 minute to bring the ingredients together into a ball. Switch to the dough hook if need be and mix on medium-low speed, occasionally scraping down the bowl, for 3 minutes, until the pre-doughs become cohesive and assimilated into each other. Add more flour or water as needed until the dough is soft and slightly sticky.

3. **Dust a work surface with flour,** then roll the dough in the flour to coat. Knead the dough by hand for 3 to 4 minutes, incorporating only as much extra flour as needed, until the dough feels soft and tacky, but not sticky. Form the dough into a ball and let it rest on the work surface for 5 minutes while you prepare a clean, lightly oiled bowl.

4. **Resume kneading the dough for 1 minute** to strengthen the gluten and make any final flour or water adjustments. The dough should have strength and pass the windowpane test (see page 84), yet still feel soft, supple, and very tacky. Form the dough into a ball and place it in the prepared bowl, rolling to coat with oil. Cover loosely with plastic wrap and let rise at room temperature for approximately 45 to 60 minutes, until it is about $1^1/_2$ times its original size.

5. **Transfer the dough to a lightly floured work surface** and form it into either a loaf pan shape or a freestanding *bâtard* (see pages 87–91 for shaping instructions). For loaf pan bread, place the dough in a greased 4 by $8^1/_2$-inch bread pan. For a *bâtard*, place it on a proofing cloth or on a sheet pan lined with parchment paper and, if you like, dusted with flour. Mist the top of the dough with pan spray (optional), cover loosely with plastic wrap, and let rise at room temperature for approximately 45 to 60 minutes, until it has grown to $1^1/_2$ times its original size.

6. **Preheat the oven to 425°F (218°C)** and, if baking a freestanding loaf, prepare the oven for hearth baking (see page 86), including a steam pan (steaming is optional for a sandwich loaf). When the dough is ready to bake, place it in the oven, pour 1 cup of hot water into the steam pan, lower the temperature to 350°F (177°C), and bake for 20 minutes. Rotate the loaf 180 degrees and continue baking for another 20 to 30 minutes, until the loaf is a rich reddish brown on all sides, sounds hollow when thumped on the bottom, and registers at least 200°F (93°C) in the center.

7. **Transfer the bread to a cooling rack** and allow it to cool for at least 1 hour before serving.

BAKER'S FORMULA	%
Whole wheat flour	72
Whole rye flour	28
Salt	1.8
Instant yeast	1.4
Water	67
Molasses	11
Oil	2.8
Anise seeds	1.8
Orange zest	1.4
Total	187.2

NUTRITION FACTS	
Calories (kcal)	93.25
Protein (g)	3.06
Carbohydrates (g)	18.83
Dietary fiber (g)	2.99
Total sugars (g)	1.45
Fat (g)	1.11
Saturated fat (g)	.13
Trans fatty acid (g)	0
Cholesterol (mg)	0
Sodium (mg)	157.31

Santa Lucia Buns

Makes 9 to 12 buns

BREAD PROFILE

Enriched, medium soft dough; delayed fermentation method; commercial yeast

DAYS TO MAKE: 2

Day 1: Soaker and *biga*, 20 minutes set up and mix; overnight autolyse
Day 2: 2 hours to de-chill *biga*; 12 to 15 minutes mixing; 2 to 3 hours fermentation, shaping, proofing; 20 to 30 minutes baking

COMMENTARY

Some traditional versions of this bread use saffron, an expensive spice that is actually the stigma of crocus flowers, to give the rolls a reddish tint. I have not included it in this formula, but should you want to use it, add ¼ teaspoon saffron to the scalded milk (or heated buttermilk, soy milk, or rice milk) as soon as you remove it from the heat and let the saffron steep in the milk as it cools. You can either leave it in or strain it out before adding the milk to the soaker (I leave it in).

Santa Lucia Day is celebrated on December 13. In Sweden, a custom arose to celebrate the day with a festival in honor of this Sicilian saint, a beautiful girl who suffered torture and blinding rather than renounce her faith. She was believed to have carried food to Christians hiding in caves, wearing a wreath of candles to light her way, and thus, during the festival, young girls wear similar wreaths and process in white dresses tied with a crimson ribbon. Sweet buns, known as *lussekatter* or *lusse brod*, are baked, coiled into various shapes to represent the blinded eyes of the young girl. As the girls in white process, they pass out their Santa Lucia buns to remind worshippers of the saint's victory over evil and of the pending return of the sun and its light (*Lucia* means "light").

Another interpretation, as told by Betsy Oppenneer in her wonderful book *Celebration Breads*, is that the breads symbolize the eyes of devil cats who pulled the chariot of the evil goddess Freya. Saint Lucy is celebrated for subduing those cats through her goodness and light.

SOAKER

VOLUME	OUNCES	GRAMS	INGREDIENT	%
1¾ cups	8	227	whole wheat flour	100
½ teaspoon	.14	4	salt	1.75
¾ cup plus	6	170	milk, scalded and cooled, or unscalded buttermilk, yogurt, soy milk, or rice milk	75
Total	14.14	401		176.75

1. **Mix all of the soaker ingredients together** in a bowl for about 1 minute, until all of the flour is hydrated and the ingredients form a ball of dough.

2. **Cover loosely with plastic wrap** and leave at room temperature for 12 to 24 hours. (If it will be more than 24 hours, place the soaker in the refrigerator; it will be good for up to 3 days. Remove it 2 hours before mixing the final dough to take off the chill.)

BIGA

VOLUME	OUNCES	GRAMS	INGREDIENT	%
1³/₄ cups	8	227	whole wheat flour	100
¹/₄ teaspoon	.03	1	instant yeast	.4
¹/₂ cup plus 2 tablespoons	5	142	filtered or spring water, at room temperature (about 70°F/21°C)	62.5
1 large	1.65	47	egg, slightly beaten	20.6
Total	14.68	417		183.5

1. **Mix all of the *biga* ingredients together** in a bowl to form a ball of dough. Using wet hands, knead the dough in the bowl for 2 minutes to be sure all of the ingredients are evenly distributed and the flour is fully hydrated. The dough should feel very tacky. Let the dough rest for 5 minutes, then knead it again with wet hands for 1 minute. The dough will become smoother but still be tacky.

2. **Transfer the dough to a clean bowl, cover** tightly with plastic wrap, and refrigerate for at least 8 hours and up to 3 days.

3. **About 2 hours before mixing the final dough,** remove the *biga* from the refrigerator to take off the chill. It will have risen slightly but need not have risen significantly in order to use it in the final dough.

FAQ ∾ *Which is better, scalded or unscalded milk, and why?*

In theory, milk that has been scalded and cooled should produce a taller loaf. This is because scalding, or bringing the milk to a simmer, definitely denatures any active enzymes that remain in the milk. Some of the denatured enzymes are proteases, which could weaken the gluten if they were fully active. This is more of an issue with raw, unpasteurized milk because raw milk is loaded with enzymes and microorganisms (this is both its strength and its weakness). Pasteurization, especially at high temperatures (ultra-pasteurization), accomplishes this same task, though does adversely affect flavor. (Buttermilk and yogurt, by the way, do not need to be scalded because of the lactic acid they contain, which also serves to control enzyme activity.) In side-by-side tests, some loaves with scalded milk performed better than those with unscalded milk, but not always. Another factor with scalded milk is that it should be weighed or measured after it has been scalded, as it loses a number of grams to evaporation during the scalding process, and this throws off the hydration of the pre-dough. The bottom line is this: If you feel that your loaf is not reaching it fullest size potential with unscalded milk, try using scalded. Be sure that the scalded milk has cooled to at least lukewarm (about 100°F/38°C) before mixing it into any soakers. It should be even cooler, less than 80°F (27°C), when used in a *biga*.

FINAL DOUGH

VOLUME	OUNCES	GRAMS	INGREDIENT
Use all	14.14	401	soaker
Use all	14.68	417	*biga*
³/₄ cup plus 2 tablespoons	4	113	whole wheat flour
⁵/₈ teaspoon	.18	5	salt
2¹/₄ teaspoons	.25	7	instant yeast
¹/₄ cup or 5 tablespoons	2.5 2.5	71 71	honey or agave nectar or sugar or brown sugar
¹/₄ cup	2	56.5	vegetable oil or unsalted butter, melted
			extra whole wheat flour for adjustments
			1 egg (or 1 egg white) beaten with 1 tablespoon water and ¹/₄ teaspoon sugar or honey for egg wash (optional; see Commentary)
			raisins for topping
Total	37.75	1070.5	

1. **Using a metal pastry scraper, chop** the soaker and the *biga* into 12 smaller pieces each (sprinkle some of the extra flour over the pre-doughs to keep the pieces from sticking back to each other).

2. **If mixing by hand,** combine the soaker and *biga* pieces in a bowl with the 4 ounces flour and the salt, yeast, honey, and vegetable oil. Stir vigorously with a mixing spoon or knead with wet hands for about 2 minutes, until all of the ingredients are evenly integrated and distributed into the dough. The dough should be soft and slightly sticky; if not, add more flour or water as needed. **If using a stand mixer,** put the pre-dough pieces in the bowl along with the 4 ounces flour and the salt, yeast, honey, and vegetable oil. Mix on slow speed with the paddle attachment (preferable) or dough hook for 1 minute to bring the ingredients together into a ball. Switch to the dough hook if need be and mix on medium-low speed, occasionally scraping down the bowl, for 3 to 4 minutes, until the pre-doughs become cohesive and assimilated into each other. Add more flour or water as needed until the dough is soft and slightly sticky.

3. **Dust a work surface with flour,** then roll the dough in the flour to coat. Knead the dough by hand for 3 to 4 minutes, incorporating only as much extra flour as needed, until the dough feels soft and tacky, but not sticky. Form the dough into a ball and let it rest on the work surface for 5 minutes while you prepare a clean, lightly oiled bowl.

4. **Resume kneading the dough for 1 minute** to strengthen the gluten and make any final flour or water adjustments. The dough should have strength and pass the windowpane test (see page 84), yet still feel soft, supple, and tacky. Form the dough into a ball and place it in the prepared bowl, rolling to coat with oil. Cover loosely with plastic wrap and let rise at room temperature for approximately 45 to 60 minutes, until it is about 1^1/$_2$ times its original size.

5. **Prepare a sheet pan by lining it** with parchment paper or a silicon mat. Divide the dough into 8 to 12 pieces. Round each piece into a tight ball (see page 91), then cover and let rest for 10 minutes. Roll out each ball into an even strand about 10 inches long. Spiral each strand from both ends toward the center, making 2 snail shapes that meet. You can leave them this way or flip one of the snails over so they form an S shape. Place the shaped pieces 1^1/$_2$ inches apart on the prepared pan. Mist the top of the buns with pan spray (optional), cover loosely with plastic wrap, and let rise at room temperature for 1 hour, until they have grown to at least 1^1/$_2$ times their original size.

The eyes of Saint Lucy, celebrated in Santa Lucia buns.

6. **Preheat the oven to 425°F (218°C),** When the buns are ready to bake, gently brush the tops with egg wash or egg white wash, place a raisin in the center of each coil if you wish (to symbolize the eyes of Saint Lucy), and place the pan in the oven. Lower the temperature to 350°F (177°C) and bake for 15 minutes. Rotate the pan 180 degrees and continue baking for another 10 to 20 minutes, until the buns are a rich reddish brown on all sides, sound hollow when thumped on the bottom, and register at least 195°F (91°C) in the center.

7. **Transfer the buns to a cooling rack** and allow them to cool for at least 30 minutes before serving.

BAKER'S FORMULA	%
Whole wheat flour	100
Salt	1.6
Instant yeast	1.4
Milk	6
Water	5
Egg	1.65
Honey	2.5
Oil	2
Total	120.15

NUTRITION FACTS	
Calories (kcal)	11.76
Protein (g)	3.65
Carbohydrates (g)	18.84
Dietary fiber (g)	2.80
Total sugars (g)	2.52
Fat (g)	3.06
Saturated fat (g)	.50
Trans fatty acid (g)	.01
Cholesterol (mg)	8.43
Sodium (mg)	144.89

Hapanleipä and Vorterkaker

Makes 2 large and 2 small loaves

BREAD PROFILE

Lean or enriched doughs; delayed fermentation method; mixed leavening method

DAYS TO MAKE: 2

Day 1: Soaker and starter, 20 minutes set up and mix, 4 to 6 hours starter fermentation; overnight autolyse
Day 2: 2 hours to de-chill starter; 12 to 15 minutes mixing; 2 to 3 hours fermentation, shaping, proofing; 30 to 45 minutes baking

Although these breads are similar, they are not exactly the same. *Vorterkaker* is Norwegian in origin, while *hapanleipä* is Finnish. Both are shaped like wheels with a hole in the center. The main difference is that *vorterkaker* is sweeter, with a licorice flavor from fennel and anise seeds. Both are wonderful with cheeses or as an appetizer or snack bread. For the versions below, everything is the same except the ingredients in the soakers.

HAPANLEIPÄ SOAKER

VOLUME	OUNCES	GRAMS	INGREDIENT	%
1³/₄ cups	8	227	whole rye flour	100
¹/₂ teaspoon	.14	4	salt	1.75
³/₄ cup	6	170	water	75
1 teaspoon	.25	7	honey or agave nectar	3
or 1¹/₂ teaspoons	.25	7	or sugar or brown sugar	
Total	14.39	408		179.75

VORTERKAKER SOAKER

VOLUME	OUNCES	GRAMS	INGREDIENT	%
1³/₄ cups	8	227	whole rye flour	100
¹/₂ teaspoon	.14	4	salt	1.75
1¹/₂ teaspoons	.16	4.5	fennel seeds	2
1¹/₂ teaspoons	.16	4.5	anise seeds	2
³/₄ cup	6	170	milk, soy milk, or rice milk	75
3¹/₂ tablespoons	2.25	64	dark corn syrup, molasses, or sorghum syrup	28
¹/₄ cup	2	56.5	vegetable oil	25
Total	18.71	530.5		233.75

1. **Whether for *hapanleipä* or *vorterkaker*,** mix all of the soaker ingredients together in a bowl for about 1 minute, until all of the flour is hydrated and the ingredients form a ball of dough.

2. **Cover loosely with plastic wrap** and leave at room temperature for 12 to 24 hours. (If it will be more than 24 hours, place the soaker in the refrigerator; it will be good for up to 3 days. Remove it 2 hours before mixing the final dough to take off the chill.)

If you happen to have any leftover potato water (see page 122), use it in the soaker; it will tenderize the bread and impart a sweeter flavor.

Many versions of these breads call for 100% rye flour and no wheat flour at all. But including wheat does give the bread a little more spring and a softer texture. You can adjust the balance of wheat and rye in either the soaker or the starter. You can also substitute a whole wheat or rye flour *biga* in place of the starter.

These flat, crisp breads are sometimes glazed with melted butter as soon as they come out of the oven. This is optional, but it does provide a nice shine and a slight buttery flavor. You can also brush the hot breads with vegetable oil, or leave them unglazed for a more rustic look.

STARTER

VOLUME	OUNCES	GRAMS	INGREDIENT	%
1/3 cup	2.5	71	whole wheat or rye mother starter (pages 67 and 69)	33.3
1 2/3 cups	7.5	213	whole rye flour or whole wheat flour	100
3/4 cup	6	170	filtered or spring water, at room temperature (about 70°F/21°C)	80
Total	16	454		213.3

1. **Mix all of the starter ingredients together** in a bowl to form a ball of dough. Using wet hands, knead the dough in the bowl for about 2 minutes to be sure all of the ingredients are evenly distributed and the flour is fully hydrated. The dough should feel very tacky or even slightly sticky. Let the dough rest for about 5 minutes, then knead it again with wet hands for 1 minute. The dough will become smoother but still be tacky or slightly sticky.

2. **Transfer the dough to a clean bowl, cover** loosely with plastic wrap, and leave at room temperature for approximately 4 to 6 hours, until the dough is nearly double in size. The dough should register between 3.5 and 4.0 if tested with pH paper (see page 77) and have a pleasant aroma similar to apple cider vinegar. If the starter has not doubled or acidified properly, allow it to continue to develop at room temperature. It could take up to 8 hours or even longer.

3. **When the starter has fully developed, knead** it for a few seconds to degas it. The starter is now ready for mixing into the final dough; however, if necessary to coordinate timing with the soaker, cover tightly with plastic wrap and refrigerate overnight (or up to 3 days). About 2 hours before mixing the final dough, remove the starter from the refrigerator to take off the chill.

FINAL DOUGH

VOLUME	OUNCES	GRAMS	INGREDIENT
Use all	14.39 or 18.71	408 or 530.5	*hapanleipä* or *vorterkaker* soaker
Use all	16	454	starter
3/4 cup plus 2 tablespoons	4	113	whole rye flour
5/8 teaspoon	.18	5	salt
2 1/4 teaspoons	.25	7	instant yeast
			extra whole rye flour for adjustments
			unsalted butter, melted, or vegetable oil for glazing (optional)
Total	34.82 or 39.14	987 or 1109.5	

1. **Using a metal pastry scraper, chop** the soaker and the starter into 12 smaller pieces each (sprinkle some of the extra flour over the pre-doughs to keep the pieces from sticking back to each other).

2. **If mixing by hand,** combine the soaker and starter pieces in a bowl with all of the other ingredients except the extra flour and the butter and stir vigorously with a mixing spoon or knead with wet hands for about 2 minutes, until all of the ingredients are evenly integrated and distributed into the dough. The dough should be soft and slightly sticky; if not, add more flour or water as needed. **If using a stand mixer,** put the pre-dough pieces and all of the other ingredients except the extra flour and the butter into the mixer with the paddle attachment (preferable) or dough hook. Mix on slow speed for 1 minute to bring the ingredients together into a ball. Switch to the dough hook if need be and mix on medium-low speed, occasionally scraping down the bowl, for 3 minutes, until the pre-doughs become cohesive and assimilated into each other. Add more flour or water as needed until the dough is soft and slightly sticky.

3. **Dust a work surface with flour,** then roll the dough in the flour to coat. Knead the dough by hand for 3 to 4 minutes, incorporating only as much extra flour as needed, until the dough feels supple but firm and slightly tacky. Form the dough into a ball and let it rest on the work surface for 5 minutes while you prepare a clean, lightly oiled bowl.

4. **Resume kneading the dough by hand for 1 minute** to strengthen the gluten and make any final flour or water adjustments. The dough should have strength yet still feel supple and only slightly tacky. Form the dough into a ball and place it in the prepared bowl, rolling to coat with oil. Cover loosely with plastic wrap and let rise at room temperature for approximately 45 to 60 minutes, until it is about $1^1/_2$ times its original size. While the dough is rising, prepare 2 sheet pans by lining the bottom (the underside) with either parchment paper or a silicon mat. Dust the lined pans with coarse rye flour.

5. **Transfer the dough to a lightly floured work surface** and divide it into 2 equal pieces (or any number of smaller pieces). Dust the top of the first piece with rye flour and roll the dough out into a 12-inch circle about $1/_4$ inch thick (you can roll it thinner for a crispier bread). Use a metal spatula to carefully transfer the dough to one of the prepared sheet pans. Repeat this process with the second piece of dough. With a cookie cutter or the rim of a drinking glass dipped in flour, cut out the center of each dough, like a doughnut hole (you can bake the centers on the same sheet pans as the larger pieces, if there is room). Dock the entire surface with a fork or a roller docker (see page 288). Cover the dough with a cloth towel or plastic wrap and let rise at room temperature for approximately 45 minutes, until it is at least $1^1/_2$ times taller.

BAKER'S FORMULA Hapanleipä	%
Whole rye flour	100
Salt	1.5
Instant yeast	1.2
Water	62
Honey	1.2
Total	165.9

BAKER'S FORMULA Vorterkaker	%
Whole rye flour	100
Salt	1.5
Instant yeast	1.2
Milk	28.5
Water	28.5
Dark corn syrup	10.7
Oil	9.5
Fennel and/or anise seeds	1.5
Total	181.4

NUTRITION FACTS Hapanleipä	
Calories (kcal)	94.85
Protein (g)	2.67
Carbohydrates (g)	19.78
Dietary fiber (g)	3.46
Total sugars (g)	.23
Fat (g)	.44
Saturated fat (g)	.01
Trans fatty acid (g)	0
Cholesterol (mg)	0
Sodium (mg)	15.27

NUTRITION FACTS Vorterkaker	
Calories (kcal)	134
Protein (g)	2.96
Carbohydrates (g)	23.67
Dietary fiber (g)	3.86
Total sugars (g)	2.28
Fat (g)	3.15
Saturated fat (g)	.29
Trans fatty acid (g)	0
Cholesterol (mg)	0
Sodium (mg)	167.38

SHAPING HAPANLEIPÄ AND VORTERKAKER

(A) Roll out the dough into a circle. (B) Cut out a doughnut-like hole from the center with a biscuit cutter. (C) You can bake the cut-out piece as a small cracker bread while baking the larger loaf.

6. **Preheat the oven to 425°F (218°C).** When the dough is ready to bake, place the 2 pans in the oven, lower the temperature to 350°F (177°C), and bake for 15 minutes. Rotate the pans 180 degrees and top to bottom and continue baking for another 10 to 15 minutes, until the breads are crisp and a rich, reddish brown.

7. **Brush the tops with melted butter or vegetable oil** as soon as they come out of the oven. Leave the breads on their pans to cool for at least 1 hour before serving.

Julekage, Panettone, and Stollen

Makes 1 large, 2 medium, or 3 small loaves

Danish Christmas bread, *julekage*, is similar to Italian panettone or German and Swiss stollen, which are more familiar to Americans. The main difference between the three is in their flavorings: *julekage* contains cardamom, panettone is more floral, and stollen has an almond flavoring. Also, each is baked in its own distinctive shape. Regardless of how you adjust the flavors or shapes, the whole grain version here makes this a healthier, heartier holiday treat.

BREAD PROFILE

Rich dough; delayed fermentation method; mixed leavening method

DAYS TO MAKE: 2

Day 1: Soaker, starter, and fruit soaker 30 minutes set up and mix, 4 to 6 hours starter fermentation; overnight autolyse
Day 2: 2 hours to de-chill starter; 12 to 15 minutes mixing; 2^1/$_2$ to 3^1/$_2$ hours fermentation, shaping, proofing; 40 to 60 minutes baking

SOAKER

VOLUME	OUNCES	GRAMS	INGREDIENT	%
1^3/$_4$ cups	8	227	whole wheat flour	100
^{1}/$_2$ teaspoon	.14	4	salt	1.75
^{1}/$_2$ cup plus 2 tablespoons	5	142	milk, soy milk, or rice milk	62.5
^{1}/$_2$ cup	4	113	unsalted butter, melted	50
Total	17.14	486		214.25

COMMENTARY

The soaker is a bit different than in other breads in this book, a bit wetter because it includes butter. As the melted butter firms up, the dough will thicken but still be wet. It will all come together, however, on Day 2, when you add additional flour to the final dough.

You can substitute an equal amount of *biga* for the starter (page 81), but the starter version will have a longer shelf life because of the increased acidity.

1. **Mix all of the soaker ingredients together** in a bowl for about 2 minutes, until all of the flour is hydrated and the ingredients form a soft ball of dough.

2. **Cover loosely with plastic wrap** and leave at room temperature for 12 to 24 hours. (If it will be more than 24 hours, place the soaker in the refrigerator; it will be good for up to 3 days. Remove it 2 hours before mixing the final dough to take off the chill.)

STARTER

VOLUME	OUNCES	GRAMS	INGREDIENT	%
5 tablespoons	2.25	64	whole wheat mother starter (page 67)	33.3
1^1/$_2$ cups	6.75	191	whole wheat flour	100
^{1}/$_2$ cup plus 2 tablespoons	5	142	filtered or spring water, at room temperature (about 70°F/21°C)	74
Total	14	397		207.3

1. **Mix all of the starter ingredients together** in a bowl to form a ball of dough. Using wet hands, knead the dough in the bowl for about 2 minutes to be sure all of the ingredients are

evenly distributed and the flour is fully hydrated. The dough should feel very tacky. Let the dough rest for about 5 minutes, then knead it again with wet hands for 1 minute. The dough will become smoother but still be tacky.

2. **Transfer the dough to a clean bowl, cover** loosely with plastic wrap, and leave at room temperature for approximately 4 to 6 hours, until the dough is nearly double in size. The dough should register between 3.5 and 4.0 if tested with pH paper (see page 77) and have a pleasant aroma similar to apple cider vinegar. If the starter has not doubled or acidified properly, allow it to continue to develop at room temperature. It could take up to 8 hours or even longer.

3. **When the starter has fully developed, knead** it for a few seconds to degas it. The starter is now ready for mixing into the final dough; however, if necessary to coordinate timing with the soaker, cover tightly with plastic wrap and refrigerate overnight (or up to 3 days). About 2 hours before mixing the final dough, remove the starter from the refrigerator to take off the chill.

FRUIT SOAKER

VOLUME	OUNCES	GRAMS	INGREDIENT
1⅓ cups	8	227	any combination of dried and candied fruits (see Commentary)
¾ cup	6	170	orange liqueur, rum, brandy, or orange juice (see Commentary)
1 teaspoon	.18	5	ground cardamom (for *julekage*)
1½ teaspoons	.25	7	orange and/or lemon extract, in any combination (for panettone)
1½ teaspoons	.25	7	almond extract (for stollen)
2 teaspoons	.32	9	vanilla extract (for all)
Total	15	425	

Depending on the bread you plan to make, stir together all the appropriate fruit soaker ingredients in a bowl, cover with plastic wrap, and leave it out overnight. It will be ready to use the following day.

FINAL DOUGH

VOLUME	OUNCES	GRAMS	INGREDIENT
Use all	15.75	425	fruit soaker
Use all	14	397	starter
Use all	17.14	486	soaker
1⅓ cups	6	170	whole wheat flour
⅝ teaspoon	.18	5	salt
1 tablespoon	.32	9	instant yeast
¼ cup	2	56.5	sugar or brown sugar
2 large	3.3	94	eggs, slightly beaten
			extra whole wheat flour for adjustments
			unsalted butter, melted, for topping (optional)
			confectioners' sugar or granulated sugar for topping
Total	58.69	1642.5	

A marzipan or almond paste filling complements this loaf nicely. For almond paste, cream together 1 cup almond paste, 2 tablespoons unsalted butter, 1 egg, and 4 tablespoons unbleached flour.

1. **Strain the fruit soaker,** reserving any liquid for adjusting the hydration of the dough. Using a metal pastry scraper, chop the starter into 12 smaller pieces (sprinkle some of the extra flour over the pre-dough to keep the pieces from sticking back to each other).

2. **If mixing by hand,** combine the soaker and starter pieces in a bowl with all of the other ingredients except the extra flour and stir vigorously with a mixing spoon or knead with wet hands for about 2 minutes, until all of the ingredients are evenly integrated and distributed into the dough. The dough should be soft and slightly sticky; if not, add more flour or water or reserved liquid as needed. **If using a stand mixer,** put the pre-dough pieces and all of the other ingredients except the extra flour into the mixer with the paddle attachment (preferable) or dough hook. Mix on slow speed for 1 minute to bring the ingredients together into a ball. Switch to the dough hook if need be and mix on medium-low speed, occasionally scraping down the bowl, for 3 to 4 minutes, until the pre-doughs become cohesive and assimilated into each other. Add more flour or water or reserved liquid as needed until the dough is soft and slightly sticky.

3. **Dust a work surface with flour,** then roll the dough in the flour to coat. Knead the dough by hand for 3 to 4 minutes, incorporating only as much extra flour as needed, until the dough feels soft and tacky, but not sticky. Form the dough into a ball and let it rest on the work surface for 5 minutes while you prepare a clean, lightly oiled bowl.

4. **Resume kneading the dough for 1 minute** to strengthen the gluten and make any final flour or water adjustments. If this dough seems stickier than others, it is because the fruit is seeping its liqueur; add more flour to compensate. The dough should feel soft, supple, and tacky. Form the dough into a ball and place it in the prepared bowl, rolling to coat with oil. Cover loosely with plastic wrap and let rise at room temperature for approximately 60 minutes, until it is about $1^1/_2$ times its original size.

SHAPING STOLLEN

(A) Roll out a ball of the dough from the center but not to the edges (leave the outer edges plump). The center section should be about $^1/_2$ inch thick. (B) If filling with almond paste or marzipan (see Commentary), place it in the rolled-out center. Otherwise, proceed to the next step. (C) Fold up the loaf into an S-shape, with one of the plump ends as the bottom, the center folded back over itself, and the other plump end folded back to complete the S. Pat the S sections of the loaf together to firm it up. (D) When you pan the folded loaf, give it a slight crescent shape (optional but traditional).

BAKER'S FORMULA	%
Whole wheat flour	100
Salt	1.4
Instant yeast	1.5
Milk	22.5
Water	27
Dried fruit soaker	66
Sugar	2
Egg	3.3
Unsalted butter	18
Total	241.7

NUTRITION FACTS	
Calories (kcal)	123.91
Protein (g)	2.82
Carbohydrates (g)	2.16
Dietary fiber (g)	2.59
Total sugars (g)	5.23
Fat (g)	3.07
Saturated fat (g)	1.77
Trans fatty acid (g)	.08
Cholesterol (mg)	7.22
Sodium (mg)	102.87

SHAPING PANETTONE

(A) Cover the bottom of the pan with baking parchment cut into a circle. Mist the inside of the pan with oil spray, and form the dough into a ball large enough to fill the pan two-thirds full. (B) Place the dough in the prepared pan, cover, and proof until the dough domes above the top of the pan.

5. **Transfer the dough to a lightly floured work surface,** divide it as desired, and form the pieces into a loaf pan shape for *julekage* (see page 87) or one of the shapes shown on page 249 and above. Mist the top of the dough with pan spray (optional), cover loosely with plastic wrap, and let rise at room temperature for approximately 60 to 90 minutes, until it has grown to 1¹/₂ times its original size. In a loaf pan, the dough should rise to about 1 inch above the rim. In panettone paper, it should rise to just above the top of the paper.

6. **Preheat the oven to 400°F (204°C).** When the dough is ready to bake, place it in the oven, lower the temperature to 335°F (168°C), and bake for 20 minutes. Rotate the bread 180 degrees and continue baking for another 20 minutes, then rotate the bread again, continuing to bake until the loaf is a rich, reddish brown on all sides, sounds hollow when thumped on the bottom, and registers at least 200°F (93°C) in the center. The taller the loaf, the longer it will take to bake.

7. **Transfer to a cooling rack and apply toppings,** as appropriate, while still hot from the oven. For *julekage* and panettone, brush the tops with melted butter. For stollen, brush the entire surface, including the underside, with melted butter, then roll in either confectioners' sugar or granulated sugar. If using confectioners' sugar, dust the stollen again after 15 minutes, using a sifter or a strainer filled with powdered sugar and tapping it over the loaves to achieve a snowlike dusting. For all three, allow to cool for at least 2 hours before serving.

Bagels are unique among breads because they are boiled before they are baked. Long before the artisan bread movement, professional bagel makers intuited the value of delayed fermentation, holding the shaped dough overnight in refrigerators so they would not overferment but also to develop more flavor. It is rare to find a true, 100% whole grain bagel in most bagel shops (even when they are labeled whole wheat or multigrain), and nowhere will you find a bagel that is made in quite the same way as these, utilizing delayed fermentation very differently than bagel shops, allowing you to make the bagels shortly after shaping them.

Flatbreads are far more common worldwide than what we know as traditional European leavened bread. Not all flatbread is flat or unleavened, of course, as focaccia, pizza, pita, and naan prove. In fact, most flatbread is fermented and leavened, even when the final product is fairly flat and dense, such as the Scandinavian and Finnish rye breads. So we will distinguish flatbreads from crisp, cracker breads even though, technically, there is a great deal of crossover.

Whole Wheat, Multigrain, and Pumpernickel Bagels

Makes 6 to 7 bagels

BREAD PROFILE

Lean dough; delayed fermentation method; commercial yeast

DAYS TO MAKE: 2

Day 1: Soaker and *biga*, 20 minutes set up and mix; overnight autolyse
Day 2: 2 hours to de-chill *biga*; 12 to 15 minutes mixing; 1¹/₂ to 2¹/₂ hours fermentation, shaping, proofing; 10 minutes boiling; 30 to 40 minutes baking

The delayed fermentation method is perfectly suited to 100% whole wheat bagels. Professionally made bagels are always held overnight before baking in order to create a better flavor and texture. The pre-dough method allows us to assemble the bagels at just the time we want to bake them yet still achieve their full potential in terms of both flavor and texture.

There are two main differences between bagel dough and other whole grain bread doughs. One is the use of malt syrup, which is necessary for the most authentic flavor, though you can also use honey. The other is that bagel dough is stiffer and less hydrated, so that the bagels do not rise too much and then fall during the boiling stage. You can make multigrain and pumpernickel bagels by simply adjusting the ingredients in the soaker, as shown in the versions on pages 258 and 259. A few special tools are required for bagel making. Before you begin, make sure you have a large slotted spoon or skimmer and a pot wide enough to accommodate at least four bagels at a time.

This method is not the same as for bagel recipes in my other books, in which the dough is shaped the day before and then refrigerated. However, if you prefer to shape and hold the bagels and bake them later, you can do so with this method, but with caution. The challenge is to be sure the shaped dough does not overferment in the refrigerator. If this happens, use less yeast the next time.

Barley malt syrup is available at most natural foods markets. It comes in light and dark versions and looks like sorghum syrup or molasses. It is not diastatic; that is, its enzymes are not active, having been denatured when the syrup was heated during processing.

This is the one dough in which even instant yeast should be hydrated before it is combined with the final ingredients (only in the final dough, not the *biga*). This is because bagel dough is less hydrated than other types of dough, so if the yeast is not dissolved in advance, specks of yeast could create "hot spots" later, leading to uneven baking.

If you use minced dried onions or garlic, hydrate them for 1 hour, then drain thoroughly before use; this will protect them from burning in the oven.

SOAKER

VOLUME	OUNCES	GRAMS	INGREDIENT	%
1³/₄ cups	8	227	whole wheat flour	100
¹/₂ teaspoon	.14	4	salt	1.75
¹/₂ cup plus 2 tablespoons	5	142	water	62.5
2 tablespoons	1.25	35.5	barley malt syrup, dark or light, or honey	15.6
Total	14.39	408.5		179.85

1. **Mix all of the soaker ingredients together** in a bowl for about 1 minute, until all of the flour is hydrated and the ingredients form a ball of dough.

2. **Cover loosely with plastic wrap** and leave at room temperature for 12 to 24 hours. (If it will be more than 24 hours, place the soaker in the refrigerator; it will be good for up to 3 days. Remove it 2 hours before mixing the final dough to take off the chill.)

BIGA

VOLUME	OUNCES	GRAMS	INGREDIENT	%
1³/₄ cups	8	227	whole wheat flour	100
¹/₄ teaspoon	.03	1	instant yeast	.4
¹/₂ cup plus 2 tablespoons	5	142	filtered or spring water, at room temperature (about 70°F/21°C)	62.5
Total	13.03	370		162.9

1. **Mix all of the *biga* ingredients together** in a bowl to form a ball of dough. Using wet hands, knead the dough in the bowl for 2 minutes to be sure all of the ingredients are evenly distributed and the flour is fully hydrated. The dough should feel very tacky. Let the dough rest for 5 minutes, then knead it again with wet hands for 1 minute. The dough will become smoother but still be tacky.

2. **Transfer the dough to a clean bowl, cover** tightly with plastic wrap, and refrigerate for at least 8 hours and up to 3 days.

3. **About 2 hours before mixing the final dough,** remove the *biga* from the refrigerator to take off the chill. It will have risen slightly but need not have risen significantly in order to use it in the final dough.

FINAL DOUGH

VOLUME	OUNCES	GRAMS	INGREDIENT
Use all	14.39	408.5	soaker
Use all	13.03	370	*biga*
2¼ teaspoons	.25	7	instant yeast
2 tablespoons	1	28.5	water, at room temperature (about 70°F/21°C)
⅝ teaspoon	.18	5	salt
7 tablespoons	2	56.5	whole wheat flour
			poppy seeds, sesame seeds, nigella seeds, coarse sea salt or pretzel salt, dried minced garlic or onion (rehydrated in water; see Commentary), or diced fresh onion tossed in vegetable oil, for topping
2 teaspoons			baking soda
			1 egg white beaten with 1 tablespoon water and a pinch of salt for egg wash (optional; see Commentary)
			extra whole wheat flour for adjustments
Total	30.85	875.5	

1. **Using a metal pastry scraper, chop** the soaker and the *biga* into 12 smaller pieces each (sprinkle some of the extra flour over the pre-doughs to keep the pieces from sticking back to each other).

2. **If mixing by hand,** dissolve the yeast in the water in a bowl, add the pre-dough pieces and the salt, and stir vigorously with a mixing spoon or knead with wet hands for 3 to 4 minutes, until all of the ingredients are evenly distributed and integrated into the dough. Add the 7 tablespoons whole wheat flour and continue to knead the dough for about 2 more minutes, until all of the ingredients are integrated and distributed into the dough. The dough should be firm and not sticky; if not, add more flour or water as needed. **If using a stand mixer,** dissolve the yeast in the water in the mixing bowl, and then add the pre-dough pieces and the salt, and mix on slow speed with the dough hook for 1 minute to bring the ingredients together into a ball. Add the 7 tablespoons whole wheat flour and continue to mix on either low or medium-low speed for 3 to 4 minutes, occasionally scraping down the bowl, until the pre-doughs become cohesive and assimilated into each other. Add more flour or water as needed until the dough is firm and not sticky. This is a stiff dough, so turn the mixer off if necessary to avoid stressing the motor.

Toppings such as poppy seeds and sesame seeds usually adhere to boiled bagels just fine, but minced onions, minced garlic, larger seeds, and coarse salt will stick better if you use the optional egg white wash.

You can substitute 14.5 ounces of wild yeast starter (page 80) for the *biga*, but if you do so, reduce the water in your elaborated starter to 3.5 ounces so it will have the firmness needed for bagels.

You will be poaching the bagels in simmering water that has been alkalized with baking soda. You can also add malt syrup or honey to the water, or food-grade lye (difficult to find but available through mail order catalogues), but baking soda will do the job. The alkalinity promotes browning and gives the crust that familiar bagel flavor. (Lye is also used in traditional pretzels for a similar purpose.) We will use the term *boil* rather than *poach* because it is the more familiar term, as in "traditional boiled bagels." Many baking companies have switched to steaming the bagels, like French bread, to save this time-consuming step, but bagel aficionados consider boiling to be the definitive aspect of a true bagel. Otherwise, it is just a roll.

3. **Dust a work surface with flour,** then roll the dough in the flour to coat. Knead the dough by hand for 3 to 4 minutes, incorporating only as much extra flour as needed to form a stiff dough that is still supple enough to shape. Form the dough into a ball and let it rest on the work surface for 5 minutes while you prepare a clean, lightly oiled bowl.

4. **Resume kneading the dough for 1 minute** to strengthen the gluten and make any final flour or water adjustments. The dough should be firm when fully kneaded and pass the windowpane test (see page 84), yet still feel supple and satiny. Form the dough into a ball and place it in the prepared bowl, rolling to coat with oil. Cover loosely with plastic wrap and let rise at room temperature for approximately 45 to 60 minutes, until it is about $1^1/_2$ times its original size. Meanwhile, prepare a sheet pan by lining it with parchment paper or a silicon mat and dusting with either whole wheat flour or cornmeal.

SHAPING BAGELS

(A) Roll out an 8-inch strand of dough; $4^1/_2$ ounces, by weight, for a full size bagel. (B) Wrap the strand around your hand, overlapping the ends by 2 or 3 inches, and then squeeze the ends together to close the circle. (C) Roll the ends on a damp work surface to seal the bagel closed. It is now ready for panning and proofing.

5. **Transfer the dough to a lightly floured work surface** and divide it into six or seven 4-ounce pieces. Roll each piece into an 8-inch rope and shape it into a circle around your hand. Seal it tight at the point where the two ends overlap by squeezing or pressing it into the counter. There should be a 2-inch-diameter hole in the center. Place the shaped bagels on the prepared sheet pan, cover loosely with a cloth towel (it's okay, in this case, if a skin forms), and leave out at room temperature while you move on to the next step. (You can also refrigerate the pan for up to 24 hours if you plan to make the bagels later, in which case you should cover it with plastic wrap or place it in a plastic bag.)

6. **Preheat the oven to 500°F (260°C).** While the oven is heating up, prepare your toppings and have them ready to apply. Line a baking sheet with parchment paper or a silicon mat,

BOILING BAGELS

BAKER'S FORMULA	%
Whole wheat flour	100
Salt	1.8
Instant yeast	1.6
Water	56
Barley malt syrup	7
Total	166.4

NUTRITION FACTS	
Calories (kcal)	25.63
Protein (g)	1.14
Carbohydrates (g)	53.43
Dietary fiber (g)	8.63
Total sugars (g)	.28
Fat (g)	1.33
Saturated fat (g)	.24
Trans fatty acid (g)	0
Cholesterol (mg)	0
Sodium (mg)	478.21

(A) Carefully lower the bagels into the alkalized water. (B) Boil the slightly proofed bagel in for about 1 minute on each side, then remove using a skimmer or slotted spoon. The bagels are now ready for garnishing and baking.

misting the parchment with pan spray (this is important if using parchment but not necessary with silicon mats). Bring 4 inches of water to a boil in a wide pot. Add the 2 teaspoons baking soda to the water when it comes to a boil; watch out, the water will foam when you add the baking soda. Lower the heat to maintain a steady simmer.

7. **The bagels should be ready to boil** within 20 to 30 minutes of shaping. Carefully lift one from the pan and lower it into the water. It should float within 30 seconds. If not, boil it until it does float and then remove it, but wait 5 minutes before boiling another, repeating the float test. When they pass the test, boil 2 to 4 bagels at a time, gently turning them over after 30 seconds so they boil for a total of 1 minute. Using a slotted spoon or skimmer, remove them from the water and transfer them back to the prepared sheet pan.

8. **When all of the bagels have been boiled,** apply the toppings, using egg white wash if needed to help the toppings stick (see Commentary). Place the pan in the oven, lower the temperature to 450°F (232°C), and bake for 15 minutes. Rotate the pan 180 degrees and continue baking for another 10 to 15 minutes, until the bagels are a rich brown on the top and bottom.

9. **Transfer the bagels to a cooling rack** and cool for 20 minutes before serving.

MULTIGRAIN BAGELS

COMMENTARY

The total weight of the grains should be 5 ounces (excluding the 3 ounces of whole wheat flour). It is especially important to weigh these grains as the volume can vary substantially. The volume measure will get you close if you don't have a scale; adjust as necessary for your next batch.

Smaller or softer grains may be used uncooked, such as amaranth, rolled oats, and flax-seeds. Precook larger or harder grains; see page 102 for cooking instructions.

BAKER'S FORMULA	%
Whole wheat flour	72
Multigrain mix	28
Salt	1.8
Instant yeast	1.6
Water	56
Barley malt syrup	7
Total	166.4

NUTRITION FACTS	
Calories (kcal)	96.79
Protein (g)	3.61
Carbohydrates (g)	2.08
Dietary fiber (g)	2.83
Total sugars (g)	.57
Fat (g)	.69
Saturated fat (g)	.07
Trans fatty acid (g)	0
Cholesterol (mg)	0
Sodium (mg)	206.22

Makes 6 to 7 bagels

SOAKER

VOLUME	OUNCES	GRAMS	INGREDIENT	%
2/3 cup	3	85	whole wheat flour	37.5
1 cup plus 2 tablespoons (approx.)	5	142	any combination of cooked and uncooked grains (see Commentary)	62.5
1/2 teaspoon	.14	4	salt	1.75
2 tablespoons	1.25	35.5	barley malt syrup, dark or light, or honey	15.6
1/2 cup plus 2 tablespoons	5	142	water	62.5
Total	14.39	408.5		179.85

1. **Mix all of the soaker ingredients together** in a bowl for about 1 minute, until all of the flour is hydrated. Let the soaker rest for 5 minutes, then mix again for 1 minute until the ingredients form a thick, porridge-like dough.

2. **Proceed as in step 2** on page 254 and onward in the whole wheat bagels.

The best toppings for bagels are poppy seeds, sesame seeds, salt, or a combination of them all, applied just after boiling but before baking.

PUMPERNICKEL BAGELS

Makes 6 to 7 bagels

SOAKER

VOLUME	OUNCES	GRAMS	INGREDIENT	%
³/₄ cup plus 2 tablespoons	4	113	whole rye flour, preferably coarse or pumpernickel grind	50
³/₄ cup plus 2 tablespoons	4	113	whole wheat flour	50
¹/₂ teaspoon	.14	4	salt	1.75
¹/₂ cup plus 2 tablespoons	5	142	water	62.5
3¹/₂ teaspoons	.75	21	barley malt syrup, light or dark, or honey	9.5
2¹/₄ teaspoons	.5	14	molasses or sorghum syrup	6.25
Total	14.39	407		180

BAKER'S FORMULA	%
Whole wheat flour	78
Whole rye flour	22
Salt	1.8
Instant yeast	1.6
Water	56
Barley malt syrup	4
Molasses	3
Total	166.4

NUTRITION FACTS	
Calories (kcal)	94.19
Protein (g)	3.50
Carbohydrates (g)	2.05
Dietary fiber (g)	3.26
Total sugars (g)	.47
Fat (g)	.48
Saturated fat (g)	.07
Trans fatty acid (g)	0
Cholesterol (mg)	0
Sodium (mg)	176.85

1. **Mix all of the soaker ingredients together** in a bowl for about 1 minute, until all of the flour is hydrated and the ingredients form a ball of dough.

2. **Proceed as in step 2** on page 254 and onward in the whole wheat bagels.

Whole Wheat Focaccia

Makes one 17 by 12-inch focaccia

BREAD PROFILE

Slightly enriched dough; delayed fermentation method; commercial yeast

DAYS TO MAKE: 2

Day 1: Mixing, 10 to 15 minutes; overnight autolyse
Day 2: 3 hours panning, dimpling, topping, and proofing; 20 to 30 minutes baking

COMMENTARY

This is easy dough to mix, whether in a machine or by hand. It is so easy, in fact, that I rarely use the mixer. Why clean up a machine when it is so much simpler to clean a mixing bowl? However, some bakers prefer to do all their mixing by machine, so I've included instructions for using a stand mixer.

You can substitute up to 25% medium or coarse whole wheat flour for fine grind whole wheat flour.

The sweetener is optional. Some people prefer to use it because it helps with browning, but the final product will be delicious with or without a sweetener.

Focaccia and and its Tuscan counterpart, *sciattiata*, are the pizzas of northern Italy, usually baked in sheet pans and with a thicker crust than pizza. Focaccia is associated with Liguria and its capital city of Genoa, while *sciattiata* is associated with Tuscany. Other than their differing names, they are similar: great crust baked with whatever you feel like putting on top. There are as many ways to top focaccia and *sciattiata* as there are to top pizza, but because focaccia takes longer to bake than pizza it is important to follow the topping guidelines on page 26 to protect against burning.

Also, because of its high hydration, this dough does not need to be made with two pre-doughs. It can be mixed and panned on Day 1 and then baked the following day (the *pain à l'ancienne* method described in chapter 1). The ideal thickness of baked focaccia is approximately 1 inch, not like the 2-inch versions found in so many supermarkets. This is like pizza, after all, not just bread with something on top. With a 1-inch thickness, you still have the option of splitting it across the middle and using it for panini-type sandwiches, for which it is the perfect bread. Or, you can simply enjoy it as a meal unto itself.

DOUGH

VOLUME	OUNCES	GRAMS	INGREDIENT
4 cups	18	510	whole wheat flour, preferably fine grind (see Commentary)
1¼ teaspoons	.35	10	salt
1¼ teaspoons	.14	4	instant yeast
2 cups plus 2 tablespoons	17	482	water, at room temperature (about 70°F/21°C)
1½ teaspoons	.35	10	honey or agave nectar
or 2 teaspoons	.35	10	or sugar or brown sugar (optional)
			extra whole wheat flour for adjustments
1½ tablespoons	.75	21	olive oil
Total	36.59	1037	

1. **If mixing by hand,** place all of the ingredients except the extra flour and the olive oil in a bowl and mix for 2 to 3 minutes. Keep a bowl of water handy and dip the mixing spoon in the water from time to time to keep the dough from sticking. Use a plastic bowl scraper, also dipped in water, to continually scrape down the bowl. You can also use wet hands to mix the dough. The dough will be sticky but fairly smooth; adjust the water or flour, as needed. Add the olive oil and mix for another 15 seconds, long enough only to coat the dough. Let the dough rest in the bowl for 5 minutes, uncovered, and then mix again for 1 minute. The dough will be smoother and stronger, but it will still be sticky. If it is too wet, that is, if it feels like a batter and does not have enough structure to hold together, add some additional flour. Even though sticky, the dough should be able to pass the windowpane test (see page 84). **If using a stand mixer,** use the paddle attachment. Place all of the ingredients except the extra flour and the olive oil in the bowl and mix on low speed for 2 minutes. The dough will be sticky but fairly smooth (if it seems stiff, drizzle in some additional water, 1 teaspoon at a time, until it becomes sticky). With the machine off, pour the oil over the dough, scrape down the sides of the bowl with a plastic bowl scraper (dip the scraper in water to keep the dough from sticking to it), and then mix on low speed for another 15 seconds. Let the dough rest in the mixer for 5 minutes, uncovered. Mix again, on medium speed, for 30 seconds to 1 minute. The dough will be smoother and stronger, but it will still be sticky. If it is too wet, that is, if it feels like a batter and does not have enough structure to hold together, add some additional flour. Even though sticky, the dough should be able to pass the windowpane test (see page 84).

Focaccia dough is a rustic bread, which means its dough is wet and sticky; if shaped into a loaf, it spreads out and loses some of its definition. While this wetness makes it a bit difficult to work with, it is also what makes this kind of dough so special, because it expands more in the oven and creates large, irregular holes, which translates into better flavor. The airier structure allows heat to more easily penetrate and thoroughly roast the grain.

To use this dough for pizza, divide it into 6- or 7-ounce pieces as soon as it is made. Toss the pieces in flour to coat, then form into small balls. Line a sheet pan with parchment paper or a silicon mat, grease with 1 tablespoon of olive oil, then roll the dough balls on the oiled surface to coat. Cover loosely with plastic wrap, slip the pan inside a large plastic bag, and refrigerate overnight. The dough will be usable for up to 3 days. Follow the instructions for making pizza on page 271.

This dough also makes excellent rustic breads. To use it for ciabatta, *pain rustique,* or *pain à l'ancienne* mini baguettes (see page 263 for shaping instructions), proceed as in step 2 and onward on page 265.

To make herbed oil, to 2 cups extra virgin olive oil, add 1 cup chopped fresh herbs (such as basil, oregano, thyme, and sage in any combination) or 1/4 cup dried herbs, 2 teaspoons paprika, 1 tablespoon kosher salt, 1/2 teaspoon coarsely ground black pepper, and 6 cloves garlic, chopped (or 1 tablespoon dried granulated garlic). Steep at room temperature for 1 hour. Herbed oil will keep, refrigerated, for 2 weeks.

Focaccia topping ideas: olive oil and coarse salt or sugar; pinenuts, walnuts, or pecans; caramelized onions, olives, or roasted garlic; high-moisture cheeses like blue cheese or feta and medium or hard cheeses (added during the last 3 to 5 minutes of the bake) like Parmesan or Cheddar; cooked ground meat or chicken. You can also brush pizza sauce over the top before proofing and make a pizza-style focaccia.

2. **Prepare a 17 by 12-inch sheet pan,** lining it with parchment paper and oiling it with 1 tablespoon olive oil (including the side walls of the pan).

3. **Transfer the ball of dough** to the pan and rub the top of the dough with olive oil. Then use the palms of your hands to flatten it. It will only cover about half of the pan; this is to be expected, as the dough has just been mixed, the gluten is still very tight, and no fermentation gases have yet developed. Cover and seal the pan with plastic wrap or slip it into a large plastic bag and immediately refrigerate it overnight. It will rise slightly as it cools down in the refrigerator.

4. **The next day (or within 3 days),** remove the pan from the refrigerator about 4 hours before you plan to bake the focaccia (3 hours on a hot day). Remove the plastic wrap or bag and drizzle about 1 1/2 teaspoons olive oil over the top of the dough. Use your fingertips to press out the dough, starting from the center of the pan and moving out to all four corners, creating pockets (dimples) as you press (shown at left). Do not force the dough to spread, simply allow it to spread as far it naturally wants to go. You can angle your fingers slightly toward the edges of the pan, but do not push the dough—it will spread on its own as you press down. The pressed dough will probably cover about three-quarters of the pan before the gluten tenses up and it begins shrinking back. When the dough starts shrinking back, stop pressing. Your goal is to preserve some of the developing gas pockets formed during the overnight fermentation. Loosely cover the dough with the plastic wrap and let it rest at room temperature for about 20 minutes.

5. **Repeat the pressing and dimpling** of the dough as before. If the dough sticks to your fingers, drizzle another teaspoon of olive oil over the dough or dip your fingers in olive oil as often as needed. This time the dimpled dough will cover about 85% to 90% of the pan before it shrinks back. Again, let it rest for 20 minutes at room temperature, covered loosely.

6. **The third dimpling will probably complete the job.** If you are using flavored oil, such as the herbed oil (see Commentary), spread 3 tablespoons over the top of the dough before the third dimpling. Otherwise, use 2 tablespoons of plain olive oil (or however much you like). Remember to start at the center of the pan and work toward all four sides and corners as you press. If the dough reaches the corners but shrinks back, do not force it; it will fill the corners as it rises. The dough will probably be about 1/3 to 1/2 inch thick and come less than halfway to the top of the pan. Again, cover the dough loosely and let rise at room temperature until it comes just to the top of the pan. This will take anywhere from 2 to 3 hours, depending on the ambient temperature.

7. **Prepare your toppings** (see Commentary) and preheat the oven to 500°F (260°C); preheating will take at least 30 minutes. Top the focaccia as desired and place it in the oven. Reduce the heat to 450°F (232°C) and bake for 15 minutes. Rotate the pan 180 degrees and continue baking 12 to 15 minutes longer, until caramelized to a light brown color on the bottom as well as the top. Add any cheeses during the last 3 minutes of baking.

8. **About 3 or 4 minutes after removing the pan from the oven,** use a pastry blade or metal spatula to transfer the focaccia from the pan to a cooling rack or a cutting board. Trace around the inside edge of the pan with the blade or spatula to loosen the dough anywhere it might be stuck to the pan. Place the tool between the focaccia and the parchment paper or silicon mat and carefully slide it out of the pan, jostling the pan as needed to move the focaccia out onto the cooling rack or board. Be careful not to spill any excess oil or burn yourself. Drizzle any olive oil still in the pan over the top of the focaccia (there is a lot of flavor in that oil, and it will be absorbed into the focaccia as it cools). Let the focaccia cool for at least 10 minutes before cutting and serving. (You can leave the focaccia in the pan to cool, but the bottom crust will soften considerably; however, some people prefer this softened crust.)

BAKER'S FORMULA	%
Whole wheat flour	100
Salt	2
Instant yeast	.8
Water	94.5
Honey	2
Olive oil	4
Total	**203.3**

NUTRITION FACTS	
Calories (kcal)	79.57
Protein (g)	2.91
Carbohydrates (g)	15.38
Dietary fiber (g)	2.56
Total sugars (g)	.39
Fat (g)	1.26
Saturated fat (g)	.19
Trans fatty acid (g)	0
Cholesterol (mg)	0
Sodium (mg)	157.33

SHAPING PAIN À L'ANCIENNE MINI BAGUETTES

Transfer the dough to a heavily floured work surface, being careful to degas it as little as possible; the key to shaping *pain à l'ancienne* mini baguettes is minimal handling. (A) Using a metal pastry scraper, cut the dough into strips 1½ inches wide. (B) Gently transfer the strips to a prepared sheet pan or floured peel. (C) Bake as described on page 266, using the steam pan *and* misting.

Transitional Rustic Bread and Focaccia

Makes 2 ciabatta or one 17 by 12-inch focaccia

BREAD PROFILE

Lean dough; delayed fermentation method; commercial yeast

DAYS TO MAKE: 2

Day 1: Mixing, 10 to 15 minutes; overnight autolyse
Day 2: 3 hours to divide, shape, pan, and bake; 20 to 40 minutes baking

This is another delayed fermentation dough that is not made in the two-step process, but in the *à l'ancienne* adaptation described in chapter 1. Again, we can do this in one mixing because the dough is wetter than standard bread dough and does not use a great deal of yeast. It is mixed, chilled overnight, and then shaped into loaves or pressed into the pan the next day. This dough makes exceptional ciabatta as well as focaccia. On page 260 you will find a similar formula, but made with 100% whole wheat. My suggestion is to make this version first, to master the technique, then try the 100% whole wheat version.

DOUGH

VOLUME	OUNCES	GRAMS	INGREDIENT
2¼ cups	10	283	whole wheat flour
2¼ cups	10	283	unbleached bread flour
1½ teaspoons	.4	11	salt
1 teaspoon	.11	3	instant yeast
2 cups	16	454	water, at room temperature (about 70°F/21°C)
2 tablespoons	1	28.5	olive oil
Total	37.51	1062.5	

COMMENTARY

This is easy dough to mix, whether in a machine or by hand. It is so easy, in fact, that I rarely use the mixer. Why clean up a machine when it is so much simpler to clean a mixing bowl? However, some bakers prefer to do all their mixing by machine, so I've included instructions for using a stand mixer.

1. **If mixing by hand,** place all of the ingredients except the olive oil in a bowl and mix for 2 to 3 minutes. Keep a bowl of water handy and dip the mixing spoon in the water from time to time to keep the dough from sticking. Use a plastic bowl scraper, also dipped in water, to continually scrape down the bowl. You can also use wet hands to mix the dough. The dough will be sticky but fairly smooth; adjust the water or flour, as needed. Add the olive oil and mix for another 15 seconds, long enough only to coat the dough. Let the dough rest in the bowl for 5 minutes, uncovered, and then mix again for 1 minute. The dough will be smoother and stronger, but it will still be sticky. If it is too wet, that is, if it feels like a batter and does not have enough structure to hold together, add some additional flour. Even though sticky, the dough should be able to pass the windowpane test (see page 84). **If using a stand mixer,** use the paddle attachment. Place all of the ingredients except the olive oil in the bowl and mix on low speed for 2 minutes. The dough will be sticky but fairly smooth (if it seems stiff, drizzle in some additional water, 1 teaspoon at a time, until it becomes sticky). With the machine off, pour the oil over the dough, scrape down the sides of the bowl with a plastic bowl scraper (dip the scraper in water to keep the dough from sticking to it), and then mix on low speed for another 15 seconds. Let the dough rest in the mixer for 5 minutes, uncovered. Mix again, on medium speed, for 30 seconds to 1 minute. The dough will be smoother and stronger, but it will still be sticky. If it is too wet, that is, if it feels like a batter and does not have enough structure to hold together, add some additional flour. Even though sticky, the dough should be able to pass the windowpane test (see page 84).

2. **For focaccia,** proceed as in steps 2 through 8 in the whole wheat focaccia on page 262. **For rustic breads** such as ciabatta or *pain à l'ancienne* mini baguettes, lightly oil a bowl with olive or vegetable oil (or pan spray), form the dough into a ball, and place the dough in the bowl (the bowl should be large enough to accommodate the dough when it rises to nearly double its size). Cover the bowl with plastic wrap or place it in a plastic bag and refrigerate it immediately for an overnight, cold fermentation.

BAKER'S FORMULA	%
Whole wheat flour	50
Bread flour	50
Salt	2
Instant yeast	.5
Water	80
Olive oil	5
Total	187.5

NUTRITION FACTS	
Calories (kcal)	8.97
Protein (g)	3.01
Carbohydrates (g)	16.74
Dietary fiber (g)	1.71
Total sugars (g)	.08
Fat (g)	.41
Saturated fat (g)	.07
Trans fatty acid (g)	0
Cholesterol (mg)	0
Sodium (mg)	179.66

3. **Gently transfer the dough** to a lightly floured work surface with a plastic bowl scraper (try not to rip or tear the dough). Form the dough into 2 or 3 rectangles for ciabatta (see below) or 4 mini baguettes (see page 263 for shaping instructions), being careful to degas the dough as little as possible when shaping it. Raise the loaves on a proofing cloth or on a sheet pan lined with parchment paper and, if you like, dusted with flour. Mist the top of the dough with pan spray (optional), cover loosely with plastic wrap or a cloth towel, and let rise at room temperature for approximately 45 minutes, until nearly $1^1/_2$ times its original size.

4. **Preheat the oven to 500°F (260°C)** and prepare it for hearth baking (see page 86), including a steam pan. When the dough is ready to bake, place it, seam side up, in the oven (either with a peel or on a sheet pan), and pour 1 cup of hot water into the steam pan (or mist the oven three times at 1-minute intervals). Lower the temperature to 450°F (232°C) and bake for 20 minutes (15 minutes for mini baguettes). Rotate the bread 180 degrees and continue baking for another 15 to 30 minutes, until the bread is a golden brown on all sides, sounds hollow when thumped on the bottom, and registers at least 200°F (93°C) in the center. The crust should be hard (though it will soften somewhat as it cools). If the crust is dark but the bread still feels soft, turn off the oven and leave the bread in for another 5 to 10 minutes. You can also cover the bread loosely with aluminum foil to prevent it from burning.

5. **Transfer the bread to a cooling rack** and allow it to cool for at least 1 hour before serving.

SHAPING CIABATTA

(A) Turn the dough out onto a heavily floured work surface. Using a pastry blade, cut off a piece of dough for the first ciabatta. Loosely fold the floured dough piece into thirds. (B) Gently roll the folded dough in the flour to coat it, but do not degas it. (C) Transfer the shaped dough to a floured pan or proofing cloth, seam side down, for proofing.

Whole Wheat Pizza Dough

Makes 5 individual-size pizzas

The best pizza dough is always made by long, slow fermentation, usually in the refrigerator. Making it with 100% whole wheat or whole grain flour can be a challenge because the dough does not have the resiliency and extensibility of white flour dough. However, the delayed fermentation method overcomes this problem, yielding a dough that is soft and somewhat sticky but with wonderful stretching qualities. This versatile dough can also be used to make ciabatta, focaccia, and mini baguettes *à l'ancienne* (see page 263).

BREAD PROFILE

Lean dough; delayed fermentation method; commercial yeast

DAYS TO MAKE: 2

Day 1: Soaker and *biga*, 20 minutes set up and mix; overnight autolyse
Day 2: 2 hours to de-chill *biga*; 12 to 15 minutes mixing; 1 hour fermentation (or hold overnight); 5 minutes per pizza, shaping and assembly; 5 to 8 minutes baking

SOAKER

VOLUME	OUNCES	GRAMS	INGREDIENT	%
1³/₄ cups	8	227	whole wheat flour, preferably fine grind	100
¹/₂ teaspoon	.14	4	salt	1.75
³/₄ cup plus 2 tablespoons	7	198	water	87.5
Total	15.14	429		189.25

1. **Mix all of the soaker ingredients together** in a bowl for about 1 minute, until all of the flour is hydrated and the ingredients form a ball of dough.

2. **Cover loosely with plastic wrap** and leave at room temperature for 12 to 24 hours. (If it will be more than 24 hours, place the soaker in the refrigerator; it will be good for up to 3 days. Remove it 2 hours before mixing the final dough to take off the chill.)

BIGA

VOLUME	OUNCES	GRAMS	INGREDIENT	%
1³/₄ cups	8	227	whole wheat flour	100
¹/₄ teaspoon	.03	1	instant yeast	.4
³/₄ cup plus 2 tablespoons	7	198	filtered or spring water, at room temperature (about 70°F/21°C)	87.5
Total	15.03	426		187.9

1. **Mix all of the biga ingredients together** in a bowl to form a ball of dough. Using wet hands, knead the dough in the bowl for 2 minutes to be sure all of the ingredients are evenly distributed and the flour is fully hydrated. The dough should feel very tacky. Let the dough rest for 5 minutes, then knead it again with wet hands for 1 minute. The dough will become smoother but still be tacky.

2. **Transfer the dough to a clean bowl, cover** tightly with plastic wrap, and refrigerate for at least 8 hours and up to 3 days.

3. **About 2 hours before mixing the final dough,** remove the *biga* from the refrigerator to take off the chill. It will have risen slightly but need not have risen significantly in order to use it in the final dough.

FINAL DOUGH

VOLUME	OUNCES	GRAMS	INGREDIENT
Use all	15.14	429	soaker
Use all	15.03	426	*biga*
7 tablespoons	2	56.5	whole wheat flour
$^5/_8$ teaspoon	.18	5	salt
1$^1/_2$ teaspoons	.18	5	instant yeast
2$^1/_4$ teaspoons or 1 tablespoon	.5	14	honey or agave nectar or sugar or brown sugar (optional)
2 tablespoons	1	28.5	olive oil
			extra whole wheat flour for adjustments
TOTAL	34.03	964	

If the dough feels soft and supple but seems too elastic—that is, if it springs back quickly and is difficult to stretch into a pizza crust—next time try swapping in an equal amount of active dry yeast for the instant yeast. In most cases, you would increase the active dry yeast by 25%, but this dough has ample yeast in the formula regardless of which type you use. (See the FAQ on page 98 for more information on this.)

1. **Using a metal pastry scraper, chop** the soaker and the *biga* into 12 smaller pieces each (sprinkle some of the extra flour over the pre-doughs to keep the pieces from sticking back to each other).

2. **If mixing by hand,** combine the soaker and *biga* pieces in a bowl with the 7 tablespoons flour and the salt, yeast, honey, and 2 tablespoons of the olive oil. Stir vigorously with a mixing spoon or knead with wet hands for about 2 minutes, until all of the ingredients are evenly integrated and distributed into the dough. The dough should be soft and slightly sticky; if not, add more flour or water as needed. **If using a stand mixer,** put the pre-dough pieces in the bowl along with the 7 tablespoons flour and the salt, yeast, honey, and 2 tablespoons of the olive oil. Mix with the paddle attachment (preferable) or the dough hook on slow speed for 1 minute to bring the ingredients together into a ball. Switch to the dough hook if need be and mix on medium-low speed, occasionally scraping down the bowl, for 2 minutes, until the pre-doughs become cohesive and assimilated into each other. Add more flour or water as needed until the dough is soft and slightly sticky.

3. **Dust a work surface with flour,** then roll the dough in the flour to coat. Knead the dough by hand for 3 to 4 minutes, incorporating only as much extra flour as needed, until the dough is soft and very tacky, verging on sticky. Form the dough into a ball and let it rest on the work surface for 5 minutes. Line a sheet pan with parchment paper or a silicon mat, then oil it with the remaining 1 tablespoon olive oil.

4. **Resume kneading the dough for 1 minute** to strengthen the gluten and make any final flour or water adjustments. The dough should have strength and pass the windowpane test

Press the dough ball with your fingertips into a flat disk. (A) Use floured hands and knuckles to gently stretch dough into a wider disk. Work from the edges only, not from the center of the dough. Let the dough rest when it becomes too elastic and then continue stretching with floured hands and knuckles, from the edges not the center, to make a 9- to 12-inch disk. (B) Place the shaped dough on a floured or parchment-lined peel or back of a sheet pan. (C) Add sauce, checking for holes in the dough to make sure it does not go through the dough to the peel, and other toppings. (D) Slide the pizza onto a preheated baking stone or the back of a preheated sheet pan. If using parchment, slide it with the parchment onto the stone and remove the parchment after about 5 minutes of baking.

(see page 84), yet still feel soft, supple, and very tacky, verging on sticky. Divide the dough into 5 equal pieces; they should weigh about 6.25 ounces each. Form each piece into a tight ball, as shown on page 89, and place the balls on the prepared pan. Roll the balls in the oil to coat the whole surface of each, then cover the pan loosely with plastic wrap. If you need to hold the dough for later baking, you can put the pan in a plastic bag and refrigerate it to slow down the fermentation; the dough can stay in the refrigerator for up to 24 hours before it must be used. Otherwise, proceed with the next step.

5. **Preheat the oven as hot as it will go** (with a baking stone if you have one; the dough will be ready to shape and bake in 1 hour, which is how long you should preheat a pizza stone). You will not need a steam pan. If you do not have a baking stone, use the underside of a sheet pan, or simply place the shaped dough on a sheet pan, assemble the pizza, and bake it on the sheet pan. Although this is the least recommended suggestion, in some cases it may be the most practical. Follow the instructions on the opposite page for shaping pizza dough. Lightly top with sauce and your favorite toppings (see Commentary).

6. **Slide the topped pizza onto the stone** (or bake directly on the sheet pan) and close the door. Wait 2 minutes, then take a peek. If it needs to be rotated 180 degrees for even baking, do so. The pizza should take 5 to 8 minutes to bake. If the top gets done before the bottom, move the stone to a lower shelf before the next round. If the bottom crisps before the cheese caramelizes, raise the stone for subsequent batches.

7. **Remove the pizza from the oven** and transfer to a cutting board. Wait 3 to 5 minutes before slicing and serving, to allow the cheese to set slightly.

FAQ ❧ *Most of the formulas call for additional flour during the final mix, as well as extra flour for adjustments. Will the dough always use all of this flour and what if it absorbs it all and still feels too sticky?*

Each brand or type of flour performs differently. You should add all the flour listed as an ingredient and use the "extra flour for adjustments" only as needed. Sometimes there will be "adjustment" flour left over, and sometimes you will need even more flour than the instructions indicate, in which case you should add it. Let the dough dictate what it needs, not the recipe. Most of the time the amounts will be accurate, but there will be times when you will have to use your own judgment. Use the pictorial guide on page 71 to give you an idea as to how the dough should look, and use the recipe instructions to understand how it should feel. Soon, you will have a good feel for the consistency of various doughs and will make any needed adjustments easily and intuitively.

BAKER'S FORMULA	%
Whole wheat flour	100
Salt	1.8
Instant yeast	1.2
Water	78
Honey	2.8
Olive oil	5.6
Total	189.4

NUTRITION FACTS	
Calories (kcal)	89.20
Protein (g)	3.16
Carbohydrates (g)	16.73
Dietary fiber (g)	2.78
Total sugars (g)	.56
Fat (g)	1.66
Saturated fat (g)	.25
Trans fatty acid (g)	0
Cholesterol (mg)	0
Sodium (mg)	154.84

My favorite toppings include a blend of three cheeses (one hard like Romano, one "melter" like mozzarella, and one wild card like blue cheese) tossed with a variety of herbs, roasted eggplant, artichoke hearts, any seafood, and broccoli rabe. I also like to drizzle herbed oil (see page 262) over just about every pizza I make. For the sauce, use your favorite recipe or brand (the thinner the better since it thickens as it bakes).

MULTIGRAIN PIZZA DOUGH

Makes 5 individual-size pizzas

SOAKER

VOLUME	OUNCES	GRAMS	INGREDIENT	%
2/3 cup	3	85	whole wheat flour	37.5
1 cup plus 2 tablespoons (approx.)	5	142	any combination of cooked and uncooked grains (see Commentary)	62.5
1/2 teaspoon	.14	4	salt	1.75
3/4 cup plus 2 tablespoons	7	198	water	87.5
Total	15.14	429		189.25

1. **Mix all of the soaker ingredients together** in a bowl for about 1 minute, until all of the flour is hydrated and the ingredients form a thick, porridge-like dough.

2. **Proceed as in step 2** at the top of page 268 and onward in the whole wheat pizza dough.

BAKER'S FORMULA	%
Whole wheat flour	72
Multigrain blend	28
Salt	1.8
Instant yeast	1.2
Water	78
Honey	2.8
Olive oil	5.6
Total	189.4

NUTRITION FACTS	
Calories (kcal)	96.21
Protein (g)	2.76
Carbohydrates (g)	16.98
Dietary fiber (g)	.89
Total sugars (g)	.95
Fat (g)	1.80
Saturated fat (g)	.22
Trans fatty acid (g)	0
Cholesterol (mg)	0
Sodium (mg)	179.88

Whole Wheat Pita Bread

Makes 6 to 8 pitas

Pita bread and other simple flatbreads from the Middle East, India, and northern Africa, such as *pide, khobaz, aiysh, zata, mella,* and *kesret* can all easily be made without using the delayed fermentation method, and they usually are. However, in keeping with the goal of evoking the fullest potential of the flavor trapped in the grain, we will apply the delayed fermentation method to produce better-tasting flatbreads. You can make transitional versions by substituting white flour for some of the whole wheat and decreasing the amount of water, but why bother when the 100% whole wheat version tastes so good.

BREAD PROFILE

Lean dough; delayed fermentation method; commercial yeast

DAYS TO MAKE: 2

Day 1: Soaker and *biga*, 20 minutes set up and mix; overnight autolyse
Day 2: 2 hours to de-chill *biga*; 12 to 15 minutes mixing; 2 to 3 hours fermentation, shaping, proofing; 2 to 4 minutes baking

You can vary the flavor and
texture of this basic formula by
substituting small amounts of
rye or other types of flour or
multigrain blends for the whole
wheat flour in the soaker.

SOAKER

VOLUME	OUNCES	GRAMS	INGREDIENT	%
1³/₄ cups	8	227	whole wheat flour	100
¹/₂ teaspoon	.14	4	salt	1.75
³/₄ cup	6	170	water	75
Total	14.14	401		176.75

1. **Mix all of the soaker ingredients together** in a bowl for about 1 minute, until all of the flour is hydrated and the ingredients form a ball of dough.

2. **Cover loosely with plastic wrap** and leave at room temperature for 12 to 24 hours. (If it will be more than 24 hours, place the soaker in the refrigerator; it will be good for up to 3 days. Remove it 2 hours before mixing the final dough to take off the chill.)

BIGA

VOLUME	OUNCES	GRAMS	INGREDIENT	%
1³/₄ cups	8	227	whole wheat flour	100
¹/₄ teaspoon	.03	1	instant yeast	.4
³/₄ cup	6	170	filtered or spring water, at room temperature (about 70°F/21°C)	75
Total	14.03	398		175.4

1. **Mix all of the *biga* ingredients together** in a bowl to form a ball of dough. Using wet hands, knead the dough in the bowl for 2 minutes to be sure all of the ingredients are evenly distributed and the flour is fully hydrated. The dough should feel very tacky. Let the dough rest for 5 minutes, then knead it again with wet hands for 1 minute. The dough will become smoother but still be tacky.

2. **Transfer the dough to a clean bowl, cover** tightly with plastic wrap, and refrigerate for at least 8 hours and up to 3 days.

3. **About 2 hours before mixing the final dough,** remove the *biga* from the refrigerator to take off the chill. It will have risen slightly but need not have risen significantly in order to use it in the final dough.

FINAL DOUGH

VOLUME	OUNCES	GRAMS	INGREDIENT
Use all	14.14	401	soaker
Use all	14.03	398	*biga*
3/4 cup plus 2 tablespoons	4	113	whole wheat flour
5/8 teaspoon	.18	5	salt
2 1/4 teaspoons	.25	7	instant yeast
1 1/2 tablespoons	1	28.5	honey or agave nectar
or 2 tablespoons	1	28.5	or sugar or brown sugar
1 tablespoon	.5	14	vegetable oil or olive oil
			extra whole wheat flour for adjustments
Total	34.1	966.5	

The formula for this dough is very similar to others in this book, but the dough should be slightly firmer than for sandwich bread or hearth bread, as you will be rolling it out. Cultural variations of this bread are often distinguished by how thinly or thickly they are rolled. If rolled too thick, they will not puff and create a pocket when baked. This is sometimes intentionally done for breads meant to be torn when eaten, or for breads used as wraps but not for pocket applications (such as for gyros or *piadine* sandwiches). As you work with this dough, you will soon develop a sense as to how thin or thick to roll it, depending on how you plan to use it.

1. **Using a metal pastry scraper, chop** the soaker and the *biga* into 12 smaller pieces each (sprinkle some of the extra flour over the pre-doughs to keep the pieces from sticking back to each other).

2. **If mixing by hand,** combine the soaker and *biga* pieces in a bowl with all of the other ingredients except the extra flour and stir vigorously with a mixing spoon or knead with wet hands for about 2 minutes, until all of the ingredients are evenly integrated and distributed into the dough. The dough should be soft and slightly sticky; if not, add more flour or water as needed. **If using a stand mixer,** put the pre-dough pieces and all of the other ingredients except the extra flour into the mixer with the paddle attachment (preferable) or dough hook. Mix on slow speed for 1 minute to bring the ingredients together into a ball. Switch to the dough hook if need be and mix on medium-low speed, occasionally scraping down the bowl, for 3 minutes, until the pre-doughs become cohesive and assimilated into each other. Add more flour or water as needed until the dough is soft and slightly sticky.

3. **Dust a work surface with flour,** then roll the dough in the flour to coat. Knead by hand for 1 minute, incorporating only as much extra flour as needed, until the dough feels supple but tacky. Form the dough into a ball and let it rest on the work surface for 5 minutes while you prepare a clean, lightly oiled bowl.

4. **Resume kneading the dough for 1 minute** to strengthen the gluten and make any final flour or water adjustments. The dough should have strength and pass the windowpane test (see page 84), yet still feel supple and only slightly tacky, almost like satin. Form the dough

into a ball and place it in the prepared bowl, rolling to coat with oil. Cover loosely with plastic wrap and let rise at room temperature for approximately 45 to 60 minutes, until it is about 1 1/2 times its original size.

5. **Transfer the dough to a lightly floured work surface,** divide it into 6 large or 8 smaller pieces, and form each into a tight ball (see page 89). Place the balls on a sheet pan lined with parchment paper or a silicon mat, cover loosely with plastic wrap, and let rise at room temperature for approximately 45 to 60 minutes, until the pieces have grown to 1 1/2 times their original size.

6. **Preheat the oven as hot as it will go** and prepare it for hearth baking (with a baking stone if you have one; see Commentary). You will not need a steam pan. On a lightly floured work surface, roll out each piece of dough into a flat disk 4 to 5 inches in diameter. Dust the disks with flour and return them to the sheet pan, stacking them if necessary. Cover with a cloth towel or plastic wrap and let rest for 5 minutes.

SHAPING PITA

Using a rolling pin, roll out the proofed dough balls (A) into round or oblong disks about 1/4 inch thick and 8 inches in diameter. Let rest for 15 minutes. Slide one disk onto a preheated baking stone (the pita bake one at time). (B) It will begin to bubble within 2 minutes. (C) Within another minute or so, it will completely blow up like a balloon. When this happens, count to 20 and then remove the pita.

7. **Return to the first disk** and, starting from the center, roll it out to the edges into a circle about $1/4$ inch thick. (The diameter will be determined by the size of the dough: a 4-ounce piece will have about an 8-inch diameter; a 5-ounce piece can be rolled to about 10 inches.) Try to keep the dough as even in thickness as possible and do not roll to thinner than $1/4$ inch. Again, dust the disks with flour and either return them to the pan or move them to a flat surface where they can rest, covered and undisturbed, for 15 minutes.

8. **Lightly flour a baking peel** (or the underside of a sheet pan) and transfer the first disk to the peel. Slide the dough from the peel onto the baking stone, as if loading a pizza, and close the door. The pita should take about 2 minutes to begin puffing, but check on it after 1 minute; if you do not want it to puff and split, dock the entire surface with a fork or roller docker just before baking. As soon as the dough puffs up, it is nearly finished baking. If it puffs and then collapses, that means the internal steam escaped from a hole, but the pita will still have a pocket. Give the puffed bread 20 seconds to finish baking, then transfer to a cooling rack.. Do not wait for it to develop a crust, or it will not flatten when removed from the oven. Continue baking all of the pieces in this manner.

9. **As the pitas cool,** the steam will gradually escape, causing them to flatten out. Pita breads are ready to eat after 10 minutes of cooling.

the top of the oven and adjust accordingly. When baking with a thoroughly preheated stone, your biggest challenge will be generating enough top heat for an even split. Some bakers like to position a second stone on the shelf just above the baking surface to create radiant heat close to the top of the dough. I have not noticed this making a difference in my oven, but if it works for you, go for it. If you do not have a baking stone, use the underside of a sheet pan and preheat it just as you would a stone, though for only 20 minutes.

BAKER'S FORMULA	%
Whole wheat flour	100
Salt	1.6
Instant yeast	1.4
Water	60
Honey	5
Oil	2.5
Total	170.5

NUTRITION FACTS	
Protein (g)	9.55
Carbohydrates (g)	51.33
Dietary fiber (g)	8.37
Total sugars (g)	2.80
Fat (g)	2.95
Saturated fat (g)	.46
Trans fatty acid (g)	0
Cholesterol (mg)	0
Sodium (mg)	417.71

Whole Wheat Naan

Makes 5 naan

BREAD PROFILE

Slightly enriched, medium soft dough; delayed fermentation method; commercial yeast

DAYS TO MAKE: 2

Day 1: 20 minutes set up and mix; overnight autolyse

Day 2: 45 to 60 minutes shaping, rounding, fermentation, final shaping; 3 to 5 minutes baking

Naan is a lot like pizza dough. It is made in many countries and cultures, sometimes with water, sometimes with milk or yogurt, and sometimes with yak's or sheep's milk. This version uses yogurt, but you can substitute buttermilk if you prefer. Unlike pita bread, this bread should not puff into a pocket, so it will be docked with a fork before baking. The best versions are baked in 1000°F (538°C) tandoor ovens, where they are slapped against the side walls and then peeled off with long tongs after just a few seconds of baking. In a home oven, a baking stone works nicely, though the naan take longer to bake than in a tandoor. Served hot and slathered with garlic butter as soon as they come out of the oven (naan cools in a matter of seconds), they are hard to beat.

DOUGH

VOLUME	OUNCES	GRAMS	INGREDIENT
3¹/₂ cups	16	454	whole wheat flour
1¹/₈ teaspoons	.32	9	salt
1 teaspoon	.11	3	instant yeast
1¹/₂ cups plus 2 tablespoons	13	369	yogurt, buttermilk, yogurt, soy milk, or rice milk
2 tablespoons	1	28.5	unsalted butter, melted
			extra whole wheat flour for adjustments
			olive oil or garlic or other flavored butter for topping
Total	30.43	863.5	

COMMENTARY

Naan does not have to be made with a soaker or *biga* because we do not need the oven spring and interior crumb we seek in regular loaves.

In many ways, including hydration and texture, this is very much like a pizza dough, and in fact, it can be used to make pizza. Simply follow the general directions on page 269.

When baking naan, the key is a very hot oven—as hot as yours will go—as well as a very hot baking surface, such as a baking stone. If you have a baking stone, preheat it for at least 1 hour.

1. **If mixing by hand,** combine the 3¹/₂ cups flour and the salt, yeast, yogurt, and butter in a bowl. Stir vigorously with a mixing spoon or knead with wet hands for about 2 minutes, until all of the ingredients are evenly integrated and distributed into the dough. The dough should be soft and slightly sticky; if not, add some of the extra flour or more milk as needed. **If using a stand mixer,** put the 3¹/₂ cups flour and the salt, yeast, yogurt, and butter into the bowl. Mix with the paddle attachment (preferable) or dough hook on slow speed for 1 minute to bring the ingredients together into a ball. Switch to the dough hook if need be and mix on medium-low speed, occasionally scraping down the bowl, for 3 to 4 minutes, until the dough is smooth and slightly sticky.

2. **Dust a work surface with flour,** then roll the dough in the flour to coat. Knead the dough by hand for 3 to 4 minutes, incorporating only as much extra flour as needed, until the dough feels soft and tacky, but not sticky. Form the dough into a ball and let it rest on the work surface for 5 minutes while you prepare a clean, lightly oiled bowl.

3. **Resume kneading the dough for 2 minutes,** adding flour if needed to make a smooth, soft, tacky dough. Place the dough in the prepared bowl, cover tightly with plastic wrap, and place in the refrigerator overnight.

4. **Transfer the dough to a lightly floured surface,** divide it into 5 pieces, and form each into a tight ball, as shown on page 89. Place the balls on a sheet pan lined with parchment paper or a silicon mat, cover loosely with plastic wrap, and let rise at room temperature for approximately 45 to 60 minutes, until the pieces have grown to 1¹/₂ times their original size.

BAKER'S FORMULA	%
Whole wheat flour	100
Salt	2
Instant yeast	.7
Yogurt	81
Unsalted butter	6.2
Total	189.9

NUTRITION FACTS

Calories (kcal)	188.71
Protein (g)	7.89
Carbohydrates (g)	35.62
Dietary fiber (g)	5.54
Total sugars (g)	2.27
Fat (g)	3.12
Saturated fat (g)	1.58
Trans fatty acid (g)	.07
Cholesterol (mg)	6.81
Sodium (mg)	371.13

5. **Preheat the oven to its highest setting** and prepare it for hearth baking (with a baking stone if you have one; see Commentary). You will not need a steam pan. On a lightly floured work surface, roll out each piece of dough into a flat disk 4 to 5 inches in diameter. Dust the disks with flour and return them to the sheet pan, stacking them if necessary. Cover with a cloth towel or plastic wrap and let rest for 5 minutes.

6. **Return to the first disk and hand stretch** the dough, as you would for pizza (see page 266), into a circle about $1/4$ inch thick and 8 inches in diameter. Try to keep the dough as even in thickness as possible and do not stretch to thinner than $1/4$ inch. Again, dust the disks with flour and either return them to the pan or move them to a flat surface where they can rest, covered and undisturbed, for 5 minutes.

7. **Lightly flour a baking peel** (or the underside of a sheet pan). Hand stretch the first piece of dough to 10 to 12 inches in diameter and about $1/8$ inch thick. Transfer to the peel and dock the entire surface with a fork or a roller docker. Slide the dough from the peel onto the baking stone, as if loading a pizza, and close the door. The naan should take about 3 minutes to bake, but check on it after 1 minute. When the dough begins to show signs of caramelization, with spots of rich brown, the naan is done.

8. **Remove it from the oven,** brush it with olive oil, garlic butter, or flavored butter of your choice, fold, and serve immediately.

Naan blisters up dramatically when it is baked in an oven as hot as you can get it.

Chapatis, Parathas, and Roti

Makes 8 to 10 flatbreads

These are nonyeasted flatbreads, so fermentation is not part of the flavor profile. The soaker technique is your one tool for generating maximum flavor in this type of bread, though you will find very few recipes that suggest using it. These are ancient breads and there was no refrigeration when they were originally developed, but that does not mean we cannot apply our newfound understanding of how flavor is evoked to use refrigeration to make an even better version. In this case, the entire dough is the soaker, and the key to flavor is simply making the dough a day ahead. It is then rolled very thinly for *rotis* and *parathas*, and thicker for chapatis. These flatbreads are baked in a skillet, not in the oven.

BREAD PROFILE

Slightly enriched, medium soft flat bread; unleavened

DAYS TO MAKE: 2

Day 1: Soaker/dough, 20 minutes set up and mix; overnight autolyse
Day 2: 2 hours to de-chill dough; 30 to 35 minutes mixing, dividing, rounding and shaping; 3 to 5 minutes baking

COMMENTARY

Some versions of *roti* use millet flour, which you may substitute for up to half of the whole wheat flour in the formula below (but if you do so, cut back on the water slightly). Because millet has no gluten, it creates a very tender, almost flaky dough. If you cannot find millet flour and do not have a grain mill, you can grind small portions of whole millet into flour in a spice grinder.

SOAKER (AND FINAL DOUGH)

VOLUME	OUNCES	GRAMS	INGREDIENT
3½ cups	16	454	whole wheat flour (or up to half millet flour; see Commentary)
1⅛ teaspoons	.32	9	salt
1¼ cups plus 2 tablespoons	11	312	water
¼ cup	2	56.5	clarified butter or unsalted butter, melted
			extra whole wheat flour for adjustments
Total	29.32	831.5	

1. **Combine the 3½ cups flour and** the salt, water, and butter in a bowl and stir for about 1 minute, until all of the flour is hydrated and the ingredients form a ball of dough. You can also make this in a stand mixer with the paddle attachment, mixing on low speed for 1 minute.

2. **Cover loosely with plastic wrap** and leave at room temperature for 12 to 24 hours. (If it will be more than 24 hours, place the soaker in the refrigerator; it will be good for up to 3 days. Remove it 2 hours before mixing the final dough to take off the chill.)

3. **Dust a work surface** with 2 tablespoons of the extra whole wheat flour, transfer the dough to the work surface, and knead for 1 minute, working in the flour until the dough is only slightly tacky. If the dough absorbs all of the flour, sprinkle in more and continue kneading until the dough feels soft and supple but not sticky, incorporating only as much extra flour

BAKER'S FORMULA	%
Whole wheat flour	100
Salt	2
Water	69
Butter	12.5
Total	183.5

NUTRITION FACTS	
Calories (kcal)	103.28
Protein (g)	2.77
Carbohydrates (g)	16.63
Dietary fiber (g)	.55
Total sugars (g)	.07
Fat (g)	2.70
Saturated fat (g)	1.53
Trans fatty acid (g)	.07
Cholesterol (mg)	6.16
Sodium (mg)	178.75

as needed, then form the dough into a ball. Let the dough rest on the work surface for 5 minutes. Prepare a sheet pan, lining it with parchment paper or a silicon mat and dusting it with whole wheat flour.

4. **Resume kneading the dough for 1 minute** to strengthen the gluten and make any final flour or water adjustments. The dough should have strength and pass the windowpane test (see page 84), yet still feel supple, satiny, and only slightly tacky. Divide the dough into 8 to 10 pieces and round each into a tight ball (see page 89). Place the balls on the prepared sheet pan, cover with a cloth towel or plastic wrap, and let rest for at least 20 minutes (or refrigerate for later use).

5. **On a dry work surface, roll out** the first ball of dough into a circle a bit less than 1/4 inch thick. The dough shouldn't stick, but if it does, lightly dust underneath it with whole wheat flour; you can also lightly mist the surface with pan spray to facilitate an easy release. For chapatis, this is all you need to do, so roll out all the pieces to this size. For *rotis*, let the rolled-out dough rest for at least 5 minutes while you proceed with rolling out the other balls, then roll or hand stretch all of the pieces until they are very thin—1/8 inch or thinner. For *parathas*, brush the top of the rolled-out dough with melted butter, fold it into thirds, then roll it out again; you may need to dust the work surface with flour. Set the first piece of dough aside and repeat this process with the other pieces. When all of the dough has been buttered and rolled, repeat the process one more time. After the second buttering and rolling out of all the pieces, return to the first piece, roll it into a circle about 1/8 inch thick, then do the same for the remaining pieces.

6. **To cook all three versions, heat a skillet** (preferably cast iron) over medium-high heat and mist the interior with pan spray or wipe it with a paper towel that has been dipped lightly into vegetable oil. Cook the rolled-out pieces one at a time; the thinner they are rolled out, the faster they cook. As soon as the underside browns, flip the flatbread and cook the other side. They will take anywhere from 1 to 3 minutes per side to cook. You can stack and wrap the cooked breads in a cloth towel to keep them warm as you continue cooking, or serve them as soon as they come out of the pan.

Injera

Makes 4 to 8 *injera*, depending on the pan size

This is different from any other bread. It is more like a pancake and is customarily served alongside Ethiopian and Eritrean foods, especially their spicy stews (*wats* and *tsebhis*), but you can make it for any occasion. I like it with hearty soups and chili. You can tear off pieces of the bread and use them as a utensil for scooping up food, or simply eat the *injera* alongside.

Teff is the traditional grain for this bread, but I have had it with various combinations of wheat flour (usually all-purpose white flour) mixed with teff, and even with no teff at all. The dough has the consistency of pancake batter and is poured into a hot skillet and made like a crepe. *Injera* is traditionally leavened with wild yeast starter, sometimes supplemented with commercial yeast and sometimes not, depending on whose recipe you use. When made with 100% teff, the starter is sufficient, but when wheat flour is used, the commercial yeast provides that extra bit of effervescence to create the correct texture, with lots of tiny holes and a wonderful springiness.

BREAD PROFILE

Lean dough, delayed fermentation method; mixed leavening method

DAYS TO MAKE: 2

Day 1: 10 minutes to make starter; 4 to 6 hours fermentation, overnight autolyse
Day 2: 2 hours to de-chill starter; 30 to 60 minutes mixing and proofing; 3 to 5 minutes, per piece, baking

COMMENTARY

In this recipe, the starter is really the dough. On Day 2 we add only salt and commercial yeast for flavor and maximum air pockets.

Instant yeast is optional, but it is recommended if you make this with a high proportion of whole wheat flour instead of teff. If you omit the yeast, proceed directly to cooking the batter as soon it becomes active and foamy and the salt has been added.

Use your largest skillet to cook the *injera*. Some Ethiopian and Eritrean families I have met use large electric skillets for this, which allows them to make breads 14 to 16 inches in diameter.

You can make the starter with any combination of whole grain flours, but use finely ground flour, not coarse meal, as this pancakelike bread is thin and needs the adhesive properties finely ground flour delivers. Millet, brown rice, barley, corn, or oat flour are all good choices.

The amount of water added to the starter will depend on the type of grain you use. Teff flour has no gluten and will absorb less water than whole wheat flour, so add the water until you achieve the desired consistency, as described in the instructions.

BAKER'S FORMULA	%
Whole wheat and/or teff flour blend	100
Salt	.75
Instant yeast	1.2
Water	150
Total	251.95

NUTRITION FACTS	
Calories (kcal)	61.46
Protein (g)	2.21
Carbohydrates (g)	13.27
Dietary fiber (g)	1.44
Total sugars (g)	.04
Fat (g)	.40
Saturated fat (g)	.03
Trans fatty acid (g)	0
Cholesterol (mg)	0
Sodium (mg)	59.85

STARTER

VOLUME	OUNCES	GRAMS	INGREDIENT
¼ cup	2	56.5	whole wheat mother starter (page 67)
1¾ cups	8	227	whole wheat or teff flour (see Commentary)
1¾ cups (approx.)	14	397	filtered or spring water, at room temperature (about 70°F/21°C; see Commentary)
Total	24	680.5	

Mix all of the starter ingredients together in a bowl, gradually adding just enough of the water to form a thin batter with the consistency of gravy or crepe batter. Cover loosely with plastic wrap and leave at room temperature for about 4 hours, until you see bubbles starting to form. If you want to make the *injera* on the same day, let the batter rest at room temperature another 1 to 2 hours, until it is bubbling aggressively and creating some foam. Or place the starter in the refrigerator overnight, in which case you should remove it 2 hours before mixing the final dough to take off the chill.

FINAL DOUGH

VOLUME	OUNCES	GRAMS	INGREDIENT
Use all	24	680.5	starter
¼ teaspoon	.07	2	salt
1 teaspoon	.11	3	instant yeast (optional)
Total	24.18	685.5	

1. **Add the salt and yeast** and to the starter and mix for 1 minute to evenly distribute the ingredients. Cover loosely with plastic wrap and leave at room temperature for at least 30 minutes.

2. **Heat a large skillet over medium heat** and wipe the interior with a paper towel dipped lightly into vegetable oil. Ladle enough batter into the pan to cover the entire surface, tilting and rotating the pan to evenly distribute the batter. Cook it as you would a crepe or pancake, but only on one side. The bread should be filled with lots of tiny air pockets, bubbles trapped by the dough. When the top side is dry and set, check the underside; it should be caramelized to a rich brown. Remove the *injera* from the pan and cover with a cloth towel to keep warm while you continue with the remaining batter. Serve hot.

I love food that crackles, crunches, and flakes. Whether it be matzo, the most basic of all breads—flour, water, and salt—graham crackers, thin wheats, or my personal favorite, snappy seeded crackers, these are a versatile, healthful means to increase fiber and to use with various spreads. They also can easily take the place of less beneficial snack foods, like fried chips, white flour crackers, and salted pretzels, to provide filling, satisfying, guilt-free munchies.

Whole Wheat Matzo

Makes 8 to 10 sheets

The mother of all breads, matzo has as much symbolic value as it does culinary importance. Bread does not get any more basic than this: flour, water, salt, and heat. There are many cultural variations on this theme under many different names, such as the Middle Eastern *ragayig*, Far Eastern *roti*, and Indian chapati, but few breads have as powerful a story associated with them as matzo.

Authentic kosher-for-Passover matzo must be made in less than 18 minutes from the moment the water hits the flour until the dough goes into the oven. With practice, this can be done at home, but there are many times when you just want to make matzo and don't need it to be the ultimate kosher version. The 18-minute rule was imposed, by the way, because the Jewish elders determined that to be the time when natural yeast begins to affect and ferment the dough. The whole key to the Passover symbolism of matzo, of course, is that it is unleavened bread. Whether the rabbis' interpretation is true or not, 18 minutes became the benchmark. Truly kosher matzo is hard to find and expensive, costing as much as $35 a pound in some cities. So, if you can master the time frame, who knows, you may be able to save money—or even generate a nice income during the Passover season.

The time frame alone places this bread on the opposite end of the spectrum, philosophically, from bread made by our delayed fermentation method. However, if breaking the 18-minute barrier is not a concern, make the dough the day before, as in the delayed fermentation method, and roll it out and bake it the next day. You will see how it becomes slightly sweeter, not from fermentation but through enzyme action. The dough becomes, in essence, its own soaker and, in accordance with our operating theory, is chemically transformed, evoking more flavor from the grain.

BREAD PROFILE

Lean, crisp flatbread; unleavened

DAYS TO MAKE: 1

8 to 12 minutes mixing; 10 to 15 minutes shaping; 5 to 10 minutes baking

DOUGH

VOLUME	OUNCES	GRAMS	INGREDIENT
1³/₄ cups	8	227	whole wheat flour
¹/₂ teaspoon	.14	4	salt (optional)
³/₄ cup	6	170	water
			extra whole wheat flour for adjustments
Total	14.14	401	

COMMENTARY

This same dough can be turned into a crisp rye cracker by using a 50-50 combination of coarse and fine whole rye flour in place of the whole wheat flour, and a higher percentage of water, as needed. Roll the dough to a ¹/₄-inch thickness and bake at 325°F (163°C) for about 30 minutes or until crisp.

1. **Preheat the oven to 350°F (177°C)** with a baking stone (or use an inverted sheet pan).

2. **Combine the flour, salt, and water in a bowl** and mix to form a coarse, soft dough. Transfer to a lightly floured work surface, dust the dough with more flour, and knead for approximately 3 minutes, adding more flour as needed to make a firm but tacky dough. It should not be sticky. Let the dough rest for 3 minutes and then resume kneading for another minute, adjusting the flour or water as needed. The dough should feel soft and satiny, not sticky, and only a little tacky.

3. **Divide the dough into 8 to 10 pieces** (the more you practice rolling matzo, the larger you can make these pieces), round each into a tight ball (see page 89), and let them rest for 3 minutes. On a work surface (use minimal flour, if any, on the surface and the dough), roll out each piece of dough into a disk or rectangle until it begins to shrink back, dusting the pieces with flour if you need to stack them.

4. **Return to the first piece** and, starting from the center, roll it out to the edges into a disk or rectangle ¹/₈ inch thick. Dust the work surface with flour only if necessary.

BAKER'S FORMULA	%
Whole wheat flour	100
Salt	1.75
Water	75
Total	176.75

NUTRITION FACTS	
Calories (kcal)	8.55
Protein (g)	3.26
Carbohydrates (g)	17.24
Dietary fiber (g)	2.90
Total sugars (g)	.10
Fat (g)	.44
Saturated fat (g)	.08
Trans fatty acid (g)	0
Cholesterol (mg)	0
Sodium (mg)	162.72

෪

You can dock the dough with a fork, but a better choice is a roller docker, available at cookware stores. A small roller with many studs sticking out of it, it looks like a Medieval torture device. This tool is useful for pie dough, naan, and for any dough that is not supposed to blister or have large air pockets. A crimping roller, also available at cookware stores (often used to seal raviolis), can be used to run perforation lines similar to what you see on commercial matzo. This can be used in place of the roller docker. If you have neither, you can always use the old standby, a fork.

SHAPING MATZO

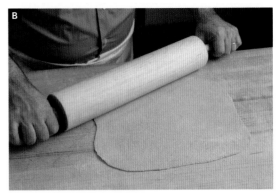

(A) Roll out the ball of dough into a round or rectangular disk. Stop when the dough continues to spring back and move onto another piece. (B) After a few minutes rest, return to the first piece and roll from the center to the edges, until evenly ⅛ inch thick. (C) Use a roller docker or a fork to create small holes over the entire surface.

5. **Lightly flour a baking peel** (or the underside of the sheet pan) and transfer the first piece to the peel. Dock the entire surface, then slide the dough onto the baking stone and bake until the matzo begins to turn a rich brown, caramelizing on both top and bottom; this could take anywhere from 8 to 15 minutes, depending on how thinly the dough is rolled. Remove the matzo from the oven, place on a cooling rack, and continue baking the other pieces, rolling out the remaining balls of dough while the earlier ones are baking. The matzo should be crisp and snap easily after it cools. If not, return it to the oven briefly to crisp it.

Lavash

Makes about 3 dozen crackers

You could say that this Armenian cracker bread is the yeasted version of matzo. It is fermented and rolled very thin, then topped with seeds and baked, either just until soft or to a crisp. It is possible to turn many of the whole grain bread formulas throughout this book into such a cracker, but the dough will be easier to roll out if it is a little less wet than most of the other formulas. Because we are not concerned with oven spring but only flavor, the following version uses only a single dough, held overnight in a cold, delayed fermentation. The following day it is rolled thin, topped, and baked.

DOUGH

VOLUME	OUNCES	GRAMS	INGREDIENT
1³/₄ cups	8	227	whole wheat flour
⁵/₈ teaspoon	.18	5	salt
1¹/₄ teaspoons	.14	4	instant yeast
¹/₂ cup plus 3 tablespoons	5.5	156	water
1 teaspoon or 1¹/₂ teaspoons	.25	7	honey or agave nectar or sugar or brown sugar
1 tablespoon	.5	14	vegetable oil or olive oil
			extra whole wheat flour for adjustments
			1 egg white beaten with 1 tablespoon water and a pinch of salt for egg white wash (see Commentary)
			seeds and spices for topping (see Commentary)
Total	14.57	413	

1. **If mixing by hand,** combine the 3¹/₂ cups flour and the salt, yeast, water, honey, and oil in a bowl. Stir vigorously with a mixing spoon or knead with wet hands for 3 to 4 minutes, until all of the ingredients are evenly integrated and distributed into the dough. The dough should be soft but firm and tacky but not sticky; if not, add more flour or water as needed. **If using a stand mixer,** combine the 3¹/₂ cups flour and the salt, yeast, water, honey, and oil in the bowl. Mix on slow speed with the paddle attachment (preferable) or the dough hook for 1 minute

BREAD PROFILE

Slightly enriched, crisp flatbread; delayed fermentation method; commercial yeast

DAYS TO MAKE: 2

Day 1: 10 to 15 minutes set up and mix; overnight autolyse
Day 2: 1 hour to de-chill dough; 1 hour dividing, resting, and shaping; 25 to 30 minutes baking

COMMENTARY

The egg white wash will hold seeds better than water alone. However, if you prefer not to use egg, you can brush the surface with plain water. Alternatively, you can use a solution of ¹/₈ teaspoon cornstarch whisked into 2 tablespoons water; this will help seeds adhere, but it will not create the shiny surface as the egg white wash does.

The most popular seeds for topping are poppy and sesame, but you can also use black sesame seeds, nigella seeds (also known as black onion seeds), caraway seeds, anise seeds, or cumin seeds (use a light touch with cumin; these seeds are very intensely flavored). Also consider dusting the surface with paprika, cayenne (with a very light touch!), garlic salt, or chili powder. A little goes a long way, but it is fun to lay down lines of different colors and flavors and then cut or break the crackers across the lines so that each cracker has a few toppings striped across it.

The baking instructions are for crisp crackers, since this is the application most people prefer. However, if you want to bake a softer cracker bread, perhaps to use for roll-ups or wraps, reduce the baking time by about 5 minutes and remove the pan from the oven before the dough caramelizes. It will soften as it cools.

BAKER'S FORMULA	%
Whole wheat flour	100
Salt	2.2
Instant yeast	1.75
Water	69
Honey	3
Olive oil	6
Total	181.95

NUTRITION FACTS	
Calories (kcal)	94.75
Protein (g)	3.35
Carbohydrates (g)	17.48
Dietary fiber (g)	2.92
Total sugars (g)	.64
Fat (g)	1.89
Saturated fat (g)	.28
Trans fatty acid (g)	0
Cholesterol (mg)	0
Sodium (mg)	203.06

to bring the ingredients together into a ball. Switch to the dough hook if need be and mix on medium-low speed, occasionally scraping the bowl, for 3 to 4 minutes, until the ingredients are well integrated into the dough.

2. **Knead the dough for 1 more minute** to strengthen the gluten and make any final flour or water adjustments. The dough should have strength and pass the windowpane test (see page 84), yet still feel soft, supple, satiny, and only slightly tacky. Form the dough into a ball and place it in a clean, lightly oiled bowl, rolling to coat with oil. Cover tightly with plastic wrap and refrigerate overnight.

3. **Remove the dough from the refrigerator** 1 hour before you plan to bake. Transfer the dough to a work surface dusted with flour, divide into 2 equal pieces, and round each piece into a tight ball (see page 89), adjusting the flour as needed; the dough should be firm and satiny, with very little, if any, tackiness. Cover with a cloth towel or plastic wrap and let the dough rest for 1 hour.

4. **Preheat the oven to 350°F (177°C)** and prepare 2 sheet pans by lining the underside of the pans with parchment paper or silicon mats. Mist the work surface lightly with pan spray or wipe it with just a touch of oil on a paper towel. Working from the center of the dough out to the four corners, roll out the first ball into a rectangle, dusting the top of the dough with flour only if needed to prevent sticking. Roll the dough out as thinly as it will allow, about $^1/_4$ inch. If the dough begins to spring back, let it rest for a few minutes and start rolling the second piece. Mist the work surface or lightly oil it each time you start a new roll out (this makes it easier to lift the dough from the surface without tearing it). Return to the first piece and roll it into a rectangle approximately $^1/_8$ inch thick. Carefully transfer the dough to the back of the first prepared sheet pan. If it does not fit the pan, trim off any excess with a pastry scraper or a pizza roller. Repeat the process with the second piece of dough. Brush the top of each sheet of dough with egg white wash and apply whatever toppings you desire.

5. **You can bake the sheet** as a single, large cracker bread or cut it into small triangles or rectangles before baking (see page 295). Bake for 12 minutes. Rotate the pans 180 degrees and top to bottom and continue baking about 12 minutes longer, until the lavash is a rich brown on both the top and the underside.

6. **Let the crackers cool on the pan** before serving. Full-size cracker breads can be snapped off into miscellaneous sizes and shapes. Precut crackers are ready to use.

Thin Wheat Crackers

Makes 18 to 24 crackers

I don't know about you, but there are some types of commercial crackers I can never seem to get enough of. Ritz, Triscuits, and Wheat Thins are among my favorites. Wheat Thins are probably the most functional and versatile, so I came up with my own 100% whole wheat version.

DOUGH

VOLUME	OUNCES	GRAMS	INGREDIENT
1 cup	4.5	128	whole wheat flour
1/2 teaspoon	.14	4	salt
6 tablespoons	3	85	milk, buttermilk, yogurt, soy milk, or rice milk
1 1/2 tablespoons	1	28.5	honey or agave nectar
or 2 tablespoons	1	28.5	or sugar or brown sugar
4 tablespoons	2	56.5	vegetable oil or light olive oil
			extra whole wheat flour for adjustments
			1 tablespoon kosher salt or sea salt dissolved in 1/2 cup water for salt water wash
Total	10.64	302	

1. **Combine the 1 cup flour and** the salt, milk, honey, and oil in a bowl and mix until the ingredients come together to form a ball of dough. Add extra flour or milk as needed to make a firm but tacky dough.

2. **Transfer the dough to a lightly floured surface** and knead for 3 minutes, adjusting the flour or liquid as needed; the dough should feel like modeling clay and have a satiny surface. It should not be soft and sticky or crumbly.

3. **If baking the crackers immediately,** preheat the oven to 350°F (177°C). Cover the dough with a cloth towel or plastic wrap and let rest for 20 minutes, then move on to the next step. If holding the dough overnight, form it into a ball, place in a lightly oiled bowl, cover loosely with plastic wrap, and leave at room temperature overnight.

4. **When you are ready to bake the crackers,** prepare a sheet pan by lining it with parchment paper or a silicon mat. Mist the work surface lightly with pan spray or wipe it with just a touch of oil on a paper towel. This makes it easier to lift the dough later. Transfer the dough to the

BREAD PROFILE

Enriched, crisp crackers; unleavened

DAYS TO MAKE: 1 OR 2 (OPTIONAL)

10 minutes set up and mixing; 20 minutes resting; 5 to 10 minutes rolling and cutting; 20 to 25 minutes baking

COMMENTARY

You can always substitute flour from other grains in place of some of the whole wheat flour, but keep the ratio at about 65% to 70% whole wheat flour and 30% to 35% other flours.

In any cracker that has a tender or crumbly texture there is, of necessity, going to be added fat. In our version, we use heart-healthy vegetable oil rather shortening. For a more buttery flavor, you can use melted unsalted butter.

You can make these crackers as soon as you make the dough, but the crackers will taste even better if you hold the dough overnight, like a soaker, allowing some enzyme activity to occur before you bake the crackers the following day.

In addition to the salt water wash, you can top the crackers with seeds and spices, as in the recipe for lavash (page 289). Replacing the salt water with an egg white wash will help the toppings better adhere to the crackers.

BAKER'S FORMULA	%
Whole wheat flour	100
Salt	3
Milk	67
Honey	22
Oil	44
Total	236

NUTRITION FACTS	
Calories (kcal)	97.68
Protein (g)	3.50
Carbohydrates (g)	2.47
Dietary fiber (g)	2.67
Total sugars (g)	4.44
Fat (g)	.88
Saturated fat (g)	.34
Trans fatty acid (g)	.01
Cholesterol (mg)	1.46
Sodium (mg)	27.84

work surface and, working from the center of the dough out to the four corners, roll it out into a rectangle, dusting the top of the dough with flour only if needed to prevent sticking. Roll the dough out as thinly as it will allow, about $1/4$ inch. If the dough begins to spring back, let it rest for a few minutes, then continue rolling until the rectangle is about $1/8$ inch thick. Brush the top of the dough with the salt water wash.

5. **Use a pizza roller or a pastry scraper to cut** the dough into whatever sizes and shapes you desire (small rectangles are suggested). Use the pastry scraper or a metal spatula to transfer the individual crackers to the prepared sheet pan. They should not touch, but they can be close together. Bake for 10 minutes, then rotate the pan 180 degrees and continue baking about 10 minutes longer, until the crackers begin to turn a rich brown on both the top and the underside.

6. **Let the crackers cool on the pan** before serving. They will crisp up as they cool.

FAQ ∽ *Why is agave nectar listed as a sweetener option? What about stevia, Splenda (sucralose), and polyol sweeteners, like sorbitol and maltitol?*

Agave is an attractive alternative to honey or sugar because, while it is primarily natural fructose (about 90%), it is assimilated into the body more slowly than regular sugar. It is becoming popular, especially among diabetics, because it does not spike blood sugar levels, as refined sugars or high-fructose corn syrup do. The usual substitution of agave nectar for sugar is 75% agave for 100% sugar; it is substituted in equal amounts for honey. Because syrups are partly water, you may need to slightly reduce the liquid in the recipe when using honey or agave to replace sugar.

As for other sweeteners, the only truly natural alternative is stevia, but the government (specifically, the Food and Drug Administration), despite having no evidence against stevia, has not officially approved it as a sweetener (some people suspect politics and lobbyists are at work); stevia has been approved for use as a food supplement. In extract form it is very concentrated, about 235 times sweeter than sugar, and its sweetness does hold up in baking. The type of stevia product you use (powder, leaf, or liquid) will determine the substitution rate, so check the package for this information. Because it is not a sugar, per se, products made with stevia will not caramelize in the same way as those made with sugar. You might also notice a slight licorice flavor if you use stevia.

Splenda (sucralose) is one of the few sugar substitutes that work equally, one for one, in place of sugar. The jury is still out as to the long-term health effects of sucralose, but it does perform like sugar, browning up nicely and caramelizing like sugar.

There is also a category of sweeteners known as polyols, or alcohol sugars, that includes sorbitol, maltitol, xylitol, isomalt, and lactitol, which are often used as sugar replacements. They are technically not sugars but can be used one for one as a substitute. Like other sugar replacements, they are more expensive and sometimes have laxative properties, but they do work well in baked goods, providing crust caramelization and good flavor.

Seeded Crackers

Makes about 3 dozen crackers

I love working with seed flours made by grinding sunflower, pumpkin, and other seeds into flour (nuts can be used this way too, but they are more expensive). The flour makes a wonderful addition to dough. One of the big advantages, besides flavor and nutrition, is that the seeds tenderize the dough because they have no gluten and are rich in natural oils. The following is one of the most popular crackers I make; when I serve them at parties and other gatherings they disappear faster than any other.

BREAD PROFILE

Enriched, crisp crackers; unleavened

DAYS TO MAKE: 1

10 minutes set up and mixing; 10 to 15 minutes rolling and panning; 20 to 25 minutes baking

COMMENTARY

Feel free to substitute flours made from other grains for some of the whole wheat, but be sure that at least 60% of the total flour is whole wheat flour.

The seeds do not have to be toasted because the crackers will be rolled so thin that the seed flour will actually toast while the crackers are baking.

If measuring by volume, measure the seeds *before* grinding.

Use a dry food processor, spice grinder, or blender to make the seed flour. But be careful to not generate too much friction, or the seeds will turn to seed butter as their oils warm up. Work in small batches in a blender or use the pulse switch on a food processor. It is okay if the seeds are not too finely ground (a food processor is not likely to grind them to a fine powder, anyway), as a little seed texture is delicious in the crackers.

You can make these crackers as soon as you make the dough, but the crackers will taste even better if you hold the dough overnight, like a soaker, allowing some enzyme activity to occur before you bake the crackers the following day.

Toppings can range from plain to salty to sweet. For salty flavors, use finely ground salt (such as popcorn salt or commercial seasoning salts), or make your own seasoned salt by blending finely ground salt with your favorite spices or herbs. Or toast 1/4 cup instant yeast in a dry skillet until it turns a medium shade of brown. (Toasting yeast turns it into nutritional yeast as it kills the living cells and leaves behind the nutrient base.) Transfer to a small bowl immediately and stir in 1/2 teaspoon finely ground salt. For sweet toppings, try cinnamon sugar, made with 5 parts sugar to 1 part cinnamon. Or use a honey glaze made by heating 2 tablespoons honey with 2 tablespoons water until the honey is fully dissolved; keep it warm until you are ready to apply it to the baked crackers. To apply dry toppings to crackers, spray with olive oil or vegetable oil pan spray as soon as they come out of the oven, then immediately sprinkle with the topping. For liquid toppings, lightly brush the hot crackers with the glaze as soon as they come out of the oven.

DOUGH

VOLUME	OUNCES	GRAMS	INGREDIENT
1³/₄ cups	8	227	whole wheat flour
6 tablespoons	2	56.5	sunflower seeds, pumpkin seeds, or a combination of the two, ground into flour (see Commentary)
6 tablespoons	2	56.5	sesame seeds, whole, preferably unhulled
3 tablespoons	1	28.5	flaxseeds, ground into flour (see Commentary)
1/4 teaspoon	.07	2	salt
1/2 cup plus 2 tablespoons	5	142	water
1¹/₂ tablespoons or 2 tablespoons	1 1	28.5 28.5	honey or agave nectar or sugar or brown sugar
2 tablespoons	1	28.5	vegetable oil or light olive oil
			extra whole wheat flour for adjustments
			toppings and glazes (see Commentary)
Total	20.07	569.5	

1. **Combine the 1³/₄ cups flour and** the seeds, salt, water, honey, and vegetable oil in a bowl and mix until the ingredients come together to form a ball of dough. Add extra flour or water as needed to make a firm dough.

2. **Transfer the dough to a lightly floured work surface** and knead for 3 minutes, adjusting the flour or liquid as needed; the dough should feel like modeling clay and have a satiny surface. It should not be soft and sticky or crumbly.

3. **If baking the crackers immediately, preheat** the oven to 350°F (177°C). Cover the dough with a cloth towel or plastic wrap and let rest for 20 minutes, then move on to the next step. If holding the dough overnight, form it into a ball, place in a lightly oiled bowl, cover loosely with plastic wrap, and leave at room temperature overnight.

4. **When you are ready to bake the crackers,** prepare 2 sheet pans by lining them with parchment paper or silicon mats. Mist the work surface lightly with pan spray or wipe it with just a touch of oil on a paper towel. This makes it easier to lift the dough later. Transfer the dough to the work surface and, working from the center of the dough out to the four corners, roll it into a rectangle, dusting the top of the dough with flour only if needed to prevent sticking. Roll the dough out as thinly as it will allow, about 1/4 inch. If the dough

begins to spring back, stop rolling and let it rest for a few minutes, then continue rolling until the rectangle is about ¹/₈ inch thick.

5. **Use a pizza roller or a pastry scraper to cut the dough** into whatever sizes and shapes you desire (small rectangles are suggested). Use the pastry scraper or a metal spatula to transfer the individual crackers to the prepared sheet pans. They should not touch, but they can be close together. Bake for 10 minutes, then rotate the pans 180 degrees and top to bottom and continue baking about 10 minutes longer, until the crackers begin to turn a rich brown on both the top and the underside.

6. **If topping the crackers,** do so immediately when they emerge from the oven. Let the crackers cool on the pan before serving. They will crisp up as they cool.

BAKER'S FORMULA	%
Whole wheat flour	100
Salt	.9
Water	62.5
Honey	12.5
Oil	12.5
Sunflower seeds	25
Sesame seeds	25
Flaxseeds	12.5
Total	250.9

NUTRITION FACTS	
Calories (kcal)	142.34
Protein (g)	4.75
Carbohydrates (g)	16
Dietary fiber (g)	3.48
Total sugars (g)	1.81
Fat (g)	7.37
Saturated fat (g)	.57
Trans fatty acid (g)	0
Cholesterol (mg)	0
Sodium (mg)	66.88

SHAPING CRACKERS

(A) Roll the dough to about a ¹/₈-inch thickness. (B) Use a biscuit cutter to cut out round crackers. (C) Or use a roller knife to cut out other shapes.

Graham Crackers

Makes 1 pan

Sylvester Graham (1794–1851) may not have created the current commercial version of graham crackers, but he did popularize the notion of making cracker biscuits from coarsely ground whole wheat flour, now known as graham flour. His idea was to separate the bran and germ from coarsely milled wheat, then grind the endosperm into a fine flour, and then add the coarse bran and germ back in. This gives it a different feel from regular coarsely milled flour. Graham was a controversial, troubled character during his lifetime, and I am not sure if he would be proud or embarrassed by the current version of graham crackers. But I like them and thought it would be nice to see if we could improve upon the commercial version. See what you think.

DOUGH

VOLUME	OUNCES	GRAMS	INGREDIENT
1³/₄ cups	8	227	whole wheat graham flour or coarse whole wheat flour
¹/₄ teaspoon	.07	2	salt
1 teaspoon	.25	7	baking powder
¹/₂ teaspoon	.12	3.5	baking soda
¹/₄ cup	2	56.5	milk, buttermilk, yogurt, soy milk, or rice milk
6 tablespoons	4	113	honey or agave nectar
1¹/₂ tablespoons	1	28.5	molasses or sorghum syrup
¹/₂ teaspoon	.14	4	ground cinnamon (optional)
			extra whole wheat flour for adjustments
Total	15.58	441.5	

1. **Combine all of the ingredients except the extra flour** in a bowl and mix until they come together to form a ball of dough. Add extra flour or milk as needed to make a firm dough.

2. **Transfer the dough to a lightly floured work surface** and knead for 3 minutes, adjusting the flour or liquid as needed; the dough should feel like modeling clay and have a satiny surface. It should not be soft and sticky or crumbly.

3. **If baking the crackers immediately, preheat** the oven to 350°F (177°C). Cover the dough with a cloth towel or plastic wrap and let rest for 20 minutes, then move on to the next step. If

holding the dough overnight, form it into a ball, place it in a lightly oiled bowl, cover loosely with plastic wrap, and leave at room temperature overnight.

4. **When ready to bake the crackers,** prepare a sheet pan by lining it with parchment paper or a silicon mat. Mist the work surface lightly with pan spray or wipe it with just a touch of oil on a paper towel. This makes it easier to lift the dough later. Transfer the dough to the work surface and, working from the center of the dough out to the four corners, roll it into a rectangle, dusting the top of the dough with flour only if needed to prevent sticking. Roll the dough out as thinly as it will allow, about 1/4 inch. If the dough begins to spring back, stop rolling and let it rest for a few minutes, then continue until the rectangle is about 1/8 inch thick.

5. **Dock the entire surface area** with a fork or a roller docker (see page 288), then use a pizza roller or a pastry scraper to cut the dough into whatever sizes and shapes you desire (large or medium-size rectangles are suggested; see page 295). Use the pastry scraper or a metal spatula to transfer the individual crackers to the prepared sheet pan. They should not touch, but they can be close together. (If you have a crimper, you can transfer the entire dough to the sheet pan and run perforated lines down and across the dough to define the cracker rectangles. This will allow you to separate the crackers after they are baked.) Bake for 12 minutes, then rotate the pan 180 degrees and continue baking 10 to 15 minutes longer, until the crackers begin to turn a rich brown on both the top and the underside.

6. **Let the crackers cool on the pan** before serving. They will crisp up as they cool.

BAKER'S FORMULA	%
Whole wheat (graham) flour	100
Salt	.9
Milk	25
Honey	50
Baking powder	3
Baking soda	1.5
Cinnamon	1.75
Molasses	12.5
Total	194.65

NUTRITION FACTS	
Calories (kcal)	116.15
Protein (g)	2.64
Carbohydrates (g)	26.94
Dietary fiber (g)	2.10
Total sugars (g)	1.27
Fat (g)	.67
Saturated fat (g)	.14
Trans fatty acid (g)	.01
Cholesterol (mg)	.54
Sodium (mg)	239.98

GLOSSARY

As we get deeper into the process of the transformation of grain into bread, the terminology can be unfamiliar and even overwhelming unless you are already a biological or cereal chemist. Here are brief definitions of some terms you may need to refer to from time to time. It is not an exhaustive glossary, as many other baking terms are also important but not as directly relevant here. However, the following will provide useful reference points as you explore this fathomless craft.

Active dry yeast: Also known as dry active yeast, this is commercial yeast (*Saccharomyces cerevisiae*) that has been dried to about 8% moisture content. Typically, 25% of the yeast is killed during processing. This type of yeast must be hydrated in warm water prior to adding it to the dough in order to dissolve the nutrient crystals on which it lives and awaken the yeast cells.

Agave nectar: A sweetener derived from the agave cactus plant. It contains fructose in a natural form that has been found to be more gradually assimilated than other sugars such as sucrose or high-fructose corn syrup. It can be used as a substitute for sugar or honey in breads (see page 292).

Aleurone: This is the layer of the pericarp (bran) that is closest to the endosperm. It is believed by some to be the most nutritiously beneficial component of flour.

All-purpose flour: Blended from hard and soft wheat to produce a flour of about 10 to 11.5% gluten. It can be purchased either bleached or unbleached. The unbleached has better flavor and aroma. It is sometimes used for bread, but more often in pastries such as cookies and quick breads. It can also be blended with higher protein flour to help soften a dough.

Amino acid: The building blocks of protein.

Amylases: The category of enzymes that helps convert starch into sugar. Alpha-amylase breaks large starch molecules into smaller pieces, while beta-amylase breaks out maltose from the ends of the starch chains.

Ascorbic acid: Also known as Vitamin C, it can be derived from plants, berries, fruits, and leaf vegetables. It is sometimes added in very small amounts to flour or to dough to improve oven spring and also to strengthen the dough structure during fermentation.

Autolyse: A mixing technique in which flour and water, and sometimes other ingredients, are mixed for a short period and then allowed to rest while the flour fully hydrates. Later, the final ingredients are added and the dough is mixed again. This method allows for better dough extensibility and development with the minimum amount of actual mixing time.

Banneton: A basket, wooden or plastic, sometimes coiled, sometimes lined with linen. It is used for the final proofing of dough prior to baking to give the dough a unique shape or design.

Bâtard: Derived from the French word meaning "bastard," this oval-shaped loaf is so named because it is neither a round (*boule*) nor a baguette.

Biga: The Italian name for pre-fermented dough. It usually is a stiff dough with a small amount of yeast and no salt, but it can also refer, in some baking systems, to wild yeast starters or any other type of pre-ferment.

Boule: A French term for a round, crusty loaf. It literally means "ball." In large versions it is sometimes referred to as a *miche*.

Bowl scraper: *See* Pastry scraper.

Bran: The layers of pericarp surrounding the endosperm of a grain. The bran is often polished off the kernel and used for animal feed or sold as nutritional fiber. Most bran contains both soluble and insoluble fiber.

Bread flour: White flour milled from hard wheat (spring or winter) with a protein content of approximately 12.5%. It can be purchased either bleached or unbleached. The unbleached usually has superior flavor and aroma. (*See also* patent flour.)

Cake flour: Fancy or short patent flour milled from soft wheat, it is low in gluten (about 6% to 8%) and usually bleached.

Cane syrup: When the liquid is squeezed from sugar cane it is usually then spun to separate the sucrose crystals from the molasses (with its minerals). Cane syrup, on the other hand, is evaporated cane liquid, retaining both the sucrose and molasses. It is sweeter and smoother than molasses and can be substituted for it in most recipes.

Caramelization: The browning of sugars, which occurs at approximately 325°F (163°C). In bread it is the primary cause of crust coloration, but it is not the same as the Maillard reaction, which requires proteins and also contributes to crust coloration.

Carbohydrate: A class of organic compounds composed of carbon, hydrogen, and oxygen. Starches and sugars produced in cereal grasses and other plants are the major source of carbohydrates in the diet.

Caryopsis: The seeded fruit of grasses and grains, including the husk, pericarp, endosperm, and germ. For example, an unhulled wheat or rye kernel.

Ciabatta: "Slipper bread," originally from the Lake Como region of Italy, where a local baker named his oblong rustic breads after the slipper worn by a local dance troupe. It is now a worldwide phenomenon, made with high hydration dough that does not hold its shape when rising but spreads out to create extremely large holes in the crumb and a creamy texture. The dough is similar to pugliese, except for the shape.

Clear flour: After patent flour is removed from straight flour, mills sell what remains as clear flour. It is obviously higher in fiber than the patent flour, but still consists of mostly endosperm with some of the aleurone and any other bran particles that ended up in the straight flour. There are three grades of clear flour: fancy (from soft wheat, used for pastry flour), first clear (from hard wheat), and second clear (also from hard wheat but considered too fibrous for baking; it is sold for industrial purposes). First clear flour is what many bakers add to rye breads because it looks a little like rye flour and is high in gluten (which the rye is not).

Compressed fresh yeast: Commercially produced yeast of the species (*Saccharomyces cerevisiae*). It comes in the form of moist bars (about 70% hydration) with a refrigerated shelf life of approximately 3 weeks. Active dry yeast is a dehydrated version of fresh yeast.

Couche: A cloth or linen bed, literally translated from the French as "layer." It is used as a proofing bed for shaped doughs, as many loaves can be lined up on a long *couche* with a small amount of cloth pulled up to divide them. The linen wicks off moisture so that the dough does not stick when it is transferred from the *couche* to the oven.

Cracked grain: Coarsely milled grain; usually the result of the first stage of milling before grinding grain into a finer flour.

Crumb: The interior structure of bread, including the structural matrix formed by gelatinized starches and coagulated proteins.

Degassing: The expulsion of carbon dioxide from fermenting dough during the dividing or shaping stages, also sometimes referred to as punching or a punch down. The degree of degassing contributes to the final crumb structure, as any pockets of gas remaining from the first fermentation can serve as a foundation for larger holes in the final rise.

Denature: To alter the properties of enzymes or other proteins by modifying their structure, either through heat or by adding another ingredient such as an acid. In baking it refers to deactivating enzymes or coagulating proteins.

Desem: An ancient style of sourdough hearth bread developed in the Flemish region of Belgium. It is usually made only of whole wheat flour, salt, starter, and water, but the starter is cultivated in a special way, at cool temperatures over a long period of time. The starter is what differentiates *desem* from other wild yeast breads, and there are now desem breads made with the starter but with grains other than wheat.

Diastatic: A product containing active diastase, a family of amylase enzymes. Usually refers to enzyme-active malt powder derived from barley or wheat.

Dietary fiber: The total amount of fiber in a food, including both soluble and insoluble fiber as well as resistant starch.

Docker: Any tool used to cut, score, or degas a shaped dough. Can be a knife or a roller with spikes. (*See also* Roller docker.)

Elasticity: Refers to a dough's ability to stretch and spring back. Glutenin is the protein most responsible for elasticity and firmness in wheat.

Endosperm: The portion of a grain that generally contains most of the starch and protein. In wheat, the endosperm contributes approximately 75% of the bulk of a kernel. It surrounds the germ and is, in turn, surrounded by the pericarp, or bran.

Enzymes: Specialized protein molecules that facilitate specific biochemical reactions. Those that break down starches are called amylases, and those that break down proteins are called proteases.

Extensibility: Refers to the ability of a dough to stretch without tearing. Gliadin is the protein in wheat that contributes to extensibility.

Extraction: The amount of flour obtained from the unmilled grain, expressed as a percentage of the original grain. White flour is generally between 70% and 75% extraction, high-extraction flour is approximately 85%, and whole wheat flour is 100%.

Fermentation: The process in which microorganisms (yeast or bacteria) convert sugar (primarily glucose) into carbon dioxide, alcohol (ethanol), or acids.

Fiber: Found in the walls of plant cells, fiber is a complex carbohydrate that, unlike other carbohydrates, is not digested by enzymes in the stomach and small intestine. Fiber may be either soluble or insoluble; soluble fiber can be fermented in the colon, allowing it to be partially digested.

Soluble fiber: Found in oat bran, pectin, and the pentosan gums of rye and wheat, as well as fruits and vegetables, this type of fiber is digested by bacteria in the colon.

Insoluble fiber: Found in wheat bran and most other grains, as well as beans, seaweed, and some fruits and vegetables such as pears and celery, this type of fiber consists of cellulose and lignins (noncarbohydrate, woody fiber found mostly in seeds such as flax). Insoluble fiber passes through the colon undigested, absorbing water as it goes. The essential function of insoluble fiber is to add bulk to digested matter and to carry off undigested food and bile for elimination.

Resistant starch: Cooking can change normally digestible starch into indigestible fiber, at least until it reaches the colon, where it behaves more like soluble fiber. Dried pasta, bread crust, and toasted bread are examples.

Flakes: Also known as rolled grain, as in rolled oats or rolled triticale. The kernels are steamed first so they won't shatter when rolled. They can often be added directly to dough but can also be cooked first, as you would for oatmeal.

Flour: Any grain, legume, or nut can be milled into a powder referred to as flour. While most flour, by volume, comes from wheat, rye, and other grass seeds, some cultures make greater use of flour from beans, roots, and seeds than we do in the United States.

Friction factor: Refers to the heat generated by an electric mixer during the mixing cycle. It is one of the factors in determining water temperature for dough.

Gelatinize: In bread making, this refers to the thickening of starches that occurs when the internal temperature exceeds 180°F (82°C). As the dough heats up, the starches absorb as much surrounding water as possible until they burst, thus thickening into a gel-like state.

Germ: The embryo portion of a grain, containing oils, vitamins, and enzymes. Because it is mostly fat, the germ can go rancid and cause spoilage in whole grain flour that isn't stored in a cool, dry area.

Gliadin: A globular short-chain protein that combines with glutenin to form gluten. Gliadin contributes to the extensibility of dough.

Gluten: A strong protein composed of two smaller proteins, gliadin and glutenin. It is formed primarily in wheat flour and to a lesser extent in rye and barley flour. Gluten provides elasticity, extensibility, and mixing tolerance to dough and traps carbon dioxide to form gas cells.

Glutenin: A long-chain protein that combines with gliadin to form gluten. It contributes to the elasticity of the dough.

Grits: Like groats, but cut into small bits rather than large. Usually refers to alkaline-treated corn (hominy), but not exclusively.

Groats: Grains that have had their hulls removed. They are sometimes, but not always, crushed into large or small bits, but not into flour. Steel-cut oats, rye chops, cracked wheat, and buckwheat bits are the most common form of groats.

Hard wheat: Wheat that is high in protein (above 11.5%). It can be grown as either winter wheat or spring wheat, and can be red, white, or durum.

High-gluten flour: Milled from hard wheat, with a gluten content in excess of 14%. It can be purchased bleached or unbleached.

Honey: Produced by bees from flower nectar, honey is about two-thirds fructose and glucose, and one-third water and other sugars.

Hydration: The water content of a dough or any product; to hydrate is the act of adding water.

Instant yeast: A fine-grained, dehydrated form of commercial yeast (*Saccharomyces cerevisiae*) containing about 5% moisture. In most cases, it can be added directly to the flour when mixing dough. Instant yeast is approximately three times more concentrated than fresh yeast by weight, and can be found under different brand names such as Rapid Rise, Perfect Rise, Bread Machine Yeast, and SAF-Instant.

Lactic acid bacteria/lactobacilli: Bacteria that produce lactic acid, and sometimes acetic acid, during the fermentation process. Many strains of bacteria fall under this general category.

Lean dough: Bread dough made with minimal fat and other enrichments, sometimes referred to as hard dough. Examples include French, Italian, and Vienna breads and rolls, and many rye breads.

Leaven: An element that has a transforming influence. In the case of bread, it is usually in the form of yeast but can also be baking powder, baking soda, steam, or air. It derives from a root word meaning "to enliven, to bring to life, to vivify."

Leuconostoc bacteria: A genus of lactobacillus organism in the streptococcocacaea family. It is able to produce carbon dioxide as well as lactic acid, and creates an an unpleasant aroma even while briefly imitating the leavening properties of yeast. It does not thrive in high acid, low pH environments so it eventually dies out as a sourdough starter establishes itself with other bacteria more conducive to good bread baking.

Levain: French term for either sourdough bread or a wild yeast starter.

Lignin: An organic woody insoluble substance, similar to cellulose, found in various degrees in the pericarp of grains and seeds. It is considered by nutritionists to be especially good for the heart and for controlling cholesterol. Flaxseeds are a major source.

Maillard reaction: A browning effect similar to caramelization. It is caused by the interaction of certain sugars, proteins, amino acids, moisture, and heat. It occurs between 212°F (100°C) and 350°F (177°C) and contributes to the distinct coloration of crust.

Malt: Malting is the germinating, sprouting, and drying of grains, primarily barley and sometimes wheat, a process that activates various amylase enzymes and allows maltose sugars to be separated from starch molecules. When malt is active (diastatic) it can be added to dough to increase enzyme activity and browning. When denatured (nondiastatic), it can be used as a flavoring agent (for example, in bagels and beer making). When barley (or wheat) is malted, dried, and ground it is sometimes listed as malted barley (or wheat) flour.

Maltose: A disaccharide, or double-sugar molecule, composed of two glucose rings. Barley is a major source.

Mash: Grain that has been hydrated in water hot enough to activate some enzymes and to deactivate others in order to bring out its sweetness without breaking down its structure completely. (See also pages 55 and 77 for a more detailed explanation.)

Meal: Whole grains that are milled to a sandy or gritty consistency not quite as fine as flour.

Meteil: A French term that properly refers to a blend of rye and corn or rye and wheat. In bread baking, *meteil* breads are usually a blend of wheat and rye, with wheat being the predominant grain.

Miche: A large, round French country hearth loaf, usually made with partial or 100% whole wheat flour (or, as in the style of the famous *pain Poilâne*, a high extraction wheat flour of approximately 85% whole wheat properties).

Mother starter: A wild yeast starter that is kept alive indefinitely in the refrigerator through regular refreshments (feeding it with flour and water), and from which other starters are elaborated to be used in dough as leavening and as a flavor enhancer.

Nigella seeds: Also known as black onion seeds, these tiny black seeds have a mild peppery flavor. They are often used as a bread topping in many cultures, from Russia and eastern Europe to the Middle East and India.

Oven spring: The additional rise that a dough undergoes when placed in the oven unless it has been overproofed. Ideally, bread dough will rise 10% to 15% during the first 10 minutes of baking.

Oxidation (flour and dough): A reaction in which atoms lose electrons when they react with oxygen. When this occurs after milling, it strengthens the flour proteins. When it occurs during mixing, it can strengthen gluten bonds (though too much oxidation can cause the dough to break down). When it occurs in the oven it promotes oven spring.

Pan spray: Oil and other ingredient blends, sold in aerosol or pump spray containers. It is used to apply a small, controllable amount of oil to facilitate non-sticking of the product to bowls, pans, or coverings such as plastic wrap. A small mist is usually sufficient.

Parchment paper: Nonstick silicon-treated baking paper that can withstand the heat of the oven.

Pastry blade: Also referred to as a bench blade or bencher, it consists of a flat rectangular stainless steel blade held by a plastic or wooden handle. It is the best tool for dividing bread dough by hand and also for scraping and cleaning work counters.

Pastry flour: Derived from fancy clear flour from soft wheat, it is about 8% to 9% gluten.

Pastry scraper: A flexible plastic tool, sometimes shaped with both a curved end and a flat end (hemisphere style). It is used to separate dough from surfaces without tearing the dough, and is sometimes also used to help manipulate dough when hand mixing. Probably one of the most versatile, often used, and least expensive tools in a baker's tool kit.

Patent flour: The purest grade of white flour, made only from the center portion of the endosperm. Even within this grade there are five subcategories: extra short or fancy (40% to 60%), first patent (60% to 70%), short patent (70% to 80%), medium patent (80% to 90%), and long patent (90% to 95%). Each category rep-

resents how much straight flour has been sifted from the center endosperm. So 100 pounds of straight flour would yield only 40 to 50 pounds of fancy or extra short patent flour (used mostly for cake flour, which is milled from soft wheat).

Pearled grain: Also known as polished grain, pearled grain is more processed than whole grain, having most of the pericarp (bran) rubbed off.

Peel: A flat, long-handled paddle (wood or metal) used to load or remove bread and pizza from the oven.

Pericarp: The jacket or skin of a ripened grain kernel or other plant seed. In grain, it consists of several layers of bran and fiber that surround the endosperm.

pH: Refers to a scale that measures acidity and alkalinity, running from 1 to 14. The lower the pH number, the greater the acidity: 7 is considered neutral, and anything above 7 is considered alkaline. Bread dough is typically 5 to 6 on the pH scale, while sourdough can be as low as 3.5.

Poolish: A French-style, sponge-type pre-ferment, usually made of nearly equal parts water and flour and a very small amount of yeast. This pre-ferment technique was brought to France by Polish bakers, thus the name. Like all pre-ferments, it acts as a dough improver for both flavor and structure.

Pre-ferment: A general term to describe any number of pre-doughs that are mixed in advance of the final dough and then added in during the final mixing stage. They improve flavor, structure, and performance. Examples include *biga*, *poolish*, *pâte fermentée*, sponges, and wild yeast starters.

Proof: A term used to describe the final fermentation of dough prior to baking. Also used to describe the hydration of active dry yeast to "prove" it is alive.

Proteases: A family of enzymes that break apart protein chains by cutting the peptide bond between amino acids.

Proteins: Organic molecules composed of amino acids linked in chains. They can assume a variety of shapes depending on their links and various side chains, and play a variety of roles. In addition to their structural functions, they participate in all metabolic processes in the body. They represent the tissue or muscle of plants or animals and are a vital food source.

Pugliese: A rustic bread from the Puglia region of Italy that is sometimes made with semolina flour. Similar in structure to ciabatta, it has large holes and a creamy texture. In Puglia, it is often baked in round rather than slipper shaped loaves.

Pumpernickel flour: A coarsely milled, whole rye flour, given this name by American millers to associate it with traditional pumpernickel-style rye breads of Germany and Poland, which are usually dense and dark.

Punching down: *See* Degassing.

Refreshing: The rebuilding of a wild yeast starter by adding fresh flour and water.

Roller docker: A small roller on a handle with metal or plastic studs that create holes in the surface of a dough. It is mainly used to prevent air pockets and bubbling of pie and pizza doughs.

Rye chops: Coarsely ground whole grain rye kernels, similar in size to cracked wheat, bulgar, hominy grits, or steel-cut oats.

Scoring: Also known as slashing, cutting, or docking, this refers to making strategic cuts in a dough to release steam during baking and to create a design on the crust, such as in baguettes.

Seigle: Technically, it is French for rye bread, but is more often used in reference to breads that contain more than 50% rye flour (as opposed to *meteil*, which connotes less than 50%).

Soaker: A nonfermented pre-dough containing grain (flour, coarsely milled, or whole, and especially useful for coarse grains), along with water or other liquid, and sometimes salt. Soaking the grain initiates enzyme activity in advance of fermenting the dough.

Sorghum syrup: Similar to molasses, this is the extract of boiled sorghum stalks, extracted in much the same way molasses is derived from sugar cane. The flavor of sorghum syrup is smoother and lighter than molasses. Sorghum itself is a cereal grain (the third most cultivated grain in the world, though most of it is used for animal feed).

Sourdough (starter): When dough is inoculated with wild yeast and lactic acid bacteria, it is considered sourdough. A small piece of this dough can be used to leaven larger pieces of dough for bread. Sourdough starter can be either in a liquid or sponge form, or firm, as in bread dough itself. It can be kept alive and healthy indefinitely by periodic feeding, or refreshing.

Spelt: An ancient strain of wheat that some people with gluten sensitivities are able to tolerate. In Italy it is called *farro*, and in Germany it is known as *dinkel*.

Sponge: A pre-ferment in batter form. Generally, it is much wetter than the final bread dough to which it is added.

Starch: A complex carbohydrate, or polysaccharide, made of numerous glucose rings. It composes between 70% and 75% of a grain kernel.

Starch damage: Refers to starch molecules that have been damaged during the growing or milling process. This damage allows enzymes to more easily access and break down starches. Most flour has a small amount of starch damage; if the damage is excessive, the dough can break down during fermentation due to too much enzyme activity.

Starter: *See* Sourdough and Pre-ferment.

Straight flour: The flour left when only the germ and bran have been sifted out. It includes endosperm and some of the aleurone layer and is typically about 72% to 75% of the wheat kernel.

Sugar breakout: The release of smaller sugar threads from more complex starch chains as a result of enzyme activity.

Thermal death point: The temperature at which any given organism dies. In terms of baking, 138°F (59°C) is the temperature at which yeast and other organisms die during baking.

Volatile flavor compounds: Fermentation, either from yeast or lactic acid bacteria, causes new and various compounds to form in dough. These compounds have unique flavor profiles, some of which volatilize, or evaporate, during baking (they disappear into aroma), while others leave trace flavors behind. This is why natural starters can produce such a wide array of flavors.

Whole grain: The whole grain consists of the bran (pericarp), the germ, and the endosperm.

Whole meal: Whole meal is flour that retains all three parts of the whole grain.

Whole rye flour: Like whole wheat flour, it is flour derived from 100% of the rye kernel. It can be purchased as coarse or fine milled, or simply as stone milled whole rye flour, which is a medium coarse grind. The pericarp fiber of rye is currently being studied for its healthful benefits, some claims ranking it ahead of oat bran as a digestive and cholesterol aid.

Whole wheat flour: Made from the whole wheat kernel, and therefore 100% extraction. It includes the bran, germ, and endosperm and must be stored in a cool, dry, place to prevent the oils in the germ from turning rancid.

Windowpane test: A way to determine whether the gluten has sufficiently developed in a dough by gently stretching a piece of the dough to see if it will produce a paper-thin, translucent membrane.

Yeast and wild yeast: A single-celled fungus. There are many strains, not all suitable for bread making. The most common form for bread is *Saccharomyces cerevisiae*, of which there are both commercial and wild varieties. Yeast leavens bread by converting glucose into carbon dioxide and ethyl alcohol (ethanol).

RESOURCES

The following are some of the best but only a fraction of the resources I consulted for this book.

WEBSITES

Every day, new resources appear online, so expect this list to be partially obsolete by the time it gets published, but also know that I will continue to provide links on my blog at **http://peterreinhart .typepad.com.**

Throughout this book, I mention others I consulted during the research and testing phase, four of whom wrote essays that I hoped to include in the book, but we simply ran out of pages. Instead, I am running them or have provided links to them on my blog. Here's the lineup: Emily Buehler, "Enzymes, the Little Molecules That Could"; Debra Wink, "The Pineapple Juice Solution and Other Metabolic Transformations" and "Yeast and Bacteria"; Jeff and Janet Ganoung, "Whole Grain Nutrition and Health"; and *desem* baker Jennifer Lapidus, "Making it Work—Where Theory and Reality Meet in the Dance of Bread."

Also, and it's not available to the public yet, but Lindley Mills mills a proprietary blend of twelve organically grown whole grains that makes one of the best multigrain breads I've ever baked. As soon as it becomes available, I will post it on my blog.

I can also be reached via my blog to answer questions regarding the information presented in this book, to troubleshoot dough problems, and to keep a dialogue going about all things bread.

Alton Spiller, Inc., www.barmbaker.com
Monica Spiller's site for all things related to barms and mashes, including her own, original version of the mash bread discussed in this book. Monica's ongoing chronicle of her work with organic whole grains, barms, and mashes can be found on a sister website for her nonprofit organization, The Whole Grain Connection, at www.sustainablegrains.org.

Anson Mills, www.ansonmills.com
The best cornmeal and other heirloom grains, including true Carolina Gold rice flour.

Asheville Bread Festival, www.asapconnections.org
Steve Bardwell and Gail Lunsford organize this event, one of the ever increasing number of bread festivals around the country (check the Bread Bakers Guild of America site for others). It

is usually held in March, and brings together many small, artisan, craft bakers to showcase their breads and take classes with teachers like Jeffrey Hamelman and others.

The Bread Bakers Guild of America, www.bbga.org
Every serious bread baker in North America, and not just professionals, should be a member of this organization. The single greatest repository of artisan and craft baking knowledge and networking access is embodied by the Guild. If you want to go to one of the Guild's Camp Bread events, don't hesitate for a second to sign up, as they sell out immediately.

The Bread Baker's List, www.bread-bakers.com
Reggie and Jeff Dwork's long-standing mailing list for bread heads who generously just love sharing information.

The Fresh Loaf, www.thefreshloaf.com
There are many excellent websites devoted to bread and discussions of bread, but this one is close to my heart. Floyd Mann, who created and maintains the site, worked as a high school apprentice at my bakery, Brother Juniper's, about twenty years ago. He continued his baking passion as a hobbyist even as he pursued a successful career as a computer specialist and established the site for others who, like himself, just love baking bread for the joy of it. Even though he worked for me, he has managed to maintain a very objective stance and has no problem calling me to task when he disagrees with something I've written. I guess I trained him well. The site also links to many other useful sites.

General Mills Health Institute, www.bellinstitute.com
All the large flour companies now offer helpful websites with baking information and, in this case, useful health news as well. See also Cargill's site at www.cargill.com and Con Agra's at www.conagrafoods.com.

Grain Mills, www.grain-mills.com
There are many excellent sites, like this one, dedicated to selling or reporting on mills for home grinding. Check the web for others. For personal testimonials, use the baking discussion groups, such as The Baking Circle at King Arthur Flour, The Bread-Baker's List, and The Fresh Loaf, all listed in this section.

Great Harvest—Charlotte, www.greatharvestcharlotte.com
Home site for Jeff and Janet Ganoung's branch of the Great

Harvest Bread Company empire; a retail, neighborhood baking company devoted to fresh milling and whole grain breads. Both Jeff and Janet are food scientists as well as bakers, so they are great people to communicate with about everything from the health benefits of whole grain, to fresh milling, and everything else whole grain. They can also answer questions about the Great Harvest philosophy and refer you to the appropriate sources within the national company for further information.

John LaPuma, MD, www.drjohnlapuma.com

I heard Dr. LaPuma speak at a bread symposium in Santa Barbara a few years ago and was impressed with his research and commitment to health through whole grains. Check out his site for ongoing discussions of healthy eating.

The Katina Thesis, www.vtt.fi/inf/pdf/publications/2005/p569.pdf

Kati Katina is a biotechnology research scientist in Finland who has written extensive, scholarly papers on the effects of sourdough on bread. This report, which can be downloaded, is not for the faint of heart, but is loaded with useful though highly technical information about how various organisms affect the flavor and quality of bread. Look Kati up on any search engine for links to other papers she has presented.

King Arthur Flour Company, www.kingarthurflour.com

Is there any flour company in this country that has done more to promote healthy baking? I can't think of one. They offer great baking classes, lively website discussion groups, a legendary catalogue, terrific books, and, if you are in Norwalk, Vermont, some of the most delicious baked goods you will ever taste.

Rose Levy Beranbaum's Blog, www.realbakingwithrose.com

Another excellent source of information, stories, and Rose's unique approach to baking of all kinds. Nobody stresses over the details like Rose, so you can be sure that if she addresses a subject, she has spilt blood, sweat, and tears over it.

San Francisco Baking Institute, www.sfbi.com

Michel Suas's school, the home site for the initial Camp Bread events, is part of a larger company that sells top of the line professional baking equipment. But most importantly, the intensive week long classes at the SFBI, are, along with those at King Arthur, the best in the country for serious bakers.

The Wheat Foods Council, www.wheatfoods.org

Useful site with links to the greater world of wheat. They also publish excellent pamphlets on wheat.

The Whole Grains Council, www.wholegrainscouncil.org

This is a real go-to site for everything whole grain. Links are always being added to extend access to more information. The site includes a link to an excellent glossary of grains.

BOOKS

What follows are some of the most useful book resources that were consulted in developing the methods, theories, and formulas presented in this book, or simply provide lively discussions and useful information. Many of the rare, older books can be found through internet used book services at reasonable prices.

Bob's Red Mill Baking Book by John Ettinger (Running Press, 2006).

The Book of Bread by Jerome Assire (Flammarion, 1996).

The Book of Bread by Judith and Evan Jones (Harper and Row, 1982).

Bread, A Baker's Book of Techniques and Recipes by Jeffrey Hamelman (Wiley, 2004).

Bread Alone by Daniel Leader and Judith Blahnik (William Morrow and Co., 1993).

The Bread Bible by Rose Levy Beranbaum (W.W. Norton Co., 2003).

Bread Science by Emily Buehler (Two Blue Books, 2006).

Celebration Breads by Betsy Oppenneer (Simon and Schuster, 2003).

Cookwise by Shirley Corriher (William Morrow and Co., 1997).

Formulas and Processes for Bakers by Samuel Matz (Pan-Tech International, 1987).

Food in History by Reay Tannahill (Crown Publishers, 1988).

Good Bread Is Back: A Contemporary History of French Bread, The Way It Is Made, and the People Who Make It by Steven Laurence Kaplan (Duke University Press, 2006).

How Baking Works by Paula Figoni (Wiley, 2004).

King Arthur Flour Whole Grain Baking by King Arthur Flour (Countryman Publishing, 2006).

The Laurel's Kitchen Bread Book by Laurel Robertson, Carol Flinders, and Bronwen Godfrey (Random House, 1984).

The Modern Baker, Confectioner, and Caterer, ed. John Kirkland (The Gresham Publishing Co., 1927).

Sprouts for the Love of Every Body by Viktoras Kulvinskas (21st Century Publications, 1978).

On Food and Cooking by Harold McGee (Scribner, 2004).

Secrets of a Jewish Baker by George Greenstein (Ten Speed Press, 2007).

Six Thousand Years of Bread by H.E. Jacob (Doubleday, Doran, and Company, 1944).

A Textbook of the Science and Art of Bread, Including the Chemistry and Analytic and Practical Testing of Wheat, Flour, and Other Materials Employed in Baking by William Jago (Simpkin, Marshall, Hamilton, Kent, and Co., 1895).

A Treatise on the Art of Bread-Making by Abraham Edlin (Prospect Books, 2004).

What's with Fiber by Gene and Monica Spiller (Basic Health Publications, 2005).

Whole Grain Bread by Machine or Hand by Beatrice Ojakangas (MacMillan, 1998).

The World Encyclopedia of Bread and Bread Making by Christine Ingram and Jennie Shapter (Lorenz Books, 1999).

INDEX

OTHER BOOKS BY PETER REINHART from Ten Speed Press

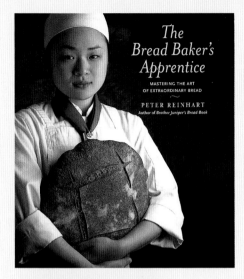

2002 JAMES BEARD COOKBOOK OF THE YEAR
2002 IACP COOKBOOK OF THE YEAR

"A detailed primer for everything from classic brioche to classic boiled bagels."

—*Wall Street Journal*

"As we continue our bread-making journey into the 21st century, Peter Reinhart's *The Bread Baker's Apprentice* should emerge as the definitive text on the subject. There is simply no other work where a student, and for that matter, many seasoned bakers, can turn to understand how the magic of breat bread baking works."

—Charles Van Over, author of *The Best Bread Ever*

9 x 10 inches, 320 pages, full color
ISBN-13: 978-1-58008-268-6

1999 JAMES BEARD BEST BAKING AND DESSERTS AWARD WINNER

"This is such an engagingly readable book that you won't want to put it down, except to run to the kitchen to bake from it."   —Flo Braker, author of *The Simple Art of Perfect Baking*

8 x 9 7/8 inches, 224 pages, two color
ISBN-13: 978-1-58008-802-2

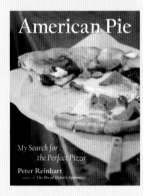

"We all know that Peter Reinhart is a great baker and teacher, but now that he's fallen in love with pizza, we can see he's also a great tour guide as he takes us to the best pizzerias in Italy and America. Secrets are divulged, expert tips provided, and stories told. Much more than a collection of recipes, this is a book that is as fun to read as it is to bake from."   —Carol Field, author of *The Italian Baker*

7 x 9 inches, 272 pages, two color
ISBN-13: 978-1-58008-422-2